# IN THE PLACE OF ORIGINS

BODY, COMMODITY, TEXT

Studies of Objectifying Practice

A series edited by

Arjun Appadurai,

Jean Comaroff, and

Judith Farquhar

# IN THE PLACE OF ORIGINS

Modernity and Its Mediums

in Northern Thailand

**ROSALIND C. MORRIS**

Duke University Press

Durham & London

2000

© 2000 Duke University Press
All rights reserved
Printed in the United States of America on acid-free paper ∞
Typeset in Minion by Keystone Typesetting, Inc.
Library of Congress Cataloging-in-Publication Data appear
on the last printed page of this book.

# CONTENTS

# ACKNOWLEDGMENTS

The enormity of debt is rarely as great and as difficult to express as when one completes a book. The longer the process of writing, it seems, the deeper the debt. As much as anywhere else, time accumulates its value here. Some debts are expiated in the citational practices by which thought or utterance is ceded to others. But there is another dimension of debt, one that asks not to be annulled but to be extended in the moment of recognition. This is the debt to teachers, to colleagues, to friends, and to others who bear our writing and attend our words, who stay with us and listen. It is this debt that binds this project and me to others. It is this debt that makes writing a pleasure as much as a duty.

I owe something profound—not this book, which I do not, in any case, properly own—to my teachers at the University of Chicago. First among these: Jean Comaroff, without whose patient supervision and mercurial intellect I would have been so much poorer in thought and in word. But also David Bunn, Norma Field, Nancy Munn, Frank Reynolds, and Raymond Smith. I benefited enormously from each of their knowledges and from their impassioned pedagogy. John Comaroff provided support, encouragement, and challenge in myriad domains. Charles Keyes gave invaluable assistance, ethnographic insight, and disciplined readings from afar when I needed them. And both Penny van Esterik and Shigeharu Tanabe augmented that assistance with the support they provided and the questions they asked at various moments.

Editorial input has proven invaluable on unexpected occasions, and I wish to acknowledge, in particular, Tani Barlow, Michèle Dominy, Yukiko Hanawa, and Carol Breckenridge for the opportunities they provided and the incitement to improvement that their comments generated at different times. Portions of the arguments that appear here have also informed essays in *positions: east asia cultures critique*, *Public Culture*, and *Social Text*. Lectures on materials referred to here were delivered at Bard College, the University of Chicago, the University of Michigan at Ann Arbor, the University Seminar on Cinema and Inter-disciplinary Interpretation at Columbia, York University, Haverford College, and at the 6th International Thai Studies Conference in Chiang Mai. Audiences at each of those venues prompted me to revisit my assumptions and made it possible for me to believe that the issues of modernity and mediumship in Thailand could speak to the concerns of this millennial moment. For that recognition and the impetus that it provided, I am indeed thankful.

In Thailand, my debts are enormous and nearly beyond what formal grati-tude can express. The many people who spoke to me, who shared their lives, their anxieties, and their visions of the future, have my undying loyalty. Monks, mediums, flower vendors, teachers, students, maids, and taxi drivers: they remain nameless here, as in the text, in deference to the promise of privacy. My only hope is that the body of this book is adequate to the promise of remem-brance that I made to them. Nonetheless, there are some who can and must be named. Anan Ganjanapan, Rujaya Abhukorn, and Kruamas Woodtikarn as-sisted me with introductions and insight, making possible the work that under-writes this project. Acharn Anan was especially generous with his own research material, and for this I can hardly express sufficient thanks. But neither would this book have been possible had Shalardchai Ramitanondh and Richard Davis not already undertaken their inaugural researches on northern Thai spirit possession and ritual practice. My debt to their pioneering efforts is, I hope, visible on every page that follows, even in those moments—perhaps especially in those moments—when I have found myself obliged to disagree with their analyses.

I also wish to acknowledge others who shared with me their friendship and time in Thailand: Bancha Leelaguagoon, Rawan Beertisawang, Alan Klima, Sara van Fleet, and Sam Van Fleet. Susan Turner endured much in order that this research be undertaken, and I remain grateful. Marriam Motamedi was my shelter during moments joyous and difficult. In this, she was matched by Jill Swan, whose home and food, conversation and enthusiastic questions I enjoyed over the years. My parents provided support with constancy, prodding me on frequent occasions by asking what I no longer had the courage to ask myself, namely, "Is the book nearly finished?"

In the five years since completing the initial research on which this book rests (during which time I have made three subsequent trips to Thailand), I have found myself excited by the work and the support of colleagues at Columbia University, many of whom have had a profound impact on my thinking about the issues addressed here. I am especially grateful for the kindness of Elaine Combs-Schilling and Alex Alland. Dorothea von Mücke and David Levin have kept me connected to other worlds, and provided that most necessary gift, friendly and fearless criticism. Mick Taussig has helped me to rethink some of what I thought I knew about magic. Gayatri Spivak has been an endlessly inspiring colleague. And Marilyn J. Ivy and John Pemberton have, in different ways, sustained my imagination and my desire to pursue this project with their own exemplary works and their inestimable friendship. I could not, of course, have accomplished anything at Columbia were it not for the challenge and the provocation of students whose works and questions have incited me again and again to go further.

The comradeship and the dialogue that is possible when one shares an institution are, nonetheless, not impossible even when vast geographical distance separates us. Indeed, the conversations that helped to transform this book, that urged it to become what it now is, have often taken place via telephone or e-mail or in the kinds of brief encounter that conferences and air travel—to say nothing of reading itself—facilitate. In this regard, I would like to thank Southeast Asianists Vicente Rafael and James Siegel and also non–Southeast Asianists Amila Buturovic, Kristine Harris, Robert Polito, and Daphne Winland.

This book rests on research conducted with generous support from the Social Sciences and Humanities Research Council of Canada, the Social Science Research Council (U.S.), the John D. and Catherine T. MacArthur Foundation for Research on Peace and International Understanding, York University, and the University of Chicago. It also benefited from a semester's leave provided as part of Columbia University's junior faculty development program.

I am indebted to Ken Wissoker and Jean Brady at Duke University Press, and to Judith Hoover, whose copyediting was both meticulous and respectful. The anonymous readers who combed both the first version of this manuscript and the book that it ultimately became are the objects of a special gratitude. Akaramunee Wannapraphrai, a widely published author in her own right, also merits my gratitude for assistance with translation from the Thai. And Deirdre de la Cruz has my thanks for her scrupulous indexing, performed at breakneck speed.

Finally, though always already at the beginning, Yvette Christiansë has borne my thinking and my writing of this book with patience and a faith that has been life giving. Her readings of this text, during a very long period of gestation, have been astute and clarifying, and it is perhaps to her as much as to anyone that I owe a sense of the poetic possibilities in ethnography.

# NOTE ON TRANSCRIPTION

In general, I have used a modified version of the Haas convention for transcribing Thai words, except where the use of a particular spelling has become so common in English-language texts as to make an alternative version discomforting for the reader. Thus, for example, I have used the now-conventional "müang" rather than the Haas-style, myaŋ, and *suai* rather than *suaj*. For reasons of typesetting, tone markers are omitted and special phonetic signs are kept to an absolute minimum. In the case of proper names, I have deferred to transcriptions that have been used in standard bibliographic reference texts, and to the styles that have been chosen by authors for their own names when these have appeared in English-language publications. English and other roman-script language titles that incorporate Thai words retain the original style of transcription.

# INTRODUCTION

Among the many stories that were recounted to me during the period of my field research on spirit mediumship in northern Thailand, the one that remains most poignant for me, being at once exemplary and irreducibly particular, concerns a wealthy Yuan (northern Thai) woman and her Sino-Thai husband from the southern part of the country. The couple, now handsomely middle-aged, is ensconced at one of the centers of Chiang Mai's revivified community of mediums. Inhabiting a luxurious suburban home that erupts on the horizon of rice fields and more modest wooden houses just east of Chiang Mai City, they are revered by other mediums and by many of the city's cultural elite, who patronize their theatricalized possession performances in both private and public contexts. The woman is the medium of several extremely powerful spirits, including King Ramkhamhaeng of Sukhothai, and her husband is a well-respected lay scholar of Buddhism and a practiced meditator.

Several years ago, while on retreat at a temple near Chiang Mai, this man experienced a loss of consciousness that inaugurated a series of crises in which he believed himself to have been possessed by spirits. His experience of displacement and psychic rupture was common enough to be recognized by others as possession, and so he enlisted ritual experts to translate the speech that passed through him. In this manner, he learned the demands of the spirits: that he become a vehicle for their continued work in the world and that he abandon his own worldly pursuits as part of a submission to their intrusions. As a rather conservative Buddhist layman who adheres to the nationalist traditions of the Thammayut sect, the man was profoundly traumatized by these possessions. Because Thammayut doctrine eschews the ritualism associated with spirits and views it as a profane and excessively visible residue of primitive and animist belief, often associated with effeminacy and penetrability, the meditator interpreted his encounters with spirits as a threat to both his Buddhism and his masculinity. With fearfully vigilant meditation and the guidance of his abbot, he determined—against all odds—to resist his seeming fate. To do so, he struck a verily Mephistophelian deal and gave over his wife to be possessed by the spirits in his stead. In return, he promised the spirits of those ancient princes who were seeking entry to his body that he would act as her assistant, aiding her in every way during her possessions, serving as the translator of their utterances and as the guardian of both the ritual traditions and the logic of Buddhist merit within which the highly Buddhicized performances of contemporary possession must take place. It is unclear how this woman, elegant and shy but renowned for her beautiful speech, entered into this contract. Neither she nor her husband, nor those who knew them, would tell me how the difficult and perhaps shameful negotiations took place: what promises or pleas were made, what hopes sacrificed, what needs and desires overcome. Nonetheless, with her husband as impresario of a ritual community mainly dominated by women, this unassumingly attractive woman was made the vessel of a double instrumentality. In her body the forces of a husband's fear and of historical transformation found the form for their own self-translation.

Complicating this story of what seems on the surface to entail spectacularly atavistic impulses are the mundane stories of everyday life. They are stories of a family on the outskirts of an eternally "new" city, itself on the outskirts of a nation's tumultuous modernity. They are stories of a "religious" colloquialism in contest with doctrinal Theravada Buddhism, and especially that of the royalist Thammayut sect. They are stories of desire torn between longings for the phantasmatic security of "tradition" and the equally phantasmatic bounty of the new. They are also stories of terror in the face of that spectral chaos that is the underside of modernity's bureaucratic rationality.

The couple have a son, now adult and emphatically secular, who has rejected them in their new life as the intermediaries between worlds. He is an only child, despite their stated desire for others, and at the time I was conducting research in Chiang Mai, he no longer lived there but had gone south, to Bangkok, in pursuit of an education. The physical separation was painful, though bearable and absolutely typical in this nation of ceaseless flux in which the ebbs and flows of internal migration are interrupted or reversed only in times of political crisis or financial collapse. However, with the death of their respectability in his eyes, the burden of mediumship had assumed a weight of unspeakable grief for the medium and her husband. And so with the melancholia of possession— which, in Chiang Mai, has become the very icon of postmodern nostalgia—has come the mourning of a personal apocalypse.

I met this couple a few months after I had begun fieldwork in Chiang Mai

City, and through my interest in their lives it seems fair to say that I came to represent the possibility of a surrogate child for them. Perhaps because I betokened both the extremity of modernity's privilege and the knowing ambivalence toward it that they desired for their own son, I assumed the awkwardly demanding honor of their affection. That affection would not have been without its price, however, including an exclusive submission to the spirits of this medium and an abrogation of my research with other mediums. It would also have entailed a willingness to answer their more personal, frighteningly ambiguous demands. It was an affection that I felt I could not fully reciprocate and one that ultimately led to my alienation from the circle of their intimacy. In the end, I determined that I could not permit myself to assume the role their grief demanded, and the ethical strictures governing me in my position seemed to make separation preferable to false promises.

In the meantime, however, I myself became the vehicle for a kind of triangulation through which this couple, and the other mediums in their circle, could translate themselves. My presence occasioned the explicitation of otherwise secreted knowledges, sometimes in the form of commentary, sometimes in the form of theatrical presentation. As a result, the delicate economy between peers and competitors that governs mediums in Chiang Mai was newly opened to negotiation and simple reaffirmation—as is the case whenever a stranger enters the space of possession. In the process of these multiple mediations, the mediums entered into those processes of self-objectification and even self-fetishization that are demanded by the ethnographically informed discourses of nostalgic cultural revival now dominating the ideological landscape in Chiang Mai. Through me and for me their partial meanings became articulate. Through me and for others their unfulfillable desires found expression. Indeed, our relationships materialized and made vividly—if sometimes painfully—clear the impossible economy of cultural translation that underwrites all ethnographic projects. Just as my presence in the home of a couple spurned by their child seemed to make palpable their own parental lack and longing, so my work as an ethnographer seemed repeatedly to remark the fact that contemporary mediumship is inextricably bound up with the wounded translation of absence and partiality.

This may seem a strange claim given the anthropological tradition of treating spirit possession in northern Thailand as a mode of presencing the past and of bringing forth the figures of originary power. After all, the spirits who possess mediums in Chiang Mai today are mainly the founding fathers of princely power. And in this regard, mediumship is supported by the recourse to origins that also characterizes the speech of public intellectuals, culture brokers, and middle-class consumers who flock to photograph studios for portraits of themselves in the period costumes of bygone days. However, the narratives of origin that circulate during periods of felt loss, such as the one in which so many northern middle-class Thai individuals now find themselves, are not so unequivocal. What strikes the observer who is willing to listen closely to the often clichéd stories of historical descent into the present is that, for every tale of origin, there is an encounter with the absence of origins. For every image of first appearances, there is a vacancy. Invariably encrypted within the tales of commencement is the realization that the origin is not one, that there are only substitutions, displacements, and translations in their stead. Thus, for example, kinship and affinity may be figured in the stories that contemporary mediums tell about their relations to spirits through the trope of the wet nurse. Here, the substitutional mother occupies the place of matrilineal firstness. Or members may explain the origins of their cult by providing an account of having purchased a tutelary spirit—who is now attached to and identified with a local site—from foreigners such as the Burmese. In this case, the origin comes from afar. Or, yet again, a romantic poet may insert dialogue in the text whose lost object is both love and home, displacing the putative unity of origins with an alterity that is both the condition of possibility of love and the source of its loss. These ironic narrative doublings, which secret difference at the very heart of identity's figure, have become ubiquitous in northern Thailand. They reveal a deep sense of homesickness and an ambivalent longing for return, as well as a logic of cultural representation in which the copy and the double have overwhelmed the poetics of originality.

In the course of this book, I will suggest that these doublings express a consciousness that occupies the moment at which the indigenous technologies of transmission—magical speech and ritual possession—have come face to face with those of reproduction: photography, printing, and writing in general. That consciousness finds difference in the place of origins, but seeks, compulsively, to heal over the breach of that original alterity by theatricalizing origination. It emerges from and indexes northern Thailand's modernity, itself forged through processes of nation formation and the monetization, then capitalization, of the economy. Here, as elsewhere, these processes and transformations are related to each other, and it is the project of this book to trace some of their linkages and effects, while also making sense of the individual narratives in which mediumship—both magical and electronic—takes place. My focus on the lives and works of spirit mediums (which is by no means exclusive) is partly a response to the extraordinary fact of its efflorescence in the past four decades. But it is also born of a sense that in mediumship one sees particularly clearly the troubled consciousness of northern Thai modernity. Partly, this is because mediumship has been valorized as the exemplary sign of a northern Thai ritualism that has itself been imagined as the index of northern Thai culture in nationalist historiography. Partly, it is because mediumship is the site that most dramatically stages the problem of origins.

It is undoubtedly necessary at this point to provide a few words of introduction to northern Thailand before proceeding further. This is a difficult task given the fact that Thailand is both a place ubiquitously represented in the global imaginary and one left opaque in the glossing of locality as the dialectical other of transnational modernity. Every serious anthropological engagement with the subject of Thailand seems, inevitably, to come up against the schizophrenic imageries of tourist brochures, which stress both its uncolonized, edenic beauty and its head-spinning technological worldliness. Narratives in which narcotraffic and prostitution are thought to drive the national economy are often improbably juxtaposed with those that fantasize newly industrial status. And discourses about the smilingness of Thai people often abut those in which the global economic crises of the late nineties are nothing but the logical end result of a Thai overinvestment in appearances. But where there are divergences, there are also confluences through which the imbrications of local worlds in broad transnational networks are effected. Shoring up Thailand's own national culturalist self-representations, for example, are the anthropological texts in which the almost uniform valorization of Thai Theravada Buddhist ideology has left questions of difference and power too often unasked. As Thongchai Winichakul's insightful writings on Thai history have made abundantly clear, no account of Thailand can afford to be ignorant of the complex but often contingent discursive linkages, the (failed) correspondences, by which Thailand and the West (to say nothing of Thailand and Japan) have been engaged with each other.[1] Thai astrology and Western empiricism, national culturalist discourse and tourist literature, localist revivalism and ethnographic inscription: all of these seemingly oppositional pairs have, in fact, been entwined in the making of Thailand's modernity. The same may also be said of a specifically northern Thai modernity.

Northern Thailand is perhaps an even more complicated object, insofar as it has become integral to the narrative of Thai nation formation only through an act of internal colonialism. The area that now constitutes the bureaucratically recognized space of northern Thailand (*phaak nüa*) was once a loosely linked set of tributary principalities, often referred to as Lannathai. For significant periods over the past five centuries, it was a vassal state of Burma, and its liberation from that subjugated status was achieved only through submissive

1. Thongchai Winichakul, *Siam Mapped: A History of the Geo-Body of a Nation* (Honolulu: University of Hawaii Press, 1994).

alliance with the Siamese, on whom Chiang Mai became dependent as a result. During the last decades of the nineteenth century, as Siam was attempting to stave off the invasive forces of both English and French imperial power, a series of treaties worked to translate tributary status into corporate membership, and Chiang Mai was inserted into what Thongchai has termed the geo-body of a new nation centered in Bangkok. Soon afterward, it became the seat of a significant bureaucratic apparatus, and as this occurred, the rationalizing and monetizing reforms of Bangkok were brought to bear in the north. They met considerable resistance; everything from capitation taxes to official antiritualism became objects of resentment and revolt on the part of northerners. Yet, from the late nineteenth century onward, the strategic deployment of a national education system, the establishment of Central Thai as the language of both government and schooling, and the performative encompassment of the north in monarchical pageantry all mitigated against the survival of a local sensibility. Today, most northerners are emphatically nationalist in their commitments, their sense of national identity (*ekkalak thai*) having been solidified through the imagination of both interior and exterior threats during the years of communist insurgency in Southeast Asia. But rising precisely, if ironically, from the certitude of national identification, an increasing number have also begun to espouse the nostalgic politics of Lanna regionalism. Chiang Mai is now the site of nearly endless state-sponsored events in which local history and a courtly rendition of Lanna culture are specularized and made the objects of visual pleasure. It has become a city of display, where ruins and shopping arcades are the altars of modernity's fetishes, foremost among which is history itself. Pastness, and specifically northern pastness, has become an object of desire. In a place that entered into modernity via the photograph and the printed text, widespread photographic literacy being achieved almost simultaneously with alphabetic literacy, almost everything can be reproduced. The most potent sign of the modern in northern Thailand may well be dusted roadsides that have become marketplaces for imitation antiques.

Home to almost a half million people, Chiang Mai receives more than a million tourists each year; yet even without that constant influx of foreigners, it is a heterogeneous city and its hybrid world receives thousands of migrant workers on both daily and seasonal bases. Among them are members of the minority highland peoples who have been marginalized by state formation and local geopolitical strife in neighboring countries. Sino-Thai immigrants, who have played a significant role in Chiang Mai since the last century, constitute a significant part of the population, but ethnically Thai Bangkokians have also moved to the city in search of relative quiet. In the small marketplaces that dot the cityscape, this diversity of people is matched by an extraordinary range of consumer goods. And in the sprawling malls that increasingly take up space along the main thoroughfares that surround and radiate out from the "old city," itself marked by ruins, goods from Japan, Europe, and the United States are as abundant as they are anywhere else in the world. Yet, the eternally "new city" of consumer desire is also criss-crossed by small roads, and these involute to form tiny neighborhoods that often seem to be diversions of an otherwise linear urban layout. In their quieter spaces, the multiple-house compounds and teak structures of another era can still be found, albeit next to cement bungalows with two-car garages. Above them and ringed by barbed wire, the mirror-encrusted façades and gold-painted spires of Buddhist temples reach skyward.

It is in this context of rambunctious juxtapositions between old and new that growing numbers of mediums practice their newly ambivalent technologies of transmission. And it is in this context that the discourses of loss and return find their most fertile ground. Longingly recalling the moment before Chiang Mai's feudal aristocracy relinquished its hold over the area, these discourses imagine the past in the screen image of courtly grandeur. Indeed, in one form or another it is this "feudalesque" image—of gorgeously excessive wealth and severe but personalized power—that gives flesh to the idea of origin now circulating in the touristified imagination that dominates northern Thailand. Occasionally providing a counterpoint to the image of bureaucratic rationality that modernism holds up as a new political ideal in Thailand, these retrospectively utopic imaginings of pre-Siamese history also efface much of the violence that defined it. Nonetheless, in their backward glances, they permit a certain denaturalization of the globally circulating forms that now pass as the natural end of world history.

The book that follows is, in part, an attempt to locate the reformed practices of mediumship in Chiang Mai in relation to historical factors, including and encompassing the ideological contest over ritual in Thai Theravada Buddhism, the transformation of gendered relations amid the upheaval that has been wrought by capitalization, and the growth of both commodity culture and the mass media in the north. But it is also deeply concerned with the relationships among commodities, writing, and mechanical reproduction, and with the specific forms of historical consciousness that have emerged in northern Thailand under their hegemonic reign. For this reason, chapter 1 begins with a reading of a text that emerges on the cusp of northern Thailand's modernity. It is a love poem in which an unlikely encounter with the rationalizing forces of economy and writing is undertaken. Indeed, in its staging of the problems of authorship and the loss of speech's performative powers, and in its ironic gesture toward autoethnography, it opens for us all of the issues to which spirit mediums will redirect our attention. Interestingly, the author of this poem, a roguish man of letters named Phayaphrom, has become one of many spectral figures who now haunt the landscape of Chiang Mai and visit mediums in the form of possessing spirits. But even if he were not to have become body in this form, his writing would speak potently to the subject at hand. Most important, he would have posed the question of subjectivity as a crucial site for the exploration of modernity and modern mediumship in particular.

It is for this reason that chapter 2, "Ruin, or What the City Remembers," returns to a historical account of the circumstances within which Lannathai became northern Thailand and the center of a distinctly regionalized tradition. My purpose here, in addition to grounding the rest of the text in the material histories of the area, is to make possible an understanding of the architectures of contemporary historical consciousness. Chapter 2 therefore is devoted to a reading of the contemporary city, with all its preserved ruins, as a writing of traces whose force can be comprehended only when one understands thoroughly the necessary theatricalization of forgetting, something that mediumship performs in particularly acute ways. Inevitably, such an approach requires that one read backwards but against the grain of revivalist discourses to both contextualize and denaturalize the reactionary representations of feudal Lannathai.

Returning to the present, then, chapter 3 moves to a consideration of one medium's possession by a spirit named Phayaphrom. In the doubling of the values of expression in possession, the performances of this medium permit me to ask what notions of representation and authenticity are at work in both poetry and mediumship. It is my hope that chapter 3 works to dispel once and for all the questions of duplicity that skeptical anthropologists and doctrinal Buddhists so regularly raise in their efforts to understand mediumship in naïvely functional or simply pejorative terms. Attending especially to the theatricalization of amnesia, I suggest that the importance of forgetting far exceeds the veiling function that it otherwise seems to perform and elaborate instead a notion of specular performativity by which the past is transformed from an object of knowledge to one of traumatic memory and, thus, of (impossible) identification.

Chapter 4 examines the structural, spatial, and temporal logics within which mediumship organizes itself and which recently have been valorized as the autochthonous forms of northern Thai culture. Extending the reading afforded by Phayaphrom's poem, I attempt to read the ambivalence of architectural form and mythic narrative against the grain of culturalist arguments in which "tradition" is represented as the principle of order. This leads to a discussion, in chapter 5, of the economy of mediumship, to the logics of gifting and debt within which it is inscribed, and to the political economy of its community in relation to that of the state within which it has grown and changed over the past four decades. The result of that movement is a return to an earlier moment, both in this text and in the national narrative. Chapter 6 begins with Phayaphrom's medium, whose lessons for reading photographs provide the occasion to consider again the relationships between magical transmission and photographic representation—as both technologies and agents in the transformation of historical consciousness. Here, I explore the rapprochement between mediums and the mass media as a particular transformation in the structure and distribution of auratic value and in the gradual reclamation of mediumship from the ridiculed category of ritual to that of tradition's sign. Tracking the convergence between photography's generalization and the rise of ethnofolkloric studies in northern Thailand, I suggest that the "revival of ritual" is, instead, the mark of its movement into the domain of representation, a movement that nonetheless generates the conditions of possibility for a restoration of magical (which is to say antirepresentational) power.

It is this strangely doubled productivity of photographic and ethnofolkloric discourse that surfaces in the accounts of chapter 7, where a narrative of conflicts over a newly valued locality and a crisis in political representation at the national level lead individuals in Chiang Mai to mobilize mediumship again. A series of repetitions and uncannily failed doublings constitute the object of this chapter, the most crucial of these being those between the aborted democratic revolution of 1973–1976 and the bourgeois democracy movement of 1992. The contemplation of these relations here demands an exploration of the nature of Chiang Mai's peripherality vis-à-vis the capital city; in response to this demand, the chapter is devoted to understanding how and why a certain ruinousness of the modern permits the constitution of Chiang Mai as the moral and historical antecedent to Bangkokian capital. In the end, these explorations confront the emergence of representation's other in the midst, from the very center of representation's hegemony. In chapter 8, I consider a new kind of mediumship that tends toward ecstasy and is riven by a metaphorics of excess. This Saivite possession is treated as the beginning of a postrepresentational practice, one that is to be understood as a function of a certain economic madness—the madness wherein equivalence is apotheosized. I call this practice ritual libertinage and with it the question of representation finds its temporary closure. There is, however, an epilogue to this long tale of mediumship's stories. It emerges from a return visit to Thailand in the autumn of 1997, at which time a famous medium from Chantaburi called on all mediums in Thailand to relinquish their duplicitous claims to spiritual presence. He did so on national television, while inviting a nation of skeptics to attend a final (televised) performance at which he would reveal all the techniques of his deception. That spectacle took place on 29 November as the Thai economy spiraled downward. It displaced for a moment the hysteria of financial apocalypticists with the thrall of a competing revelation that promised technology's truth but ended in the boredom that accompanies mere technique. This book closes with an attempt to comprehend the circumstances in which such a public renunciation becomes thinkable, and what the implications of such renunciation are for an anthropological understanding of the linkages between political and economic discourses of transparency and the forms of representation within which mediumship has historically been staged.

Each of these momentary engagements with the questions of mediumship rests on an analysis in which commodity processes are understood to be specifically potent factors, both as material forces in the histories of Chiang Mai and as representational logics that are explicitly linked to language. The political economies of gender also figure centrally in this history; in many ways, the book narrates a process of transformation whereby reproductivity has been transferred from feminine to masculine domains and men have become the enframing agents of women's nonproductive transmissions. Like many other histories of modernity, this book also tells the story of bourgeoisification, and hence of women's domestication, even as it narrates the growing disparity between desire and its possible satisfaction in an economy that requires proletarianization. Nonetheless, I have not used the rubrics of class and gender or ethnicity to organize the text, fearing that a hypostatization of those categories occludes rather more than it reveals about the complex processes by which different subjects have been so multiply and contradictorily interpellated within northern Thai modernity.

There is, finally, a repetitive stuttering in the very structure of this book that deserves some remark. Many of the chapters begin anew at the same place: with Phayaphrom, who is variously rendered as poet, merchant, prophet, and spirit; or with that moment in Thai history that has come to signify the rupture of the modern, namely the mid–nineteenth century. I should say here that this first repetition is neither an homage to the medium of that character nor an insistence on his paradigmatic status. And it is because I believe hybridity to be anterior to the modern in northern Thailand, rather than to remark the absoluteness of the temporal threshold, that I continue to tell the story of modernization from so many different locations but with reference to the same false origin. In the end, both of these gestures of return are part of an effort to suggest something about the impossibility of absolute translatability in ethnography and an attempt to give voice—without meaning—to the residual silences and irreducible differences whose intractable actuality would otherwise be effaced by a more seamless narrative. In the end, I hope that such a strategy makes palpable the difficulty of finding a place of commencement in a genre where beginnings are at once the introduction to myriad other narratives and the first gesture in a process of typification. The problem of typification, Adorno tells us, is the problem of the relation between actuality and its concept.[2] Often, that is the relation of actually local events and the notion of locality, a relation that is of particular concern to me in this book. Between them an abstraction enters, but although that abstraction is a general property of representational language, it assumes particularly significant dimensions under capitalist conditions, when language begins to lose its capacity to be marked by the specificities of its object. This loss is thematized in Phayaphrom's poetry in especially poignant ways, and, as will become apparent, his writing is addressed to precisely those economic conditions under which abstraction has become generalized and writing has become both the site of loss and the instrument for representing that origin that representation itself has made distant.

2. Theodor W. Adorno, *Negative Dialectics* (1966), trans. E. B. Ashton (New York: Continuum, 1994).

# 1 WRITING, EXCHANGE, TRANSLATION: A POETICS OF THE MODERN

A wet nurse. A tutelary spirit bought from foreigners. A poet's dialogue with himself about home. These figures were alluded to briefly in the introduction of this book, and I shall soon have occasion to explore them more fully. Yet, even before more careful reading, it is apparent that they contain within themselves a narrative, or at least a flashing symptom, of the problem of translation. For, whenever one encounters a figure of origins and finds something other at the place of commencement, one is engaged with translation, with the effort to forge substitutional and supplementary relations that both remember and overcome the difference that demanded them.

One hardly needs to remark that, whenever the origin (of one's relationship, of one's cult or clan, of one's humanity) turns out to have been something secondary, it is experienced as a site of loss. But in such cases, loss is already repetitive, encountered after the fact and, more important, as something already repeated. The absent mother, the lack of a local spirit, and the homelessness at home that make self-narration a kind of return—these figures share a structure we may call phantasmatic. They partake of that logic in which events emerge to consciousness only through their deferral, through the screen of a conceptuality in which the event is an idea.[1]

To be sure, the phantasmatic nature of representation makes all efforts to speak of origins ones of loss, but when the figure of origin is already a displacement or a substitution, as in these stories, something more is at work. In these

---

1. On the question of phantasm, see Marilyn J. Ivy's lucid account in *Discourses of the Vanishing: Modernity, Phantasm, Japan* (Chicago: University of Chicago Press, 1995), esp. 22–23. Also see Jean Laplanche and J.-B. Pontalis, *The Language of Psychoanalysis*, trans. Donald Nicholson-Smith (London: Hogarth, 1973).

cases, an ambivalent self-consciousness seems to be at play. Later in this book, I hope to show how such thematizations of loss in repetition are linked to the technologies of mass reproduction in Thai modernity. My project, in brief, is to trace the means by which representational practices, both aesthetic and political, are encompassed by the technologies of mass mediation and the economies of exchanging. Before considering the historical context and the conditions of possibility within which these processes occur and the figures of substitutional origin begin to circulate, however, I would like to linger on the topic of translation.

### On Translation, Again

It is, of course, neither incidental nor unusual that the problematic of translation (and of my own specifically ethnographic translation of that problematic) should emerge at sites of lack and longing such as those identified in the narratives of wet nurses, purchased tutelary spirits, and the epistolary romances of jilted lovers. The pairing of these two terms, "loss" and "translation," will almost inevitably summon the ghost of Babel, and with it a theological genealogy that is not, properly speaking, immediately relevant to a discussion of northern Thailand. This does not mean, of course, that anthropological discourse can ever fully escape this haunting by a myth—and a philosophy—of translation that is fundamentally Judaic. Indeed, although the rhetoric of translation has been central to social and cultural anthropological self-reckoning only since the fifties, when it acquired real currency for British anthropologists, its practice has been an inextricable part of the discipline since its emergence.

Such gestures toward a disciplinary tradition notwithstanding, "translation" has received renewed and redirecting energy as a metaphorics for ethnography in recent years, particularly in the wake of contemporary conversations with both Frankfurt School materialism and French poststructuralist thought.[2] Of course, what is meant by translation in, say, Benjaminian or Derridean terms is very different from that assumed in the pragmatically oriented works of Godfrey Leinhardt or Edmund Leach, to name two exemplary English writers on

---

2. By "poststructuralist" I mean to encompass a variety of philosophical projects, all of which have emerged since the late 1960s and that share a sense that the "subject" is both a historically particular mode of identification and something best understood as an effect of discursive processes rather than the originary site of consciousness within which discourse is received. The term is to be strongly distinguished from postmodern/ist, which I understand to operate primarily within the aesthetic domain. It is broader than deconstructionist, a term that I identify mainly, if differently, with the thought of Jacques Derrida and Paul de Man.

the topic.[3] And every ethnographer must choose from among the various philosophies of language and their axiomatics, no matter how familiar the "object" of one's ethnography. This book is informed by a belief that a post-structuralist valorization of difference and indeterminacy, as being at once the limit and the enabling condition of translation, is supported and even demanded by the reading of modern northern Thai texts. The present chapter, which is devoted to a reading of Phayaphrom's nineteenth-century love poem, *Khao Sii Bot* or *The Poem in Four Songs*,[4] provides the argument for such a position and attempts to demonstrate that the reach for what is, in the Anglo–North American context, a markedly "foreign" theoretical apparatus can be an act of fidelity, albeit one doomed to ultimate inadequacy. But lest this text appear to be a mere substantiation of that theory's validity, a deployment of ethnography in the interest of poststructuralism, let me say that the readings of Phayaphrom and of Derrida (and of Phayaphrom via Derrida, but also Derrida via Phayaphrom) are intended to displace both authors from their seeming centrality in equally seeming self-same traditions. They displace each other, but only to reveal their own lack of singular origins.

Written on the cusp of northern Thai modernity, prior to Bangkok's encompassment of the Lanna principalities and before the effects of Siam's treaties with Britain had opened the new nation to the forces of international free trade, *The Poem in Four Songs* is striking for many reasons. In it, literature is already split, already destabilized by a multiplicity of tongues, and already torn between the antinomies of gifting and the rationalizing effects of economization. Submitting to its poetic logics and its rendition of a locality that, it seems, is imagined by its author as always already heterogeneous, one is confronted by a crucially important, historically particular truth. That truth might be simply put as follows: In the beginning, in the place of origins, there was translation.

The full ambiguity of this expression "in the place of," which connotes both a location and a substitutional relationship, cannot be decided in English. But neither can it be decided in Thai, where the term *thii* indicates at once a place, an instance, and a being in (a) place or relationship.[5] Rather, as I shall argue

---

3. For a discussion of the history of translation theory in British social anthropology, see Talal Asad, "The Concept of Cultural Translation in British Social Anthropology" (1986), in *Genealogies of Religion: Discipline and Reasons of Power in Christianity and Islam* (Baltimore: Johns Hopkins University Press, 1993), 171–99.

4. Phayaphrom, *Khao Sii Bot [The Poem in Four Songs]: A Northern Thai Tetralogy* (1861), transcription, English translation, and vocabulary by Søren Egerod (Stockholm: Scandinavian Institute of Asian Studies Monograph Series Number 7, 1971).

5. For a full account of this word's forms and definitions, as well as combinatory terms in which it

later, the practices of modern spirit mediums can be understood as part of a heroically translational effort to mobilize the manifold possibilities of being "in the place of origins." For now, however, I want to explore *The Poem in Four Songs*, that text whose astonishing radicalism and uncanny prescience seem not only to respond to such readings, but to demand the detour through "foreign" theory. The point, of course, is not simply to prove that one can indeed undertake such a reading and, as a result, draw secreted logics from what could, in another reading, appear to be merely sentimental romance. Rather, it is that such readings enable one to better comprehend the actual historical relationships among local discourses on representation, the histories of ritual theatricality, the political economies of the colonial moment, and the transformations of consciousness that the mass media have effected over the past century.

This will perhaps seem a strange tactic: the location of a poststructuralist project in northern Thai ground. And yet, such a transplanting or grafting of foreign philosophy and foreign object is not only suggested by the "local" material, it is the subject of that material. Not surprisingly, there is a certain melancholy that afflicts the texts to be read, and this melancholy is redoubled by the notion of translation that emerges from it. For to be so beholden to the need for other representations of one's own otherness is a nearly unbearable condition. For many, including many of those in contemporary northern Thailand, such a condition finds its most perfect theatricalization in the laments of bereft lovers or forsaken parents and abandoned children. One of those laments has already been suggested in the preceding account of a Chiang Mai medium, but there are others. There are also many other narratives of loss in which the "missed" but eternally recurrent colonial encounter with the West is identified as the slayer of northern Thai autonomy. These songs of longing reflect what is undoubtedly a bourgeois sentimentality. However, my attention to them ought not to be construed as an attempt to buttress their ideological claims to total representativeness.

In northern Thailand, as elsewhere in the country and around the world, there is a variety of resentment and criticism directed toward those who are so tender about the past. Among elders who see modern technology as a liberation, among laborers who know their history to have traversed generations of servitude, among televisually enthralled youth who have no patience for their parents' fantasies of departed cultural values, the distinctly northern Thai concern with loss has little allure.[6] Nonetheless, as the discourse of the cultural

---

serves as root, see the entry in Mary Hass, *Thai-English Student's Dictionary* (Stanford: Stanford University Press, 1964), 240–44.

6. Many other fieldworkers who have conducted their research elsewhere in Thailand have shared

elite, it has enormous force in the local arena. Nor should we be surprised that the theatrical form of a modern translator's credo would entail such bourgeois sentimentality. For northern Thais inhabit a world in which global capital and the proximity it has forced between previously remote others have also created new forms of distance and generated a profoundly felt need for self-translation. Such felt need is inequitably distributed, to be sure, and its burden is probably felt most by the most disempowered inhabitants of the global periphery.[7] But it encompasses us all, and in no way can anthropologists escape its call.

James Merrill, whose astonishing poem, "Lost in Translation," inspired Clifford Geertz's own essay by the opposite name, "Found in Translation," continues to speak, at once ambivalently and hopefully, to anthropology:

> But nothing's lost. Or else: all is translation
> And every bit of us is lost in it . . .
> And in that loss a self-effacing tree,
> Color of context, imperceptibly
> Rustling with its angel, turns the waste
> To shade and fiber, milk and memory.[8]

with me their sense that northern Thailand and especially Chiang Mai are the sites of a nostalgia that has no parallel elsewhere in the nation. That Chiang Mai constitutes a historically retrojected object of desire for many wealthy Bangkokians is undoubtedly part of the reason for this seemingly exceptional imagination. That Chiang Mai is an especially coveted tourist destination that has substituted "authentic culture" for beaches in its advertisements to foreigners undoubtedly is another factor. But equally important is the insistence on a history that is prior to and independent of Bangkok's.

7. Vicente Rafael and James Siegel provide exemplary studies of this predicament and the politics of translation associated with it. See Vicente L. Raphael, *Contracting Colonialism: Translation and Christian Conversion in Tagalog Society under Early Spanish Rule* (Durham, NC: Duke University Press, 1992; originally published by Cornell University Press, 1988); James T. Siegel, *Solo in the New Order: Language and Hierarchy in an Indonesian City* (Princeton, NJ: Princeton University Press, 1986).

8. James Merrill, "Lost in Translation," in *From the First Nine: Poems 1946–1976* (New York: Atheneum, 1981), 352. The poem provides the title for Clifford Geertz's "Found in Translation: On the Social History of the Moral Imagination," in *Local Knowledge: Further Essays in Interpretive Anthropology* (New York: Basic Books, 1983), 36–54. It should be noted, however, that the poetics to which Geertz subscribes and those manifest in the poem are not entirely compatible. Geertz's essay, which occupies the uneven terrain between a woman who has no voice (the widow who is to be burned before the Danish man's horrified eyes) and one who has only her languages, ultimately refuses translation in his insistence that Bali is, well, Bali. For Geertz, it seems, difference is to be found only between and not within cultures. Merrill, by contrast, seems to subscribe to a much more radical poetics, his object being the split subject rather than the colonial encounter.

Merrill's poem belongs to the present of this book. It speaks to those, like the stranded figure around whom it is organized, who knows "little more" than "her languages. Her place."[9] More than this, it speaks to readers for whom language is home, to mobile subjects dislocated from territorial affiliation in the globalized afterlife of the nation-state. Merrill's character is not, however, cosmopolitan. She does not know, as does Merrill and his ideal reader, that her languages are not original but destined for translation. And it is this ignorance that plagues her and makes of "her place" the site of absolute loss.

For Merrill, in contrast, loss is itself productive, at once demanding and anointing translation. He inhabits an utterly secular world from which has passed (were it to have existed) the sense of a divine unity between name and thing. It is a world that no longer even laments its exile from that mute self-sameness that the ur-languages, Hebrew, Pali, and Sanskrit (among others), attempt to recall. Merrill's poetics, no less than modern anthropology's poetics, rest on a structuralist understanding of language, if by structuralism we follow Foucault to mean "the troubled consciousness of modern thought" and the means by which subjects are both alienated and emancipated as individuals.[10] For Foucault, it is a consciousness that emerges with the generalization of the commodity form, one in which language has become a matter of exchanging, and words, like money, have come to derive their value from their "pure function as sign."[11] But the "troubled" status of that consciousness derives from the fact that the function is ambivalent, and more, falsely premised on the fantasy of actual substitutability. The dream of absolute contingency gives way to one of difference. For if value's abstraction is the moment in which differences are overcome, it is a moment always haunted by the possibility that difference will return, by the fact that difference takes the form of hauntings. And as Marx well understood, the unity of the commodity is also its internal and irreducible

9. Merrill, "Lost in Translation," 346.

10. Michel Foucault, *The Order of Things: An Archaeology of the Human Sciences* (1966; New York: Vintage, 1970), 208.

11. Ibid., 170. The generalization of the commodity form is to be distinguished from the emergence of capital, despite the fact that capital "invariably takes the form at first of money" (Karl Marx, *Capital* [1887; Moscow: Progress, 1954], 1: 145). This is true both in principle and in northern Thai history, capitalism coming to the area only in the twentieth century. In *The Order of Things*, Foucault is concerned with the relationships between language and money, and less with capitalism, although there is some tendency to conflate monetization with capitalism in Foucault's early work, a failure that Jacques Derrida reproduces in *Specters of Marx: The State of the Debt, the Work of Mourning, and the New International* (1993), trans. Peggy Kamuf (New York: Routledge, 1994). For an excellent critique of this slippage, see Gayatri Chakravorty Spivak, "Ghostwriting," *Diacritics* 25, no. 1 (1995): 65–84.

difference, the difference between the sensuous particularity of the thing and the principle of equivalence by which it will become fantastically exchangeable. Even under capitalism, in which money is the origin of exchange, different kinds of commodities circulate. So too, translation is marked by the fact of identity's absence.

Foucault's discourse on economy and representation is, of course, devoted to the history of modern Western Europe, and I will have occasion to return to his discussion of language as exchanging in the latter part of this chapter. At this point, however, it is necessary to consider what the arrival of language's economization looked like from within northern Thailand. To this end, I turn to *The Poem in Four Songs.* I shall be treating it as an archive of sorts, seeking in it the traces of a transformation that was not fully realized at the time of the poem's writing but that, in retrospect, Phayaphrom seems to have anticipated with uncanny foresight. This transformation was not, it should be emphasized, one in which purity or singularity was displaced by plurality, for the language world of the north was plural long before modernity penetrated it. It is, indeed, the transformed nature of a plurality that preceded the modern to which Phayaphrom's poem turns us.

Archives, as Derrida has remarked, are structures of commencement, but they are also houses of sorts, the domestic places in which records of a commandment are kept.[12] This at least is the meaning that Greek etymology gives us, but it is also the meaning that Thai etymology gives us. For the *hong kep ekkasaan*, the "room for keeping important documents," also contains within itself a sense of the first. *Ekkasaan*, which may be translated to mean documents, especially primary or important documents, has its root in the word for first, *aek*, in the doubled sense of priority and significance. *Saan* translates as message, letter, or writing and suggests that which is communicated in a public domain.[13] An archive is therefore a place where one goes for first things, but only those that have relevance to the public. It is a source of originals that derive their significance from their imbrication in processes of dissemination, a *domos* whose interiority is made possible by the fact of a public. In this sense, then, it is a place of origins that, like the others to be discussed in this book, is also one of removal.

12. Jacques Derrida, *Archive Fever: A Freudian Impression*, trans. Eric Prenowitz (Chicago: University of Chicago Press, 1995), 2.

13. According to the Domnern-Sathienpong Thai-English dictionary, *saan* is the root for several terms denoting published information, including *saanakhadii* (story or article), *saantraa* (document under seal), *saanbob* (register), *khaosaan* (news), and *songsaan* (to send a message or letter). See Domnern Kaandaen and Sathientpong Wanapok, *Thai-English Dictionary* (Bangkok: Amarin, 1994), 499.

### The Poem in Four Songs: *The Poet, Authorship, and Subjectivity*

Strangely enough, *The Poem in Four Songs* was composed by Phayaphrom after he had ostensibly abandoned poetry for the life of a trader. Comprising four distinct "songs" and written in a relatively free but internally rhymed verse form called *khao*, Phayaphrom's tetralogy is, in fact, an epistle to his departed wife and lover, Chom. As narrated in the poem, Phayaphrom ventures out on what is supposed to be a brief trip to call in his debts so that Chom will be able to pay back her own relatives for loans they have extended her. Although his trip grows longer and longer, Phayaphrom assumes that Chom will be waiting for him upon his return to Laplaeng. However, in the place of an adoring and attendant wife, he finds his house empty. Panicked and beleaguered by doubt, he rushes to his neighbors in search of news and learns that Chom has returned to her home in Phrae at the bidding of her relatives. He also learns that she has done so accompanied by a mysterious man, and although many explanations are proffered by friends and relatives, this man becomes the point around which all of Phayaphrom's fears focus. The abandoned poet imagines a love affair between the two and, in spite of his efforts to sustain the image of his wife's purity, he is consumed by a madness-inducing rage.

In truth, it is the second marriage for both of them, Chom's former husband having died after saddling her with his gambling and opium debts. Both in historical actuality and in the poem, Chom and Phayaphrom meet at the palace in Phrae where Chom has been sent as guarantee for a loan made by an aristocrat named Phra Indra.[14] For his part (although this dimension of the story is not recounted in *The Poem in Four Songs*), Phayaphrom had gone to Phrae to inspect and possibly purchase an elephant for his king, but had recklessly gambled away the king's money on his return journey. For this crime, he was sentenced to death, his offering of an explanatory poem, "Unpropitious Elephants," having complicated matters enormously. Escaping by returning and seeking asylum under Phrae's King Wichairaachaa, Phayaphrom was later sentenced to death by this new benefactor when he was accused of an illicit relationship with a young woman in Wichairaachaa's court. Again eluding the death penalty—in part because he is granted time to write another poem—Phayaphrom and Chom flee to Laplaeng and set up house together.[15] It is thus

---

14. The fact that Phra Indra shares the name of Brahmanism's originary deity permits Phayaphrom to play on the reasons for Chom's departure, suggesting that it is like a death and that she has been called back to the place of her origins: "Lady, whom Indra descended to create / he took you / to Phrae, beautiful as a gem, / the City of Silk [also known as the City of Indra]" (IV. 606–9). Note that I have modified Egerod's translation slightly, to retain more of the ambiguity of the original.

15. Egerod, introduction to *The Poem in Four Songs*, by Phayaphrom, 5–7.

in exile from debt and the threat of death that the two live out their furious passion. The story of Phayaphrom's own difficult relations with kings and princes does not make its way into *The Poem in Four Songs*; instead, he figures as a creditor. In this regard, the poem reflects the poet's actual assumption of a new mercantile role in Laplaeng. In the poem, the possibility that Chom has been called back to pay her debts is raised only to be quickly abolished by the malignant fear of betrayal, but the historical record suggests that she had been summoned by Phra Indra, who held rights in her under the law of Phrae.[16]

Phayaphrom mourns his loss in hyperbolic fashion, even to the extent of ridicule from his friends. The poem is his effort to persuade Chom to return, and it is full of both poignant remembrance and acidic questioning. It is a profoundly vacillating text, which moves among different narrative possibilities and different forms of representation. Written in an epistolary style marked by direct narrative, it also contains recountings of other people's remarks, and it is embedded with citations of imagined dialogue, spoken first by Phayaphrom's traveling comrade, then by Chom, her niece, and other Laplaeng neighbors. Each song begins with a desperate wailing, a declaration of grief, confusion, and mad despair. Then, as if to stage the madness into which its author is descending, the poem spasmodically alternates between pleas for Chom to hear his poetry and insinuations that she has forgotten her own words.

The author of *The Poem in Four Songs* was born in 1801 and given the name Phrommin by his parents, Prince Saen Muangma of Lampang and his wife, Peng. Becoming a novice at the age of seventeen, Phayaphrom achieved considerable notice for his literary talents, and his renown as a student permitted him to go to Chiang Mai, where he continued his Buddhist education. There, he studied at Wat Chetiya Luang, an extremely important center of Theravada Buddhism that was soon to be caught up in the colonial conflict between the reform Buddhism of the Siamese kings and their Thammayut order and the deeper lineage of the northern Mahannikai sect.[17] Honing his exceptional skills as a writer before returning to Lampang, Phayaphrom nonetheless earned a living as a copyist of legal documents and a scribe of love letters. He acquired fame and his more exalted name after he was asked to revise a poem (*Hongsa*

16. Ibid., 7.

17. For an account of the Thammayut order's emergence in Mongkut's reign, see Stanley J. Tambiah, *World Conqueror, World Renouncer: A Study of Buddhism and Polity in Thailand against a Historical Background* (Cambridge: Cambridge University Press, 1976), 200–229. Also see Peter Jackson's discussion of the relationship between ideologically and rhetorically valorized differences between the orders and the actual lack of practical differences in *Buddhism, Legitimation, and Conflict: The Political Functions of Urban Thai Buddhism* (Singapore: Institute of Southeast Asian Studies, 1989), 85–91.

*Hin*) by the renowned author, Phaya Lomawisai, who had offered it to King Wolayanrangsi of Lampang.[18] Thus from an act of revision did Phayaphrom emerge as a writer.

The question of the relationship between writing and repetition, between the copy and the original, emerges here where biography and social history intersect each other on the eve of mechanical reproduction. In the copying that is also the writing of *Hongsa Hin*, Phayaphrom signals what is, in northern Thailand, a new problematic of representation but also a new problematic of authorship. The poet is himself caught halfway between the orator, who tells only his own story and bears responsibility for it, and the copyist, who is the mere vehicle of another's telling.[19] Though Phayaphrom worked as a copyist, there was something in the famously extraordinary act of poetic revision that, even then, was understood to be more than mere copying in the sense that monks, for example, copied the *suttas* or other Buddhist texts for the purposes of doctrinal dissemination. Indeed, Phayaphrom's mastery of the poetic principles was so impressive that Wolayanrangsi made him poet laureate of Lampang,[20] and his talents are abundantly evident in the complex marriage of Northern Thai colloquialisms with Pali, Khmer, and Central Thai loan words that defines *The Poem in Four Songs*.[21] This is true despite the fact that such scriptural copying was itself the site of considerable invention and redaction, as evidenced in the multiplicity of palm leaf manuscripts whose "different" inscriptions purport to be precise replications of original texts.

For those more familiar with post-Romantic visions of the writer as hero, the revision and even rewriting of another composer's work might seem to threaten the very concept of authorship, but it was common in Thailand at this time. One may glean from this fact that "authorship" in mid-nineteenth-century northern Thailand was conceived as being a complex technology of writing at the boundary between repetition and newness rather than an originarily creative act.[22] The porosity between the life of the man and that of the

---

18. Egerod, introduction, 5.

19. Jacques Derrida, *Of Grammatology* (1967), trans. Gayatri Chakravorty Spivak (Baltimore: Johns Hopkins University Press, 1974), 305.

20. Egerod, introduction, 5.

21. It is worth noting in this context that northern Thai literature continues to mark its own authenticity through the staging of plurality. Thus, the recent SEAwrite Award–winning novel, *Cao can phom horm* [Princess of the fragrant hair] by Chiang Rai writer Maalaa Khamjan (Bangkok: Khathataron, 1992), was praised for its dialogical usage of northern dialect and formal Siamese language.

22. In his account of the history of the Indonesian lingua franca Melayu, James Siegel argues persuasively that the institution of authorship emerges from that of copying in the moment that

narrator in the poem bears out this claim. Only in those moments when the poem features the citation of another's speech and marks it as having a status different from his own inscribed text does the poet's authorial voice become audible and, indeed, visible as such. This is not merely because there is an imagination of different speakers, but because Phayaphrom writes himself into the text as the recipient of a speech over which he has no control and that he hears himself hearing in the act of writing. At the general level, *The Poem in Four Songs* precedes that line between text and context that is, indeed, the condition of authorship in the modern sense.[23] Yet, it has already passed into a new domain of writing and irrevocably transgressed the category of poetry as it was understood in the north until that time.

Until this moment, and notwithstanding the differences between Thai and Lanna literary traditions, the discourse of poetics was concerned primarily with meter and verse forms and with phonology, the values of verbal propriety and beauty having been understood as mutually determining. Although the nineteenth century would see the displacement of poetry by prose, and of cosmologies by geographies,[24] that very displacement would generate a reactive revival of "traditional poetics" in the early part of the twentieth century.[25] Phayaphrom was undoubtedly familiar with the standard texts on poetics, including the fourteenth-century ur-text of national literature, the *Cindamani* of King Narai's reign.[26] The first *Cindamani* relied heavily on Pali verse forms

---

the copyist copies himself or herself into the text and introduces both displacement and deferral: "The copyist, the author, is someone who speaks the text of who writes it down. He is the one who, hearing what he copies, is moved to speak. And to speak not only the exact words, but sometimes other words beyond those that he reads or hears in the extended sense of the word 'hear'" (24). The case of Thai is not entirely analogous to that of Melayu, and the specificities that would accrue to an author writing in a language that is always—and always already—not his or her own mark an untraversible distance between the two. Nonetheless, Siegel's rich account of Indonesia suggests that the significance of the copyist and of the relationship between inexact copying and authorship in Thai history bear close attention and further inquiry. See James T. Siegel, *Fetish, Recognition, Revolution* (Princeton, NJ: Princeton University Press, 1997).

23. Ibid., 64.

24. Thongchai Winichakul, *Siam Mapped: A History of the Geo-Body of a Nation* (Honolulu: University of Hawaii Press, 1994).

25. Manas Chitakasem, "Poetic Conventions and Modern Thai Poetry," in *Thai Constructions of Knowledge*, ed. Manas Chitakasem and Andrew Turton (London: SOAS, 1991), 37–62; Nithi Aeusriwongse, *Paak kai lae' bai rua* [Quill and sail] (Bangkok: Amarin Kanphim, 1984).

26. Phra Horathibodi, *Cindamani, lem 1–2 lae' banthuk ruang nangsu cindamani lae' cindamani chabap phrachao borommakot* [Cindamani, volumes 1 and 2, with a note on the Cindamani and King Borommakot's edition]. (Bangkok: Sinlapa Bannakhan, 1979); hereafter referred to as *Cindamani*.

despite the fact that it assigned Sanskrit names to them, but it was devoted mainly to the provision of a poetic vocabulary and to a rather obsessively didactic insistence on correct spelling. This valorization of spelling initially suggests the primacy of writing, but it was actually part of an (impossible) effort to ensure the unity of writing and speech at the moment that poetry was transferred to the text from its previous residence in aurality and the traditions of oratorical performance. How is this possible? The seeming primacy of speech in writing perhaps can be better understood if one recalls that the use of particular, visually distinct but like-sounding consonants determines the tone of vowels in Thai, and thus correct spelling is, for the authors of the *Cindamani*, correct speech and, more important, beautiful speech.[27]

Significantly, the demand for properly poetic vocabulary is also, necessarily, a demand for multivocality. It requires that a poet "build a store of appropriate poetic vocabulary—homonyms, synonyms, and high-style words deriving from many foreign languages (Pali, Sanskrit, Khmer, Mon, Burmese and Thai)."[28] Indeed, according to the *Cindamani*, the perfect Thai language of poetry is named with a term of Khmer origin (*phro'*) indicating melodious sound. Not only must a writer possess the language of metaphor, but he or she must own it in several languages, any of which can be mobilized and made to enter the text as needed, where need is understood as a function of aurality. The substitutability of words and languages seems, in this context, to suggest a sign with no relationship to the object. But this would be a misleading and anachronistic interpretation, because in this case, the possibility of intralingual movement lies in the presumption of a divine connection between word and thing. In the *Cindamani*, the thing named retains its glorious autonomy, immune to what Benjamin would later call overnaming.[29] Meaning lies there, with the object and in the object, not in the infinite play of signification. Its proof is beauty, a beauty that poets will strive for with varying success but that will, in its sheer luminosity, be immediately recognizable to the one who beholds it. Because all poetic language is thought to be marked by the world and indeed to be an emanation of it, one language can be substituted for another according to the logic of the *Cindamani*, though not any substitution will suffice. Melodiousness, then, is the sign of an appropriate but temporally contingent substitution.

27. Ibid., 29.

28. Manas, "Poetic Conventions," 39. As Manas observes in a footnote (39 n. 4), poets actually compiled their own vocabularies, inventing new pairings and sets of homonymic or rhyming terms that could then be used whenever the need arose when composing a verse.

29. Walter Benjamin, "On Language as Such and on the Language of Man" (1916), in *One-Way Street*, trans. Edmund Jephcott and Kingsley Shorter (New York: Verso, 1997), 122.

That it is overdetermined by a text whose drive to canonicity and regularization emerges contemporaneously with the rise of a newly bureaucratized and hierarchized state should perhaps be borne in mind, and we will want to recall the fully political dimensions of this desire for unity as we consider the life of a poet whose verse brought him so close to death at the hands of state power.

Even within the confines of the *Cindamani*'s poetics, however, the imagination of a poetry in which the world could be spoken ran into obstacles. Consider, for example, the fact that Pali, the language from which Phayaphrom derived so much of his poetic vocabulary, was imagined to be something other than a language, in the strict sense of the term. In the premodern cosmologies of Thai Buddhism, the child who did not acquire any language was said to speak Pali. His or her mute tongue was imagined as the instrument of a truth in which word and thing were identical.[30] What can language that is not *a* language be when it is treated as *one* language among others? Truth—as the reconciliation of word and thing—is not translatable, and yet Phayaphrom (and other poets like him) makes Pali the cohabitor of a thoroughly interlingual text, one that demands constant translation. Are we to read this as an effort to insert truth, unadulterated, into the text? Or is it possible that the poem recognizes that the one who inhabits language can never approach truth except through language, and therefore that even Pali must be subject to translation by human beings? These questions will become crucially important as our reading of the poem proceeds, but it is necessary first to attend to the question of authorship. As will become clearer, however, authorship has everything to do with translation.

At the close of his poem, Phayaphrom apologizes for his failure to achieve correct rhyming (IV.1089). Yet, he is certain of his composition's future: "The fame of my poem will spread and shake people / all over the southern kingdoms / and everyone will talk about it" (IV.1118–20). The extravagance of the gesture is unmistakable, and we may remark this shamelessly self-appraising moment in the text as a gesture of signature. Elsewhere, Phayaphrom has named himself, asking his lover if she thinks of him the way he, Phrommin, thinks of her (IV.684), but more often, he refers to himself according to the northern Thai custom of relative seniority. Speaking of himself, he is *pii* (Central Thai: *phii*),

---

30. In the *Traiphum Phra Ruang*, we encounter the following passage: "When the child hears his parents, speaks their particular language, he copies their language. If the little one is born, grows up, and becomes strong, but does not learn any language at all, he will speak Pali, which is the language of truth" (122). See Frank E. Reynolds and Mani B. Reynolds, trans. and eds., *Three Worlds According to King Ruang: A Thai Buddhist Cosmology* (Berkeley: University of California Press, 1982).

the "elder" or, in Egerod's translation, "older brother." In such a relational form, the "I" of Phayaphrom's text seems unstable, fluid, irreducibly bound to an other. Yet, the redoubled signature at the poem's end, appearing first as the name and then as the flamboyant prophecy of fame, marks this poem's embrace of a historically new mode of subjectivity. It is unlike the religious texts of the time in which composition can serve only to spread the word of Buddha. This poem announces Phayaphrom, already infamous in his life as a rogue who jousts with words and tempts the king's patience with ironic verse. In his vanity, Phayaphrom gives voice to an autonomous, creative subjectivity—paradigmatically figured as a kind of heroic authorship—that is beginning to emerge and even to compete with the demands for an adherence to form as the criterion of artistic excellence. Still spectral in *The Poem in Four Songs*, this kind of subjectivity is nonetheless introduced in the form of a "leave-taking" by which the poet is able to extract himself from absolute loss and achieve perspective on his world. It is a poignantly ambivalent perspective that not only lets him imagine a future for his name, but that, as we shall see, leads him to ethnographize himself in the voice of another.

The irony of the relationship should not be passed over. Indeed, the infamous totality of modernist narrative is made possible in this moment of leave-taking, and few texts are more beautifully redolent of the ambiguity entailed by such a structure than Phayaphrom's is. As in other, more famous poems of the period, Phayaphrom's work thematizes the process by which a subject emerges in a romantic idiom. Sunthorn Phu, the more famous and slightly older poet of Bangkok during this period, wrote one his most famous travel poems, or *nirat*, on the occasion of being banished from the city and from his own lover. Forced apart without the opportunity for proper words, Sunthorn Phu describes the moment of separation as one in which the lovers were left with "only our eyes in place of words."[31] As in Phayaphrom's poem, the unspeakability of loss is tied, for Sunthorn Phu, to a moment of alienation that, oddly enough, permits a visionary return to the scene of loss and indeed renders it *as a "scene"* in a newly scopic economy. The poet speaks of the occasion from a remove, in the shadow of memory, and the scene is gathered up in his account as an object. Tacking back and forth between the moment of loss and that of a fantasized return, the alienated lover of the *nirat* is a protosubject, one who has acquired what Heidegger would call a "world view."[32] For him, the

---

31. Sunthorn Phu, *Nirat Muang Klaeng* [*Poem of the Middle Country*], trans. H. H. Prince Prem Purachatra (Bangkok: The National Identity Board, Office of the Prime Minister, 1984), p. 1, line 6.
32. Martin Heidegger, "The Age of the World Picture" in *The Question Concerning Technology and Other Essays* (1936), trans. William Lovitt (New York: Harper & Row, 1977).

world becomes that scene from which sense is derived and that against which his will is always poised. This is why the love poem may well be the first truly modern form of Thai literature. And this is why the love poem may be the proper object of any anthropological engagement with modernity. Quite simply, the love poem is the symptom of modernity. In any case, the leave-taking that makes authorship possible also calls up language again, this time as the belated medium of both a promise and a solicitation.

### Promises and Debt: Writing Loss

Words have a double status from the very beginning of *The Poem in Four Songs*, being at once solicitations and promissory statements. Those that Chom has forgotten are words of promise, words that bear the status of oath. They are her marriage vows, her promises of fidelity, and her offering of time to Phayaphrom. The fiction of the oath, of course, is that word and deed can be made identical and that speech can be made immune to time. The oath does not simply predict, it governs its speaker's future. But the performative utterance can be annulled after the fact; indeed, it can be seen to be operative only retrospectively. Chom's promises have proven false and hence the inauthenticity of her speech has been revealed. This is the source of Phayaphrom's madness, his delirious despair. For if the performative as such cannot be known in advance, if promises do not necessarily mean anything at the time of their utterance, then nothing can guarantee any performative in particular.

The doubt to which this realization quietly gives birth appears first in the poet's compulsive assertion of his own fidelity. It is a repetitiveness that, as the saying goes, protests too much. It conceals a haunting that the poem cannot, finally, banish: namely, that the desecration of a marriage vow will mean that Phayaphrom himself cannot be sure of his own capacity to resist traitorousness. For this reason, then, he commits himself to the future once again through the gesture of solicitation and commences a cycle of compulsive repetition. If Chom will hear his words and return, returning as much to her own promises as to Phayaphrom's invitations, that magical unity of word and deed may be restored. It matters not that the restoration takes place after an apparent breach. The truth of a promise is always a function of futurity, and there is no means of quantifying the deferral that binds speech and deed together in this performative logic. Thus, in the space of doubt, there remains the ironic possibility that Chom will prove herself true to her word. To have faith in his beloved, Phayaphrom must risk the deferral of her answer. The poem inhabits this space.

The aporia between the poetic inscription and its hearing is remarked from the beginning of the poem, when Phayaphrom writes: "I have begun my poetry / just wait and listen, my dear" (I.17–18). He does not ask Chom to wait in order that he be able to begin his poem, but rather, he states that he has begun already, and that after such a beginning, she must wait. The line break performs temporality here, inserting itself between the poem's commencement and its reception. A seemingly innocuous space, it assumes intensified significance through repetition and variation in myriad ways. That Chom does not read and that she is dependent on monks to tell her of Phayaphrom's writing is just one of these ways (I.108–110).

*The Poem in Four Songs* can be said to properly commence with the single phrase "Afterwards" (*lun lang naaj*, I.31), which appears, mimetically, after a thirty-line invocation of the poem's addressee, Chom.[33] Everything that follows, which is to say the poem itself, occupies this place of being after. Phayaphrom's agony is redoubled, however, by the fact that, in being after, he is also before the response that he seeks. The return for which he so desperately longs is suspended in the poem and by the poem. Endlessly deferred by her forgetting, Chom's literal return could nonetheless not dislocate Phayaphrom from the time of being after. He has already been wounded. That is the condition of his writing.

How much more painful, then, is the lurking possibility that though she receives his message, Chom will not respond to him. Indeed, it is this possibility of a withheld response that becomes the abyss across which the poet must stretch himself. How will he traverse this space of a possibly ruptured reciprocity? Not by direction, not with honesty, not "without shame or fear / like a seasoned rogue" (II.399–400), though he vows this much and promises a "letter/telling the complete story" (I.88–89). Rather, he will reach toward Chom through metaphor: "My words will be figurative / set forth in wellrounded poetry / mixed with comparisons" (I.14–16). With these lines, Phayaphrom implicitly declares his education, his training in the techniques of poetic composition, and his familiarity with the demands of the *Cindamani*. But he also stages the concept of metaphoricity as being at once part of the magical aspiration to overcome the abstraction of language and the irredeemably plural product of that emergence.

It is no accident that the figurative gesture and the poetic comparison will enter Phayaphrom's poem most insistently when he is attempting to "represent" the purity of his beloved. An awkward and clichéd loquacity afflicts the poet in these moments, and he is reduced to summoning his departed lover in

---

33. Egerod translates *lun lang naai* as "afterwards," but includes a parenthetical reference to the more literal and fuller meaning, which would be "After you had left." See Phayaphrom, *The Poem in Four Songs*, 11.

the imagery of gold, silk, gemstones, lotus blossoms, moonlight, and stars. Though elegantly composed and skillfully rhymed, these descriptions cannot hide their own failures to contain what they designate. Chom, in her original state, is pure, and her purity is inimical to its representation, which necessarily requires the invocation of something other than Chom and hence the very corruption of Chom. Does this mean that Phayaphrom has himself become implicated in the debasement of his lover? In the poem's paradoxical approach to Chom, we cannot avoid observing that the poet addresses her purity only from the perspective of loss. More important, insofar as his metaphors cannot help but fail her, Phayaphrom reproduces that loss in his own writing. The only possibility of a true presentation of Chom's purity would be her bodily presence in the text as such. However, the better his imagery, the less visible will it become and the more palpable will Chom be for the reader of these pages. Unfortunately, if Phayaphrom could restore Chom to the text in her luminous presence, his imagery and indeed his poetry would have become imperceptible, verily photographic. Not only would his authorship as a poet vanish, but Chom would have become the image of the image's ideal. She would not merely have returned to her own original words; she would have effaced Phayaphrom's.[34] Hence his ultimate embrace of a contaminating similitude: language "mixed with comparisons."

It is with profound grief that the reader comes to recognize with Phayaphrom that his romantic poetry must risk his lover's substitutability in language. Any comparison, of course, contains a moment of abstraction in which one object can be made to stand for another. This is the inherent potential of language to become an economy, a matter of exchanging. However, Thai poetry in general, and Phayaphrom's poem in particular, bridles against the possibility of infinite substitution. In this regard, they share something of the apparational, as Adorno defines it. They resist exchangeability by maintaining within themselves an awareness of the dissonance between the real and its representation.[35] Metaphoricity itself embodies this awareness, with each substitution operating only by virtue of the recognition that Chom is not, for example, really gold. As a result, Phayaphrom is spared Midas's fate. Yet, the poem's rhyming play of sound bespeaks something else as well. It is not simply in the play of absence that the poem operates. The poet also endeavors to introduce actual presence into the text, and the significance of voice as utterance, as the

---

34. For a discussion of this supplementary logic of the image, see Derrida, *Of Grammatology*, esp. 270–302.

35. Theodor W. Adorno, *Aesthetic Theory*. Gretel Adorno and Rolf Tiedemann, eds.; trans. Robert Hullot-Kentor. Minneapolis: University of Minnesota Press, 1997.

audible materiality of a speaking, cannot in the end be fully translated. This is why *The Poem in Four Songs* is so thoroughly embedded with citations.[36] And this is why there is such an insistence on rhyme. Each citation belies a commitment to the possibility of an absolute, irreducibly specific presence in the text. In the citation of speech, the poem aspires to flesh and to the dense bodiliness of a voiced speaking. But here again, written citation ironically undoes itself, for in the effort to make present another voice, the poet must encounter the status of his own text as secondary, belated, and ultimately supplementary. Ironically, then, it is when the poem seems to come closest to a sentimental poetics of presence that it opens onto a confrontation with exchange and the economies of substitution. In fact, *The Poem in Four Songs* stages a quite extraordinary dialogue between a nostalgically poetic desire for identity between the word and the world and the possibility that language is absolutely arbitrary and incapable of being marked by its object even in the moment of representation. In this face-off, poetry will be on the side of the gift, prose on that of economy. Separating the two will be a matter of memory.

*The Poem in Four Songs* summons the image of purity with enormous ambivalence and, indeed, as much to mark its corruption as to suggest its wished-for continuity. In its most severe form, this corruption is rendered as a molestation (I.173), but more often, it takes the form of a forgetting. Forgetting itself is the source of this corruption, and *The Poem* lays blame for it at Chom's departed feet. Repeatedly, Phayaphrom accuses Chom of forgetting her "original" words. But what can such forgetting mean in a poem so elegiac, so obsessed with remembrance as return? At the poem's beginning, forgetting has a rather innocent inflection, but it quickly becomes the idiom for betrayal. Thus, Chom is accused of "discarding" her words (I.408), until, in the poem's final song, her words have "vanished, gone away, disappeared completely" (IV.304). It is clear that the possibility of remembrance is the possibility of return—which is not yet to say that remembrance is return. This return, however, is not to be understood in crudely nostalgic terms. For there is an economy at work here, which, like the economy of goods and material exchange, is premised on the fiction of reciprocity, despite the fact that it operates on the basis of an irredeemable indebtedness. This impossibility of pure exchange enters into economy in the form of time, and memory is the figure through which that time can be experienced. It is an imaginal return that exists precisely because the absolute return is impossible.

---

36. The mark of the citation in Thai is not diacritical, but linguistic. In this poem, it takes the form of *waa*, a word meaning "that" which is often used in such constructions as *bok waa* (said that). However, the verb can remain implicit, and *waa* on its own signifies reported speech, either the speech of another or the earlier speech of the narrator.

Phayaphrom pleads, "Even if you do not remember / please listen / to the poem about my grief" (I.28–30). Not remembering is here written as *bo' cam*, using a poetic form that resonates with the simple Northern Thai (*kam müang*) form of the negative, *bo'* being the Northern Thai term for the negative, which is indicated by *mai* in Central Thai. *Cam* is common to both languages, and in both this form and in its pairing with *daaj* (as in *camdaaj*), it means to remember or recall, but also to confine or retain. Combined with *pen* (*campen*), it is usually translated as "being necessary," in which term memory is buried as the force of a demand. A series of related terms reveals the memory of all debt. It is a logic that underlies both the poetics of an impossible economy and the context within which Phayaphrom's poem more literally takes place. *Camnorng* means "to mortgage," *camnan* "to pawn or mortgage" (conventionally, *camnan* appears as *cam* only). In Central Thai, *camnaaj* is an elegant term used to mean "to sell or be sold."[37] Finally, *camnaeg* is a formal term to indicate the verb "to divide or separate." It will come as no surprise, then, to realize that the poem of mourning is utterly saturated with the politics of debt, with the remembrance of a receipt that must be repaid or that has not been repaid but haunts now, as a trace of the having-been-given of a gift that was not one. Mauss would perhaps have called this the *hau* of the poem: self-fetishizing, the poem seeks to transfer to itself that "spiritual power" that inhabits things given and that yearns to effect a return.[38] Phayaphrom offers credit, but "something other than utility," and in his lines, a "mystical and practical force resides."[39] The *hau*—of the gift and of the poem—represents (re-presents) the force of obligation, or indebtedness, in its material form. His poem might then also be read as the impossible "memory" of the gift of love.

As is well known by theorists of the gift, the remembrance of a gift is forbidden by the ideology of charity. In its pure form, gifting requires the absolute forgetting of the gift by the giver. To give knowingly would be to anticipate a return, and the fiction of the pure gift demands that it be given freely and without interest. This is why individuals, usually women, who give alms to monks in Thailand must do so without any acknowledgment from the recipients. No monk ever thanks or even looks upon the person who feeds him. In fact, the silence of the monk whose bowl is filled makes possible the merit that will accrue to the giver. That this silence emanates from an exclusively male institution and that it mainly constitutes a "field of merit" for women, who are the principal almsgivers in Thailand, suggest that the economy of the gift is

37. Hass, *Thai-English Student's Dictionary*, 117–19.

38. Marcel Mauss, *The Gift: Forms and Functions of Exchange in Archaic Society* (1925), trans. Ian Cunnison (London: Routledge and Kegan Paul, 1966), 9–10.

39. Ibid., 70–71.

never a purely formal matter, but that it is also a deeply political one. Women are here relatively obligated to give. And they are relatively unable to refuse a gift. As in the case of Chinese mothers discussed by Angela Zito,[40] Thai mothers are in complicated relations with their sons, who seem to be indebted as the recipients of their mother's gifts but whose receipt of such gifts indebts mothers. The *Traiphum Phra Ruang* extols the values of maternity at great length, but also provides the framework within which sons come to be the masters of their mothers. Insofar as women must make sacrifices to acquire merit to move up the ladder of rebirth, passing through masculinity into the asexual domain of the *thewada* and the enlightened ones, their sons are the ones who enable progress. First, as children, they receive their mother's generosity. Then, as monks who do not recognize their mothers' gifts, they facilitate the transformation of an interested offering into a sacrifice. As monks, sons escape the debt that maternal gifts would produce (and, until recently, most males were ordained at least temporarily). And, having escaped this debt, young men who exit the *sangha* are then able to enter into marital arrangements. The *sangha* is thus the structural switch-point in a society that historically has been organized by the principles of lateral exchange in the institution of marriage. However, encompassing this economy is an overarching system of debt, gift, and sacrifice, otherwise known as kinship and descent. According to this logic, women remain forever indebted to their sons, who will, in the end, permit them to give. Perhaps this is why the elderly women to whom I spoke in Chiang Mai invariably said that the task of women is "to give and to suffer." And perhaps this is why Chom could not, ultimately, refuse the call to stand in for another's loan. As one who was always already indebted, she not only guaranteed the loan, she was its sign.

Of course, modern marriage works as an economy only by effacing itself in the idea of mutual debt and by contrasting itself to something else: an interested exchange, concubinage, prostitution, or, in Thai, *kaan pen soopheenii* (prostitution). In this context, it is worth considering Marcel Mauss's attention to the dubiousness of the gift's freedom, and hence to its generosity, when he states that it is "the sovereign right to *refuse* a contract . . . which lends an appearance of generosity to the circulation of goods."[41] Sovereignty belongs to the recipient. Once accepted, the gift enslaves its receiver in a relation of debt. The giver is then always at risk in the moment of giving, for a refusal to receive will liberate the other person from all bonds. Phayaphrom, whose romantic fantasy is most modern in its refusal to admit the economics of marriage, confronts this risk

40. Angela Zito, personal communication.
41. Mauss, *The Gift*, 71, my emphasis.

profoundly when he solicits Chom to return, and her refusal appears to be an emphatic rejection of love's debt. This is made unequivocal when Phayaphrom remarks that he could have borne the departure of a mistress much more happily than that of a wife, for in having exchanged marriage vows, the two have ostensibly forged an eternal mutual debt. In leaving him, Chom has rendered her relationship to Phayaphrom as contractual and as self-interested as mere concubinage. She has threatened the possibility that the gift of love was merely an exchange, and in so doing she has introduced the possibility that sentiment was merely the counterfeit of money.

How then, does a gifting relation differ from one of more mundane exchange? Mauss's original formulation was not based simply on a categorical opposition. Rather, it suggested a historical development in which modern societies become increasingly economized, albeit with increasing moral value being attributed to the gift in proportion to the diminution of its prevalence and significance. There is an extent to which Phayaphrom's poem shares this sense and sees the burden of economic relations as that which threatens and ultimately annihilates the purity of his relationship with Chom. But in *The Poem in Four Songs*, the line between gift and economy is a difficult one to sustain, in both categorical and historical terms. Nor should this be surprising, given the tendency for a similar collapsing of oppositions in Mauss's own text.

Mauss's use of the term "appearance" leads Jacques Derrida to probe the precise relationships of transference and displacement by which the gift is bound in and to the circular economy. He writes, the "very appearance . . . of the gift annuls it as gift, transforming the apparition into a phantom and the operation into a simulacrum."[42] For Derrida, the recipient's recognition of the gift constitutes the moment in which it is transformed into debt. Hence, a true gift would rest upon the forgetting of the gift and, moreover, a forgetting of the act of forgetting. Indeed, as Derrida says, "Forgetting and gift would . . . be each in the condition of the other."[43] The correlate of such an argument is, therefore, that memory and economy are also "the condition of each other." If the equivalence postulated between gift and forgetting is itself an economizing one, it nonetheless permits us to return to Phayaphrom's poem with an enlarged perspective from which to read the dynamics of memory and debt. Ultimately, Derrida's argument will center on the place of time in the definition of economy. Time becomes, for him, the one thing that distinguishes gifting from other kinds of economic exchange, even as time is the one thing that cannot

42. Jacques Derrida, *Given Time: I. Counterfeit Money*, trans. Peggy Kamuf (Chicago: University of Chicago Press, 1991), 14.

43. Ibid., 18.

finally be banished from rational economy.[44] Time as interval (what he calls "the temporization of temporalization") is the principle of *différance* through which the gift seeks its restitution and becomes other than itself.[45] Phayaphrom's text is also structured by the time of the gift, even though it negates that time with a plea for remembrance.

Bearing within themselves the traces of memory (*cam*), *camnaeg*, the Thai transitive word for partition or division, and *camnaaj*, the word for sale and/or distribution, somehow capture the complex relationship between remembrance and debt. To be sure, these are rather special constructions, even in Central Thai, but Phayaphrom's own play between colloquial Northern Thai and formal Central Thai calls up precisely this reading of the other shadows around words. From the moment he tells Chom to attend him, even if she does "not remember" (*bo' cam*) (I.28), Phayaphrom's poem is marked by precisely this haunting of memory by separation and debt. Prior to undertaking his own journey to call in the monies owed him, to force memory on those for whom he is creditor, Phayaphrom asks Chom for time and promises "not to be slow" (II.345). He himself is unable to sustain this commitment, but it is because Chom does not remember her promise to give him time that Phayaphrom later asks, "Where did the vows vanish?" (II.548). The relationship between terms and principles is not, however, merely an etymological one. It is also thematized within the poem as a narrative about the condition of being multiply beholden to other people's memory and their call to restitution.

To begin with, Chom is beset by the accusations of her relatives, who "were afraid . . . that their property would be forfeited" (I.660) and therefore "were in a great hurry to retrieve their property / which they had loaned to [Chom] on that occasion / in the past" (I.687–89). This indebtedness is, itself, only a secondary one, caused by an earlier indebtedness that Chom's first husband had "poured upon" her (II.144). In the poem, Phayaphrom writes, "Those were not debts for rice, / incurred to fill the innards and feed the belly. / Nor were they debts for sacrifices and offerings, / nor debts for buying / betel or food / nor for meritorious deeds. . . . / Those were debts to raise money for Yunnanese opium" (II.145–53). A corrupt indebtedness, this memory of a receipt that has been without righteousness from the start dooms Chom to being recalled by her other relatives. There are at least two senses in which this fateful logic works itself out. First, the poverty and despair into which her ex-husband's debt drives Chom leads her to a renunciation of more proper ritual indebtedness. Thus, instead of making ritual offerings to the spirits of place and to the spirits of the

44. Ibid., 41–43.
45. Ibid., 40.

deceased—as would be customary for her in this historical context—Chom says (or is reported by Phayaphrom to have said), "If I would eat all [the offerings] / it would be better, my stomach would be full" (II.235–36). By refusing to acknowledge her eternal ritual debt to these spirits and the powers they embody, Chom becomes subject to the profane indebtedness that she inhabits in relation to her relatives. It is the mark of Phayaphrom's self-professed love that he agrees to answer this debt by calling in the monies owed to him by ethnically Mon and Tai traders. Around this transference of debt, Phayaphrom and Chom took an oath, "pledged each other" (II.344). Phayaphrom himself is sure that he will be repaid because he holds in his hand the words, the "signatures" of those who owe him. Insofar as proper names are the form of words closest to the sign of absolute singularity, and insofar as they approach an identity between signifier and signified, they guarantee for Phayaphrom that the money given will be returned and the original value restored. Even with such certainty and even after their oath, however, Phayaphrom must ask permission to "go and demand what is owed me / from my many debtors / in the many villages and houses" (II.315–17). He asks in order to demand, signaling his own debt to the woman he loves.

Before taking his leave, however, Phayaphrom is prevailed upon by Chom to consider redeeming her elder cousin, Bao. Bao is in debt-bondage, and her daughter, "young and lovely," would come to live with Chom and Phayaphrom in the event that they took over Bao's debt. The two also discuss another young woman, Chanta, who is in need of redemption and desirous of their protection. They decide between these two on the basis of "ancient customs," recalling as they do so the case of a "dishonest deal" concerning the "redeeming of a slave" (II.507–16). Finally, they determine that Chom will indeed pay for her cousin's freedom.

A seeming digression in the middle of the poem, this conversation about debt and redemption is indicative of the local labor economy, and it indexes a world in which everyone is indebted (women much more so than men) by virtue of a transcendent hierarchy in which only the king and the spirits have sovereignty. The conversation about Bao and Chanta is also an allegory of the transference that Phayaphrom wants to arrange for his wife's debt. His fantasy of a debt redeemed by love, by a union that dissolves difference, proves impotent, however. And it is this failure that then leads to the necessary remembering of a relationship defined by difference. That difference was sustained rather than sublated in the metaphorics of translation.

On several levels, the poem is torn between these two trajectories of Phayaphrom's desire. On the one hand, the poet consciously longs for a pure restoration of his lost love, and in this regard, he dares to wish for a negation of time.

Love is here on the side of the impossible, figured also as gift. On the other hand, he inhabits the "afterwards," the time after loss, and, in his recognition of this subjection to time, he embraces the only possibility for survival, namely, the economy of difference in time (which is to say *différance*) wherein translation is possible and even necessary. This is the time of memory, not the time of the gift—which is forgotten. Language itself mediates this conflict.

As the poem gathers itself toward an end in "Song Four," metaphor struggles against the possibility that purity will simply exceed language and make a mockery of all representation. Having repeatedly invoked his grief-induced delirium, Phayaphrom describes his confusion before the phantasmatic image of Chom: "I see the likeness of your face / . . . but then you have disappeared from my sight" (IV.698–702). Absence becomes excess as Chom, the pure beloved, begins to appear, impossibly, like "twenty-five carat gold" (IV.885). Here, a space opens up between language and its object, the impossible image marking its own inadequacy to the task of re-presentation more than anything else. For this very reason, because the disjuncture between language and object has been staged in Phayaphrom's effort to convey Chom's singularity in terms of a standard value, metaphor can be redeemed.

In the last song, Phayaphrom bespeaks the strange but unequal intimacy that he continues to desire despite Chom's departure. He proclaims, "I love you / like a water buffalo is loved by the minah bird / which picks its lice and pulls out its ticks" (IV.317–20). A surprising tenderness infuses these images of the bird feeding on the "eggs and maggots" that infest the buffalo's back. Tellingly, the love pictured here is not so much a desire for unity as it is the oblivious coexistence of two very different beings. That is to say, it specifically resists dissolving into an image of oneness. In this respect, it departs markedly from the mutually annihilating passion Phayaphrom described in "Song One" as the desire to consume each other: "We were so much in love / that we felt like eating each other up, / like swallowing one another" (I.359–61). It is also a rather irresistible gesture of self-translation.

### Dialogue and the List: The Ethnography of Economy

Having cast himself in an image of such extreme otherness, Phayaphrom opens up the possibility of rereading his representations of locality as being infused by difference. More important, he links this possibility to a reading of difference as being the condition of possibility for representation. This conceptualization emerges most visibly and perhaps most awkwardly in the fulsome cataloguing of local attributes and practices in "Song Three." The labor of description devoted to the poet's hometown would seem, on first sight, to be addressed to the now distant Chom, the poem's intended hearer, and to other readers who are perhaps less familiar with it. Ironically, however, it is Phayaphrom himself who receives these passages in the poem. The descriptions are, in fact, part of the cited speech attributed to Chom's niece, who attempts to soothe Phayaphrom by reminding him of the local bounty she can access for him.

Initially, the plenitude that is being summoned in the description of Laplaeng wants to be read in terms of a compensatory logic. The verbosity and the aspiration to completeness of these passages seem to respond merely to Phayaphrom's loss, suggesting to him the possibility of a substitutional value. It is a violent substitution, of economy for affect, of consumable produce for love's sentimental eternity, and, not surprisingly, the poet is horrified by such an offering. But even this reading seems to beg others, for there is an excessiveness in this passage—one feels burdened by its length—that demands to be asked why this veritably ethnographic depiction has been written in a dialogic form and addressed to the poet himself. In the end, the passage seems only to dislocate the poet from his own home by bringing to the level of explicit discourse what ought to be taken for granted, what ought to form the mere ground on which the text is written. Rhetorically, we might ask: Does it not alienate a domain that would be assumed by its inhabitants as part of a naturally cultured landscape? Does it not objectify what ought to be a tacitly known habitus?

To be sure, Chom's niece would have had relative claims to this place in the context of matrilineal descent, where property is passed through women, as was the case in this area during the nineteenth century. Hence, Phayaphrom's possession of such knowledge might be said to come from his wife and her matrikin and thereby be foreign to him. But such a baldly functional anthropological reading does not finally permit an adequate confrontation with the fertile strangeness of the text or with the centrality of such strangeness in the poet's rendering of the relationships between debt and translation. Let us turn to the text itself. I quote at length to give readers a fuller appreciation of the poem's own extension. Prior to the passage cited here, Chom's niece has told Phayaphrom that he is pitied by his relatives but that he need not worry for his future.

> In this glorious city of Laplaeng
> we shall never die of famine.
> Coconuts and pith of palms,
> betel nuts and betel leaves, pigs and wine,
> as well as food and all the spices —
> if you feel like eating and drinking these,
> you need not worry —
> [the country] flows with these things, they pile up plentifully,
> there is always enough.

Topknot oranges, smooth oranges, and crow oranges,
tiger eye fruit, and durian,
we have plenty of all of these.
Ripe jack-fruit,
fragrant fleshy mangosteen
known for its taste all over Thailand
—if you want to have those
there is no need to go far away,
we have them right here
in the country and villages of Laplaeng.
The three-year-mango
with its very delicate taste,
the three-vermilion-mango, the si'daa mango, the horse mango,
the mango-which-the-crows-sit-around,
the cotton-like mango with the awful smell,
the kun citrus, the Kaffir lime, the orange, the tangerine, the lemon,
hog plum and myrobalan,
pomelo with the white meat,
jack-fruit with the elongated pulp,
pomegranate and sour plums,
the sweet pineapple,
tamarind with the short sections,
—there is always enough of everything sweet.
Cug fruit and kiang fruit
rose apples covering the tree all around
sugar apple and buffalo kween fruit
and ripe citrus fruits
—we have plenty of all of these.
We plant them in rows
we fill the orchards of each village with fruit trees.
Whatever you want to eat,
please just let me know,
and I will go and search for it.
The green-ripe banana and the sandal-wood banana,
the dwarfed golden banana and juicy banana of Lawa
as well as the Southern egg-banana and the Chaing Mai banana,
the dirty abandoned banana,
and the sour banana with many hands
stand close together in rows
fencing in the orchards as far as the eyes reach.

The dwarfed golden banana,
which is black when ripe and has blunted ends
—these are abundant everywhere.
The milky banana
with the fiercely bitter blossoms,
nice and sweet when fully ripe,
all kinds of fruit,
whenever the right season has come
they are all in the region.
Some are sweet and some are sour,
whether you wish to eat fruit unripe
or fully ripe,
there is indeed plenty.
When the fruits reach the stage of maturity
there's enough for some to rot.
Please yourself, uncle.
Even though my aunt
has left you and run off
don't be upset about it at all,
I will not let you starve.
The glorious Laplaeng
has not gone under but still stands firm.

.   .   .   .   .   .   .   .   .   .   .   .

Even if you wish to eat cake
mixed and kneaded in the Southern way,
it shall be according to your heart's desire.
Drops of gold [sugared egg yolk dropped in boiling lard], or pinches of
    gold [sugared egg yolk in small cups]
placed on a banana leaf tray,
rice dessert with intestines in it, or mixed dessert,
according to your wish
and desire,
piles of round cakes
fried in lard and dipped in molasses,
custard cakes
put in a little cup
such as they sell at temple festivals and at Chinese gambling places,
oily rice mixed with Dioscorea root,
lotus dessert floating in water resembling a seed,
popped rice, molded and mixed with sesame,

cakes baked in a pan with depressions like mortar holes,
and Indian egg custard,
rice crushed and powdered with sesame
agar in syrup cut up into diamond-shaped pieces,
—and the syrup covering it is saturated with scents
of granulated sugar, which has been made into a heavy mixture during
    stir-boiling
and is poured over and sipped—
cookies
which are even tastier,
cakes in the shape of monitor eggs, sago dessert,
Chinese balsam cake
with pork inside,
the cake of the Wise one [the Buddha]
made with Southern molasses
—if you want to eat any of those
I will make them for you.
Thai desserts have many names
like squeezed-through-a-hole-so-it-has-a-tail
and seeds of sweet basil. (III.652–775).[46]

One is tempted to read the anticipation of Boasian method in these lists. So many details and so little image. Boas aside, it is clear that in this poem, lack summons the mimetic performance of plenitude. The poem makes visible this bounty by naming it, by making a performance out of such naming. The nearly absurd distinctions among kinds of bananas and oranges reflects a multiplicity that marks language in the process by which language remarks diversity. But formally, the list is the manifestation of pure quantity (for which reason Walter Miller made it the only trace of modernity in the postapocalyptic landscape).[47]

46. In excerpting this portion of the text, I have omitted some rather difficult but brief passages in which Chom's niece speaks about the kinds of women Phayaphrom might desire, likening them to various kinds of ghosts (III.724–26). Much could be said about the categorization of divorced and widowed women as being like ghosts. For in likening them to this kind of malevolent spirit (which is the connotation in these passages), Chom has suggested that these women are, like ghosts, excessively receptive to the communication of desire. They are the women who would not refuse solicitations, and they seem uncannily able to hear desire even before it has found itself expressed in language. In referring to ghosts in this manner, I am indebted to the work of James T. Siegel and his analysis of ghosts in *Fetish, Recognition, Revolution*, 76–93.

47. In Walter A. Miller Jr.'s novel, *A Canticle for Leibowitz* (New York: Bantam, 1961), the only link to the twentieth century consists of a series of lists, one itemizing a "pound pastrami, . . . can kraut, six

In Phayaphrom's poem, the list marks the translation of multiplicity into quantity, of difference into an exchangeable value. As such, it is the very instant at which the commodity enters, the point at which language becomes a matter of exchanging and qualitative differences are dissolved into the abstraction of the value-sign. The economy in which Chom could be offered as a guarantee for Phra Indra's loan had not yet made her entirely exchangeable. Indeed, it is her very uniqueness, her human immunity to exchange, that makes her the perfect guarantee for a loan. Something about the difference between a monetary loan and the bodily presence of a young woman gave the creditor security. Ironically, when Chom's niece advises Phayaphrom to forget her and to take solace in the objects of his hometown, she has gestured even more radically toward the substitution for Chom by commodities. Chom's niece liberates her aunt from one bondage and delivers her into another. It is this niece who is cast by the poet as the one who will perform the role of trader. A violent repression and projection, perhaps. Phayaphrom has rendered her in the role of the man of whom I wrote earlier in this book. She gives over a woman to the economy of pure instrumentality.

Something more enters the list, however, because despite the appearance of taxonomic totality, a surplus is also introduced. There is, as Chom's niece says, more than enough of everything. Indeed, there is "enough for some to rot." The image suggests an almost Bataillean analysis of value-production as something that occurs in the moment of destruction or waste.[48] However, this would be a slightly anachronistic reading, and, although it is clear that excess produces value for the sovereign subject, it is not clear that such destruction would be allowed to displace satiety in Phayaphrom's world. The word "some" secures the poem against a truly postrepresentational reading.[49] Only "some" can rot. Not all. First, there must be satisfaction, even totality. The transgressive gesture, which would risk everything for value in destruction, was not yet thinkable at the time of the poem's writing (and we will encounter it only briefly, in chapter

---

bagels," and another containing columns of numbers and percentages. Phayaphrom's poem is not apocalyptic in the literal sense that Miller's novel is, but it shares the temporal location of being uttered "afterward" and, likewise, shares an insinuation that the loss of the absolute is effected by the gesture to substitute commodities for sentiment.

48. Georges Bataille, *The Accursed Share: An Essay on General Economy*, Vol. 1, *Consumption* (1967), trans. Robert Hurley (New York: Zone Books, 1991), esp. 19–41.

49. I use the term postrepresentational in Foucault's sense as it appears in *The Order of Things*, 208–11. The practice of destructive value production, which I allude to here, is discussed at length in Foucault's essay, "Préface à la transgression," *Critique: Revue Générales Publications Françaises et Étrangères* 19, nos. 195–96 (1963): 751–69.

8 of this book, when we consider the recent emergence of Saivite religiosity in northern Thailand).

The fiction of totality, of closure, will enable and underwrite the notion of general economy, just as it will enable and underwrite the structuralist imagination of language as a finite set of signs within which the play of meaning and value can occur. However, the rationalization of the world that accompanies the fiction of totality is not immediately apparent in the lists of fruits and cakes, despite the fact that the list seems to contain within itself an aspiration to completeness and orderly arrangement. Rationalization lies elsewhere, in the oblique references to agricultural technique by which the landscape has been rendered textual.

There are two brief moments that call for attention in this regard. The first is when Chom's niece departs her lists to remark on the planting of trees. She tells Phayaphrom, "We plant them in rows" (III.689). Second, and in quick succession, she reiterates her claim when she remarks, only ten lines later, that the bananas with "many hands / stand close together in rows / fencing in the orchards as far as the eyes reach" (III.698–700). What can be meant by this particular detail, so mundane but so precise? "We fill the orchards of each village with fruit trees" (III.690), she says. In this statement, there can be no doubt that the orderly fullness of the village orchards produces that bounty that exceeds need and negates desire. The rows are the sign of a measured conversion of the field from the place of bodily movement and habitation to a rationally ordered, homogeneously distributed space. This racinated space, whose origin is agriculture, already suggests that abstract territoriality that is, at the time of Phayaphrom's writing, informing the constitution of the national geo-body and the transformation of tributary galactic polities into a territorially coherent state.[50]

The rows are, apparently, the sign of economy. They are also the sign of writing. The furrows of the farmer who moves from one end of the field to another and then back, wasting no return journey without planting along the way, are the prototype of a certain kind of writing. As Derrida says, this order presages geometry, even if it is driven by the original needs of manual inscription.[51] Of course, Phayaphrom knows that his poem will not be read by its intended audience, but heard in recitation. So rhyme performs the line, but the fact of lines is still remarkable in the poem. Chom's niece repeats her statement to this effect, and insists that this manner of planting is the source of fecundity in the cultivated world of Laplaeng. Properly productive, they are also the fence

50. Thongchai, *Siam Mapped*.

51. Derrida, *Of Grammatology*, 288.

against alterity in the form of excess. The many hands of bananas bound the orchards and stave off that other kind of productivity that, in its wildness, would exceed need, becoming either value or malevolence.

The opposition is clear from the niece's perspective. The economy of the furrowed field is the alternative to Phayaphrom's madness. In the line, in the abstractions of a rationalized productivity, in the exchange of quantity for the priceless singularity of romance, Phayaphrom is to find his salvation. However, the offer is being made to Phayaphrom as a merchant, not a poet. Chom's niece is appealing to the already economistic sensibility of the man whose poetry has, in fact, long ago sentenced him to death. It was, after all, his mercantile activities that were to furnish the couple with the means to liberate Chom from her debts.[52] In this regard, then, Chom's niece is merely asking Phayaphrom to pursue his initial inclination to economize his relationship, an inclination that was premised on profound misrecognition and, as a result, was utterly doomed to destroy what it wanted to redeem. Having realized too late that Chom's gift of time could not be commensurated against the return of his loans, that he could not ask her to wait longer in hopes of more money, Phayaphrom returns to himself as a poet, seeking origins in the spoken word. And it is too late. This is the realization from which he shies and against which his delirium rages. For the writer, it is always too late. For the writer, voice will always follow writing.

## A Traffic in Language: The Problem of Printing

"The alphabet," writes Derrida, "is commercial, a trader." This is because the "movement of analytic abstraction in the circulation of arbitrary signs is quite parallel to that within which money is constituted."[53] Not only within a single society but between different societies and economic organizations, money permits movement. It is not insignificant in this regard to note that Phayaphrom's journey to collect debts is specifically a journey across cultural boundaries. He is going to call in dues from both Mon and Tai traders. Ironically, this movement amid and between different groups is one that causes Phayaphrom to tack back and forth between the two communities who now vie in the imaginations of spirit mediums for the status of original inhabitants of the area

52. It is possible to discern in this poem the grounds for arguing both that debt bondage constituted an alienation of women's bodies and that it is not identical to the prostitution of today in which a more total exchangeability can be seen. For an excellent and judicious account of the history of prostitution and women's changing status in Thailand during this period, see Suwadee Tanaprasit-patana, "Thai Society's Expectations of Women, 1851–1935" (Ph.D. diss., University of Sydney, 1989).

53. Derrida, Of Grammatology, 300.

around Chiang Mai. In fact, the Mon moved into what is now Thailand from Burma in a series of migrations, beginning sometime around the sixteenth century. Speaking dialects of Mon-Khmer, which has its own script and system of writing, these immigrants have been largely assimilated into the dominant Tai-speaking communities, and although a clear sense of ethnicity seems to have been a feature of Mon society at the time of Phayaphrom's writing, this no longer obtains.[54] Most nationalist historians now read the Mon as having been foreigners whose entry into the Thai community was facilitated by Burmese imperial wars, but contemporary spirit mediums often turn to the Mon as an aesthetic point of reference and a source of linkage to what they imagine as the celestially inspired Buddhism of Khmer's Angkor Wat. In Phayaphrom's time, they clearly represent a site of difference and, with their own sets of "totem-like spirits,"[55] their own language and their own script, they demand of him not only travel but translation. Phayaphrom must seek them "north and south," and he does so with the instrument of money.

In its staging of money as the instrument and object of travel, Phayaphrom's poem is marked by the moment of its writing. Currency at this point in time is still hard to come by and incompletely nationalized. Indeed, the lack of coinage and of liquidity in general can be seen in the ubiquity of debt relations and in the still dominant practices of corvée labor. Both were about to be displaced by capitation and other forms of taxation.[56] Coinage from the surrounding empires, from China, and from Bangkok moved awkwardly but regularly across the area and were converted according to need, although most debts were paid in kind until the middle of the nineteenth century. England's forced opening of the markets in Thailand in 1855 had precipitated a need for more cash in the national treasury—as imported products began to fill the markets of Bangkok— and systematic accounting of conversion rates became equally necessary. The procedures for achieving this, including tax farming by minority ethnic Chinese, were developed during the reigns of Rama IV (1851–1868) and Rama V (1868–1910). Quickly enacted in Bangkok, these procedures traveled swiftly but unevenly into the remoter regions of Siam (where they were frequently enacted by Haw Chinese). The same can be said of nationally standardized writing.

Efforts at systematizing Thai writing were occurring almost simultaneously,

54. Brian L. Foster, "Ethnic Identity of the Mons in Thailand," *Journal of the Siam Society* 61 (1973): 210–13. Also see the discussion of Mon language and cultural history in William A. Smalley, *Linguistic Diversity and National Unity: Language Ecology in Thailand* (Chicago: University of Chicago Press, 1994), esp. 225–32.

55. Smalley, *Linguistic Diversity and National Unity*, 225.

56. Charles F. Keyes, *Thailand: Buddhist Kingdom as Modern Nation-State* (Boulder, CO: Westview, 1987), 45.

with the introduction of formal Thai-language textbooks in the 1870s.[57] The first dictionary, a Thai-Latin dictionary by Bishop Pallegoix, had been part of an effort at translation rather than standardization, and was written in 1854, but it would be some time before a rationalization of the alphabet would be deemed essential for national development (as it was in the 1930s and 1940s under Phibul Songkhram's cultural nationalist administration, when the number of consonants was reduced from forty-four to thirty-one).[58] Nonetheless, King Rama IV had already expressed a concern with linguistic deterioration and especially the improper use of lower Thai in printing. It was under his auspices that the problem of language came to be understood as a problem of writing and printing.[59]

As Nithi Aeusriwongse has so convincingly argued, Rama IV's concern with writing was a concern with the improper juxtaposition of lower and formal or royal usages and with what he perceived to be the deterioration of Thai in print. It was a concern born of a sense of loss: a loss of proper placement and of the appropriate recognition (from Rama IV's perspective) of hierarchical difference in the social order.[60] One cannot help but note that Phayaphrom's text, with its weaving of Pali and Northern Thai, was itself in violation of the purity Rama IV desired. Nonetheless, it shared the nostalgic desire for a return to origins even as it made such a return impossible except through translation— across time and between tongues.

In Rama IV's mind, the loss of linguistic propriety and the revolutionary risk that it seemed to entail was effected in and through the mechanization of writing.[61] Populist publications had a physical layout premised on the juxtapositions of different stories. Their intelligibility (and hence salability) necessitated that the speech of and about the monarchy be translated from its royal form, *phraraadchadamrad*, to formal but common Central Thai. Until this moment, the king's authority was supposed to be inviolable and untranslatable, for translation would suggest also the possibility of substitutability. Similarly, His Majesty was supposed to be invisible, and this is why, until Rama V's reign—

57. Anthony Diller, "What Makes Central Thai a National Language," in *National Identity and Its Defenders: Thailand, 1939–89*, ed. Craig J. Reynolds (Chiang Mai: Silkworm, 1991), 102.

58. Ibid., 104.

59. Ibid., 101.

60. James T. Siegel discusses a similar crisis in Java, where the juxtapositions of photographs of royal personages with commoners and mundane objects in popular magazines and newspapers led to concern about the loss of social enframement and proper relations. See *Fetish, Recognition, Revolution*, esp. 84–86.

61. Nithi Aeusriwongse, "Phasaa thai mathathan lae' kaan müang" [Central Thai language and politics], *Phasaa lae' Nangsü* 17, no. 2 (1984): 31.

when the photograph was no longer a risk but a seduction—commoners were not permitted to look upon the king.[62] At the time, in the 1850s and 1860s, however, the indiscriminacy of the print medium seemed to constitute a threat to the old order. It would be some time before the monarchy would embrace the mass media as a means of translating absolute authority into popular mandate. Indeed, the full transformation would take almost a century to complete itself. At the beginning, in the first years of mass-produced literature, Rama IV would attempt to subject it to the kinds of purifying reforms that he had introduced in the realm of religion. Ironically, when considered in relation to his concerns about language, Rama IV's attempts to effect the rationalization and deritualization of Buddhism can be seen less as part of a "protestant" populism than as a reactionary bid to restore the authority of the institution that sacralized his own power. That these efforts had precisely the opposite effect is only testimony to the contingency of history and to the fact that Rama IV was himself a medium, rather than an inventor, of a modernity whose time had come.

It may be useful to pause here and reconsider the arguments about language and exchanging to which Foucault introduced us in the opening section of this chapter. It will be remembered that Foucault equates modernity with a structuralist orientation in which both language and money have lifted off from material reality and come to appear autonomous. In this regard, he relies heavily on Marx, whose work on the generalized commodity first made possible the analysis of money as an abstract form, "distinct from the palpable body form" and "purely ideal."[63] Thus dislocated from the substance in which it is coined, money operates only as the medium of exchange, being at once productive and dependent on desire. Money in this sense is thus akin to language in two senses. First, like language, it functions as a designator of value, though its form is at once arbitrary and temporarily fixed. Second, money is the conceptual representation of exchangeability just as language is the conceptual representation of translatability.[64] Within structuralism, both money and language presume an abstraction on the basis of a universal standard, whether that be value or meaning. And both permit circulation.[65]

Foucault refers to this fantasized universalism under the rubric of *representa-*

62. Christine E. Gray, "Royal Words and Their Unroyal Consequences," *Cultural Anthropology* 7, no. 4 (1992): 448–63.

63. Marx, *Capital*, 1: 98.

64. On language as translatability, see Walter Benjamin, "The Task of the Translator" (1923), in *Illuminations*, trans. Harry Zohn, ed. Hannah Arendt (London: Fontana, 1973), 70–82; and "On Language as Such and on the Language of Man," 107–23.

65. Derrida, *Of Grammatology*, 300.

*tion*. For, in the seventeenth and eighteenth centuries of Western Europe from which he draws his analysis, there is still the fantasy of a "system of signs that would be transparent to the continuity of being."[66] The representability of the world is, at this time, not in question, has not yet been displaced by mere syntax. Later, the violent introduction of will, or desire outside of the law, will rupture this aspiration to transparency and, according to Foucault, bring about the apotheosis of representation.[67] As always, the obstetric narrative in Foucault's writing turns out to be more complicated than a first glance might suggest. One episteme never completely displaces the other, but only comes to dominate its antecedent in his analysis; thus, the episteme of representation survives even after the interventions of transgression's philosophers: Sade, Bataille, Genet, Klossowski, and, of course, Foucault himself. And despite the emergence of what Foucault describes as a Quixotic libertinage, the logic of representation continues to inform a great deal of social life in the West.

The demand of representation is, suggests Foucault, that appearance and being be somehow adequated. This is why a structuralist understanding of language requires that meaning be temporarily fixed and that currencies be said to truly represent the value of a product (rather than the desire for it, for example). Representation becomes a problem as soon as one admits that meaning might be totally arbitrary or absolutely unfixable by virtue of time's intrusions into the relations of difference between signs. Because representation remains committed in some sense to what is perceived to be the true order of things, and because it secures itself with reference to something outside of itself, it is the point from which the consciousness of loss emerges. Only from within representation can the plenum of experience become an object of knowledge and thus a point of departure. Only from within representation can one become aware of the disarticulation of language from the world. That is to say, only in loss can a sense of origin be perceived.

But can one assume that the impact of Western epistemes and the money economy in Thailand would have the same consequences? Can one believe that representation has taken hold there as well? And if it has, what are its forms? Perhaps the most obvious argument against the assertion that money and writing introduced the problem of representation to Thailand would take the form of a reference to the discourses of appearance and face (*naa*). Culturalist anthropological and autoethnographic portraits of Thailand invariably suggest

---

66. Foucault, *The Order of Things*, 208.

67. For Foucault, this development is most fully manifest in the works of Sade, and it is through his own insertion in the lineage leading from Sade, through Lautréamont, Genet, and Klossowski, that he asserts his stake in the "end of representation."

that, even today, one is required to maintain the appearances of ideal cultural order in Thailand. At the same time, this performance (this masking) need have no particular relationship to one's subjective thoughts or commitments. If this were true, would not the claim for representation's hegemony ring hollow? Without disingenuousness, one can counter this culturalist argument by making recourse to the now pervasive laments in Thailand (laments that occupy newspaper editorials, restaurant chatter, and the concerned gossip of mothers) that young people no longer feel obliged to respect the "norms" of ideal Thainess. But this would be an anachronistic gesture, despite the fact that the social transformations of which we are speaking move at glacial paces even when they are felt to be sudden. More convincing are the anticipatory traces of these changes in Phayaphrom's poem and in the other literature of the late nineteenth century. After all, one of the maddening qualities of Phayaphrom's unrequited love is that it leaves him incapable of sustaining the social forms that are expected of him. It leaves him looking mad in the eyes of his friends and neighbors, and it leaves him vulnerable to the rationalizing inducements of Chom's niece. He reveals too much, and he is mad for doing so. If Chom's promise of an economy seems to be the very antithesis of a love in which appearances are collapsed into sentiment, it is nonetheless the case that economy produces the difference between contract and love, the one being representational, the other expressive. And this is the point. The economy of writing and the writing of the economy in Phayaphrom's poem reflect the fact that representation can seem adequate only from without, only after a separation has been wrought between the world and its image. That separation is partly and perhaps largely the effect of mass reproduction and, more specifically, of the mechanization of writing.

The mechanization of writing is, I want to argue, the means by which writing achieves its hegemony. Moreover, this hegemony is imagined from within representation's economy to be the alienation and representation of language and the seeming loss of voice. Now, it is clear that there is no language without writing, if by writing we mean a systematized code. And the hegemony of writing is not, it must be asserted, the sacrality of writing. To the contrary, where writing appears sacred it is because it is indistinguishable from speech, unmediated and therefore capable of transforming the world. However, where one can speak of writing's hegemony, speech has been displaced as the site of transcendent authority.

The absolute form of such hegemony would be a world in which all language has become algebra: a pure abstraction, in which the code is represented as such but without content. Short of absolutism, however, prose—especially the prose of science—moves toward this end with its contempt for figurative language and the repression of its own metaphoricity.[68] This is as true in Thailand as anywhere, and it is important to understand that Phayaphrom's poem circulated in a time when the cosmologies of old were being displaced not only by geographies, as Thongchai tells us, but also by ethical tracts and books that eschewed the notion of divine intervention and indeed of any relation to divinity that would be perceptible to humans. In 1867, Thipakhorawang published his *Nangsü sadaeng kitchanukit* (Book explaining various things), a treatise devoted to the explanation of the natural world.[69] In every way, it embodies the prosaic writing against which poetry would be compared in the modern era. As Phayaphrom's citational practices make clear, poetry moves toward the presencing of voice and the voicing of presence. Its valorization of figurative language is an acknowledgment of both the disjuncture between language and world and the drive toward resemblance. Ironically, in its claims to transparency, the prose of science dislocates poetry from its putatively privileged relationship to the world only to then reinvigorate its retrospective claims to authenticity. In this belated condition, however, authenticity is not veracity and figurative speech is not natural. It is artificial: an art. Its truth is metaphorical and can be granted only if one believes that things are other than they appear, which fact positivism denies. Thus, poetry acquires its value as a site of presence only after what Derrida calls the "becoming-prose of the world."[70] And this because it bears the mark of the poet's voice, not because it expresses the world. Though it will claim to be a residual whisper of the primordially singing voice, poetry in the modern world can only be understood as a nostalgic medium of impossible return. It exists in the irrevocable afterward of a dialectic with prose.

It is in this context that we can understand the strange lists of *The Poem in Four Songs*, with their references to a rational (and ultimately prosaic) economy of the landscape-turned-page as being the figuration of loss and, moreover, the ironic origin of loss. At the end of his poem, Phayaphrom, the merchant, admits that he has been unable to sustain the demands of the *Cindamani*, of correct rhyming. Voice has passed out of his poem, and writing has been his instrument. Writing as traveling, writing as exchange: at once corrupt and productive, translational and originary, writing is here the birth of a strange autoethnography. Why else would Phayaphrom write to himself through the voice of another in order that he be given what is his again? Dispossessed, he

68. Derrida, *Of Grammatalogy*, 303–4.

69. Thiphakorawong (Chaophraya), *Nangsü sadaeng kitchanukit* (1867; Bangkok: Khurusapha, 1971). Also see Thongchai, *Siam Mapped*, 40–42.

70. Derrida, *Of Grammatology*, 287.

renders another as his medium, not knowing that, in alienating himself this way, he will be doomed to return again and again as a stranger at home.

### The Poem as Ethical Ethnography

What does it mean to be a stranger at home? At several points in *The Poem in Four Songs*, reference is made to locally unique products, attributes, or practices. Chiang Mai banana, southern molasses, Indian egg custard, cake made in the southern way, Chinese balsam cake, and even the kinds of cakes that can be found at festivals and in Chinese gambling dens: these items signify both a cosmopolitan wealth in Laplaeng and the difference between Laplaeng and other places. Elsewhere in the poem, we find distinctions among forms of currency (II.473),[71] an insistence on the difference between debt-bondage in the north and the system of slavery in Bangkok (I.610), and reference to the customs of both Phrae and Laplaeng (III.524, 538). It is through this repeated gesture of distinction among localities that Phayaphrom's poem reveals what might be called a prototypically ethnographic dimension. The depiction of Laplaeng emerges here only through its enframement by difference. In this context, however, the internal dialogue of the poem assumes importance as the instrument through which locality itself is displaced. For, as I suggested earlier, the explicitation of the Laplaeng environment for Phayaphrom can only denaturalize it. Phayaphrom is pried away from himself in this moment, as he becomes the listener in his own poem and, moreover, the one who is asked to see what is already before his eyes. In this regard, Chom's niece forces Phayaphrom to look again, and in this forced repetition of a gaze, the world is gathered up for him as a view of plenty, of wealth in abundance. There is abundance "as far as the eyes reach" (III.700). There is, in fact, a world view being offered to Phayaphrom.

In speaking of a gathering up of the world before Phayaphrom, I mean to invoke again Heidegger's conceptualization of the world picture. There is something in this conscious, explicitly intensional look that makes of Laplaeng a kind of reserve for Phayaphrom and something of which he can have a "world view."[72] As a generalized orientation, Heidegger sees such a structure of perception as being specifically modern, and, as I have already stated, this would not

---

71. Egerod translates these two lines (from Chom and Phayaphrom's discussion about redeeming Chanta's debt) as "three tamleung / in Southern ticals" (II. 472–73). However, this is a historical correction on his part. The text actually reads "in the currency of Thai baht" (*pen ngeun baad taj*).

72. Heidegger, *The Question Concerning Technology and Other Essays*. See especially "The Question Concerning Technology" and "The Age of the World Picture," 3–35 and 115–54.

be an incorrect interpretation. One of its most revealing symptoms is the positioning of Phayaphrom as the subject of a representation of origin.

When Chom's niece tells Phayaphrom that he ought to cease roaming and take what is available at home, rendering Laplaeng as the site of an organic plenum whose fecundity is precisely cultivated, she essentially implores him to take up the politics of localism. She generates what might be termed an aura for Laplaeng insofar as it becomes the authentic site from which Phayaphrom's travels can only alienate him. Aura would be understood here in Walter Benjamin's words as a "unique existence" and a "presence in time and place."[73] It would be a source of cultic value, something to which one might, as the poem itself suggests, make offerings. Yet, as Samuel Weber has perceptively observed, "What holds the aura . . . in place, as it were, is the subject as its point of reference, just as, conversely and reciprocally, the subject is ensconced, 'embedded,' held in place and at rest, by the scene that it both observes and 'breathes in.' "[74] Weber goes on to remark that Benjamin's subject is always at once "in the scene" and somehow departing from it: "Distance and separation are therefore explicitly inscribed in the scene, or even the scenario of the aura. . . . The aura would from the start be marked by an irreducible element of taking-leave."[75] We can discern this necessary separation being forced on Phayaphrom in the poem through the fact of dialogue, which introduces the ambivalent space between subject and object. And as Laplaeng acquires its value through this representational expulsion, the poem dramatizes a fundamental aspect of the auratic or authentic object: namely, that it becomes visible only in the moment of its disappearance. The same can be said, of course, about the love poem in general.

What needs to be asked in this context is how the authenticity-generating separation becomes, in this poem, the impulse toward ethnography and translation. These are, fundamentally, questions of the poem's intention. The poem's narrative contains within itself a conception of representation in which loss, debt, time, and memory are enmeshed with each other. Metaphoricity operates within it as a mode of translation, of traversing difference. It needs to be clear, however, that the poem is proposing a notion of translation that entails more than a relationship between origin and end, more even than an ethics of trans-

73. Walter Benjamin, "The Work of Art in the Age of Mechanical Reproduction" (1936), in *Illuminations*, trans. Harry Zohn, ed. Hannah Arendt (London: Fontana, 1973), 70–82.

74. Samuel Weber, "Mass Mediauras, or: Art, Aura and Media in the Work of Walter Benjamin," in *Mass Mediauras: Form, Technics, Media*, ed. Alan Cholodenki (Stanford: Stanford University Press, 1996), 86.

75. Ibid., 86, italics in original.

formation. For, in subjecting himself and his own home to the alienating (the leave-taking) effects of representation, Phayaphrom suggests what will appear to be an extremely modern conception of the already translated status of "the original." Blended from a dialect of northern Thai, Pali, Central Thai and Khmer, the poem requires from the start a play between and across languages. Each word is linked in a chain of signifiers to at least four languages and is ghosted by homophonic resonances and etymological remembrances. Readers and listeners must embrace this multiplicity if they are to comprehend the text, which seems to be driven toward enlargement in difference. And this is true even before the poem is translated into, for example, English.[76]

The passage of lists demands to be recalled in this context. For if Phayaphrom's text is at once already translated and intended for translation (within the languages of the text and beyond them), the reader is immediately burdened by the need for an adequate, which is to say, richly enlarging translation. What will make possible the reading of this text and the other texts that follow in this book? Simple transliteration and literal translation will not suffice. One needs a certain context, of both the text and its production, so that its sense can be transmitted. Such contextualization, which ought to be both political and historical, cannot fully mitigate the violence of a translation that otherwise tears the text from the site whence it derives its authenticity. However, it can constitute the enframement by which we take our distance in order to comprehend it. This taking-leave is made possible, as I have suggested, by Phayaphrom's poem and even advocated there as what might be termed an ethics of ethnographic reading.

When Phayaphrom returns now, as he is said to do every day when he takes over the aging body of a female medium on the periphery of Chiang Mai, he does so as the figure of an endless exile. He seems to return, and he appears as the very emblem of a return to the era of courts and courtly power. Yet, he is as strange now as he became in the writing of his poem. Now, as then, he embodies the uncanny strangeness of home. Contemporary mediumship is not, however, a mere continuation of the representational politics that inform *The Poem in Four Songs*. The text is a confrontation with the mediations of writing and print, with rational economy and with forms of debt that gifting is impotent to overcome. Mediumship itself, though utterly imbricated in the changes that have been effected by the mass mediation of Thai life in general, seeks to overcome these forces. Its staging of voice responds reactively—which is not to

---

76. Indeed, the ideal translation into English would mobilize loan words and rhymes from other languages. It would entail the production of a fabulously hybridized English, something novel and manifold, like that achieved in French by Aimé Cesaire.

say resistantly—to the hegemony of vision that writing and the economy of representation in *The Poem in Four Songs* entail. It constitutes an aspiration to poetry in the form of a ritual theater. After the scripturalizing reforms of Rama IV's Thammayut Buddhism, what we shall come to understand as the "becoming prose" of the Thai world, theater of all kinds assumes the appearance of *mere* representation. Its staginess becomes either fabulous or ridiculous, but always extraordinarily other. Hence, in the drive to restore immediacy, whether in the form of political clientship or magical efficacy (as mediums appear to be princes endowed with curative knowledges), mediumship is doomed to inhabit the exile of mediation. Even without the precise etymological identity that defines the English vocabulary of spirit possession, we have reason to believe that the rebirth of mediumship in the late twentieth century has its roots in the rise of writing's mechanization and in the displacement of its hegemony by other forms of mass media. For this reason, I have commenced a book about contemporary spirit mediumship in Chiang Mai with *The Poem in Four Songs*.

It will be admitted that the poem of an elite, multiply literate man of aristocratic lineage can in no way be said to "represent" or "typify" the period from which it emerges. Precisely because of its singularity, the poem demands to be read historically. It calls into question the act of generalization by which the notion of typicality—which is another way of saying culture—is produced. An exceptional text, *The Poem in Four Songs* demands that we imagine an ethnographic method that neither reduces the poem to its informational content nor loses its sense. But this merely returns us to our earlier question of what needs to be known in order that such a translation perform its task.

Later in this book, I will return to many of the issues raised in the poem: to debt and loss, to translation and economy, to authenticity and retrojection. The return will be part of an effort to historicize these issues and the forms in which they appear at the moment of the poem's writing in the middle of the nineteenth century. The time is significant, marking a radical shift in the organization of both political economy and cultural imaginaries in northern Thailand. Although the mid–nineteenth century appears, from the perspective of the present, to be one of loss, it is currently the object of longing in the nostalgic discourses of Lanna cultural revival. Indeed, it is precisely the courtly world of individuals such as Phayaphrom that now provides the imagery of a putatively lost paradise for contemporary mediums and culture brokers. In their desire for a return to origins, many northern Thai individuals also long for more intimate forms of debt, imagining that in the severe and personalized power of the caos they would also find protection and freedom from the tyrannical indifference of rational bureaucracy. The revalorization of spirit possession in Chiang Mai forms a crucial site at which this desire is articulated. It is not the only site, of course, and I want to make clear that I am not suggesting a unique or even primary role for spirit possession in the response to either reform Buddhism or modernity in general. In fact, spirit mediumship is a rather marginal theater for the enactment of a representational politics that can also (and more commonly) be discerned in the proliferation of alternative Buddhisms. It is one medium among many. However, as far as mediums go, the real may well be the true. Appearances can be everything.

# 2 RUIN, OR, WHAT THE NEW CITY REMEMBERS

Chiang Mai, the city to which Phayaphrom fled after the failure of his marriage to Chom, was in many ways the city to which contemporary mediums would turn more than a century later for the image of Lannathai's golden era of autonomy. It was, in fact, a new city, its name ensuring an eternal youth. Not in the sense that it had once been a new city, built on the ruins of an old one, but in the sense of having been renewed after years of subordination to Burmese powers. After more than two hundred years of occupation, Chiang Mai had been restored in 1775, when Siam's King Taksin responded to the local prince's request for assistance. This prince, Cao Kawila, had initiated a rather bloody rebellion against the Burmese and murdered the local representative, a certain *sitké,* Siri Cò Su (also known as Thir-ri-kyaw-thu).[1] His courage and audacity seem to have earned him the respect of his southern counterpart, who had himself led a heroic war of recovery against the Burmese after the fall of Ayutthaya.[2] In any case, Taksin responded to the letter of invitation Kawila sent when it became clear the latter could not oust the Burmese on his own, and

1. David K. Wyatt and Aroonrat Wichienkaeo, trans., *The Chiang Mai Chronicle* (Chiang Mai: Silkworm, 1995), 144, also n. 102; hereafter referred to as *The Chiang Mai Chronicle.*
2. There are a significant number of histories that deal with Taksin's rise to power from the position of merchant to that of warrior-liberator and, through alliance with the ethnic Chinese in the cities east of Bangkok, the founder of a new kingdom in Thonburi. But Taksin the Great, as official historiography represents him, also suffered ignominious defeat after making that fatal error of conflating his own person with the institution of monarchy. For a brief and lucid account of this rise and fall, see David K. Wyatt, "The Subtle Revolution of Rama of Siam," in *Studies in Thai History* (Chiang Mai: Silkworm, 1994), esp. 135–39. On Kawila as military strongman, see Ratanaporn Sethakul, "Political, Social, and Economic Changes in the Northern States of Thailand Resulting from the Chiang Mai Treaties of 1874 and 1883" (Ph.D. diss., Northern Illinois University, 1989), 14–15.

certainly not without the help of his siblings who had sided with the occupiers. Though revisionist history would remember this moment as the beginning of a process that could be termed one of internal colonialism, the cleric who probably authored *The Chiang Mai Chronicle* in about 1827 described it thus: "Then, Cao Kawila sent a letter/ asking the Cao Duan Thip, his younger brother, to go down and meet the Southern army and throw them all on the mercy of the king of the South. Chaophraya Cakri and Phraya Surasi the commander, together led by King Taksin, were pleased, and raised/an army and sent it up to Lampang, and encamped it there."[3] In the aftermath of this victory, Taksin appointed Cao Kawila as the "ruler of Lakhòn" and "put the whole domain in the charge of [him]."[4]

The victory did not bring peace, however. The last lines of the section of *The Chronicle* titled "Siam Reorganizes Government of the North" remark in ominous tones, "At that time, war was everywhere."[5] Nor was the conflict with Burma settled. Even more important, the brief alliance with Siam dissipated. Within two years of the expulsion of the Burmese and Kawila's ascent to power in Lakhòn Chiang Mai, conflict broke out, apparently in response to the oppressive surveillance that Taksin's minions enacted. Taksin's commissioners visited the cities of Phrae, Nan, and Lakhòn [Chiang Mai] following the defeat of Vientiane in 1778, ostensibly to inspect the area. However, as the author of *The Chronicle* put it, "Those commissioners came and oppressed [the people], confiscating goods, gold, silver, and cloth. They grabbed the young, the unprotected infants and widows, to serve them."[6] Kawila responded with murderous revenge, which he then made up for by attacking Müang Lò and Müang Thoeng and extracting slaves whom he then presented to Taksin.

The Siamese king was not thoroughly placated, however, and Kawila was found guilty of murder and failure to "heed repeated summons to pay attendance [to Taksin]." He escaped the punishment of lashings and the removal of part of his earlobe by offering to attack Chiang Saen instead, something Taksin welcomed. Thus was he able to return to Lakhòn, his small army of three hundred men now starving. And thus began the very tumultuous relations between Siam and Lanna that would continue into the next century, as Siam converted the form of its dominance over Chiang Mai from one of tribute to one of provincial membership in a newly centralized state.

It is important to recognize that the region over which Siam would exercise

3. *The Chiang Mai Chronicle*, 145.
4. Ibid., 146.
5. Ibid.
6. Ibid., 149.

its increasingly territorialized sovereignty was not a totalized political entity. It was dispersed, fluctuating, and fragmented into numerous smaller polities that, despite being linked to each other in a system of nesting and overlapping dependencies, were relatively autonomous. Chiang Mai, one-time center of Mengrai's empire (r.1259–1317), was perhaps the most volatile of all. Even after its liberation from Burmese forces in 1775, Chiang Mai would be attacked several more times, and it is safe to say that in the moment of its restoration, it was but ruin. The description of the city that appears in *The Chronicle* is permeated by images of desolation and chaotic instability: "villages and fields were deserted, all wild and overgrown. To the south there were tigers; to the north were elephants. The land was unstable, as there was no lord or ruler to take charge. . . . The list of able-bodied men came to [only] 700."[7] It is difficult to imagine that a city so despoiled by war that its labor force counted only seven hundred men could rebound so quickly and become the jewel without which, as King Rama V would say less than a century later, the Siamese nation could not be complete. But Chiang Mai's recovery was extraordinary in both speed and extent. In part, this has to do with the nature of political order in the area and the dominance of the *müang* system by which the centers of power could draw into themselves the labor power and product of surrounding areas. But it is also the legacy of a politics of violent appropriation. Like other cities of the area, Chiang Mai was populated and depopulated repeatedly over the centuries as defeating armies captured and enslaved the city's residents, while local leaders responded by raiding the surrounding territories and bringing back with them the men and women who had been unable to flee quickly enough. It is this policy of brutal population management that Kraisi Nimmanhaeminda identified in the telling aphorism, "Get the vegetables into baskets, put the slaves into towns" (*kep phak saaj saa kep khaa saaj müang*).[8]

Kawila's Chiang Mai would change little, even after his death in 1816 at the age of seventy-three,[9] until the administrative reforms of Rama IV and Rama V were brought to bear on the area in the middle and later part of the century. This is not because it enjoyed particular stability but, to the contrary, because it continued to shudder and retreat into relative calm as quarreling siblings from aspiring aristocratic families fought for control and lost it, while attacks from

---

7. Ibid., 151.

8. Kraisi Nimmanhaeminda, "Put Vegetables into Baskets, and People into Towns," in *Ethnographic Notes on Northern Thailand,* ed. Lucien M. Hanks, Jane R. Hanks, and Lauriston Sharp (Ithaca, NY: Cornell University Press, Southeast Asia Program Data Paper No. 58, 1965), 6–9; Ratanaporn, "Political, Social, and Economic Changes," 25.

9. *The Chiang Mai Chronicle,* 187.

neighboring principalities and awful visitations of disease continued to take their toll on the city. If there was a norm in the political life of Chiang Mai it was this sense of radical instability. Indeed, there is an odd continuity in the discontinuity of Chiang Mai's history, in the impossible tradition of disintegration and disruption that afflicted the city so regularly and rendered it the ruinous memory of another era's aspiration to futurity.

This chapter attempts to provide an account of the uneven trajectory that passed through Chiang Mai as it was engulfed by the histories of other nations, their imperial aspirations, and their neocolonial desires. It seeks to mediate between the materials that have survived time and those that continue to be woven into the fabric of daily life. Needless to say, the writing of such a history is not an easy task. Chiang Mai is a city in which the signs of antiquity are constantly being produced anew and where the monumental aspirations of newly empowered classes produce ruins of glass and cement much more quickly than did the builders of stone and brick fortresses of earlier eras.

Any account of northern Thailand must move back and forth between the unstable values of newness and antiquity. It must also vacillate between the historical valuation of locality that was so characteristic of the area and the new infatuation with globality that has simultaneously dislocated Chiang Mai from its past and rendered that past an object of longing. The terrain is therefore a terribly unsteady one, and genealogies refuse to surrender themselves easily. What follows, then, by way of temporary solution to the dilemmas posed by this complex structure of time and place, is a history of the literature and the landscape of the city, a reading that has sought the signs of history and of value as much in the streets and alleys as in the texts and the narratives of that city's residents. My purpose has not merely been to walk the city, as Certeau would say,[10] though it is important to imagine the meanderings that constitute the Chiang Mai of people's experience. Rather, it is to find in the architectures of desire and remembrance the ghosts of other times, their forms and logics, their structures and irrational undersides. And of course, the objective of my own textual peripatetics between places and the textual spaces within which Chiang Mai has been written is to provide readers with a historical context in which the rest of this book's stories of magical transmission and mass mediation can make sense.

### Trains and Other Stations of Entry

Most visitors to Chiang Mai and returning residents approach the city from its eastern end, where the train arrives from Bangkok and other Thai cities. An

10. Michel de Certeau, "Walking in the City," in *The Practice of Everyday Life*, trans. Steven F. Rendall (Berkeley: University of California Press, 1984), 91–110.

international airport occupies the other end of the city's sprawl, but it is in the train station that one feels most acutely drawn into the possibility of walking and therefore of knowing the city as a place in which to move. Walter Benjamin once wrote of Moscow, "The city delivers itself at the outset, at the station."[11] This, of course, is the seduction of the station, though like all seductions, it rests on a certain resistance to satisfaction. Arriving, a self-conscious foreigner is humbled by the recognition of how familiar the colonial desire for transparency can be, and by how simultaneously trite and significant the train station is as a trope for arrival. But it was not always thus. The first survey for the train between Bangkok and Chiang Mai was drawn up between 1887 and 1889,[12] and until long after that initial cartographic enterprise, the travel between the central plains and the north was so onerous and time consuming that, as Ingram has remarked, it was probably "cheaper to ship a ton of cloth from England to Bangkok than from Chiengmai [sic] to Bangkok."[13] Yet, even today, the foreigner can be humbled by the degree to which Chiang Mai retains its particularity in the face of all other transformations. Benjamin was spurned by Moscow at the moment that he sought his first word. The Chiang Mai train station is more accommodating, being well posted in English. Arrows attempt a strange perspective as they point from flat signs toward the Night Bazaar and Thapae Gate. But once one has departed the train and its incarcerating mobility,[14] the sounds of a local language, kam müang,[15] itself imperfectly scripted in Central Thai, opens wide the space of difference.

I suspect that only Westerners experience the melancholic suspension that Certeau attributed to the train's glass windows and the unnatural rhythms of steel. But perhaps everyone is subject to its desensitizing properties, which deafen travelers to the specters of those who worked on these tracks, the mainly Chinese laborers who carried iron and breathed creosote, attempted to orga-

11. Walter Benjamin, "Moscow" (1928) in *One-Way Street*, trans. Edmund Jephcott and Kingsley Shorter (London: Verso, 1979), 178.

12. Thongchai Winichakul, *Siam Mapped: A History of the Geo-Body of a Nation* (Honolulu: University of Hawaii Press, 1994), 124.

13. James Ingram, *Economic Change in Thailand 1850–1970* (Stanford: Stanford University Press, 1971), 114.

14. I owe the notion of the train's incarceration to Michel de Certeau's brief essay, "Railway Navigation and Incarceration" in *The Practice of Everyday Life*, 111–14.

15. There is some debate as to whether kam müang ought to be called a language or a dialect. It differs from Central Thai in its script and in having six rather than five tones. Educated residents of Chiang Mai speak Central Thai more than Northern Thai, though the latter has enjoyed something of a revival in the past three decades. Outside the city, however, kam müang is more frequently spoken.

nize against foreign capital, and disappeared into the history of a territorializing project that required rapid transport to the borders of a new nation-state. Nonetheless, their brethren can be seen on the tracks today, cleaning and repairing the way of the trains or pausing to eat while still in boots of black rubber. These are the ones who move, and not the "flying trees," as George Herbert Mead remarked in his discourse on spatial perception,[16] nor the flowing rice fields. That trompe l'oeil[17] of the winged landscape dissipates as one takes the first step down onto the platform.

The drive from the station to the city center is often taken in motorized tricycle cabs called *tuk-tuks,* which sound like chainsaws. This route follows Charoen Müang Road past rows of shop houses and industrial supply stores, as well as noodle shops and more than one medical office specializing in plastic surgery. I recall walking this path to the post office and being struck by the juxtapositions of sun-bleached posters to "remedy oriental eye-lids" and the hundreds of differently sized nuts and bolts at ground level whose steel grays seem always already soiled by the dust that clouds from under the wheels of trucks. On that first passing, however, it was the single bulbs illuminating baskets of mangosteen and star fruit and the fronds of men around the streetside whiskey stalls that caught my eye.

Initially, everything seems present to the street, seems public and intimate at the same time. However, the tiny lanes or *soi* that exit the main road provide evidence of a depth behind the frontal displays of shop houses. Above it all, next to billboards announcing new condominium developments, whiskey, and shampoo, white signs with green crosses announce all-night clinics for family planning and the treatment of venereal diseases.[18] The latter are easily confused by the English speaker with the v.d.o. signs, which indicate video rentals and not the treatment of sexually transmitted diseases. For northern Thai residents, the untranslated names of automobiles, soft drinks, and cosmetics call out, signifying alterity and the cultural capital of the West.

In Chiang Mai, English is one of the languages of public space, but despite its ubiquity, it inhabits that domain in an ironized form. Magazines and restaurants, clothing stores and banks often sport signs in boldly lettered English. Shadowing the initial word, the Thai script often mimics the English name in homonymic form, and in resisting translation, the Thai signs testify to the

---

16. George Herbert Mead, *The Philosophy of the Act,* ed. Charles Morris (Chicago: University of Chicago Press, 1938), 556–59, 579.

17. Certeau, "Railway Navigation and Incarceration," 112.

18. Originally, green lights were signs of prostitution districts. The green cross carries this history within itself and is read as a sign of both treatment and cause.

miraculous power of singularity that is the myth of the untranslatable proper name. Through such intralingual mimicry, brand names appear to be proper names and to bear within themselves that which cannot be imitated. To a certain degree, Thai and indeed all Thai products are subordinated here in this gesture, as the billboard aspires secretly to a transcendance of its linguistic being as a sign.[19] One is struck by the juxtaposition of these omnipresent announcements of cosmopolitan authority (with their implicit claims to the value that comes from afar) and the relative absence of spoken English in Chiang Mai (compared, for example, to Bangkok or the former English colonies of Delhi, Singapore, Kuala Lumpur, and Hong Kong). Yet, in other ways, English is ubiquitous, ironically disseminated in the well-practiced solicitations of tourist curio vendors ("Hey, America, cheap watch, you buy") and in the scraps of cliché-turned-nonsense ("cute day is smile") that accompany the demonically gleeful cartoon characters on schoolchildren's notebooks, most of them imported from Japan. Cuteness is a popular cultural value in Thailand, one that competes with the more obviously modernist values of scale and pastness. It reasserts the primacy of the surface even as the discourses of transparency are everywhere drawing people into the pursuit of hidden truths. One encounters it in unexpected places and in mundane venues, such as in the rear windows of the luxury cars that travel up Charoen Müang Road and in the comic books that compete on local newsstands with magazines featuring forensic photographs of mutilated bodies and scandalous tales of sexual adventure. These juxtapositions elude one on first entry into the city, however. They cannot be seen from the main road as it cuts across the landscape and drives toward the neon glow that ends each day.

Charoen Müang Road crosses the Ping River and then becomes Thapae Road, the main tourist strip in Chiang Mai. Like the city's other tourist strips, it is crowded with shops selling antiques (real or faked), locally crafted silver, and musty textiles of either northern Thai, Lao, or minority ethnic (Karen, Hmong, Akha, etc.) design. There are numerous camera stores, and, instead of trees, the sidewalks are spiked by racks of postcards. Most of the latter feature smiling "hill tribe" models, saffron-clad monks, or gorgeous mountain vistas. That is to say, they serve as the visual currency of authenticity in a picturesque mode.[20] In

19. One can say that, on the billboard, the brand name/icon refuses to be one among many signs, resists being the representation of a class, and seeks instead to be that through which the class is expressed by being beyond classification. See Claude Lévi-Strauss's discussion of proper names in *The Savage Mind* (1962; Chicago: University of Chicago Press, 1966), esp. 182–83.

20. Susan Stewart, *On Longing: Narratives of the Miniature, the Gigantic, the Souvenir, the Collection* (Durham, NC: Duke University Press, 1993), 137–38.

addition to such a traffic in original beauty, Thapae Road and its offshoots are also home to several nightclubs that offer contemporary beauty—or its parody and the promise of sex. There are also restaurants, which serve American, Indian, Mexican, Italian, and French cuisine, and department stores stocked with cosmetics, clothes, and housewares with foreign labels and extravagant price tags. Eventually, Thapae Road leads to Thapae Gate, a reconstructed ruin that opens the walls of the ancient city. Plaques telling the story of the walls' erection and their restoration are embedded in the red bricks, which, in their restored but ruinous state, seem to rise and fall at the same time. The walls embrace the enormous wooden doors that stand perennially open, but that are constantly suggestive of the possibility of a closure. It is here that public city-sponsored festivals have their center and here that political rallies are held. Here too, the young men gather on warm evenings to play *takraw* while the hawkers of hill tribe treks open their picture books to bored tourists.

The construction of buildings more than four stories in height is prohibited inside the walls, and the old city's quiet is further preserved by the fact that there are no thoroughfares cutting completely through it. Instead, traffic is forced to circle the walls in a complicated track of parallel one-way streets that run along a moat. Thus, driving through Chiang Mai is a coerced encounter with the presence of the old city. It shapes all movement, either as the frame within which one drives or as the unseen form of a detour. Inside, there are still multihome compounds, much like those described in missionary journals of the past century. A famous abundance of wats or temples with mirror-encrusted nagas and glittering spires recall King Chulalongkorn's description of Chiang Mai as the jewel without which the Siamese crown could not be beautiful.[21] Yet, it would be wrong to imagine this space as one of pristine calm. Within the walls, as outside, there is ceaseless construction and involution, and amid the knotted alleys, new shops and petrol stations protrude from beneath the bougainvillea on razed lots.

At the end of the 1990s, in the wake of a financial crisis that has rocked all of Southeast Asia, the boom of the decade's early years is in apparent retreat. The towering condominiums, whose nighttime lights had out-dazzled the stars ten years ago, are now losing their luster. Paint and cement are now cracked and stained by monsoon rains and smog, and electric lights gutter. The impression is one of decline. Further out, suburban developments that were the fruit and the fantasy of a speculative economy in overdrive are now becoming ghost towns, home only to dogs and the memory of desire. Doors swing open in some developments where luxurious dwellings of four and five bedrooms are

21. Ratanaporn, "Political, Social, and Economic Changes," 87.

empty, mocking the billboards that soar above the peripheral highways with gigantic promises of bourgeois domesticity and monstrously sized faces of Thais in Edwardian attire.

The giant and unblinking eyes of these flat surfaces preside over all of Chiang Mai. And they seek other eyes, the covetous eyes of consumers and the approving gazes of tourists. Few sites of local history are unremarked by signs explaining their official historical significance and beckoning a second look. A constant address from brass plaques speaks in inaudible tones, but calls unmistakably for recognition. The inverse of spirit possession, in which an invisible presence speaks audibly to those who will overhear it, these emphatically visible signs of mass mediation communicate silently and ambivalently with the possibility of their being heard. An exemplary case is to be found at the King Mengrai Shrine which was constructed by the Chiang Mai Bankers Club. There, a sign reads: "The people of Chiang Mai built this shrine in 1975 in memory of the King who founded Chiang Mai in 1296. King Mengrai was killed by lightning around 1311 in the middle of the city. This new shrine was built because the older shrine is not suitably located for the public to pay homage and reverence." The sign demands a pause, despite its banality. For it indicates that the shrine was not only brought into the public domain by the holders of new capital in Chiang Mai, but that it became the site at which new capital came to constitute the voice of a city's residents. This was achieved by inserting local history into the economy of commodity aesthetics in a translated mode.

It is surely ironic that these signs, which seek to render history visible, go almost wholly unremarked by either local residents or tourists. Indeed, the nature of the sign's publicity is such that the extraordinary event announced there is almost completely annihilated by the fact of its display. The death by lightning, so fantastic and portentous an occurrence, seems normal. The sign of power and of its destruction in excess disappears. It is buried by the new shrine and outshone by the importance that the year 1975 claims for itself. But publicity should not be confused with visibility. The glare of too much light is often an inducement to distracted oblivion. Indeed, the signs themselves seem to be waiting, attending a future in which their memorial function will be actualized again. In the meantime, they are the detritus of an aspiration toward history that has been turned on its head by the processes of commodification. Looking at them, one cannot resist wondering about the person who polishes their brass surfaces often enough to maintain a sheen in which the squinting eye of the curious reader can catch its own reflection.

The domination of Chiang Mai by commodity aesthetics is most apparent on Thapae Road, but although the latter is somewhat unique in the level of its commercialization and in its almost exclusive devotion to tourist consumption, there are few areas of Chiang Mai City where one is more than a block from a commercial establishment. It would not be unfair to say that the entire city is saturated with the ethos of the market. And if the fortress walls delimit old and new, recent development projects constantly spill over the boundaries of the new perimeters. The knotted labyrinths of condominiums, houses, shop houses, and marketplaces are circled not by walls but by a large highway that encompasses the city and then splits off to permit transport between Chiang Mai and other northern centers, especially Chiang Rai, Lamphun, and Lampang. The international airport, on the southwest side of the city, receives daily flights from regional centers and occasional flights from China, Singapore, and Laos. In addition to the thousands of day laborers who arrive each day, the city swells with the arrival of tourists and shoppers. The latter are drawn by the truly international consumer opportunities that Chiang Mai offers; with the development of three major shopping complexes, a movie theater, and vast parking lots, to say nothing of several new hotels, Chiang Mai City is now the destination of choice for shoppers from throughout the north.

Given this aggressive modernity, and the attendant orgy of urban consumerism that it facilitates, one is surprised to find Chiang Mai portrayed in the discourse of the national tourist organ, the Tourist Association of Thailand (TAT), as a quaint, rustic city, where the ways of a vanishing world are still present. One is almost as apt to find parallels between Chiang Mai and fin de siècle Paris, as described by Benjamin or even Baudelaire, as to encounter the city of feminized traditionalism usually conjured by tourist promotionals (in which women in "traditional" Lanna dress are the standard instruments of seduction). The irony is made especially pungent when one considers the fact that the name Chiang Mai means "new city" and that its newness has been a key sign in local representations from the time of the thirteenth century. Yet, its peculiar status as the center of a national periphery ensures that Chiang Mai is a receptacle for notions of both centrality and marginality, as well as authenticity and otherness, depending on the location of its beholder in the series of nested and overlapping political spheres that define and cross-cut Thailand in the late twentieth century. Let us, then, look briefly at the nature of such nested relationships, first in terms of the *müang* tradition in which Chiang Mai emerged, and then in terms of the rural-urban dichotomy by which centrality and peripherality are so frequently understood.

### Chiang Mai: Müang, State, and Ideas of Order

Today, Chiang Mai City is the bustling, metropolitan capital of Chiang Mai province, one of nine provinces, including Chiang Rai, Mae Hong Song, Phayao, Phitsanalok, Phrae, Sukhothai, Tak, and Nan, in the bureaucratic region called northern Thailand or *phaak nüa*. Although its status as a region within the Siamese/Thai state dates to the nineteenth century, Chiang Mai City is perhaps the most successful heir to the tradition of the *müang* in northern Thailand. Northern Thai people, particularly those of Chiang Mai, usually refer to themselves as *khon müang* (people of the *müang*) and, as stated earlier, speak a dialect/language called kam müang. Although historical anthropologists often identify *khon müang* in terms of a pan-Asian Tai language group, under the rubric of Tai Yuan, the term *müang* also designates a political form that emerged at the confluence of indigenous histories and expanding Brahmanic-Buddhist states.

So much has been written about this political form that it is difficult to do anything but paraphrase the works of those who have been synonymous with the phenomenon. As Tambiah defines it, the *müang* is "centered or center-oriented space (as opposed to bounded space) and typically stands for a capital or town or settlement with the surrounding territory over which it exercised jurisdiction."[22] Condominas describes the definitive characteristic of all Tai-speaking peoples as "systèmes à emboîtement," by which he designates a political logic of relative and ascending oversight.[23] Historically, more local *müang* retained their autonomy and their organization around central images of power, but they also acknowledged more encompassing structures of similarly centered power. They paid tribute, offered labor, and provided military manpower in times of need while "enjoying" legal and military protection against foreigners in return. This accords well with Tambiah's analysis of the more elaborate states of Southeast Asia, such as Cambodia and Ayutthaya, in which peripheral entities were imagined as moral and spatial miniaturizations of a universal order that was represented and manifested by the person of the king in the context of his divinely patterned palace. Richard Davis is probably correct to distinguish between the ornate ritual centralism of Ayutthaya and the more fluid kinds of centeredness of early Lannathai,[24] but the more theatrically oriented discourse of the exemplary center that was so developed in Ayutthaya then moved to Bangkok and was firmly embraced by the local princely powers.

The ubiquity of the *müang*, with its loose but highly personalized power, should not, however, be imagined as evidence of either an essential trait of

22. Stanley J. Tambiah, *World Conqueror, World Renouncer: A Study of Buddhism and Polity in Thailand against a Historical Background* (Cambridge: Cambridge University Press, 1976), 112.

23. Georges Condominas, "Essay on the Evolution of Thai Political Systems," in *From Lawa to Mon, from Saa' to Thai: Historical and Anthropological Aspects of Southeast Asian Social Spaces*, trans. Maria Magannon (Canberra: Department of Anthropology, Australian National University, 1990), 35–36.

24. Richard Davis, *Müang Metaphysics: A Study of Northern Thai Myth and Ritual* (Bangkok: Pandora, 1984), 30.

northern Thai and Southeast Asian culture, nor as the sign of knowing complicity with hierarchy on the part of subordinates. At the macropolitical level, the *müang* operated by coercing submission through the violent extension of "protection" and the threat of alienation or outright warfare, while representing that coerced submission as a mode of divinely inspired mimesis. Clifford Geertz's apologies for the ideology of the charismatic center notwithstanding,[25] the notion of a theatrically mimetic political logic has tended, in the case of the Thai *müang*, to obscure the material mechanisms by which distant individuals and polities were forced into subordinate positions and then made to sacrifice (their labor, their product) on the basis of an extreme debt that they owed for the protection and the supposed beneficence received from higher powers. When contemporary writers—anthropologists or local culture brokers—invoke the notion of the *müang* as an ideally personalized mode of power and counterpoint to the bureaucratized rationality of the modern state, they do so at the risk of valorizing autocratic regimes. Later, as we consider the risks of a nostalgia in which the personal becomes the guise for totalitarianism, we will want to consider how the notion of the *müang* is currently deployed within the debates about Chiang Mai's history and future. For now, it is important to understand how the ideology of the *müang* operated and what effects it had in the actual political economies of northern Thailand.

At least in the official doctrine of the Ayutthayan state, and probably in sixteenth-century Chiang Mai, the king himself was supposed to constitute an embodied axis that served not only as the pivot for the turning world but also as a vertical link between the realms of sensate experience and the formless heavens. He was also a moral vector. As Tambiah describes it, the Theravada Buddhist kingdoms that inherited the transposed logic of Brahmanic India redefined the ideas of divine kinship (P. *dhammaraja*) by infusing them with the values associated with the bodhisatta or future Buddha. In crude terms, this meant conceiving of the king as a being who had deferred the goals of rebirth for the purposes of distributing merit among mortals. As it worked itself out in more or less orthodox forms, and with the particular precedent of King Aśoka, the ethicized notions of *dhammaraja* are said to have led to a mode of conquest followed by guilty appeasement, of assault and "tolerant incorporation," rather than destruction.[26] Hence, the leaders of even defeated kingdoms could retain

25. Clifford Geertz, "Centers, Kings, and Charisma: Reflections on the Symbolics of Power," in *Local Knowledge: Further Essays in Interpretive Anthropology* (New York: Basic Books, 1983), 121–46; *Negara: The Theatre State in Nineteenth-Century Bali* (Princeton, NJ: Princeton University Press, 1980).

26. Tambiah, *World Conqueror*, 39, 97; John Strong, *The Legend of King Aśoka* (Princeton, NJ: Princeton University Press, 1983), 4.

royal titles and positions of political power if they agreed to acknowledge and thereby to evidence the supreme authority of the conqueror. It is clear, however, from *The Chiang Mai Chronicle* and other documents, that the ideal of the repentant conqueror was rarely manifest in actuality. At its best, the ideology of the *dhammaraja* provided the justification of indirect rule and sustained the system of tributary principalities until the nineteenth century. At its worst, it was the veil behind which the cliques and armies of powerful men laid siege to cities and extracted not only blood but subservience, securing loyalty through a complicity with local elites, whose dominance over common people was entrenched for the price of loyalty to foreigners.

This, of course, does not mean that there were no questions brought to bear upon kings. The possibility of sustaining claims to divine authority received challenge from both within and without polities, and it was a primary ritual task of the *sangha* to collectively validate and sacralize the person of the king, whose role then included the protection of the *sangha*. In a discourse that construed the king as the most meritorious of men (merit being a store of goodness accumulated from previous lives), and where merit was thought to permit access to truth, failures in mundane politics—poor judgments, military defeats, contentious orders—evidenced a failure of insight and the illegitimacy of the king's reign, opening up the possibility for revolt.[27] Indeed, the history of Southeast Asia is everywhere a tale of the rise and fall of kingdoms, of the consolidation and dispersal of power, depending on the shifting allegiances of subordinate princes and their capacity to persuade disgruntled commoners to join them in rebellion, as they often did. The *sangha* often split over allegiances to individual mortals who were supposed to be divinely authorized. Thus, if ideal order was one of a transcendentally stable center, experiential order was frequently unruly and profoundly decentralized, to say nothing of brutal for those outside of the courts.[28] It is this rather more tumultuous world of contest and violence—of shifting, captured, and enslaved populations, of men's mobility and women's vulnerability to movement—that lies at the heart of Chiang Mai's history.

### Social Orders, Spatial Logics

Who were the people in whom these tumultuous histories worked themselves out? Kawila's city building took the form of violent enslavement and forced

27. Peter A. Jackson, *Buddhism, Legitimation, and Conflict: The Political Functions of Urban Thai Buddhism* (Canberra: Institute of Southeast Asian Studies, 1989), 45.
28. Michael Vatikiotis, "Ethnic Pluralism in the Northern Thai City of Chiang Mai" (Ph.D. diss., Oxford University, 1984).

emigration,[29] and it is to his reign that the ethnic diversity of contemporary Chiang Mai can be traced. In an effort to repopulate the city and to diversify its labor pool, Kawila had people of Mon, Burmese, Karen, Tai Yai, Tai Lue, and Tai Khoen brought to Chiang Mai to perform particular professional services. They lived in physically isolated communities around the city's peripheries, forming a body politic whose "organic solidarity"[30] was spatially manifested in communities centered in ethnically particular wats.[31] The form of the polity changed little following Kawila's ascension until Siamification, and was divided into strata of aristocrats or *cao,* and commoners or *phrai,* as well as slaves (*khaa*).[32] It was governed by three levels of bureaucratic authority, including those of the paramount *cao*s, the council of lower *cao*s, and the village leaders.[33] At the top level was the *cao luang,* or "lord of life," who represented the city and its tributaries in relations with Bangkok or other foreign states, while also controlling translocal trade, determining state policy, and occasionally adjudicating major civic disputes. From him emanated a law that protected the person and the property of the prince rather than a generalized public. He granted prebendal rights over key land resources to lower *cao*s and they, in turn, granted usufruct to the other main class of people, the common *phrai,* through forms of patronage. Patronage under the *cao*s took the form of military and economic oversight. *Cao*s promised protection from bandits (*naaklaeng*) and raiding armies as well as access to the judiciary, offering solutions to sudden losses and

29. Ratanaporn, "Political, Social, and Economic Changes," 25.

30. The notion of "organic solidarity" comes from Emile Durkheim, and refers to the interdependence of unique and specialized labor in a rationalized social formation. See *The Division of Labor in Society,* trans. George Simpson (New York: Free Press, 1933), esp. 70–229. For a discussion of this concept in the central Thai context, see Richard O'Connor, "Mechanical and Organic Solidarity in Bangkok," *Contributions to Southeast Asian Ethnography* 6 (1987): 13–26.

31. Vatikiotis, "Ethnic Pluralism," 47–51.

32. The use of the term *khaa* to denote "slave" has a long but ambiguous history. Frank Proschan has noted that the term has two histories, and is at once an ethnonym describing Mon-Khmer peoples and a designator of social class. There is some debate about whether or not the ethnonym precedes the pejorative connotation attached to the term, but as Proschan observes, the associations of *khaa* with enslavement or dependency is at least a century old. See Frank Proschan, "Who Are the Khaa?" in *Proceedings of the 6th Annual International Conference on Thai Studies: Theme Four: Traditions and Changes and Local/Regional Levels* (Chiang Mai, 1996), 2:391–414. Also Amphay Doré, *Aux sources de la civilization lao: Contribution ethno-historique à la connaissance de la culture louang-phrabanaise* [On the sources of Lao civilization: Ethno-historical contributions to the understanding of Luang Prabang culture] (Paris: Cercle de Culture et de Récherches Laotiennes, 1987), 35; Condominas, *From Lawa to Mon,* 53.

33. Ratanaporn, "Political, Social, and Economic Changes," 17; Holt Hallett, *A Thousand Miles on an Elephant in the Shan States* (Edinburgh: William Blackwood and Sons, 1890), 134–35.

agricultural failure through forms of debt bondage. In turn, they extracted labor through corvée and taxes in kind, and legitimated their authority by claiming exclusive rights to tend state spirits, especially those associated with the *lak müang* or city pillar (see below).[34] Today, the descendants of the *caos* form part of a new cultural aristocracy, and the spirits of the *cao luang* possess mediums as part of a loose but hierarchical pantheon of possessing spirits.

The *lak müang*, northern Thailand's version of the lingum, is frequently represented by ethnographers as the phallic image of a patriarchal political formation that was inserted into the autochthonous matrilineal traditions of the area. Today it is the center of an annual ceremonial complex whose ostensible purpose is to renew the city and whose implicit effect is to reproduce the discourse of ritual within which the city can legitimate its claim to historical authenticity. Cloistered for most of the year in a shrine that occupies the ground of the city's oldest wat, Chetiya (Cheddi) Luang, it is strictly forbidden to women at all times. But on an annual basis, in a week-long rite of urban renewal, it is opened to those men who wish to seek its power and to make offerings. For many, the *lak* and the temple constitute the spiritual center of a city that is not only a social and residential site but also a glyphic topography. Not only the city but all landscape in northern Thailand has this mnemotechnical dimension and is rendered in local myth and legend as the narrative space in which history has its location. But it is more than this, and the overt prohibitions that make the *lak* a risk to vision, especially to women's vision, suggest a complex logic whose more complete disentanglement will be the project of chapter 5. As an icon, it is perhaps the densest node in the severely masculinist politics of Brahmanism. Supposedly surrounded by the corpses whose sacrifice consecrated it, the *lak* signifies a patriarchal power so potent that it cannot be looked upon. It is the point of origin even of that masculine agency that it signifies. Indeed, it is its own sign, and for this reason, the spirits of the *lak* do not possess mediums and require no other representations. In the context of matrilineal inheritance, the patriarchy that is signified by the *lak* has produced rather profound contradictions, and the effort to imagine northern Thailand as a space of relative freedom and mobility for women has been constantly thwarted by the fact that the political domain seems always to have been masculinized.

As the symbol of the *müang*'s masculine origination, the *lak* has also been the site at which the representation of national purity has been produced. In the chronicles and *tamnan* (legends) of Lannathai, the development of the *müang* is intimately associated with the Tai groups, whose assertion of political hegemony in the area was carried out in opposition to the indigenous Mon-Khmer

34. Aroonrat Wichienkaeo, *Lanna Syksaa* [Lanna studies] (Chiang Mai: Teacher's College, 1982), 83.

groups. The residues of an ethnic expulsion are perhaps contained in the history of the word *khaa,* a term that historically is torn between its designations of "slave" and the linguistic and cultural group of Mon-Khmer speakers who resided in the area prior to the ascent of the Tai.[35] Given the fact that military conquest entailed the enslavement of local populations, the conflation of ethnic and social positions is not at all unlikely. Nonetheless, the model of ethnopolitical differentiation as one of total spatial and social separation, a model that is utterly intrinsic to nationalist historiography in both official texts and colloquial allegory, begs some scrutiny. As Richard Davis notes, King Mengrai is the first person of *The Lannathai Chronicle* to be identified without the term "Lao" or "Lwa," a term that generally designated Mon-Khmer peoples.[36] Sila has gone so far as to argue that Mengrai's patrilineal ancestors were Mon or Khmer,[37] and Condominas notes that the mode of conquest in which the Tai ascended to power often entailed marriage rather than the displacement of local political struggles.[38] It is thus entirely possible to read the emergence of the *müang* in northern Thailand as something achieved in the processes of contact and conversion that were later ethnicized. This, in fact, is one of the narratives told by members of spirit cults who describe their Mon spirits as having been obtained through purchase and domesticated through conversion to matriliny.[39]

Stories about the domestication and naturalization of others through the submission to matriliny are extremely common in northern Thailand. Michael Rhum's description of the cults of Ban Čom Ping (a Yuan village near Lampang) provides an exemplary instance. These cults, which are devoted to ancestral spirits termed the "Lords of Ava," are said by Rhum to be structured by a division between the cognatically organized cults of the public shrine in which men dominate and the matrilineally organized cults of the household where women predominate. Beginning with the structuralist's vision of a system in which marriage and emigration are encompassed by the principles of descent,[40] Rhum maps a society in which a form of kinship schizophrenia devolves into

35. See Proschan, "Who Are the *Khaa?*"

36. Davis, *Müang Metaphysics,* 35.

37. Sila Viravong (Maha), *History of Laos* (New York: Paragon, 1964), 77–78.

38. Condominas, *From Lawa to Mon,* 38.

39. Shigeharu Tanabe, "Spirits, Power and the Discourse of Female Gender: The *Phi Meng* Cult in Northern Thailand," in *Thai Constructions of Knowledge,* ed. Manas Chitakasem and Andrew Turton (London: SOAS, 1991), 193–94.

40. Michael R. Rhum, *The Ancestral Lords: Gender, Descent, and Spirits in a Northern Thai Village* (DeKalb: Center for Southeast Asian Studies, Northern Illinois University, Monograph Series on Southeast Asia, Special Report No. 29, 1994).

seeming complementarity between matriliny for women and patriliny for men.[41] Nonetheless, his account of the cults suggests some continuity between the ontopological gestures of Mengrai's historians and the practices of a society short in labor that sought to absorb foreigners and to naturalize and enthrall them with the myth of origin.

By "ontopology" I mean, following Derrida, the "axiomatics linking indissociably the ontological value of present-being [*on*] to its *situation*, to the stable and presentable determination of a locality, the *topos* of territory, native soil, city, body in general."[42] Put more straightforwardly, ontopology refers to the processes by which one lays claim to a natal home, giving rise to the being whose essence lies in its origin at a particular and definable place. Although Derrida links the spread of ontopological gestures, and their ethnonationalist formations, to the very contemporary processes of "tele-technic dislocation," one can perhaps extrapolate from his text to suggest that all discourses of national rootedness, and in the northern Thai case, we might say all discourses of localism, have their origins in "the memory or the anxiety of a displaced—or displaceable—population." To be sure, such memory is incited by the newly alienating, if virtual, proximity to others that the transnational mass media induces; to this extent, the memory of loss precedes the desire for the *natio*. But nor should we be surprised that the anxiety of loss would produce emphatic and even compulsive (dare we say ritualized?) assertions of autochthony. Anxiety almost always seeks to cover itself over with the repetition of what it fears is most lacking. Hence the relentlessness with which the story of a pre-Thai Lanna tradition is remarked in Chiang Mai.

In the narration of this tradition, however, there is often a great deal of ambivalence infusing the relationship between Buddhism and the other practices and discourses of spirits that are said to be indigenous to northern Thailand. Both the Buddhist histories and the ethnographic literatures on northern Thailand are full of efforts to mark the line between the indigenous and the foreign, and they do so by producing a space in which the practices that are thought to originate in pre-Indic, pre-Buddhist history appear as excesses: loud and intrusively visible signs of a literalism that is without virtue and unlit by *dhammic* truth. The propitiation of tutelary or ancestral spirits and the belief in spirits of local topography are said to be aspects of autochthonous religions.[43]

41. In this, Rhum is taking up Gehan Wijeyewardene's original assertion that matriliny in northern Thailand applies only to women. See "Northern Thai Succession and the Search for Matriliny," *Mankind* 14, no. 1 (1984): 286–92.

42. Jacques Derrida, *Specters of Marx* (1993), trans. Peggy Kamuf (New York: Routledge, 1994), 82.

43. Davis, *Müang Metaphysics*, 34–35.

Over and above this, the universe of the northern *müang,* with its political cults of the *phii müang* (spirits of the city) and the *lak müang,* is a centralized structure represented as the point of origin of true state formation.[44] The devotion to locality is seen as Mon, that to centralized power proto-Thai. Theravada Buddhism enters this narrative as the source of an encompassing force, the newly "dominant element of *müang* ritual," and a discourse of political centralization that far exceeds the parochial centeredness of the Lanna tradition.[45] From Davis's perspective, the expansionist dynamic inherent in Theravada Buddhism threatens to entirely displace the residue of the Tai *müang* and the Mon-Khmer cults of local spirits. Thus, he writes, "Theravada is encroaching upon other ritual forms at an ever increasing pace and can be expected to usurp the roles of Brahmanistic and spirit-oriented ritual in the future."[46]

Of course, state Buddhism did not simply enter the north in the form of temple ritual. And one is startled to read in so otherwise subtle an ethnographer the claim that, in the latter half of the twentieth century, it is Theravada Buddhism that is displacing the Brahmanism and spirit cults more proper to northern Thailand. After all, when Mengrai emerged as the preeminent *cao* in thirteenth-century Lannathai, he was already four centuries from the founding of the first Buddhist civilization in the territory.[47] The Dvaravati empire centered in Lopburi had spawned, in the ninth century, a peripheral dynasty called Haripunchai in Lamphun (approximately twenty-six kilometers south of

44. Condominas, *From Lawa to Mon,* 35–36.

45. Davis, *Müang Metaphysics,* 36.

46. Ibid., 37.

47. Mengrai was himself the product of a political marriage between the royalty of Chiang Saen (Ngeun Nuang) and Sipsong Panna in the north, having moved his own capital from Chiang Rai after defeating the Mon kingdom of Dvaravati and subduing the Mon-Khmer populations. See Georges Coedès, *The Indianized States of Southeast Asia,* trans. Susan Brown Cowing (Honolulu: East-West Center, University of Hawaii Press, 1968), 226–27. According to legend, Haripunjaya was actually established by holy men and former monks who requested a leader from the ruler of Lopburi. He sent his famous daughter, Camadevi, who arrived in the new city with an entourage of Mons who assisted her in establishing what is reputed to have been an extraordinarily strong and enlightened reign. On the history of Haripunjaya, see David K. Wyatt, *Thailand: A Short History* (New Haven: Yale University Press, 1984), 24. Queen Camadevi is the subject of numerous rather hagiographic accounts. Notable among them is Thamthaat Phaanich, *Phra Naang Camathewii* [Queen Chamadevi] (Bangkok: Thamthaanmulinit, 1950). By far the most superior English account of the legend is now available in Donald K. Swearer and Sommai Premchit, *The Legend of Queen Cāma: Bodhiramsi's Cāmadevīvamsa, a Translation and Commentary* (Albany: State University of New York Press, 1998).

Chiang Mai). Renowned for its temple architecture and its cultural achieve-
ments, Haripunjaya was anything but a parochial center of cultic affiliations.
The trajectory of Buddhist monarchism was not even, of course. But following
the fading of Chiang Mai's early glory after Mengrai's spectacular death, King
Tilokaraj (r.1441–1487) restored the city and established it as a global center of
Buddhist monasticism and scholarship. In 1477, the eighth World Synod of
Theravada Buddhism was held there, making Chiang Mai the focus of a pre-
modern but eminently transnational traffic in knowledges and commodities.
As already suggested, there would be many subsequent ebbs and flows in
Chiang Mai's fortunes, and in those of all of Lannathai, but even in times of
relative dissipation, the force of Theravada Buddhism imprinted itself on all
aspects of political life.

What Davis and other ethnographers tend to imagine as the recent
(twentieth-century) effect of Theravada Buddhism then, is to be understood in
other terms. There is no doubt that changes of a most profound sort have
afflicted the area, unraveling and at times reforming the social worlds within
which individuals have experienced their families and their fortunes. But these
changes are the consequences of more recent political developments. They are
the consequences of Siam's policies of internal colonization and nation formation, and the subjection of the local Buddhist tradition to a rationalist sect
whose formation under King Mongkut in the nineteenth century ushered in
the modern era. They are also the result of the militarization of the state and the
renewal of the monarchy during the middle of the twentieth century, a process
deeply imbricated with the phenomenon of mass mediatization. And of course,
they have everything to do with the profound economic transformations by
which the markets of Chiang Mai have been inserted into that global market in
which Chiang Mai is itself an object of desire and consumption.

The "tele-technics" of which Derrida writes in his post-Marxian lament are
worth remembering here. And we will want to recall his very Benjaminian
sense that the mediated proximities and mutual televisuality of the electronic
information age are themselves the sources of dislocation and new distance.[48]
This new distanciation is inextricably bound up with both the delocalization of
(spiritual) power and the return of locality as a value in an increasingly globally
mediated space. It is perhaps the literalist misconstrual of the mass media's
effects, the mistaking of virtual proximity for intimacy, that explains why the
prophecies of ethnoreligious homogenization have proven so incorrect. Spirit
cults and the practices of magical transmission are not only not disappearing in

48. Walter Benjamin, "The Work of Art in the Age of Mechanical Reproduction" (1936) in *Illuminations*, trans. Harry Zohn (London: Fontana, 1973), 70–82.

northern Thailand, they are efflorescing along with the discourses of ritual, albeit in a specularized mode. Distinguishing between these many layers of difference and the appearances of proximity, between the markets of Chiang Mai and the marketing of Chiang Mai, will take us far from the city to which Phayaphrom fled in the middle of the nineteenth century, but his postal fantasy and his entrepreneurial ambitions were already intelligible there, even if they were blind to what they would become in the space of a century. What kind of city, then, is Chiang Mai?

### City Limits

Then, as now, Chiang Mai City is situated in an area referred to as the upper north of northern Thailand, in one of several mountain-cordoned valleys that run from north to south. The mountains that embrace its northwestern and northern peripheries are branches of the Himalayan range, and from them, the four main valleys of the region are carved by the descending Ping, Wang, Yom, and Nan rivers (in easterly order). The seasonal environment is typical of upland areas in Southeast Asia, with winds from the Bay of Bengal bringing moisture to create a rainy season between June and September, a cooler season that stretches from October to February, and a period of blistering heat in the months preceding the monsoon, when temperatures reach into the upper 30s Celsius and humidity declines to about 55 percent. Although the effects of deforestation are being felt in dwindling water supplies, the valleys are well irrigated and relatively fertile. In the 1990s, they continue to sustain significant crops of both glutinous and nonglutinous rice, maize, fruits, vegetables, garlic, peppers, ground nuts, mung and soy beans, and sugarcane, all of which are traded on the local market or transported throughout the country.

The name given to the Mengrai empire, Lannathai, means million rice fields, and it suggests what is widely accepted as fact: the premodern economy of the Chiang Mai Valley was focused on rice production. Yet, the abundance suggested by so extravagant a name did not come easily. Local myth expresses the onerousness of rice agriculture by telling of a time before time when rice grains were large enough to sate a man, and only after the failure to propitiate the rice mother spirit (*mae posop*) was humanity cast in the miserable position of having to harvest rice with the back-breaking labor that it now requires.[49] In the Chiang Mai valley, the majority of the land is actually unfit for cultivation, and the soil is sandy in many places. Rainfall is seasonal, but rarely exceeds 175

---

49. On related rites, see Anuman Rajadhon, "Me Posop, the Rice Mother," in *Popular Buddhism and Other Essays on Thai Studies* (Bangkok: Thai Inter-Religious Commission for Development and Sathirakoses Nagapradipa Foundation, 1986), 135–42.

centimeters per year and is subject to extreme variations.[50] Thus, agriculture in the area is dependent on irrigation, and indeed, there is archaeological evidence of organized irrigation as far back as the thirteenth century.[51] This does not mean that irrigation has been able to satisfy all needs, however, and there are numerous accounts of famine in the *tamnan* and in missionary texts even in the early twentieth century.

The gradual commercialization of rice production and more recent land speculation have had a significant impact on the political economy of the entire northern region, exacerbating class differences and consolidating land owner-ship in the city and in transnational banking systems.[52] In relatively rural areas and the surrounding towns, landless, near-landless, and marginal households accounted for more than 70 percent of the population in the mid-eighties.[53] By the late nineties, these statistics had grown even further to reflect the continu-ing dislocation of agriculturalists. A decade ago, many landless and cash-poor farmers had become migrant laborers, moving into the larger cities as perma-nent members of an urban underclass. Even in Chiang Mai, shacks of corru-gated tin have become visible under the sun on the razed lots where con-dominiums sprout. But most landless farmers have become day laborers who are trucked into the major cities every morning to work on proliferating con-struction projects.

Today, as these same projects sit silently, accumulating the dust of unfulfilled promise, the laborers are returning to their own uncertain homes. In more optimistic years, dump trucks and transport vehicles cruised toward the city at daybreak, crammed with dozens of men and women who appeared only as straw hats and face scarves between slats of wood. It was a quintessentially modern sight, but the rural-urban trajectory that these ironically mobile bodies followed is not in and of itself a new feature of northern Thai life. Nor was it the ground of the city's phenomenal growth in the early nineties, most such la-borers moving in and out of the city on a daily or temporary basis and remain-ing invisible in national census projects. Indeed, although Chiang Mai's recent growth has been partly attributable to rural-urban migration, much is due to the influx of entrepreneurial and technical professionals from other cities. Yet, the ceaseless movement between agricultural and commercial domains and the

50. Ratanaporn, "Political, Social, and Economic Changes," 48.

51. Ibid., 47.

52. On the history of rice agriculture and its commercialization, see Anan Ganjanapan, "The Partial Commercialization of Rice Production in Northern Thailand (1900–1981)" (Ph.D. diss., Cornell University, 1984).

53. Adis Israngkura and Leuchai Chulasai, *Profile of Northern Thailand* (Chiang Mai: The Manager Company, Siam Studies and Chiang Mai University, 1990), 43.

shifting locus of land ownership renders the boundaries between rural and urban extremely porous. In this context, the very notion of the city needs to be clearly separated from those nostalgic habits of the postindustrial mind that would oppose it to "the country."[54]

The impossibility of this categorical opposition between rural and urban in Chiang Mai is not a merely postmodern phenomenon. It has a history that far predates the spatiotemporal compressions that Harvey and others associate with flexible accumulation.[55] Since its repopulation in the early 1800s, Chiang Mai has been the site of vigorous trade. In fact, the exuberant and cosmopolitan commercialism that marks Chiang Mai today is an extension and an elaboration of the city's long-standing status as a market center and as an entrepôt on trade routes between Bangkok and Rangoon, northern Thailand and Yunnanese China.[56] During the past century, Chiang Mai traders sought and obtained tobacco en route to Nan[57] and received from Haw caravaneers opium, copper, and iron.[58] From Burma came brass, sticklac, cutch, gum, buffalo, and varieties of silk,[59] and from Bangkok, silk as well as dried fish. Leaving Chiang Mai with Haw caravans and local traders was cotton, betel, rice, and myriad agricultural products.

There is considerable difference of opinion about how this trade was organized. Some describe the northern Thai economy as one of subsistence and self-sufficiency in which trade was a secondary activity, initiated and largely undertaken by outsiders.[60] Others, however, have countered this image, claiming that local peasants were also desirous of the profit that trade offered and were quick to traffic in goods when opportunity presented itself in the agricultural off-season.[61] Katherine Bowie has further complicated this picture with a reconstructive history of the Chiang Mai valley that argues for much more

54. On such habits of mind and their imbrication in the ideological projects of industrial modernity, see Raymond Williams, *The Country and the City* (Oxford: Oxford University Press, 1973).

55. David Harvey, *The Condition of Postmodernity: An Enquiry into the Origins of Cultural Change* (Oxford: Oxford University Press, 1989).

56. Carl Bock, *Temples and Elephants* (1885; Bangkok: White Orchid, 1985), 229–30; Ratanaporn, "Political, Social, and Economic Changes," 53–73.

57. Ratanaporn, "Political, Social, and Economic Changes," 48.

58. Hallett, *A Thousand Miles*, 172.

59. Ratanaporn, "Political, Social, and Economic Changes," 62.

60. Chayan Vaddhanaputi, "Cultural and Ideological Reproduction in Rural Northern Thailand" (Ph.D. diss., Stanford University, 1984); Ingram, *Economic Change in Thailand*.

61. Michael Moerman, "Chiangkham's Trade in the 'Old Days,' " in *Change and Persistence in Thai Society*, ed. G. William Skinner and A. Thomas Kirsch (Ithaca, NY: Cornell University Press, 1975), 152.

interregional trade than has otherwise been assumed; she depicts a patchwork of widely different means and subsistence levels knit together by elaborate trade networks.[62] As for taxation (either in kind or in cash), one British observer claimed that there was no tax on anything,[63] but others have listed elaborate monopolies on betel, opium, and whiskey.[64] Long-distance trade was the purview of men, but the local markets seem to have been dominated almost exclusively by women,[65] a fact that has been central in the analysis of gender relations in northern Thailand and in more generic arguments about women's relative empowerment in Buddhist Thailand.[66]

As Phayaphrom's poem made abundantly clear, the world of nineteenth-century Chiang Mai was one of extraordinary fluidity, in which the laws of a market economy were seeping quickly into all domains of the social world. Despite its monetization following Kawila's return to the city in the early 1800s, currency was not abundant and was laced into the relations of debt and credit whose histories had deeper and more potent calls upon local residents. Currency itself was an issue of prime concern among the *cao*s, whose treasuries had control over such matters. By midcentury, Bangkok journals were officially publishing exchange rates on a regular basis, suggesting a deeply regularized control of cash flows. In Chiang Mai, however, there seems to have been a protracted period of transition in which various coinages competed with and were substituted for each other on an ad hoc basis. Palm leaf manuscripts of the decisions passed down by local *cao*s evidence the severity of response to these practices and to the production of currency itself. Anyone having unauthorized minting technologies or knowledge of counterfeiting methods could be executed and his property confiscated.[67] Death to the one who would claim for himself the right to coin value and thereby to undermine the exclusivity of the state as the source of that value. Or debt, which can be a kind of death.

62. Katherine Bowie, "Peasant Perspectives on the Political Economy of the Northern Thai Kingdom of Chiang Mai in the Nineteenth Century: Implications for the Understanding of Peasant Political Expression" (Ph.D. diss., University of Chicago, 1988).

63. Ratanaporn, "Political, Social, and Economic Changes," 42; also Davis, *Müang Metaphysics*, 30.

64. Bock, *Temples and Elephants,* 340; Ratanaporn, "Political, Social, and Economic Changes," 42.

65. Bock, *Temples and Elephants,* 229–30.

66. A. Thomas Kirsch, "Economy, Polity, and Religion in Thailand," in *Change and Persistence in Thai Society,* ed. G. William Skinner and A. Thomas Kirsch (Ithaca, NY: Cornell University Press, 1975), 172–96.

67. Prasert N. Nagara, project advisor, *Basic Research on the Ancient Lanna Law: An Analysis of Its Legal Structure and Texts as Inscribed in Palm Leaves from Time Immemorial,* 12 vols., trans. (from Pali and Thai Yuan) Pitinai Chaisangkasukkul and Aroonrut Wichienkaeo (Bangkok: Thammasat University Press [in Thai], 1989), 28.

There is ample room for more research on this topic, but in considering the histories of representation and iconoclasm, one is intrigued to note that contests over image making and the claim to an exclusive authorship of meaning find their most fertile ground not in relation to the representation of divinity but in the space where the entire function of representation is abstraction, namely, economy. And insofar as commodity economies operate through the production of standard desires, it is clear that the monetization and standardization of the northern Thai economy threatened both to dissolve the residual oppositions by which rural and urban domains were imagined as the sites of different value systems and to summon new differences at the level of class and the possibility of economic satisfaction. In this new set of oppositions, the rural would be reimaged as a space of lack rather than plenitude, and its inhabitants would be drawn more firmly into the aesthetic web of the city even as it became the phantasmatically ambivalent site of improper indulgence and a satiety that could only bespeak gluttony.

We can therefore speak of an incomplete dialectic. The plethora of currencies and the diversity of goods in Chiang Mai's nineteenth-century marketplaces suggest an economic cosmopolitanism that went hand in hand with the valley's primary agricultural orientation. It is a persisting relationship. One of the most important lessons of this local history therefore is that Chiang Mai's urbanity is a kind of centrality more than anything else: not something fixed in opposition to the rural, but a position in tension with a periphery propelled by the economies of lack and desire. What distinguishes Chiang Mai's modernity is therefore not its status vis-à-vis the rural but rather the new nature of its centrality in the context of the new Siamese/Thai state. For it is as that profoundly ambiguous entity, the regional center, that Chiang Mai is now mapped onto the "geo-body" of Thailand.

Conceiving of Chiang Mai in this way permits us to escape a tendency, endemic in cultural studies, to read modernity in terms of the city and the city only in terms of display. Chiang Mai City seen from within its market appears as an orgy of goods and commodities. But the political logic of the pre-Siamese *müang* rested on the recognition that goods and commodities did not spring full-blown from the brows of market women. They had to be attracted, purchased, bartered, demanded as taxes or corvée, or stolen—from the people who produced them, even though the networks of power and obligation within which such traffic took place were naturalized as the effect of a *cao*'s authority and hence merit.

Among other things, it is this post facto centrality, this capacity to attract goods that are then the source of one's own powers of attraction, that is thematized in the contemporary performances of charismatic power in northern Thai spirit mediumship. Mediumship entails the fantasy of a fecundity without production, of value without labor, of a representation without origin. In short, it entails a fantasy of magic's rebirth in an age when the fetishization of newness has made instantaneity a value. This age, as Walter Benjamin well knew, is also the age in which history assumes the commodity form.[68] So, in the effort to effect that pure presence of the magical gesture in which there is no space between the mark and its effect, contemporary mediumship specularizes itself and is specularized as the return of the past. That such a return is literalized in the arrival of the spirits of deceased princes and warrior heroes suggests much about the representational economy in which mediumship now operates, and we shall turn to that issue in the following chapter. For now, I hope it can suffice to say that such thematizations are but the flip side of a technology that denies all mediation in the very process of transmission. They seek inscription without interval, travel without time. They are the end points of that train journey in which two immobilities, that of the passenger and that of the world outside, are juxtaposed in miraculous transport.

I began this chapter in the railway station, not merely to suggest the obvious and now compulsively remarked relations between anthropology and coloniality, but because the desire for magic is here the end point of the train journey. It was the train that so materialized Thailand's aspirations to modern urbanism, and that reconstrued the nation as a series of centers embedded in a regularized landscape across which steel could move simply in being laid down. So inseparable from the imagination of modernity as the space of movement and so inextricable from the conflation of time with space, the train is that which leads to the fantasy of enormity and the desire for locality. Now, as the railroad itself becomes a sign of a passing era, displaced by the greater power of planes and cars and by their respective regimes of flight and randomness, the past comes back from the future as the destination of a reactionary power's ambition. Mediumship indeed.

---

68. Walter Benjamin in Susan Buck-Morss, *The Dialectics of Seeing: Walter Benjamin and the Arcades Project* (Cambridge, MA: MIT Press, 1989).

# 3  FIRST, FORGETTING

Virtually every literary critic who has written about Phayaphrom has paid testimony to the fact that he was an unusual man, and *The Poem in Four Songs* is singled out as a singular text, one without parallel in its historical milieu.[1] I have tried to indicate the extent to which this singularity was a function of the poem's modernity, a feature of its uncanny anticipatory powers. For, in the longing verses of the poem, we detect the emergence of a profoundly changed representational economy in which writing has lost its magic and the logics of abstraction and general substitutability dominate instead. Although these principles would not take firm hold in northern Thailand for another two or three decades, they were already gripping Bangkok, where King Mongkut (Rama IV) had led the way in embracing the sciences of mechanical reproduction and the technologies of rationalization, if only to lament their democratizing effects. It is therefore significant that, at the time he wrote *The Poem in Four Songs*, Phayaphrom was already heavily influenced by the aesthetic trends of his urban Siamese contemporaries.[2] With its exilic wanderings and splendid longing, his

1. There are several fine works on the literature of northern Thailand that treat both the *khao* form and Phayaphrom's particular departures from it. See, for example, Chatrayaphaa Sawatdiphon, "Laksana Wannakam Khao So" [Analysis of Khao So literature], *Lannathai Khadii* [Lannathai research] (1978):156–74; Chusit Chuchat, *Lokathaat Chao Lanna Syksaa Caak Khao Phayaphrom* [Lanna worldview based on the study of Phayaphrom's poetry] (Chiang Mai: Chiang Mai Teacher's College, n.d.); Manii Phayomyong, *Prawat lae' wannakhadii Lanna* [Lanna history and literature] (Chiang Mai: Mitron Raakaan, 1973), esp. chapter 2; Saenhaa Bunjarak, *Wannakam Khao Khong Phaak Nüa* [Khao literature of northern Thailand] (M.A. thesis, Chulalongkorn University, 1976); and Prakhong Nimmanhaeminda, *Laksana wannakam phaak nüa* [An analysis of northern Thai literature] (Bangkok: Faculty of Social Research, Institute of Thailand, 1980).

2. Chusit, *Lokathaat Chao Lanna.*

romantic epistle parallels the more famous (and slightly older) Sunthorn Phu's *Nirat Müang Klaang* [Poem of the Middle Country], just as the professionalization of his writing mirrored that of its author. And if, in his ongoing interest in magical curing, he parted company from many Siamese moderns (including Sunthorn Phu, who versified his impatience with spirit doctors), he was nonetheless a distinctly pragmatic man. With mercantile interests, authorial aspirations, and an occasionally irreverent relationship to princely power, he seems, in many ways, to be a prototypically modern subject.

Phayaphrom would go to Chiang Mai at the end of his life, marry again, and be present when the treaties of 1874 and 1883 formalized the encompassment of that city by Bangkok.[3] He would become subject to a new rule of law and "the first modern judicial system," forcibly instituted by the Siamese government when the British demanded that its disputes over logging concessions in the area be mediated in an international court.[4] Over the following decades, these changes would be accompanied by the end of trial by ordeal and of witchcraft accusations. And the *caos*' personal authority to adjudicate legal disputes would give way to a judiciary institution that was categorically separate from the administrative apparatus. Throughout a vast web of distinct but related domains, the processes of generalization and abstraction overtook the north—no less in language than in economy.

As befits his almost uncanny journey toward the hegemony of writing, and its apotheosis, Phayaphrom ended his life in the city where Presbyterian missionaries were beginning work on the area's first printing press, a project that would result in the utter transformation of writing of northern Thailand. The new press demanded the standardization of the northern alphabet. And, like all presses, it permitted the unprecedented distribution of written materials and the multiplication of copies. For a brief moment, northern Thai literature seemed poised to enjoy a florescence that would enhance its autonomy in relation to the competing literature of Rattanakosin Bangkok. However, the mission could fund its primary project, Bible translations, only by contracting out a substantial portion of its production. Most of the work it took on for profit came from the Siamese government and from commercial advertisers. Between the years 1860 and 1905, for example, more than 60 percent of its production was used for nonreligious purposes.[5] Ironically, then, its effort to

---

3. The poet died in 1887, when he was eighty-five years old.

4. David Engel, *Code and Custom in a Thai Provincial Court* (Tucson: University of Arizona Press, 1978), 11.

5. Herbert R. Swanson, "This Seed: Missionary Printing and Literature as Agents of Change in Northern Siam," unpublished manuscript, R-MS 2/50–10, Chiang Mai, Phayap University Archives.

reach a specifically northern Thai audience had the unintended consequence of making that same cultural space vulnerable to penetration by other forces. Printing advertising copy and the texts of new Siamese laws, the press not only permitted the diffusion of commodity aesthetics, but became a major vehicle for the dissemination of Siamifying policy. When the Siamese government finally banned the use of Northern Thai language in the schools and in state bureaucratic contexts, it could count on the Presbyterians as its instrument and ally.[6] Phayaphrom had long since died by the time Central Thai had become the mandatory vehicle of formal business in Chiang Mai, and it is unclear how his own, inimitably multilingual compositions were viewed from within the new hegemony of the nationalized language. But for all of his attractions to the poetics of Rattanakosin Bangkok, it seems doubtful that he would have done anything but lament the suppression of Thai Yuan. And yet, in innumerable ways, he was there at the beginning of those transformations that would mark the closure of Lannathai's independence and the commencement of its complete immersion in national narratives and transnational economies.

What defines Phayaphrom's modernity is not, however, his physical proximity to the heart of change. Rather, it is the fact that his tragically heroic effort to effect the restoration of a lost love took the form of a postal fantasy, of an aspiration to presence at a distance. He was, in short, an unconscious advocate of technologized mediation. In sending his letter and imagining it read aloud to Chom, Phayaphrom produced the medium of his own transmission, with his voice substituted for by his script. Yet, though the letter aspires to performative power, seeking the reinstatement of that fidelity that the marriage vow was supposed to have generated, *The Poem in Four Songs* is troubled by the pos-

---

6. Although there is a great deal of irony in this alliance, there were also more pragmatic and intentional convergences. These were the result of the fact that the Siamese government had granted religious freedom and claimed to protect the right of Christians in its territories, something the northern *cao*s were less predisposed toward. When the Presbyterian mission, led by Dr. McGilvary, disputed accusations of witchcraft against some of their members in a case that seemed motivated, in part, by economic jealousy (the Christians had access to commodity trading and educational opportunities that other northerners lacked), they were forced to seek protection from the Siamese. Not surprisingly, they championed the establishment of the new court, where an English representative was permitted to assure the "judiciousness" of the proceedings; in so doing, they constituted a sturdy pillar of support for the Siamese efforts to oust the local *cao*s from their seats of authority. See especially Daniel McGilvary, *A Half Century among the Siamese and the Lao* (New York: Fleming H. Revell, 1912); also Herbert R. Swanson, *Krischak Muang Nua* [The northern Thai church] (Bangkok: Chuan, 1984), and Ratanaporn Sethakul, "Political, Social, and Economic Changes in the Northern States of Thailand Resulting from the Chiang Mai Treaties of 1874 and 1883" (Ph.D. diss., University of Illinois, 1989).

sibility of a failure. This much has already been argued. What has not been made clear, however, is the degree to which this skepticism marks the birth of a kind of writing that is no longer sacred, a writing that is indeed terrified by its own loss of magicality. Phayaphrom knows that, in and of itself, his letter guarantees nothing. It can produce no automatic effect. In this sense, the poem is quite unlike the kinds of writing that historians claim dominated northern Thailand until this moment, writing that was accorded a materiality beyond signification and a magical power that emanated from the script itself.[7] For Phayaphrom, all that writing can hope to do is stabilize a relationship of difference and mark an absence where the poet longs to be. It is after and secondary to the writer's presence. Indeed, it was to prevent writing from becoming the site of power and from overtaking the one who writes that the author asserted his primacy at the end of *The Poem in Four Songs*.

What the poet as modern author cannot abide is being overtaken by his writing, appearing as the mere medium of writing itself. This would be as unbearable as being the instrument of another's voice or of an agency that comes from outside of representation—something that magic demands and makes possible. Both writing and magic threaten to annihilate the author or the agent, but for opposite reasons. In writing, the author can be subsumed by the fact of textuality and appear to be its effect. However, in magic, where there is no interval between the act and its product, the agent vanishes as the mere vessel of a spectacular power. Either the medium is everything, and the space of deferral is eternal, or it is no thing, and the time of the act is forgotten.

A little more than a century after Phayaphrom's death, writing has become precisely that which produces the effect of an authorless voice. This, at least, is what we see in the possession performances of mediums, who theatricalize writing at the same time that they claim to be vacated of any subjectivity capable of memory. How is this possible? What has happened to the representational economy (including that of poetry, mediumship, and the more prosaic business of business) to permit the inversion of relations between writing and voice, between authorship and subjectivity, between memory and forgetting? I would like to suggest that these changes result, at least in part, from the fact that writing has passed through the stage of its hegemony. It has been surpassed and transformed by other technologies of representation, especially by photography. Photography is the institution in which the magic that was banished by secular writing has found the source of its greatest risk and its greatest possibility for renewal. Accordingly, it has been associated with the efflorescence of a tradi-

7. Swanson, "This Seed."

tion—namely, spirit mediumship—that the theorists of modernity thought would have vanished in the midst of bureaucratic and economic rationalization.

### Affliction and the Onerous Citizenship of Survival

Unlike Phayaphrom, who was caught halfway between the orator, who tells only his own story and bears responsibility for it, and the copyist, who is the mere vehicle of another's telling, spirit mediums are less like copyists than actors. They claim no responsibility for the words spoken through them.[8] Indeed, mediumship is a mode of effacement, perhaps the ultimate aspiration of the signifier for subsumption by its signified. To wit, the medium who is possessed retains absolutely no memory of the events that transpire during possession, and in fact must be told the words that have emanated from him or her. This, at least, is the claim that mediums make, and the authenticity of possession may be said to depend on the degree to which claims to forgetting are sustained and made believable to audiences. It is not necessary to endorse these claims to insist that they be seriously acknowledged and even taken at their word. For only in the wake of a submission to the fictions that mediums themselves inhabit can one ask what work forgetting performs and, thus, how mediumship itself works. What follows here is the narrative of a series of encounters with mediums and their performances, with considerable attention focused on a woman called Naang Khao, who is the medium of a vaguely familiar character named Phayaphrom.

Naang Khao lives on the outskirts of Chiang Mai, in a tangle of potholed dirt roads that curl between new suburban houses and decrepit wooden residences of older vintage. A widow whose children have long since left home, Naang Khao is not her real name. I call her that to ensure her anonymity, fabricating the appellation from two words, *naang* being a term for married or mature women, and *khao* meaning white, which is the color of her dominant spirit's attire. Although the title of this spirit, Caopuu, indicates high status, deriving from the terms for prince or king (*cao*) and grandfather (*puu*), Caopuu Phayaphrom has modest powers and a small sphere of renown. His seniority is relative only to the other spirits that also possess Naang Khao.

Caopuu Phayaphrom's medium is a timid and brittle-looking woman, neither abjectly poor nor particularly wealthy, though certainly on the lower end of the spectrum of Chiang Mai's mediums. Her compound is occupied by two separate structures, one a modest, whitewashed house, the other an open, peaked building made of wood but elevated on massive cement posts. The latter

---

8. On the distinction between oration and acting, see Jacques Derrida, *Of Grammatology* (1967), trans. Gayatri Chakravorty Spivak (Baltimore: Johns Hopkins University Press, 1974), 305.

structure is the shrine to which the spirits descend and the site of a small therapeutic and advisory practice. Residents of the neighborhood (*muu baan*) come daily for advice about finances and love, for curing in cases that biomedicine has failed to remedy, and for lucky lottery numbers, leaving their shoes in neat rows on the perpetually swept steps outside. Innumerable studies have been conducted to determine who seeks what kinds of assistance, and what social or historical factors influence the approach to mediums. But mediums themselves are as quick to point out patterns in patronage as are sociologists, and their conclusions rarely diverge from those of the more schooled analysts. Stereotypically, those seeking advice about love and beauty are young women, those wanting luck and physical prowess, young men. Business advice is as often the concern of middle-aged women as of men, but healing is a universal need, although mothers and wives are more likely to seek assistance on behalf of their sons and husbands than are the men themselves. For many Buddhist men, mediumship still has the rank odor of the feminine and emanates the aura of a not-yet-recuperated primitiveness. Though many would follow the advice of mediums in private and be grateful for blessings in business, they are likely to be circumspect about public acknowledgments of their dependency on occult knowledges that are not specifically presided over by monks and other literate officials of the *sangha*.[9] At issue are the forms of knowledge and the legitimacy accorded to them. Monks, who are believed capable of achieving magical powers through the study of texts and meditation practice, often deride mediums for a lack of learning, and mediums and their clients point to the relative merit of their possessing spirits (most of whom are supposedly highly learned Buddhists) as the sources of their own relative potency. Because literacy is associated today with a certain scientificity, the claims of monks have dominant status in the field of competing knowledges.

Many of the clients who visit Naang Khao, most of whom come from the

9. The traffic in sacred waters, which are thought capable of remedying the same issues, is widespread in Thailand. Recently, the Sangha Council ordered the abbot of Wat Sanam Chand to close down what it called a "holy water supermarket." The market served as a national distribution center for two hundred different bottled waters, each made from the formulae of well-known monks. Although the closure of the Wat Sanam Chand market was partly motivated by a political conflict between its abbot and Phra Phyom of Wat Suan Kaew, who had criticized such practices and attributed to them the same negative status he accords mediumship (see chapter 8), the Sangha Council initiated a public poll on the subject of holy water sales. The poll indicates the general public awareness of such traffic and remarks the ambivalent place of miraculous commerce in orthodox Buddhism. Whatever the outcome of the poll, it is likely that holy waters will continue to represent the legitimate end of the spectrum of magical healing in most Buddhist men's eyes, and that mediumship will retain the stigma of the unenlightened. See "Abbot Told to Shut Store," *The Bangkok Post*, 27 July 1998, Internet ed.

local neighborhood, have placed themselves under the protection of one of her spirits and pledged themselves to a relationship of exclusive dependency on him. Those who believe themselves to be under the spirit's protection are called *luuk sit* or, more commonly, *luuk liang*. The latter means, literally, the children whom one feeds. More generally, it is translated to mean step- or foster children. Here, language reveals the fact that feeding can constitute powerful bonds of familial relation which can mimic and even substitute for blood ties. But such individuals, who may also refer to themselves as devotees (*khon nap thyy*), have themselves paid a standardized fee for the privilege of the spirit's regal patronage, and they have agreed not to seek the services of another *cao* nor to allow any other *cao* to *suu khwan* (a rite of blessing normally performed by elders and people in authority). It is not difficult here to find the remembrance of previous eras and the kinds of debt patronage that defined the political economy of the old *müang*. When clients enter the circle of a spirit's power, they replicate the forms of citizenship that existed under the *cao*s of old Lannathai, when common people submitted themselves (or were forced to submit) to the personal rule of an individual and were promised protection in return for exclusive devotion.

Naang Khao's spirit shrine has a split level; on its elevated eastern side, beneath an open window, is a seat with a triangular pillowed backrest, the kind that pretends to be a relic of ancient courts and that can be found in any tourist market in Chiang Mai or Bangkok. Although it lacks the eight-tiered white umbrella that marks Buddhist monarchy, the seat is clearly a miniature throne, and it remains vacant except when the spirit has descended and the medium is possessed. Provocatively, it is termed the *thii deum*, the "place of origins." Above the throne, on a long wooden shelf, are dozens of vases full of dried and drying flowers, as well as joss sticks, several glasses of water, an occasional bottle of whiskey, and several unopened boxes of Marlboro Reds cigarettes: offerings to the spirits. From the shelf hang brilliantly colored streamers, and the window itself is draped with plastic, fuscia-colored lace. To the left or southern side of the seat is a veritable forest of statues and icons, with Buddhas, Indic deities, boddhisattas, and Chakkri dynasty monarchs all jumbled together. Usually, these images are shadowed by a wafting cloud of cheaply pungent incense smoke. When the smoke clears, one can see that there are four postcard photographs of King Rama V (Chulalongkorn), two with his locally adored Chiang Mai consort, Dararasmri, and several photographs of the present king and queen, as well as their daughter, the nationally revered Maha Chakkri Sirindorn. There is also a single photograph of the possessed medium, along with a dozen or so other possessed mediums. Behind all of these images is a locked glass cabinet, about four feet in length, full of clothes in cotton white and day-glo satins, these being the attire of the spirits. Their jumbled massness, barely contained by the folded order, suggests opulence and the power to consume in magnificent quantity.

When I first met Naang Khao, having learned of her from neighbors, she greeted me shyly. Another woman was with her at the time, and they were conversing in the strangely mediated intimacy that many women enjoy during the hotter hours of the day, watching television soap operas in the darkened interior of Naang Khao's house. An apocalyptic blue light was shaking the shadows of the hallways, which opened away from the screen door. Later, I would have occasion to wonder about the relationship between television and mediumship, but at the time I had no idea that some mediums had themselves become national celebrities and movie stars of a sort or that television stars have themselves become mediums. Naang Khao received me outside and led me to the shrine, where we sat on the cool linoleum of the lower level. What was second nature to her was notable to me. She sat with her body bent and perfectly enclosed, her knees tightly together and her eyes cast down. I imitated her, awkwardly, all the while trying to see.

Anthropologists are inevitably strangers, but in Chiang Mai they are also always familiar figures. Their (our) thirst for culturalist tales is rather infamous, and their (our) investment in the discourses of tradition form part of a redoubling circuit in which ethnography and localist politics intersect and reinforce each other with sometimes unsettling effects.[10] It was because of this abstract familiarity that Naang Khao told me the story of her earliest possession with only slight prompting in this, our first conversation. She knew already that I wanted to hear this story, and she was obliged—as are all mediums—to validate the fact of possession with a tale about its origins.

Naang Khao claims she had been in early middle age when she became ill with stomach cancer. It was then that the spirit first visited her. Only shortly before, a physician had diagnosed her as terminal and given her a prognosis of six months to live. The diagnosis was devastating, although it offered explana-

---

10. In Thailand, as elsewhere, one may speculate without much imagination on the relationship between ethnography and politically conservative cultural politics. Indeed, Thailand provided the scenario for the most forceful critique of such conservative alliances when it was discovered that some anthropologists actually engaged in anticommunist activities and deployed ethnography in the service of counterinsurgency efforts by both the U.S. and Thai governments during the years of the Vietnam War. But other, less visible convergences between nationalist and anthropological interests also merit attention. In his penetrating historical study of the discourses of tradition in Java, John Pemberton provides an exemplary exploration of this relation. Implicitly, *On the Subject of "Java"* (Ithaca, NY: Cornell University Press, 1994), calls other ethnographers to a more skeptical reading of traditionalism, and I take my cue from Pemberton in this regard.

tion and confirmation for her fears and suspicions. For months she had been unable to eat, her body withering until, as she recalled, she was "only eyes" (*mii tae taa*). The expression suggested a kind of identification between Naang Khao and a ghost, for spirits, especially malevolent spirits, are popularly remarked for their maniacally burning and hypertrophied eyes. Evil spirits are beings who cannot *not* see and whose eternally open-eyed state reflects a gluttony for the sensual world. The same gluttony, the same incapacity to recognize or impose limits on the physical world, leaves them blind to the moral economies within which they could achieve merit and move forward in the cycle of rebirth. Here, and in other domains, a visual metaphorics informs northern Thailand's moral universe such that the world is hierarchically schematized, divided between the visible and the unthinkable. The ethical decision to turn away from evil possibilities is construed here as a necessary blindness, and the wide-eyed specter is the sign of a failure to achieve the cataract of virtue. Naang Khao feared that she was on the verge of becoming such a specter, feared that evils committed in past lives were causing her to suffer in this and that they might continue into the next. She vomited constantly and was in excruciating pain. She begged the gods for release from her suffering. Then, as she says, the spirit "came down."

Initially, by her account, there was terror (*klua maak*). There was the pure unknowing of self, a radical loss and a total forgetting of the events that transpired during possession. Naang Khao's descriptions echoed those of the other mediums with whom I have spoken and with the friends who have endured this trauma with them. Even in hindsight, long after mediums have come to believe that accommodated possession has saved them bitter illness, the initial experience of possession is often likened to a kind of violation, a dispossession of self-knowledge and of memory. It comes, they all say, unsolicited: without warning, without omen, lacking all precedent. Somewhat unbelievably, they all insist that the one who becomes a medium has never before known a medium, is virgin to the forms and techniques of possession. Mediating between the obvious fact that most northern Thai people have seen or know of mediums, and the necessity for innocence in the dramatization of inspiration, mediums generally refuse to acknowledge their immersion in lineages of possession technique and in communities of other mediums. Despite this generic profession of ignorance, however, there are occasions when the fact of such sociality is acknowledged, namely, rites of accession to the role of professional medium and annual Praise Ceremonies in which possessed mediums meet and address each other as (relatively senior or junior) members of a spiritual community. The acknowledgment is not necessary for the commonality of forms to become obvious to outsiders, however. Many observers, both Thai and non-Thai, see such typicality as evidence of fakery. But for mediums and their followers, the tendency toward standardization is read not as proof of chicanery but as evidence of the actuality of the spirits who come from afar. It is because spirits are alike that the forms of their manifestation are also similar.

There is little divergence in the descriptions of the events that precede possession. Mediums universally identify the first experience of possession as "not knowing one's own self/body" (*maj ryy tua*), an expression more commonly translated as "losing consciousness." One of them described it thus: "I didn't know what was happening. I didn't know my own self. My eyes, my ears . . . it was as if everything closed. I don't remember it. After, they told me what I did. It was like someone else." To be like someone else is, to say the least, a radical experience of fracture, an absolute dissipation of subjectivity. Nor is this estrangement mitigated over time. Always, the return is foreign. It is experienced as an eternally new phenomenon. After each possession, the medium must be told what has happened, and she often asks what the spirit has said, what he has requested by way of new clothing or the ritual propitiations of spirits (the latter are known as *kae bon*), what instructions for merit making and what guidance in the matter of herbal or other healing techniques he has handed down.

Like many of the mediums to whom I spoke, it had taken years for Naang Khao to come to terms with possession. That is to say, it had taken years for the possession to become regularized, controllable, and, ultimately, professionalized. And like others, she spoke of this time of adjustment as a period of tumult and unpredictability. During the early stages of possession, when the spirit comes sporadically and without speaking, it is, in fact, incorrect to speak of mediumship in any general sense, for the status of medium is slowly acquired. It is only recognized by other mediums after the identity of the spirit has been clearly articulated and the medium has come to accept the professional obligations that attend possession through the acquisition of a *khan* dish.

The meantime is described by mediums as a period punctuated by days, weeks, and months of unexplained illness, often of paralysis but always of some sensory loss. Many times, this loss is mundane: a chronic absentmindedness (*khwaampen khiilyym*) that makes mediums vulnerable to the monstrous devices and events that would normally go unnoticed in the course of daily living. One medium told me that she had crushed her own hand while using a large pestle, for no apparent reason and despite the fact that the motion had been utterly habitual for her after years of making curry paste. One spoke of business failures caused by repeated but costly accidents: the spilling of cooking oil and the spoilage of food. Another recalled forgetting her own name. Yet another spoke more dramatically of total paralysis. These initial traumas, however, were not fully grasped in the moment of their experience, but each was the source of another. For it was in the return to sense that the mediums came to feel themselves to be disoriented. The recovery from possession thrust them into the world in a manner that rent the veneer of nature from daily existence and made of the most innocuous gesture a newly shocking encounter. Simple technologies became demonic, conveniences became burdens, and proportion was so distorted that a kitchen could appear to be an abattoir and a city backstreet the very image of chaos.

In each case, habit had been rendered the object of scrutiny. It had ceased to be part of what Pierre Bourdieu would call the medium's practical consciousness.[11] For the newly possessed vehicle, then, the return to consciousness, the always belated and unknowing arrival in the mundane world, begs to be recounted and makes of survival a kind of affliction. Not merely illness, as Susan Sontag would have it, but survival constitutes that "onerous citizenship" of mediumship.[12]

Although it took four years before Naang Khao's cancer finally abated, her recovery seemed to her friends to be utterly miraculous, evidence of a spiritual intervention that had begun to announce itself in the speech that was gathering coherence during possession states. The more dramatic the medium's illness, the more powerful must be the curative powers of the spirit, and ailing individuals who have been unable to find healing in the biomedical tradition that now dominates Thailand often seek out spirits who have proven themselves capable of curing the most intractable of illnesses in their mediums. Thus, the illness of the medium is exemplary and in many ways authorizes the spirit's claim to curative power. Curative techniques themselves may involve a host of different practices, from herbal remedies, forms of massage, and the laying on of hands, to the ritual propitiation of spirits and dietary interventions. More often than not, patients who seek the aid of mediums are given combinations of these techniques as part of their therapy (see chapter 8). It will come as no surprise to learn that mediums whose spirits are renowned as herbalists attract large audiences and compete with other traditional pharmacists for clients. Such professional practices generally come to mediums long after their entry into the world of mediumship, however, and are developed over the course of years. Naang Khao had been a medium for nine years by the time we met and she was famed more for her powers of divination, especially for reading joss sticks, than for medicinal knowledge.

On my first visit, I asked questions of the medium that were intended for the spirit. I got silence, frustration, and an explanation that the *cao* comes down

---

11. Pierre Bourdieu, *Outline of a Theory of Practice* (1972), trans. Richard Nice (Cambridge: Cambridge University Press, 1977), esp. 1–30.

12. Susan Sontag, *Illness as Metaphor* (New York: Farrar, Straus & Giroux, 1978), 3.

only when he chooses to. Fortuitously, on that occasion, the spirit arrived in the medium almost immediately upon her saying that she could not anticipate his descent. And coming without warning, as he did, he seemed both to legitimate her claim about sudden arrivals and to mock her suggestion that the spirit was not responsible to earthly calls even if he was responsive to human needs.

I recall it as a shuddering, a low growl, like the sound of a mad dog. Naang Khao's body went stiff, her arms shot out, and her eyes rolled backward. She wretched and convulsed momentarily, as her friend held a cup for the excrescence that leaked over her dry lips. Then a calm descended. Almost as absent of life as a corpse, Naang Khao seemed a mere body, the silhouette of a person, as she turned away and went to the cabinet, unlocking it with a key from a ring so full it looked appropriate for a jailor. Still silent, the newly vacated medium pulled out a white Mon-styled suit and slowly, with back turned, put on a buttoned tunic, sarong, sash, and white headscarf. To finish the transformation, the medium donned a pair of thick, black-rimmed spectacles. Only then did a voice emerge. It was an unfamiliar voice: deep and throaty and nothing at all like the shrill and nasal tone that normally emitted from Naang Khao's mouth. It was, remarked Naang Khao's friend, Caopuu Phayaphrom.

In later visits, I would learn that my initial profession of awe in the face of this transformation seemed ridiculous to people more familiar with such things. Unlike my own obsequy, clients of mediums fill the space of possession (which usually takes thirty or forty seconds, but can last for several minutes) and the period of waiting for an audience with chatter and laughter, drawing on cigarettes and catching up on local gossip. There is nothing stereotypically sacred (in the Weberian sense) about this occurrence or this space. Nonetheless, there is a distinct mode of embodied relation that is required in dialogue, for the *cao* is royal and therefore deserves to be *wai*-ed respectfully (a *wai* is a bow of the head with hands clasped before one's face). He may also look upon and touch clients in a condescending manner, even touching the heads of older adults.

On other days, earlier in the morning, Caopuu Phayaphrom would have other visitors, women and men who would ask him for advice about when to take school examinations, about the potential success of a business investment, about how to remedy the fissures in a marriage or how to win back the affection of a child. These individuals would be workers or middle-class housewives, entrepreneurs or college students. It is often remarked that times of fiscal crisis elicit the patronage of those most economically vulnerable, and although I believe this to be true, one ought not confuse economic vulnerability with poverty. In a speculative economy, such as that which has dominated Thailand for the past few decades, seeming wealth dissolves quickly and the richest people are quickly subject to the indebtedness (or the fear thereof) with which they leveraged their apparent wealth in the first place. Real estate and currency speculation propelled Thailand to the top of the list of the New Tigers in the mid-1980s and caused its spectacular plummet in the late 1990s. In this context, one is apt to encounter bankers and real estate entrepreneurs in the homes of mediums during good times and bad. On that first day, however, there was no one to attend the spirit other than Naang Khao's friend and me. After a brief and perfunctory conversation, a reprimand for having brought the wrong color flowers (red rather than white), and a prognostication of my own future failures and successes, Caopuu Phayaphrom disappeared. Shortly thereafter, Naang Khao came back to consciousness with a dazed look, as though she herself had been stumbling through the netherworld in search of a body.

*Inscriptions*

Whether the exile from practical consciousness makes possession possible, disorienting the medium sufficiently to make her vulnerable to the alterity of spirits, or whether it is merely symptomatic of a loss or a disjuncture that has already been effected is unclear in the testimony of mediums. The minute but terrifying facts of disorientation were always narrated to me as stubbornly meaningless and frightful signs. They were the starting points of all the possession narratives. And, as initially nonsignifying signs, it is perhaps inevitable that they would demand the heroic narration that is the medium's life history. It is notable that these experiences indexed the immanence of the possession only after the fact. In this regard, they marked a temporal detour, both anticipating what had not yet occurred (possession) and suggesting that it had already been determined by the spirit. Like prophecies, the minor catastrophes in the lives of mediums partake of a general feature of mediumship, namely, a disruption of the consciousness of time. This structure is manifested in myriad ways, but it is metaphorized most dramatically in the narratives of the voice's emergence.

In Naang Khao's case, the spirit's possessions continued without voice for several months before the rough "ejaculated sentences," as Carl Bock might have described them,[13] became regularized and the fits of convulsive unconsciousness were accompanied by a speaking. The accounts of that process provided by Naang Khao's friends suggest the extraordinary miraculousness not only of the speech that came from outside of consciousness but of the capacity, on the part of others, to comprehend it as such.

From Naang Khao's tremulous and vacated body, the spirit began to address those who gathered around her in broken and irregular spurts. Gathering the

13. Carl Bock, *Temples and Elephants* (1885; Bangkok: White Orchid, 1985), 340.

scraps of sound from these periodic events, Naang Khao's friends say they were assisted by the spirit and by another medium so that they could finally translate the happening into words and recognize the language of the possessed body as that of Caopuu Phayaphrom, though the identity of this spirit remained opaque and confused at the time and continues to this day to be an assemblage of unrelated ideals: those of literary genius, of princely power dating back to the time of Chiang Saen's dominance (sometime before the thirteenth century), and of Brahmanic purity. To her friends, Phayaphrom explained that he had come to assist Naang Khao, whom he claimed had assisted him as his wet nurse in a prior life. More important, he claimed a protective interest in all humans in what he describes as the era of bad deaths. The notion of a bad death is common and long-lived in local myth and legend. Unexpected deaths, premature deaths, deaths by accident, and those of a violent and dismembering nature are thought by many Thai people to leave a spirit disoriented to such an extent that it may be unable to move on from this world into the next. Confused in both space and time, such spirits may intentionally or unintentionally cause harm to the living, wounding survivors by holding too fast to those who remain in a material world for which the spirit is no longer equipped. However, it is the notion of an era marked by bad deaths, one that is in fact typified by bad deaths, that makes Phayaphrom's speech both notable and representative of contemporary mediumship.

In my experience, Phayaphrom's reference to bad deaths is not only typical of mediums' discourse, but it constitutes one of the most widely disseminated idioms within which ambivalence toward modernity is articulated by laypeople in general. For many, the most obvious and therefore frequently cited evidence of this phenomenon is the rise in traffic accidents. In conversation after conversation, death on the road was described to me as the very icon of modernity's caprice, one that challenged all efforts to find causal factors or malevolent intention behind otherwise random misfortunes. There is ample reason for the prominence that traffic accidents enjoy in the iconography of spirit mediums' moral discourse and in the imagination of modernity in general. They are such omnipresent facts of Thai life that cars are sometimes referred to as "the feet of ghosts." And few roadsides are not lined by small spirit shrines sheltering the souls of the many who die daily in cars and buses or who fall from motorcycles in awful, body-splitting crashes. Perhaps not even Andy Warhol could have imagined a national space so haunted by traffic death, or roadways so bloodied by the truncation of possible futures. Nor the businesses that, in Thailand, thrive on such catastrophe: the wildly popular magazines such as *191*, whose photographs of limbs and mangled cars provide the currency of visual pleasure for (mainly) male audiences throughout the country. One surmises that only the enclosures of premodern palaces and the stately pace of premodern travel could have kept princes immune to the tragedies of untimely death and specularization by desirous looks. And for this reason it was not, in the end, surprising to learn that, in the same breath that he remarked the violence of highways, Caopuu Phayaphrom informed Naang Khao's audience that he would require the accoutrements befitting northern Thai royalty: not only the material stuff of a regal abode—a throne, a shrine in the image of the royal palace, icons of all sorts—but clothing of old Mon fashion, made of white cotton fit for a Brahman. He also indicated his affection for *miang* (fermented tea leaves) and, somewhat anachronistically, for Marlboro cigarettes. Finally, he asked for a book in which to write.

Then, as now, the friends who accompanied Naang Khao scribbled the utterances down, made notes of the spirit's demands, and kept careful records of the commodity offerings, monetary transactions, and exchanges that Phayaphrom demanded. Filling notebooks with the citations of the spirit and achieving an almost Benjaminian fantasy in the form of a book of quotations, Naang Khao's friends and assistants came to occupy the role of scribe that the nineteenth-century poet Phayaphrom had himself performed. But whereas the poet's pages had been made of palm leaf, the medium's notebooks were of the kind that students buy at corner stationery stores: blue-lined with margins of red, their covers composed of gawdy pastiches and protected by cheap plastic. Whereas the poet's task was the transcription of speech into verse according to the rules of *Cindamani*, the attendants used a practice of inscription more common among accountants, making their marks in neat, dated rows.

When I spoke to her in 1991 and 1992, Naang Khao's spirit was using a notebook covered with images of coins and bills from around the world, something on which the possessing persona frequently remarked. In our many encounters, he showed off the worldly knowledge that permitted him to identify English pounds, French francs, and Italian lire with great bravado. As important as the currencies, however, were the images of royalty that appeared on their face. The kings and queens (and inventors whom he imagined to be regal figures) were objects of intense curiosity, and he often asked me about them: what were their names, were they very wealthy, what would they think of Thailand. Beyond occasioning this parade of news hour worldliness, however, the book had clearly fetishistic qualities for Phayaphrom. It was a part object, signifying far more than it manifested but containing within itself the power of all that was absent.

I was often amused by the seeming literality with which these signs of princely power were appropriated by Phayaphrom. The rather ostentatious gestures that invariably accompanied the notebook, or the demand for it, rendered it an almost ridiculously important part of his treasury. He kept it wrapped in richly decorous fabric, as would be appropriate for a religious text, and he exaggerated the gestures of writing to such an extent that one wondered whether he knew how to make letters at all—which he did, in the manner of a schoolboy. Indeed, with his numerous references to the beauty of the monied cover, Phayaphrom acted as though the notebook were made of actual bills and coins (as though money could ever occupy the place of the really real) and that it somehow instantiated an antiquated tributary logic by which the leaders of these myriad nations had sent their wealth, or at least the signs thereof, in recognition of his modest court. Actual tribute, the kind sent in the premodern era, would not have consisted of money, of course. It would have taken the form of rare and high-priced local goods—silk, woven cotton, white elephants, spice, varieties of seed or rice—and the inimitable, priceless miniature trees made of gold and silver that constitute the pinnacle of Southeast Asia's tribute. Replicas of such offerings are still given (to both monasteries and mediums), but as we shall see in later chapters, even money can be momentarily removed from its normal residence in the economies of general exchange and rendered as a sacred object in the context of mediumship. It will therefore be necessary to consider the literalization of economy's signs and the vast complex relations between the logics of gift and exchange in which they and the mediums are embedded. For now, it is the fetishization of the book, and of writing itself, that demands attention.

Phayaphrom himself wrote down many instructions for the circle of Naang Khao's assistants and for the medium herself. His determinations of auspicious dates for rituals of all kinds, including donations to wats and annual tributes to the tutelary spirits, were noted there. So were the particular objects—the number, maximum cost, color, and qualities—that were to be purchased for these occasions. The dates by which invitations to tributary rites had to be sent to other mediums were carefully written down, with great effort devoted to the precise and formal inscription of the envelope in which these invitations were delivered. At other times, instructions for curative therapies were registered and then copied out for clients. The notebooks remained under the watchful eye of the spirit, and they were consulted by *luuk sit* in the manner of an almanac.

Though treated respectfully, the inscriptions of Phayaphrom's attendants differed significantly from those that were more properly magical, the astrological signs and talismanic letters, usually of old Thai Yuan script, that were given to clients seeking protective amulets and other objects of power. Such magical writing contains within itself the memory of the sovereign performative, of the curse and the blessing and the first naming. The letters are things in themselves, and their straddling of the space between effectivity and representation opens up the possibility of miracles. The fact of such magical, thinglike status can be discerned in the manner that the texts are kept: wrapped in silks, rolled and inserted into amulets, or placed on altars. One does not ask (though I tried) what such writing means or how it might be translated. Indeed, mediums unfailingly denied being able to translate or interpret the signs their spirits left behind. One can only ask of such writings how to use them, what they do, how to keep them. This is because the inscription of such signs (we cannot really call them words) is truly a gesture of transmission on the part of the spirit possessing the medium. The materiality of the sign garners awe in clients because it is the trace of the sovereign, and indeed of the principle of sovereignty, which is to say of origination. Although Phayaphrom rarely engaged in such magical writing, many mediums produce magical letters for their clients on a regular basis (thereby competing with monks), and I have often been shown such texts as evidence of the power and antiquity of the spirit who can make them. In contrast, the notebooks, like the lists of Phayaphrom's *Poem*, resemble registries and the logs of bureaucratic functionaries rather more than the sacred texts of religious figures.

### Finding a Voice: Trauma, Writing, and Recognition

What can one say about these seemingly but ironically modern notebooks in a theater that is so grandiosely atavistic in other regards? For there can be no doubt that the *cao* who comes through the centuries to assist the wounded subjects of modernity is a figure invested with nostalgia's most potent longing. But why would a sign that seems so pregnant with the forms of colonial and national administration, the accounting notebook, find its place here, where everything else seems to aspire to antiquity and where magicality is the goal? The fact that the pen most loved by Phayaphrom, and by many other mediums, is a mock feather quill and the icon of writing before mechanization complicates the picture somewhat, but it does not mitigate the realization of modernity's force within mediumship. The juxtaposition of forms, old and new, may well suggest some historical confusion on the part of mediums, but it also reveals the complicated relationship between the logics of magical represencing and those of mnemonic inscription. In the moment that the spirit takes pen in hand, he acknowledges that his own descents leave no trace for the medium or for clients to hold on to.

One might want to read the inscriptions that both the spirit and Naang Khao's friends made as the memorialization of prior utterances, and Naang Khao certainly perceived them this way. They appeared to her almost as prostheses, the instruments of a memory that, by exceeding or substituting for hers, would make experience available as knowledge while at the same time giving to the words of the spirit both an eternity and a mobility beyond that of the localized utterance. Certainly, they permitted Naang Khao access to events she had missed in the breach of time that is possession. But they were more than note taking. They were also the renarrations demanded by trauma, the displaced speech that witnessed what was, in effect, a wound in her consciousness and, more specifically, her consciousness of time.[14]

I use the term trauma in the strict sense of the word, for Naang Khao's possession performance manifested many qualities of the structure of trauma as Freud described it. It compulsively reiterated the event, her illness, that had come so unexpectedly to overwhelm her. Like a nightmare, possession caused her to die over and over again, as signaled by her vomiting or retching and the shuddering departure of her consciousness with each arrival. It did not work to accommodate or master these experiences. In fact, rather than compensating her, it made of her survival a constant encounter with death. Such repetitions are perhaps the source of that resentment that seems to afflict so many mediums, the reason for the stubborn insistence on the burden of possession. Indeed, some of the most painful conversations I have heard have been between mediums, especially senior mediums, and those who are just beginning their journey to professionalization. In these intimate dialogues, younger mediums complain not only about the interruptions to their working lives, to their families (and the occasional abandonment by children, as mentioned in the introduction to this book), but also of the agonies of possession and the constant feeling of being lost in time. That successful mediumship sometimes compensates these individuals with wealth and renown never seems to adequately mitigate the experience of disorientation—at least for those mediums who have been inhabited by possession's discourse sufficiently to believe themselves the vessels of real specters. And of course, those who consciously fake the event are unlikely to bemoan its consequences.

Reading trauma into spirit possession in northern Thailand is a risky endeavor, of course, not least because it presupposes the concerns and, quite possibly, the psychic structure of the bourgeois subject in fin de siècle Europe.

---

14. As Cathy Caruth explains in her subtle reading of both the story of Tancred and Freud's response to it in *Beyond the Pleasure Principle*, trauma is a breach that "appears to work very much like a bodily threat but is in fact a break in the mind's experience of time" (61). This breach is "not . . . a simple and healable event, but rather an event that, like Tancred's first infliction of a mortal wound on the disguised Clorinda in the duel, is experienced too soon, too unexpectedly, to be fully known and is therefore not available to consciousness until it imposes itself again, repeatedly, in the nightmares and repetitive actions of the survivors" (4). See *Unclaimed Experience: Trauma, Narrative, and History* (Baltimore: Johns Hopkins University Press, 1996).

Yet, an interesting comparison can be drawn between the exemplary tale with which Freud explores the notion of trauma and the narrative of possession that Naang Khao's life gives us. In this context, what catches the eye, and the ear, is the fact that in Tasso's story of Tancred and Clorinda, what dooms Tancred to repeat the injury to his beloved is the lack of a sign that would permit him to recognize the repetition. He first strikes Clorinda by accident when she is disguised in the armor of his enemy, and then strikes her soul again when he flails unknowingly at a tree in which it has been lodged. Blood issues from the tree and a voice sings out from the wound to announce the doubled injury. But it is too late, and Tancred suffers the agony of having slain his beloved twice over, though it is the second wound that allows him to apprehend the first. It goes without saying that, had Clorinda been wearing her own clothing, Tancred would not have struck her. Masked by a sign that refers elsewhere, she is doomed to go unrecognized and therefore to be wounded. A tragically simple matter of attire, Tasso's story nonetheless theatricalizes something about the logic of signification in general.

Freud's own analysis of the tale is well-known and need not be repeated here, except to note that he sees in the unknowing repetition a generalizable structure in which an individual unconsciously repeats the event that was utterly un-knowable in the moment of its occurrence.[15] Though different in so many significant ways, the story of Tancred and Clorinda converges on that of Naang Khao in this one regard: perhaps more like Clorinda than Tancred, the medium is subject to a repetition that seems constantly to reenact the death from which possession has ostensibly saved her. More important, in mediumship, as in Tasso's tale, it is the repetitious gesture that makes the voice audible. Voice emerges, becomes recognizable, only when a point of differentiation has been elaborated. Whether this differentiation takes the form of the slash or the mark, of the material injury or the sign of writing (whose mutual and possibly ety-mological affinity has been remarked and debated by poststructuralist philoso-phers) is perhaps a moot question. The point is that it seems to come after the fact, while making it knowable for the first time. The second mark is the point at which a phantasmatic kind of writing is produced, and it is through this writing that voice becomes possible. Although much can be made of the fact that Clorinda speaks in a cry, one should not confuse her calling out with any primal utterance. In both Freud's retelling of the Tasso story and in northern Thai spirit mediumship, it is not really voice as primal sounding or as the

15. Sigmund Freud, *Beyond the Pleasure Principle* in *The Standard Edition of the Complete Psycholog-ical Works of Sigmund Freud*, trans. James Strachey, with Anna Freud, Alix Strachey, and Alan Tyson, 24 vols. (London: Hogarth, 1953–74), vol. 18.

expression of an originary and irreducible singularity that emerges through the repetition, but language itself: language as difference and as the always deferred system of differences within which recognition becomes (provisionally) possible. In other words: writing.

As Siegel has said in his account of spirit possession in Atjeh, the medium lends a voice to the language that comes from elsewhere, and all language comes from time's elsewhere.[16] The medium is not utterly transparent, is not mere instrumentality. In the case that Siegel describes, however, mediums are possessed generically and not by spirits whose biographies can be known, nor by those associated with definitive places in the landscape. In northern Thailand, by contrast, spirits are said to be particular, are named, and often are famously known for their historical deeds and their monumental achievements. There is, in fact, considerable effort made to claim that the voices that emerge in mediumship are particular to an individual. In this sense, it is not language but voice, not the system but origination that is dramatized in the development of speech in the medium. Yet, if the drive toward biography and the individuation of spirits suggests a logic in which speech has primacy, the theatricalization of writing and the generic qualities of the voices as well as the typing of possessing characters pulls in the opposite direction, toward an unconscious dramaturgy of writing's more basic status.

In the case of Naang Khao, the gathered scraps of utterance became coherent and recognizable to her clients as *a* voice only in the wake of their inscription. Moreover, the first attribute recognized was that of the spirit's generation, of his generic social category. Only secondarily did Phayaphrom name himself. In Naang Khao's performances, the process of inscription took on a life of its own and was metamorphosed into the gesture of the bureaucrat—that functionary of writing's generalization and even its aspiration to mathematics—but it needs to be understood in more than a literal sense. It is not only the physical alphabetical gesture that constitutes the writing of the voice, but audience in general: the recognition of language.

In mediumship, writing permits the sedimentation not only of a persona but the very possibility of speech; in this way, possession constantly reenacts the drama of language's origination. Of course, on a historical level, we need to carefully attend the theatricalized and laborious gestures that Phayaphrom makes on the pages of the money-covered notebook. In these gestures, it is not just language but the history of writing and its relationship to other technologies of representation that become visible. Indeed, the denaturalizing em-

16. James T. Siegel, "Curing Rites, Dreams, and Domestic Politics in a Sumatran Society," *Glyph* 3 (1978): 28.

phasis on the physical techniques of writing in Phayaphrom's possession not only draws attention to the act, but renders it seemingly supplemental to speech. Speech thus gains in authenticity precisely to the extent that writing becomes the object of elaboration.

It is because of this split between speech and writing, effected by a parodized inscription, that mediumship can seem both to require writing and to dramatize the primacy of speech. In another time, before photography could claim the title of pure reproduction, writing might have appeared to have a more transparent relationship to speech, in which case the specularization of inscription in possession performances would perhaps have been irrelevant and certainly would not have enhanced the presence of voice. In another time, too, the possibility that spirits of the past are actually inhabiting the bodies of mediums might not have been subject to doubt, and accordingly, the dialectical drama through which writing produces speech as real and relative presence (in opposition to writing's alienation) might not have been necessary. One cannot be sure, and there is no comparative data with which to support such far-reaching speculation. Nonetheless, it seems likely that the relations between speech and writing have been differently imagined over time. And there is no question that mediumship now exists within a context of doubt, the kind of doubt that is the ground of miracles.

### Knowledge without Subjectivity

For believers and devotees, part of the marvelousness of possession depends on the ignorance of the medium in relation to the historical knowledge that seems to be speaking through him or her. Thus, when an illiterate old woman is possessed by a Buddhist saint and enabled to write—entranced—in an old Lanna script, or when an uneducated medium is able to recite with perfection the verses of a Pali sutta that she cannot read, a miraculous aura surrounds her. The verisimilitude of the possession performance depends on the unexpected detail that reveals a secret knowledge; this verisimilitude then constitutes the authenticity of the possession. However, the fragmentariness of these details, and the seeming forgetting or not knowing of crucial information—such as Phayaphrom's poetry in the case of Naang Khao—also threatens to undermine the realness of the event. Like the imagery of Phayaphrom's (the poet's) own poem, the perfection of verisimilitude entails the effacement of the figure and, in this case, the disappearance of the medium. Total mediation appears to be no mediation. However, if the poet could not resist the fame of spectacular metaphoricity, pure transmission is the goal of authentic mediumship. Here, as elsewhere, the medium must appear to be the unknowing instrument of historical knowledge and thus the limit of personal memory. Inadequate knowledge on the part of the possessing spirit therefore appears to be the effect of a surfeit of knowledge, which is to say remembrance, on the part of the medium. It is the sign of her intervention, her disruptive mediation. All the inadequacies that belong to the medium enter to corrupt the truth of the spirit, and where the truth is veiled or fails to make itself apparent to audiences, clients will accuse a medium of fakery. If she mispronounces a word, if she recites a sutta incorrectly, if she gives incorrect advice or merely mistakes a date in the history of a king, she is vulnerable to attack for having pretended to knowledge that the spirit would possess in totality. When, however, there is no resistance, when another's story passes through her uncontaminated by her own memory, the medium seems to her audiences to be the instrument of perfect represencing, to be real (*cing*).

But mediums are rarely so thoroughly absented in their possession performances, and, in any case, the competition among mediums would require mutual accusations to the contrary. Mediums themselves sustain their claim to relative authenticity by raising the rumor of duplicity among others and by keeping open the question of veracity. Indeed, it is my experience that every stranger who visits a medium will at some point face the question of belief, often in a blunt interrogation: "Do you believe or not?" For the ethnographer as for the miracle seeker, the only fatal answer to such an inquiry is an unequivocal yes. To respond skeptically, and even evasively—as I did unwittingly, while attempting to circumvent the issue altogether—by claiming to believe only sometimes, is to demonstrate a capacity to distinguish between fakery and genuine possession, to know that appearances cannot always be trusted but that the specter of the past can indeed arrive in the present and look like something modern. Mediumship desires doubt, but only in order to have faith. Similarly, fakery and authenticity require each other.

One might go so far as to say that the lines between fakery and authenticity are tendentious not because possession is or is not actually possible, nor even because total historical knowledge is unavailable as the measure of veracity. Rather, it is tendentious because, as Lévi-Strauss learned (but misunderstood), the perfect fake *is* the perfect transmission.[17] The artistry of the medium is the artistry of self-effacement. This effacement is remarked relatively, through the clumsy inscriptions that are, by contrast, visible.

We get some insight into this logic by reading Susan Stewart's meditation on speech, writing, and the commodification of spirit in the mass-produced book.

---

17. Claude Lévi-Strauss, "The Sorcerer and His Magic," in *Structural Anthropology*, trans. John Russell (New York: Doubleday, 1967), 161–80.

In many ways, she articulates the ideology of voice's primacy when she writes: "Speech leaves no mark in space; like gesture, it exists in its immediate context and can reappear only in another's voice, another's body, even if that other is the same speaker transformed by history. But writing contaminates; writing leaves its trace, a trace beyond the life of the body. Thus, while speech gains authenticity, writing promises immortality. . . . If writing is an imitation of speech, it is so as a 'script,' as a marking of speech in space which can be taken up through time in varying contexts. . . . Writing has none of the hesitations of the body; it has only the hesitations of knowing, the hesitations which arise from its place outside history—transcendent yet lacking the substantiating power of context."[18]

Stewart sees the mass-produced book, the pure commodification of writing, as the quintessential reduction of the multiple signified to a single signifier. And she notes, provocatively, that the horror of the mass-produced volume is that it transforms spirit into matter.[19] Of course, the notebooks of mediums are not mass-produced volumes, even if they evoke that process of bureaucratized standardization and regularization that is the other side of mass production. Nonetheless, Stewart makes it possible for us to ask about the conditions under which a citation is known as such and when it appears not as a repetition (which is to say a temporally deferred gesture) but as a pure represencing. Mediumship can similarly be understood as a theater in which the voice of others cannot be delimited by quotation marks. It is as though the moment of citation and the moment of first utterance were indistinguishable.

It is perhaps useful to remember here that, in contrast, authorship in *The Poem in Four Songs* took the form not merely of the poet's self-assertion but also of the citations of Chom's niece. Indeed, it is in these citations, marked by the Thai sign for quotation, *waa*, that the speaking persona is most clearly differentiated from Phayaphrom. Had there been no quotation mark, no *waa* in the text, we would not have known so unambiguously where the poet ceased and the character began. For the medium, one can say, the *waa* is missing. The cited speech is not known as such, but takes over her body and her voice and is heard as though for the first time. "Without the mark there is no boundary, no point at which to begin the repetition," says Stewart. The mark exists only for listeners.

To speak and not be the subject of speech, to know and not be the subject of knowledge: this is the medium's predicament. But it is not merely a question of being rendered object, which is certainly a dimension of mediums' experience.

18. Susan Stewart, *On Longing: Narratives of the Miniature, the Gigantic, the Souvenir, the Collection* (Durham, NC: Duke University Press, 1993), 31.
19. Ibid.

In addition, the medium is also made to suffer time's expulsion. All utterances are made in the present. Mediums do not travel in their disembodied state to bring the words of spirits back from elsewhere in the form of reported speech. Their bodies provide the voice in which the spirit speaks. And because they are not the subject of that speaking, memory is out of the question.

In the end, the insistent display of "forgetting" operates to simultaneously reveal and conceal that which is its ground and its object. Indeed, forgetting is not the ruse through which mediums can (disingenuously) identify themselves with another kind of power, namely, that of sacral kingship. Rather, it is the logic of that kingship and of performative power in general. I mean to use the term performative in its technical, linguistic sense here, to designate the "re-iterative and citational practice by which discourse produces the effects that it names."[20] In Austin's founding exploration of the concept, performativity defines speech acts that are undertaken in very specific contexts and with specific limiting conditions, such as the homogeneity of assumptions in the audience, the precise and even ritualistic replication of previous speech acts of the same type (marriage vows and the like), and the recognized authority of the person who enunciates the performative.[21] The seeming paradox at the heart of performativity relates to this latter issue of authority, for the one who utters the performative appears to be the origin of a magically efficacious power. He or she speaks and the world changes accordingly. The quintessential locus of such sovereign speech acts is, of course, the origin myth. But in all cases, the performative announces itself as an absolutely precise replication of previous speech acts, forming a chain of impossibly identical repetition that leads back to an endlessly receding first event. It works by banishing remembrance of the interval between itself and its predecessors and by prohibiting even the thought of difference. Colloquially, it operates through reference to tradition, to what "has always been done," has been "handed down for generations," was "there in the beginning," there in "the place of origins."

One might say that performative power is the afterlife of charismatic authority, which, as Weber well knew, properly "exists only at the point of origination."[22] It is the impossible eternity of that origin, the form of a return that is

20. Judith Butler, *Bodies That Matter: On the Discursive Limits of "Sex"* (New York: Routledge, 1993), 2.

21. J. L. Austin, *How to Do Things with Words*, 2d ed., ed. J. O. Urmson and Marina Sbisa (Cambridge, MA: Harvard University Press, 1975).

22. Max Weber, "The Types of Authority and Imperative Co-ordination" (1947), in *The Theory of Social and Economic Organization*, ed. and introduced by Talcott Parsons, trans. A. M. Henderson and Talcott Parsons (New York: Free Press, 1964), 358–63.

always blind to the fact of its own repetitiveness. Not surprisingly, we find it potently manifest in the speech of all sovereigns. Northern Thailand's pre-constitutional monarchs are no exception, being men whose every word became deed and whose proclamations preceded and, in some respects, negated the need for law in its generalized form. The great risk of performative power is, however, that it tends to rest on a conflation of the institutions and the occupants of power in a manner that threatens to undo the very logic of citationality on which it works. The speaker appears to be the source of that power he claims to cite, and in the process becomes his own terminus. This is particularly true in the case of monarchy, where the king's two bodies—his temporally contingent, material being and his symbolic or institutional image—are constantly threatening to collapse into one phantasmatic potency.

In Thailand, where the monarchy was constitutionalized in 1932, the king's two bodies have been variously related over the past two centuries. However, the current dynasty was born precisely out of the recognition or the belief that the person and the institutions of kingship must be separated. Taksin the Great, who defeated the Burmese after fleeing Ayutthaya in 1767 and established Thonburi as the new capital of what would become Thailand, was deposed after having laid inappropriate claim to being a *sotâpanna*—a stream-winner who is advanced on the path of Enlightenment—and for his "overidentification of monarch and monarchy."[23] Among other things, he asked monks to pay him obeisance, something that dominant Siamese opinion forbade at the time, given that the Buddhist *sangha* was thought to grant the king his recognition rather than receive its authority from the monarch.[24] After Taksin's deposition, the man who would become known as Rama I, Phraphutthayotfa Chulalok, established the new Chakkri dynasty in Bangkok, and commenced what David Wyatt has called a "subtle revolution." His reign was characterized by the first gestures toward bureaucratic rationalization in legal and religious domains and the seeds of a modernity that would not acquire full momentum until the middle of the nineteenth century, under King Rama IV. Yet, beyond his move toward "Buddhacization" and his insistence that spirit belief assume a secondary place in religious life,[25] Rama I undertook the "restoration" of the corona-

23. David K. Wyatt, "The Subtle Revolution of Rama I of Siam," in *Studies in Thai History* (Chiang Mai: Silkworm, 1995), 139; also see Craig J. Reynolds, "The Buddhist Monkhood in Nineteenth Century Thailand" (Ph.D. diss., Cornell University, 1972), 30–35; and Lorraine Gessick, "Kingship and Political Integration in Traditional Siam, 1767–1824" (Ph.D. diss., Cornell University, 1976), 101–9.

24. Gessick, "Kingship," 101–9.

25. Wyatt, "The Subtle Revolution of Rama I," 156.

tion ceremony. His concern was the proper investiture of the king and the legitimate insertion of the regal person into the monarchical institution. The rite that he ostensibly "revived" on the basis of remembered practices in the era of Ayutthaya would ultimately publicize the irreducible tension between charismatic and performative power, between originary and citational speech. But it could not mitigate the fact that, in the effort to "re-member" the Ayutthayan forms of state ceremony for Bangkok, Rama I's coronation ceremony would have to dramatize the forgetting of that space—of war and chaotic exile—between the two eras. The forgetting of state ritual caused by the war and its dispersals had, in fact, seemed a threat to the monarchy, and the failure of proper investiture was one explanation offered for the ignominious descent of Taksin's reign. It was this rupture that was effaced with the claim to the restitution of original ceremonial forms, which nonetheless had been substantially changed in the process of purification. An amnesiac drama, in which forgetfulness was itself forgotten, Rama I's new coronation ceremony transposed and specularized the logic of performativity. It guaranteed that he would be seen as "acting" his part rather than pretending to a throne that was not his.

Let us remark that forgetting that makes possible both a man's assumption of regal position and the medium's assumption of monarchical identity. The consciousness or intentionality of the forgetting is, in the end, quite irrelevant. Quite simply, performativity demands acting if, by acting, we mean the absolute subsumption of one's being by another's part, which is to say, by a role.[26] Every performance of course is subject to failure, and when the space between the actor and the act, between the person and the institution becomes visible, performance will seem to be an act of *mere* copying. The successful performance, by contrast, will occur when technique vanishes and when it is no longer possible to even think the question of an individual's acting ability. In more than one sense, then, the successful performance is magical. For this reason, we can expect to see the dissipation of performative or magical power when technology becomes visible and when performance comes to appear representational or, in some degree, mimetic.

Explicit conversations about technique mark the demise of magicality. And when magic itself can become the object of a discourse—as it did in the latter part of the eighteenth century, at the end of the nineteenth century, and as it has again on the cusp of the new millennium—forgetting also becomes visible as a technique and a contrivance. In the process, kings become naked pretenders and mediums become fakes. Performativity, we might say, becomes mere performance, theatricality in its baser form. The consequence is an unquenchable

26. Derrida, *Of Grammatology*, 305.

longing for either an identificatory return or a narrative repossession, the latter taking the form of fetishistic historical knowledge. In these moments, one hears of either the desire for real mediumship or the ethnographic aspiration to a catalogue of "traditional practices," both of which now fill the columns of newspapers and academic journals in Thailand.

# 4 THE APPEARANCE OF ORDER

For mediums, the counterpart to the king's investiture ceremony is the *phithii jok khruu*, or Praise Ceremony. It is here that new mediums receive the dish (*khan*) on which to make offerings to the spirit and to which the spirit descends to receive them. Here, the anxious and abject imitation of monarchy assumes its public face, and here the identification with power and hierarchy becomes the ravishing demand for submission to teachers and elders. Praise Ceremonies provide the occasion to honor tutelary spirits, although they can be performed for any great teacher. They are not simply celebrations of tutorial privilege, however. More than this, they constitute an elaborate pedagogy of order in which the volatile potential of possession by the radical alterity of death is overcome in a submission to the socialized and individuated forms of the dead—or, indeed, of the undead spirits. In accepting the *khan* dish, new mediums signal their acquisition of the forms that are necessary to prevent their own dissipation. They are also publicly inserted into ritual lineages and thereby made subject to the law of a patriarchal sociality.

To a large extent, the Praise Ceremony seems to theatricalize the ideal order of the premodern *müang*, replicating the investiture ceremony of kings and enacting cosmological geometry in a delirium of miniaturization. The aspiration of that miniaturization is, it seems, to draw homologous correspondences among the various domains of body, house, and nation and, in its reach, the Praise Ceremony seems to enact a representational system for which there is no outside. In this respect, it is truly baroque.[1] The mediums who are its attendants

---

1. By "baroque" I mean a discursive and aesthetic practice dominated by the fold, that line that turns in on itself to produce something that seems to be an inside but is, in fact, only one side, the interior, of the line. The best description of this logic is to be found in Gilles Deleuze, *The Fold: Leibniz and the Baroque* (1988), trans. Tom Conley (Minneapolis: Minnesota, 1994).

extol the values of locality, binarity, and hierarchy with verily compulsive assertions of normatively Buddhist identity. And yet, the Praise Ceremony's fantastic
drive to universality does have an outside. Nor is this merely the outside Other
of an official Buddhism that rejects it. To the contrary, the Praise Ceremony is
constantly haunted by a radical exteriority whose excess and difference it seeks
to contain through gestures of thematization and disavowal.[2] The haunting that
the Praise Ceremony domesticates as "mere" possession is, I hope to show, the
source of its pejorative status in the eyes of scripturalists for whom its performances are always, and always already, excessive. That excessiveness is variously
imagined in the idioms of verbosity, naïve artistry, and sexual perversity. Such
accusations do not reject the order to which mediums aspire, it should be
noted. They simply valorize it as the ideal for which mediums are poorly suited.
The terms of meaningfulness are here historically overdetermined, for which
reason an ironic convergence can be discerned in the discourses of both mediumship and the more doctrinally oriented forms of Theravada Buddhism in
Thailand. This despite the fact that doctrine frowns on mediumship as fiercely
as mediums claim to be good Buddhists. And where the objects of anxiety for
orthodox Theravadans are empty gesture and sexual polymorphousness, mediums fear madness and simultaneous possession. Both find threat in indeterminacy and the ethnically other despite the different ways in which they allo-
cate those risks.

Many ethnographers and folklorists have been complicit with the longings
for order that mediums display, effacing their validations of hierarchy by imagining that attention to the popular suffices as a refusal of hegemony.[3] What I
hope to accomplish here is an alternative reading, one that comprehends the
Praise Ceremony not in a dialectic with dominant readings of authorized texts
(wherein it constitutes the popular) but as a performative assertion of order
that cites and flirts with alterity in a gesture toward transcendence. In short, I
want to explore the possibility that the Ceremony both recognizes and rejects
the radicality of signification and that, in the process, it offers instruction
beyond its own ambition. In what follows, I consider not only the forms of the
Ceremony and the cosmic cartography that guides its dramaturgy but also the
intertextualities and discursive linkages within which disorder gets figured. All

2. In *Negative Dialectics* (1966), trans. E. B. Ashton (New York: Continuum, 1994), Theodor Adorno
distinguishes between the concept, in which the dialectic between universality and particularity
occurs, and that radical singularity that is before and beyond language. Lacan would call this
singularity the Real.

3. The notion of "popular Buddhism" has long been used to designate a syncretism in which
supposedly pre-Buddhist animist practices are copresent with the properly antiontological teachings of Buddhism.

of this to understand how a fantasy of hierarchy comes to appear as the commandment of the flesh, and how the workings of language can be construed so that a multiple inheritance gets transformed into a demand for sexual and national identification.

## Preparing for the Dish

Historically, one is told, the Praise Ceremony was performed in the ninth lunar month, which corresponds roughly to June of the Western calendar. However, because the number of mediums has grown so much in recent years, the rites now begin in mid-March and run almost continuously (excepting *wan phra'* [day of worship]) through the end of June. During the months preceding the monsoon, when boys and young men enter the monasteries to take temporary vows, the city is dotted by these rites. They are always discernible by the slow tumult of gongs and the relentless rhythms of the modified, sometimes electrified *phiphat* orchestras that drift over neighborhoods; by the bright tents and the wheeled food carts selling snacks and sodas; by the constant stream of *tuk-tuks* and briefcase-toting mediums that approach and depart from them; and sometimes by the felt-pen arrows and directional scrawls that are posted on telephone poles to point the way. Often, they appear celebratory in tone, so much so, indeed, that Gehan Wijeyewardene has condescendingly described them as "a party at which the *caw* [*sic*] enjoy themselves."[4] Although pleasure is certainly an important part of the occasion, and although the pursuit of bodily satisfaction, both violent and sexual, occasionally overruns the ceremony, the business of "elevating" one's teachers is as serious as any disciplinary rite can be. I attended several dozen such events during 1991 and 1992, at the homes of the wealthiest and the poorest of mediums, in the old city, and in neighboring suburbs. Despite the differences in grandeur and the levels of attendance—the latter almost always being contingent on the former—the protocols and the basic forms of tribute were similar in all of them.

The express point of the Praise Ceremony is, clearly, to honor the spirits, and this is done through offerings of food, flowers, and incense and through forms of tributary dance called *forn phii*. In preparation for the rites, a medium and her or his assistants gather the necessary offerings. These may be as modest as two chickens, a small bottle of Thai whiskey, and a plate of fruit with twelve joss sticks, two wreaths of jasmine, and a handful of bought candles. Or they may be

---

4. Gehan Wijeyewardene, *Place and Emotion in Northern Thai Ritual Behavior* (Bangkok: Pandora, 1986), 225. Wijeyewardene compares the rites unfavorably to the *kataragama* of Sri Lanka, referring to them as "dull" and "unobtrusive" (162). The former accusation seems a rather personal matter of taste; the latter does not concur with my own observations.

as extravagant as two full pigs, a bottle or two of imported Johnnie Walker red label scotch, tables full of fruit, whole branches of young coconut trees, and arms full of flowers, joss sticks, and real beeswax candles. Not surprisingly, the richness of the offering testifies to the greatness of the spirit, and there is enormous pressure to make fabulous displays of it. The medium's capacity to earn money in his or her professional practice is, in turn, largely dependent on the wealth and correlative status displayed in such moments, and for this reason, mediums of means often display photographs of their offerings at Praise Ceremonies to impress visitors. It is also for this reason that mediums are associated in the minds of more ascetic Buddhists with sinful wastefulness. At every turn, they seem to earn only by expending.

There are generally two loci of activity at the Praise Ceremonies that are held at private shrines: that of the throne (*thii deum*, sometimes called *thii keut*), and that of the dancing. Usually, the former is inside the medium's home or in his or her shrine, and the latter takes place under tents, in an area that has been carefully circumscribed by threads of unspun cotton tied at eye level. At the periphery of this domain, a plate of rice will have been placed matter-of-factly on the ground. This is for the maternal spirits of the earth and sometimes for the Rice Mother or *mae posop*. Another offering will have been elevated and placed on a stand from which four differently colored flags will hang to mark the four directions of the universe and the four continents of the cosmos. This is for the emphatically masculine spirit of Phra Indra, whose mythified capacity to smite evil is sought to protect mediums from unwanted spiritual intrusions on the occasion of their tutelary spirits' descent.

If the shrine is within the private house of an individual medium, or even in a shrine built on a medium's domestic property, the offerings will be laid out inside. At Praise Ceremonies to the higher spirits of more public sites, such as the northeast corner of the city, where the spirit of Caopuu Luang Kham Daeng is said to reside (see chapter 5), long tables are usually placed outside in public view, where passersby and devotees can (and do) contribute to the collective offering. In both cases, the space is meticulously cleaned the day and night before. It is swept, scrubbed, purified with burning herbs, and sprinkled with holy water (purchased at wats, where it is bottled by monks who imbue it with personalized, if formulaic, power). Most public shrines prohibit women's entrance, and even when the medium of the spirit associated with that shrine is female, the rites of possession will have to be held in a place that is considered sufficiently removed to not offend the spirit's masculinity. In the private spaces of individual mediums, however, no such prohibitions are observed. This is because the ritualized architecture of the shrine actually transforms the domesticity of the house, the *domos*, into the universal publicity of the palace.

The hosting medium (usually a woman) commences the Praise Ceremony by lighting joss sticks before she *wais* and "takes refuge" in the "three jewels" of Buddhism, namely, the Buddha, the *dhamma,* and the *sangha.* She then sits in quiet, meditative prayer. Often, she is surrounded by other, not-yet-possessed mediums, who chat and smoke and greet each other on arrival. If the Praise Ceremony is to be an occasion at which a new medium receives the dish, then it will begin at dawn and all of the mediums of a lineage will be present. In Chiang Mai, it should be noted, the lineage is not one of blood, and although one sometimes finds more than one medium in an extended family, it is a profession of inspiration to which one is called and which cannot be sought through apprenticeship. This lack of blood relation distinguishes professional mediumship in Chiang Mai from rural cults, and from the Mon *phii meng* cults in neighboring cities, both of which are emphatically associated with matrilineality.[5]

Seen from the bottom, the "lineage" is a tenuous thread of affiliation and identification with senior figures who are themselves identified with yet higher powers. Despite the fact that the logics of seniority eventually translate themselves into those of the family in both Northern and Central Thai, through the terms of *phii* and *norng,* mediums and possessing personae generally refer to each other in that other language of mastery and submission, as teachers (*khruu*), lords or masters (*cao naaj*), and their devotees (*khon nap thyy*) or adoptive children (*luuk liang*). It is a relative and therefore unstable order that gets articulated in such positional languages, but one that is nonetheless premised on an attraction to the economies of profoundest debt and obligation. Senior spirits and their mediums can demand of their junior counterparts attendance at Praise Ceremonies and at *thord phaa paa* rites, where they are required both to donate money and to witness the generosity of their senior peers. Implicitly, juniors are also required to extend the renown of the senior teaching spirits and their mediums. Their own Praise Ceremonies will include a reference in the form of an offering to the more senior members of a lineage, and they will stage the presence of those spirits with the display of specifically named *khan* dishes to which they will be invited to descend.

The exclusivity of the senior spirit's power over others is materialized in the right that he has to *suu khwan* for his "students." *Khwan* are considered to be distinct essences that together constitute the being of a person. People are said, by those who believe, to have thirty-two such essences. Other animals and

---

5. See Shigeharu Tanabe's account of the *phi meng* in his essay, "Spirits, Power and the Discourse of Female Gender," in *Thai Constructions of Knowledge,* ed. Manas Chitrakasem and Andrew Turton (London: SOAS, 1991), 183–212.

entities, including everything from kitchen implements to water buffalo, are also comprised of *khwan*, but these are fewer in number. After an illness or an emotional trauma, one's *khwan* are said to be destabilized and occasionally even lost. They must therefore be called back, as suggested by the name of the apotropaic rite, *riak khwan* ("to call the *khwan*"). The one who performs the *suu khwan* or *riak khwan* rite for another thus has enormous power over that person's well-being. And if we take seriously the notion of the *khwan* as dispersed and volatile essences that have to be repeatedly restabilized in their interrelations, then the one who conducts this rite literally coheres the subject in relation to himself or herself, albeit in a temporary manner.[6] Some dominant mediums actually use the occasion of the *suu khwan* to advise their students on how to comport their bodies, how to meditate, and what offerings to make at which wats, but most do not engage in such disciplinary, biotechnological politics.[7] Nor is it necessary. The acceptance of the *khan* dish, and the submission to the binding rite that attends it, signals the new medium's agreement to a relationship of subservience, and it can thus be understood as the performative enactment of subjugation, albeit one in which the forgetful fact of possession ensures that there is no unified or temporally stable subject who can cross the

6. Phaya Anuman Rajadhon, "The Khwan and Its Ceremonies," *Journal of the Siam Society* 51, no. 2 (1962): 19–64; Sukhrot Phanwilai, "Bot suu khwan: wannakam thii kiaw khong kap prapheenii lae' phithiikam" *Eekasaan prakob kaan samomnaa Lanna khadii syksaa: Phasaa lae' Wannakam*, 4–6 August (1987); Prakhong Nimmanhaeminda, "Khwan lae' kham riak khwan" *Lannathai khadii* (Bangkok: Caroenwit Press, 1978), 106–36.

7. I mean to invoke Foucault's distinction between the power of the monarch who holds the right of death over his subjects and that of one who has, instead, the right over life. In Foucault's arguments, the latter is associated with the techniques of biopower, the regulation of productivity, and the state's increasing intervention into the bodily lives of its subjects. Foucault associates the latter with modernity in the West, and there is some reason to believe that a similar distinction has relevance in Thailand. However, as should be clear in the present passage and throughout this book, there is more than one modality of disciplinarity now operative in Thailand. Indeed, Thailand's modernity is defined as much by a doubled episteme (if not outright "double consciousness" in W. E. B. Du Bois's sense) as by the displacement described by Foucault in *Discipline and Punish: The Birth of the Prison* (1975), trans. Alan Sheridan (London: Penguin, 1979), or in *The History of Sexuality*, vol. 1, (1976), trans. Robert Hurley (New York: Vintage, 1990). I am somewhat hesitant to draw a parallel between the experience of African Americans in the United States and the history of northern Thais as they have been encompassed by both Siamese nation formation and the global economy of late capitalism. Nonetheless, there is an extent to which the self-Orientalization that now characterizes so much self-representation in Thailand shares that "sense of always looking at one's self through the eyes of others" that Du Bois identified in *The Souls of Black Folk* (1903; New York: Fawcett, 1964). It is, however, not so much "contempt and pity" that defines this discursive circuit as objectification and desire. On this issue, see John Nguyet Erni, "Of Desire, the *Farang* and Textual Excursions: Assembling 'Asian AIDS,' " *Cultural Studies* 11, no. 1 (1997): 65.

threshold of the Praise Ceremony and claim, as might a shaman, to possess the knowledge gained therein.

At the Ceremony itself, the acquisition of the dish seems primarily to be a matter between two mediums, the vehicle of the tutelary spirit and the new medium of the recently revealed spirit. At the initiating Praise Ceremony that I attended in 1991, other mediums professed little interest in the young host and hardly even acknowledged her presence. Yet, the gazes of these mediums were quietly inspecting and, in seeming anticipation of their approval or condemnation, the performance was especially extravagant. Not only did the medium wretch and vomit, but from a sitting position, her body leapt into the air and she flew several feet before landing, again on crossed legs. The newly possessed medium then stood, spinning, but with eyes that seemed to see nothing of the walls and windows, the shelves of Buddha statues, the icons of kings and Indic deities, or the faces of other mediums that were passing so rapidly before her. When, finally, a voice emerged in grunting spasms, other mediums began to feel the force of their own possessing spirits, filling the room with a cacophony of coughing. The young medium proceeded obliviously nonetheless, dressing from bottom up before reaching down to pick up the *khan* dish on which flowers and candles had been laid. In a newly male body, the possessed medium held the dish to his forehead, turned to each of the room's four corners, and, like the not-yet-possessed vehicle, prayed to Buddha and to the tutelary lord under whom he was to serve. This time it was Caopuu Mokkhalaan, the great teacher of Buddha's time.

The dish is the place at which the possessing spirit receives offerings and where he lays his gifts, be they the knowledge of divination or the power to cure sorcery's victims. Other dishes, which are arrayed on the sides of the room, are associated with other spirits, not all of whom will possess the medium but all of whom will receive prayers on this day. For each spirit, there is but one dish, named for the one who will descend there. The possessed medium (now masculine) picks up each and holds it to his head. Typically, he asks the Buddha for knowledge and for magical eyes and ears that will empower him to communicate properly with clients. He asks the senior tutelary spirit to give him amiable speech so that clients will be impressed. He invokes the spirit of Indra, reputed to have subdued devils in the primordial time of myth, and asks for assistance in thwarting evil. From other, lowlier spirits, he requests graceful manners, knowledge of incantations, and magical power.[8] Finally, he asks to be blessed with a large entourage of clients, who will bring him money and make offerings to the spirits, as he himself is doing.

---

8. Shalardchai Ramitanondh, *Phii cao naaj* [Spirits of the lords and masters] (Chiang Mai: Faculty of Social Sciences, Chiang Mai University, 1984), esp. chapter 4.

These requests are made before the medium mounts his throne, which sits unoccupied until now. The moment is a strangely doubled one in which the spirit seems both to be in the body of the medium and to constitute an immanence whose location will be the silk-covered seat. Both the mount and the throne are described as the sites of a birth (*keut*) and in this doubling the possibility of simultaneous origination can never be completely banished. Indeed, the medium is always vulnerable to a competing possession, and if she has failed in her efforts to learn the forms of the profession, this is precisely what will occur. The result, inevitably, is madness, called *phii baa* or *phii porb*. If the spirits cannot be evicted through the apotropaic interventions of another medium or a monk, or, in some cases, through violent injury to the medium (which jars the spirit), it is believed that the now-mad victim will die in a state of absolute dissipation. Such dangerous ambiguity reflects the fact that the spirits are many, and only through time and the discipline of the sequence can mediums eventually receive other possessing personae. But an even more radical difference, the plenitude that is tamed in the concept of the multitude, is suggested in the diversity of names and faces that are associated with a given spirit. Some spirits, such as that of King Ramkhamheang, are actually said to have thousands of faces. Others simply appear differently in different cities. Thus, for example, the spirit of Phrom Saeng Atthit claims also to be the exalted being who watches over the supreme teacher and Buddha's acolyte, Mokhalaan. At the same time, he identifies himself as Phra Phrom Erawan, though he assumes that guise only when he appears in Bangkok (at least one medium of this spirit travels back and forth between cities, appearing in one or the other of his forms depending on the location of the possession).[9]

Despite the fact that possession is constantly threatened by an inheritance of radical difference, the Praise Ceremony comes to a point in the moment of approach to the throne, when the new medium dances with swords as part of his tribute to the highest of his spirits. It is here that the Ceremony achieves its most profound exaltation of hierarchy. The dance seems to slay the competing spirits and, indeed, to allay the very possibility of competition. As that occurs, military-monarchical power is made terrifyingly voluptuous and acquires the aura of purity in a process of intense gestural abstraction.

## The Dance, the Throne, and the Axial Universe

It is now nearly two hours into the Ceremony. The room is hazy with the smoke of cigarettes and loud with conversation. Nonetheless, the music from the

9. Ibid.

orchestra outside can be heard clearly, and as the sound of the electronic keyboard entwines with that of gongs, the new medium begins to *forn*. I have seen such rites very rarely, but on each occasion, I have been moved by the grace of the dance and by how the slow wielding of the sword and the extreme stylizations of the slash conspire to lift off from the battle that is its oblique referent. A foot is raised, is held in the air. A hand opens into taut, arced fingers, and moves but a fraction of an inch in a gesture that is likened by observers to the threading of silk. A sword passes by another sword and turns inward, metal strikes metal, brashly. The medium moves forward, dipping ever so slightly. A foot returns to earth behind the axis of the body, the other rises. In one smooth continuum comprised of an infinite number of points, each the pure abstraction of the entire dance, the accomplished medium achieves the very limit of bodily signification. Now the medium is possessed by the dance, and in this moment, the allegory of the monarch's extreme power makes itself felt.

The possessed medium grows intent upon the throne, dances only for the throne. The throne, in turn, commands him. The spirit in the medium seeks only to be born there, as the one who will sit upon the throne. Others continue their conversation, spit and cough, but the medium goes on, repeating the same gestures, over and over again. Time seems to turn on itself as the dance simultaneously reveals the reason for the spirit's being present and disappears it. The gesture that sheds blood becomes one of bodily homage. *Bap* (demerit) is here transformed into *suai* (tribute), if not immediately into merit (*bun*). And in the homonymy that makes beauty a mode of tribute (*suai* means both tribute and beauty), the origin of possession is recuperated as the means to negate the condition that first demanded the spirit's return. Pure spectacle: a violent origin disappears in the moment of its display. (No wonder, then, that many of the monks who spoke to me about mediums laughed off the Praise Ceremony in particular as a "confused" occasion at which evil returns and receives the obsequious devotion of people who simply want power.)

The possessed medium who mounts his throne does so, one imagines, to become the point of universal orientation, to occupy the place of the "world-turning monarch" (*cakkravartin*). His shrine, and that of all the mediums I met, is thus treated as the miniaturization of celestial form. One cannot help but be dazzled by the baroqueness of its interior, the myriad icons, the array of dishes, the countless joss sticks that burn. Here is the status of the fasting Buddha, of the Buddha in meditating position, of the Matreya Buddha of the future. Here is the iconic protector of businesses, Gwan Yin, the bearer of financial luck. There is the image of King Chulalongkorn, and of King Mongkut, of Taksin. Here is Queen Camadevi. One marvels. Nor is this response peculiar to the foreign ethnographer. Clients remark vociferously at the mass of icons and the richness of decor, though they recognize that the cheap grandeur is but poor imitation of monarchical wealth. Mediums do their best to satisfy the needs of spirits and to honor them appropriately, although the pursuit is endlessly compromised by the very materiality in which the spirits and their mediums must communicate on this plane. Shalardchai Ramitanondh has observed that the requirements for maintaining the appearance of royal power ensure that professional mediumship is the prerogative of the middle classes, for no royal spirit would humiliate itself with poverty, and wealth must always be visible to function as such.[10] However, there is a certain incommensurability between the spirit's ethereal needs and the medium's worldly means. It is a distance whose transposition often gives the impression of an insatiable desire on the part of spirits, one that would seem to border on gluttony were it not for mediums' insistence that such sin is incompatible with the very being of possessing spirits. Still, spirits make constant demands for new statues or more candles or new pillows while in the bodies of mediums. The instructions, which are recorded by *luuk sit*, have the force of a command and are always obeyed, even at the risk of incurring great personal debt.

Very few, if any, mediums have any personal experience of royal abodes, of course, and the mediating paradigm for this miniaturized palace (in addition to other mediums' shrines) is probably the interior of the Buddhist temple, its mural paintings of heavenly palaces, and the office or seat of its abbot. The throne, the clutter of votive candles and floral offerings, as well as the forest of statues are all to be found in Theravada temples. And in any case, local markets abound with photographs and picture postcards of Thai monarchs on their thrones. Only the particular palladium of the Chakkri monarchs seems exempt from imitation in mediums' shrines, perhaps because it would approach too closely the category of lèse-majesté (the prerogatives of the reigning monarch being heavily guarded).[11] It is worth noting in this context that the reproduc-

---

10. Ibid. In pointing out the identification with middle-class aesthetics that characterize urban mediums, Walter Irvine claims that most mediums come from rural peasant backgrounds and that their performance of middle-class status is part of a claim to urbanity. My own research did not corroborate the claim to rural origins, though it is clear that many mediums narrate a movement toward the city, and toward Chiang Mai in particular, in their accounts of their spirits. Some do inhabit the periphery of the city, to be sure, but most seem to have deep roots in the urban world, even when that world is thought to be one in which the authentic values of northern rurality have been lost. See Walter Irvine, "The Thai-Yuan 'Madman,' and the Modernizing, Developing Thai Nation as Bounded Entities under Threat: A Study in the Replication of a Single Image" (Ph.D. diss., University of London, 1982), 245.

11. In Thailand, monarchy is entitled to control its own representation, and the battle to do so has been actively pursued by various kings and by those acting on their behalf. It is doubtful, however, that mediums would ever constitute a political threat to the monarch, and they are therefore

tion of the divine palace is not exclusive to mediums' shrines. Many male ritual specialists, especially ex-monks (often bearing the honorific title *luang phor*), own similar shrines from which they carry out the roles of spiritual advisor and purveyor of spells (but without recourse to performative inspiration).[12] In fact, it would be virtually impossible to distinguish between these shrines if it were not for the tell-tale photographs that mediums keep of themselves and the glass cabinets in which they, unlike the monks, stock their princely costumes.

Most shrines, whether modest like that of Caopuu Phayaphrom or grandiose like that of the spirit of King Ramkhamhaeng, are in many ways enlarged versions of the tiny spirit houses or *hor phii* that one sees at the corner of residential and commercial plots throughout Thailand. These minute edifices are erected to house the *caothii* or "lord of the place," a kind of spirit that otherwise would be dislocated and thus rendered dangerous when land is taken up by humans. I know of few people who admit to believing that such spirits exist, and the structures are mainly installed for the sake of appearances, but at the same time, one rarely sees a *hor phii* that does not have offerings of food and water refreshed on a regular basis. In this, as in so many areas, the spirits receive gestures of the hedged bet.[13]

Like many spirit houses, mediums' shrines are modeled after Cambodia's Ankor Wat, but some imitate less formidably majestic abodes, and in Chiang Mai, many even have the forked *kalae* (a crossed beam said to represent buffalo horns) that tops the roofs of old and falsely antique northern Thai buildings.

---

unlikely targets for repression. Indeed, the very acknowledgment of mediums that such a disciplinary gesture would entail is probably beneath the king and the Buddhist sect, the Thammayut, with which he is associated. By contrast, charges of improper use of the king's image are regularly used to legitimate politically motivated charges of criminality. Recently, for example, charges were brought against a group of Meo refugees, an estimated twenty thousand of whom live at Wat Tham Krabok, for improperly installing a statue of the king. The Meo were under scrutiny because of accusations that they had been engaged in active opposition to the Laotian government, with whom Thailand was then attempting to restore bilateral relations. The wat itself was established as a drug rehabilitation center in 1957, and some Meo residents there are known to have received U.S. support for their anticommunist activities. They are also publicly accused of narcotics trafficking and prostitution. It would seem, then, that the state has already given itself ample reason to evict the Meo. However, the question of improper representation of the king is one that gives the charges of criminality a moral and indeed religious authority, displacing the issue of a possible collusion between the state and the Meo in the past. See *The Nation*, 6 August 1998, Internet ed.

12. On the status of ex-monks, see Thomas A. Kirsch, "The Thai Buddhist Quest for Merit," in *Southeast Asia: The Politics of National Integration*, ed. John McAlister (New York: Random House, 1973), 188–201.

13. On the question of belief regarding spirits in modern northern Thailand, see Jack Bilmes, "On the Believability of Mediums," *Journal of the Siam Society* 83, nos. 1–2 (1995): 231–38.

The northern architecture is ironic in this case, or at least anachronistic, insofar as the housing of the *caothii* is a practice whose origins are distinctly Siamese. However, this does not stop many northerners from assuming that the architecture, like many spirit beliefs, is local and indeed, a mark of northern Thailand's difference from Siam. Whether originally northern or not (and what can that mean in the twentieth century, when northern Thailand is also nationally Thai?), mediums' shrines are carefully structured to enact something like a fractal geometry of the heavens, to permit the transformation of the medium's own body into the axis and casement for spiritual presencing. They attempt to actualize that "deep structure" of radial centricity which Tambiah identifies in the "galactic polity."[14]

It is, of course, the mandala that provides Tambiah with the concept on which he bases his interpretation of premodern Siamese political organization. And like others before him, Tambiah understands the mandala as a transcendental form of almost Platonic stature which is realized in such diverse political realities as acephalous segmentary systems and mature city-states.[15] The term itself designates an Indo-Tibetan concept that expresses the unity of a core and its container,[16] but it is also an exercise in cartographic miniaturization. In effect, it maps a world conceived in terms of four cardinal directions and a single vertical axis. The premodern Siamese tradition imagined this world as one of three planes, which were thought to be arranged vertically in a moral universe that encompassed all being. The middle world, in which humans were thought to reside, contained four continents that lay around the base of Mount Sumeru (sometimes referred to simply as Meru), a peak that not only jutted out of the earth but that actually ascended into the heavens.[17]

Like that same universe, the shrine is organized around directional axes that are marked by house posts, with east and north being the most auspicious.

14. Stanley J. Tambiah, *World Conqueror, World Renouncer: A Study of Buddhism and Polity in Thailand against a Historical Background* (Cambridge: Cambridge University Press, 1976), esp. 102–31.

15. Ibid., 104. For the precedents of this argument, see R. Heine-Geldern, "Conceptions of State and Kingship in Southeast Asia," *Far Eastern Quarterly* 2 (1942): 15–30; S. Moertono, *State and Statecraft in Old Java: A Study of the Later Mataram Period, 16th to 19th Century* (Ithaca, NY: Cornell University Press, 1968); Paul Wheatley, *The Pivot of the Four Quarters* (Chicago: Aldine, 1971), and, more recently, *Nāgara and Commentary: Origins of the Southeast Asian Urban Traditions* (Chicago: University of Chicago Press, 1983).

16. Tambiah, *World Conqueror, World Renouncer*, 102.

17. See Thongchai Winichakul, *Siam Mapped: A History of the Geo-Body of a Nation* (Honolulu: University of Hawaii Press, 1994), for an analysis of this logic and its narrativization of the moral universe in relation to the forms of cartography that would later displace it.

Indeed, the shrine shares the same structure as the house in this fantastically fractal universe, although northern Thai houses had some rather distinct features. Traditionally, space was divided according to use, with distinct sleeping areas for married couples and their children, and other spaces designated for unmarried men, for childbirth and the postpartum staying-in of women, for cooking and for storing grain. The *hyyn*, or sleeping area (which included both the *toen* for unmarried men and the larger sleeping space of the married couple) was itself bisected on north-south and east-west axes, although the terms for north and south also mean downstream and upstream and the directions are somewhat relative. Two posts, one identified as the Woman's Post (*sao naang*), the other as the Auspicious Post (*sao mongkon*), marked the western and eastern center-points of the *hyyn*, respectively. The significance of the *sao naang* is somewhat unclear in the ethnohistorical record, except that it seems to have delimited the sleeping quarters for members of the matriline. On the other hand, the significance of the *sao mongkon* seems to have received more explicitation. As Davis describes it, "The Auspicious Post is the ritual center of the dwelling."[18] According to Sanguan Chotisukharat, "It contains the *khwan* or psychic energy of the house."[19] By contrast, the spirits of the matriline are said to reside on a shelf that protrudes from the southeast wall of the women's sleeping quarters.[20] Prior to the implementation of Siamese law (and long afterward), it was this shelf that constituted the eye of the matriline, the point from which sexual relations were policed and generational obligation commanded through fines that were demanded from men who violated its women within sight of the shelf.[21]

Davis remarks that the household is "the very lowest level of the *müang*

18. Richard Davis, *Müang Metaphysics: A Study of Northern Thai Myth and Ritual* (Bangkok: Pandora, 1984), 49.

19. Sanguan Chotisukharat, *Phrapheenii thai phaak nüa* [Thai traditions of the northern region], 2d ed. (Phranakhon: Odeon, 1969); Santi Chantasawon, "The Spirit Cults and Superstition in Thai Habitation: A Case Study in the Northern Region" (Ph.D. diss., University of Michigan, 1987), 93–94. The *khwan*, it will be remembered, are manifold essences, which together constitute an entity but, at the same time, are vulnerable to dislodgment and imbalance. Rites in which the *khwan* (of houses, buffalo, and people) are tied together or simply strengthened in their harmonious interrelation are commonly performed by elders on the occasion of calendrical celebrations and at times of risk or injury.

20. Kraisi Nimmanhaeminda, "*Ham Yon*, the Magic Testicles," in *Essays Offered to G. H. Luce*, ed. Ba Shin et al. (Ascona: Artibus Asiae, 1966), 134.

21. Needless to say, the spirits possess a vision that penetrates the material world, and so the oversight exercised by the matrilineal spirits was not limited to those that occurred in the room. One nonetheless imagines that some liaisons could be had in secret.

hierarchy."[22] Its beams run in the same direction as do the streets of the city, and a misaligned house is considered to "cross the city." The same is true of the spirit house, but where the household is the lowest level of the *müang*, the spirit house of mediums is a doubled image of order. It may be useful to recall here Bourdieu's assertion that the house is the line of inversion, the point where inside and outside are forever turning around each other.[23] The spirit house partakes of both the lowest and the most exalted levels of the *müang*. In a cosmological architectonics that renders the house a miniaturization of the palace and the universe, the Auspicious Post would be the domestic counterpart to Mount Sumeru. It would be the axis of verticality and unity, not the "still point" but the point of endless origination. Not surprisingly then, it is at the Auspicious Post that the possessed medium usually sits, his throne acting as a kind of gate through which the spirit of the past enters. It is there that the medium becomes the shaft of transcendence. And it is to this point that the dancing medium proceeds in anticipation of a placement in which he will become the point of that inversion that Bourdieu identifies, the inside—and indeed the womb—through which the outside can enter. A door. A portal. The threshold but also the eyes for a house that is also a body (eyes are often termed "doors," *pratuu*, to sensation). And this body is a casement for another, a place of origin after the fact.

### The Sex of the Gate and the Spacing Between

The appearance of order seems to be gorgeously repeated in a line of miniaturization that concentrates the very universe in the body of a mortal being and makes of human eyes the doorway to both heaven and hell. And yet. A pause demands to be inserted here. For surely this dream of geometrical perfection begs the question. Does not every order constitute itself against some other, against the possibility of a disorder whose eruption it seeks, constantly, to contain? Let us then inquire a little more skeptically into the divine concentricity of ethnography's mediumship and the anxious alterity that it seeks, so compulsively, to expel.

Every house, as Mark Wigley says, is haunted by that which it seeks to hold outside.[24] But there are two senses in which one can speak of an outside. The first is merely the opposite of the inside. This outside has substance and exists in

---

22. Davis, *Müang Metaphysics*, 47.

23. Pierre Bourdieu, *Outline of a Theory of Practice* (1972), trans. Richard Nice (Cambridge: Cambridge University Press, 1977), 119.

24. Mark Wigley, *The Architecture of Deconstruction: Derrida's Haunt* (Cambridge, MA: MIT Press, 1993), 68.

perfect dialectic with the inside. Hence the possibility of speaking of an exterior spatial *domain* (the outside relies on the inside). The other exteriority, however, is the condition of possibility of that opposition: the principle of spacing within which the difference between these signifiers can, in fact, signify.[25] Derrida describes this principle as one of *différance*, although he refuses it any totalizing explanatory power, admitting that the fact of spacing does not, in any way, determine the form that those spaces will take in a particular language at a particular time.[26] I would like to consider both the logic of that spacing and the particular efforts to contain and stabilize it in northern Thailand. What I want to suggest is that the practices of spirit mediums can be seen to *literalize* this logic, to translate it into a theater of both architectural and bodily occurrence. This literalization of both the principle of spacing and the haunting that is its corollary seems worth pursuing here because it helps to explain how possession by spirits can appear simultaneously to be a performance of both order *and* its dissipation, of masculinity *and* its effeminization, of national unity *and* the fear of displacement. It also goes some way to explain how these otherwise diverse discourses have come to be entwined with each other in the fantastically globalized history of a nation.

As in so much of mediumship, spacing, the principle of difference in language, is contained by being rendered literally: by being figured as a door and as a substitutional passage through bodies. In fact, the literalism—the excessive gesture of saying what is supposed to be obvious—is part of the reason for mediumship's denigration by orthodox Buddhists. But the accusation does not stop there, and the putative imbrication of representational excess with sexual polymorphousness is a recurrent trope in the accusations that more conservative Buddhists make against mediums. Cults are often said by anthropologists to be disciplinary formations, policing the sexuality of women.[27] But northern Thai people are more likely to comment on what they believe to be the promiscuity of female mediums and the effeminacy of male mediums than on any ideal order of gender binarity. Mediums share this metaphorics, speaking of their practices in a language of palpitant sexuality. The medium who ascends the throne becomes the shaft and is shafted in the process. Similarly, the spirit mounts his throne as he mounts his medium. Nor can the English language make more delicate what is, in Northern Thai, an emphatically sexualized metaphorics. Mediums are called *maa khii*, "the rider's horse," in Northern Thai. The formal Central Thai word for medium, *khon song* or *raang song*

25. Jacques Derrida, *Positions*, trans. Alan Bass (Chicago: University of Chicago Press, 1981), 81.

26. Ibid.

27. Ann Hale, "A Re-Assessment of Northern Thai Matrilineages," *Mankind* 12 (1979): 138–50.

(meaning "vehicle," the closest literal translation to medium that I can think of), can be read, very literally, to mean the body of sending, and it cleanses to a certain extent the implication of sexual penetration. Nonetheless, mediums, especially those of low status, speak of possession as a riding, as a being ridden, and they do not conceal what is clear to all: that the medium is made productive, is made a site of origination, and is made eligible to sit at the place of origins only when he or she is entered (penetrated, ravished, fucked) by an ascetically disciplined (which is to say emasculated) masculine power whose directed productivity overcomes and transforms the volatile fecundity of the medium's body.

Some female mediums actually identify with that masculinity outside of possession, meditating and observing the five Buddhist precepts in an effort to mitigate or even to negate their menstruation and to seal up the orifices of a body they perceive to be dangerously porous.[28] However, as will become apparent, that identification is less with ideal masculinity, which in northern Thailand always signifies fertility, than with the asceticism or emasculation of the monk.[29] In this respect, mediumship seems to inherit a tradition deeply inscribed in local myth and legend. Donald Swearer, for example, has observed a similar pattern in the *Cāmadevīvamsa*, the legend of Queen Chamadevi that was composed by the northern Thai monk Bodhiramsi in the early fifteenth century. Noting the degree to which a surface structure of binary oppositions between hot and cold, city and wilderness, male and female gives way to the more complex logic of fecundity made productive through discipline, Swearer has suggested that the Buddhism of northern Thailand's golden age attributed enormous and similar potency to the bodies of both women and Buddhas. And, he argues, at least in the northern legends from which Bodhiramsi drew his narrative, this potency had to be "channeled by the charisma of ascetics and kings."[30] It is the "overlapping polarity of asceticism and fertility" that seems to resurface in contemporary mediumship, even as the ambiguity of that overlap is bracketed by the emergent bourgeois discourses of more radically binary gender.[31]

---

28. Irvine, "The Thai-Yuan 'Madman,' " 250.

29. Charles F. Keyes has provided a thoughtful account of the requirement for men to pass through a period of ambiguous gender in becoming monks. See "Ambiguous Gender: Male Initiation in a Northern Thai Buddhist Society," in *Gender and Religion: On the Complexity of Symbols*, ed. Caroline Walker Bynum, Steven Harrell, and Paula Richman (Boston: Beacon, 1986), 66–96.

30. Donald K. Swearer and Sommai Premchit, *The Legend of Queen Cāma: Bodhiramsi's Cāmadevīvamsa, a Translation and Commentary* (Albany: State University of New York Press, 1998), 7.

31. Swearer goes so far as to claim that "Buddhism as currently practiced in the Chiang Mai valley closely resembles Bodhiramsi's description of fifteenth-century northern Thai Buddhism. The fluid ambivalences that characterize the narrative world of the [*Cāmadevīvamsa*] naturally charac-

In part, the complex identification with disavowal (the medium's aspiration to emasculation) is made possible by the fact that the porosity of the feminine is passed through another metaphorics and described in the idiom of the door and the gate. The *khan* dish effects the opening of that gate just as it opened the house of the matriline in previous times. Historically, when a man went to a woman's home to ask for permission to marry her, he offered betel and areca as well as money on a dish (*khan*) to the spirits of her matriline. He fed her spirits to avoid being eaten by them. The offering itself was termed *khan*,[32] and it opened both the house (specifically, the *hyyn* sleeping quarters) and the woman's body. So it is with the medium's *khan*, which signals her availability for the spirit, who will bear himself in her again and again.

In many ways, it is possible to see this practical discourse as an empowered appropriation of Buddhist ideology, in which the very liabilities of a culturally construed femaleness are valorized and elaborated to glorious excess. Yet, the fetishism of the womb is here carried out with an ironic twist in that the medium is emptied even of fecundity. She becomes the mere receptacle of the spirit and its power (*ittharit*), not its progenitor nor even its master (as are monks). In this, one can speculate that she is rendered *kathoey*, neither female nor male, but the dominant discourse's figure of emasculation. Indeed, to the extent that she is made the site of a passing, she is even more like the door than herself, as vagina.

Structuralist fantasies of left- and right-handedness notwithstanding, somatic architecture is a messy business in northern Thailand. In the moment that the language of the house maps itself onto the body, the crystalline geometry of divine order gives way to one of consumption and excretion, eating and vomiting, desire and consummation. It is, in fact, equally possible to read the medium's spirit house as the instantiation of sexual polymorphousness as of cosmic order. Everything hinges on the door, as it were. Kraisi Nimmanhaeminda, perhaps the most famous and widely read of northern Thailand's auto-ethnographers, has noted that the doorway of the premodern *müang* house had above it a lintel called the *phor pratuu* (father of the door) or *ham yon*. This usually consisted of a carved slat of wood with the image of a serpent or, more

---

terize the relationship between Buddhism and non-Buddhist systems of belief and practice" (ibid., 13). I do not wish to go so far as to endorse a narrative of continuity; as has been argued elsewhere in this book, the historical dislocations that afflicted northern Thailand seem to prohibit such narratives of linear descent. Nonetheless, I do share Swearer's sense that certain tropes and practical discourses have recurred, among them a certain ambiguity in the organization of gendered difference and a deeply hybridized reading of the *tipitaka*.

32. Prasert N. Nagara, project advisor, *Basic Research on the Ancient Lanna Law*, trans. Pitinai Chaisangkusukkul and Aroonrut Wichienkaeo (Bangkok: Thammasat University Press, 1989), 17.

properly, a *naga*. The term *ham yon* actually means "magical testicles," a term with productive but not necessarily phallic connotation.[33] The threshold at the base of the door was called the *mae pratuu*, meaning mother of the door but also, in colloquial terms, vagina. The term *mae pratuu* is still widely in use, and because masculinist readings of women's bodies associate them with volatility, men are frequently instructed not to sit there. Being a raised ledge between rooms on which people occasionally stub their toes, the *mae pratuu* is the subject of much ribald humor.[34]

Uterine imagery, which is the extension of the vaginal metaphor, is explicit in much Thai architectural discourse, its significations including not only fecundity but also capaciousness and receptivity. Virtually any space that contains anything else is termed uterine. Even the *cheddi* of the Buddhist *stupa*, a structure built to house Buddha relics, is termed *dhatu gabbha*, meaning "relic womb."[35] Relics, whose ostensible purpose is to carry memory, also appear to have properties of fecundity and are considered to be the receptacles of merit and virtue. Tambiah refers to them in the relatively phallocentric language of fertilization, but it seems more in keeping with his own architectonic symbolism (and his later work on amulet fetishism) to read them as wombs within wombs.[36] And houses themselves are described thus. This is not to say that there is an inward progression toward ultimate fecundity, although the most guarded interior space in pre-Siamese Lannathai was that of the matrilineal spirits and hence of a certain kind of generativity. Rather, each interior is to be read as *relatively* uterine and thus *relatively* subject to penetration.

The penetrability of female space is often expressed, as the ethnography of Buddhist gender ideology constantly remarks, as softness or pliability. Thus, women are deemed within dominant ideology to be soft-souled or maleable (*caaj orn*) as well as volatile. This latter quality is associated with the fact of menstruation, because blood is deemed heating and women are said to have too much of it.[37] Nor is this a quaint residue. Contemporary women are still

---

33. Kraisi, "*Ham Yon.*"

34. The same metaphorics has been used for pedagogic purposes because it hides what it intends to convey while leaving no doubt about its meaning. For example, a popular promotional advertisement for condoms and AIDS awareness in 1991 featured a personified condom pulling back the explicitly labial drapes of a mysterious entrance. The caption claimed that only condoms would be permitted to "open the door" (*peut pratuu*), or have sex.

35. Adrian Snodgrass, *The Symbolism of the Stupa* (Ithaca, NY: Southeast Asia Program, Cornell University, 1985), 200.

36. Tambiah, *World Conqueror, World Renouncer*, 97.

37. Still powerful, this ideology of blood and heat leads many women to take medications called *yaa*

encouraged to expel physical excess through the use of herbal or pharmaceutical agents called *yaa khap pracam dyan* ("medicine to drive the period"), which supposedly speed the passage of menstrual blood but which are generally more effective as nervous stimulants. Cosmological Buddhist texts generally inscribe women as being innately rooted in physical experience, by nature more subject and more attached to sensuousness than men. For this reason, they are said to be particularly unsuited to the ascetic traditions of Buddhist meditation and particularly likely vehicles for spirits.[38]

A seeming paradox emerges here, but one that is amply familiar to feminist ethnographers and philosophers. Fecundity is represented not merely as generativity or productivity. Rather, in its propensity to excess, it is treated as an abyssal negativity. The inside of the womb is here represented less as the inside of an outside than as a space of alterity, of an undefinable, always excessive otherness that will not stand still in a dialectical relationship with the Same. In other words, it contains the power of death, and it threatens to annihilate whatever comes into contact with it. Or so Buddhist cosmology would have it. Not incidentally, the *P. dhatu gabbha*'s capacity for memorialization is also linked within the same system to this morbid womb. In both cases, the uterine position is associated with the traces of a death that is both manifold and indeterminate. One might say that the very fertility of the womb makes it available for a haunting, for a visitation by the dead, or rather, by a death that will not adhere to the binary oppositions in which the living and the dead can be divided from each other. It is, in short, haunted by the specter of the undead. Indeed, it is precisely the strangely undead quality of the spirits that makes them potentially malevolent. The fact that they cross the line dividing the realms between living and dead makes them threatening to a body in which the inside is supposed to be radically discrete.

In this context, I am struck by a memory of northern Thai folktales in which

---

*khap pracam dyan* ("medicine to drive the period"; the word "drive" is the same as that used for cars). Although these were probably herbal concoctions in their original formulation, *yaa khap pracam dyan* are now produced en masse by the local pharmaceuticals industries and are potent alcohol-based stimulants.

38. There is some difference of opinion on this. Kirsch, for example, argues that women are restrained by Buddhism on the basis of their putative worldliness and, hence, a relative propensity to sin. Keyes, in contrast, claims that women's perceived capacity to care for the suffering makes them eligible for merit making and actually facilitates their movement toward *nibbana*. See A. Thomas Kirsch, "Buddhism, Sex Roles and the Thai Economy," in *Women of Southeast Asia*, ed. Penny van Esterik (Dekalb: Northern Illinois University, Center for Southeast Asian Studies, 1996), 16–41; Charles F. Keyes, "Mother or Mistress, but Never a Monk: Buddhist Notions of Female Gender in Rural Thailand," *American Ethnologist* 11, no. 2 (1984): 223–41.

the *mae pratuu* prevents the passage of spirits into the house. She can do this because spirits are said to have jointless legs and backward feet. Hence, they cannot climb over the *mae pratuu*. But in these tales, the feminine is a threshold and an obstacle distinct from the passage itself. And, contrary to feminist narratological theory that identifies the two (the obstacle and the passage),[39] northern Thai folk stories implicitly recognize that the door *frame* is not the *space* through which one passes to enter the house. It surrounds that space and, strangely enough, marks it off and even holds it *in* place. These tales give us to understand that the frame thematizes that space, is the literalization of a spacing that, in fact, "designates *nothing*" but merely opens between and thereby constitutes the opposites of interior and exterior.[40] In this, the northern Thai folktale seems to align itself with Saussurean semiotics and its assumption that the spacing between linguistic signifiers, like the signifiers themselves, has no content. However, the fact that this space is simply a distance or, as Derrida would say, a movement, does not prevent the space(ing) from being represented in concrete terms nor, in fact, from being imagined as a locus into which alterity, the manifold, can enter. Indeed, this very *localization* constitutes the production of order, the stabilization of language in its broadest terms. The house (domestic or ritual, somatic or architectonic) is then opposed to radical difference, and is the mark of an effort to banish that difference. As every Thai cosmology says, beyond the domos (*baan*), outside of the *müang*, is the wilderness (*paa*). And that is a place full of evil. By all accounts, the wilderness is either a productivity without form—the malignant excess that threatens all life—or the multiplicity and unstable appearance of spirits.

Now, the paradox of this sexualized semiotics lies in this: that the woman whose womb is thought to be inherently impregnated with death must be domesticated in mediumship, through the Praise Ceremony in particular, by being situated in the place of this frame. This means, strangely enough, that she must occupy the structural position that in northern Thailand is named *ka-thoey*. Let me try to clarify what I mean by this statement, which seems to fly so indecently in the face of most other writings on Thai gender in which the neat oppositions of masculine and feminine, hard and soft, cold and hot, closed and open, predominate. Fortunately, a few others have already begun to part from

39. Teresa de Lauretis identifies this conflation with the concept of the "woman/boundary/space," and although this term has enormous utility for an analysis of Hollywood cinema, the virgules already suggest what the northern folktale knows to be a more complex heterogeneity. See "Desire in Narrative," in *Alice Doesn't: Feminism, Semiotics, Cinema* (Bloomington: Indiana University Press, 1984), 121.

40. Derrida, *Positions*, 81.

the naïveté of this residually structuralist reading and have drawn attention to the ways in which it reinscribes the ideologically dominant and distinctly patriarchal readings of sexual difference. Thus, for example, both Peter Jackson and Charles Keyes have noted the place of ambiguity in northern Thai gender formations, each observing the degree to which dominant modes of masculinity are produced through the encounter with emasculation, either in sexual relations with *kathoeys* or in the very desexualizing process of becoming a monk.[41] More directly relevant here, Shigeharu Tanabe has written about the *phii meng* cults devoted to ancestral spirits and argued that the rites associated with them imagine that "women's sexuality and reproduction are . . . akin to untamed power, which are first put on stage to be destroyed."[42]

In Tanabe's careful reading, the negation of the feminine permits matrilineal and matrifocal spirit cults and the women who belong to them to aspire to a moral authority that is "comparable to men's in religious, political and economic fields."[43] He describes as contradictory and incoherent the discourses that permit women to negate the very biological principles on which matriliny rests in their effort to acquire moral power. In this, and in his insistence that the rituals arrive "at a terrain where neither femininity nor masculinity but only transcendental authority dominates,"[44] Tanabe makes an extremely important move, one that informs my own effort to comprehend the sexual economies of mediumship. However, his focus on the resistant capacities of gender ambiguity in mediumship forecloses a consideration of the ways in which the seeming aspiration to neutrality on the part of mediums is cast, in dominant discourse, as a sexual impropriety, and one whose excessiveness is metonymically represented through the figure of the *kathoey*. In that representation, which is so ironically opposed to ambiguity, we find the assumption of a causal relationship between the performative excess of *kathoeys* and the birth of the supplement in writing. Mediums are not outside of this discourse, even when they embrace the abject status of being *kathoey* in marvelously parodic forms. For this reason, it seems necessary to inquire further about what the relationship between sexual polymorphousness (and not merely neutral transcendence) and mediumship might entail. To do so, I turn to a Lanna creation story that, though formalized as *tamnan*, circulates throughout the north in oral stories about the origin of the world.

41. Peter A. Jackson, *Dear Uncle Go: Male Homosexuality in Thailand* (Bangkok: Bua Luang, 1995); Keyes, "Ambiguous Gender," 66–96.
42. Tanabe, "Spirits, Power and the Discourse of Female Gender," 205.
43. Ibid., 204.
44. Ibid., 204.

*Excess, Writing, and the Figure of the Kathoey*

I begin here not with an homage to the Enlightened One, as does the *Pathamamūlamūlī*, but with the story of Naang Itthang Gaiya Sangkasi. According to the *Pathamamūlamūlī*,[45] a Buddhicized but deeply syncretic tale of origins that narrates not only the emergence and order of the world but the subsumption of animism by Buddhism, the first being to occupy the universe was a female named Nang Itthang Gaiya Sangkasi. In the version of the myth that survives in the redacted palm leaf manuscript of 1961, this being is imagined to be as ethereal as the *thewada*, and she feeds only upon the scent of flowers. However, the fragrant plants that grow in this same universe, and that she requires to sustain herself, proliferate at such an extraordinary rate that they actually threaten to suffocate her. To save herself, this first "female" being determines to create other beings who can feed upon and thereby control the otherwise nurturing flowers. And so she does. Through her creative gesture, a reproductivity that has become malignant is tamed by another but antithetical kind of (re)productivity. The animals do not, however, provide salvation. To the contrary. The creatures that the Naang fabricates from clay and sweat continue to be reborn after their death into the same realm. As a result, their rapidly multiplying numbers soon consume so much of the flora that Nang Itthang Gaiya Sangkasi is threatened by starvation. She is overwhelmed by the consequences of her efforts at self-preservation and perplexed about how she can prevent those who had already died from being reborn into her world. Unable to solve the problem for herself, she puts it to a male being, a certain Pu Sangaiya Sangkasi, who seems to appear miraculously in the text for the purpose of responding and who extracts from her a promise of marriage (read sex) in return for his solution to her riddle. He suggests that what is needed is a being who will not return following death, one whose actions in life can facilitate movement to higher or lower planes. Such a being will be human, one in whom ethical capabilities and an ability to make merit will ensure movement out of, and beyond, the world that Naang Itthang Gaiya Sangkasi must continue to inhabit. Human life is thereby brought into being.

Ethics and death go hand in hand in this story, and death saves reproduction from becoming mere malignancy. Or rather, choice in the face of infinite ethical possibilities (which is what human beings are constantly faced with) permits

45. This myth has been made available by virtue of the extraordinary translational efforts of Anatole-Roger Peltier, who worked from a palm leaf Thai-Yuan manuscript made in 1961 by Phra Adikan Som Samano and now kept at Wat Phuak Hong. Peltier's publication includes the original Thai-Yuan, a Central Thai transliteration, and English and French translations. See *Pathamamūlamūlī: Tamnan khao phii Lanna* [The Origin of the World in the Lan Na Tradition] (Chiang Mai: Suriwong Books, 1991).

death to be a principle of division and order rather than one of overwhelming and chaos-inducing presence. Merit-making and demerit-producing acts stave off the haunting that had so threatened Naang Itthang Gaiya Sangkasi, and this is true despite the fact that humans initially lack consciousness of their own agency and its effects, remaining ignorant until the Buddha comes to enlighten their world. One of the more interesting features of the human race that comes to save the world by making death meaningful is its tripartite nature. In the myth, humanity is composed of three sexes: male, female, and *kathoey* or, as Peltier translates the term, "hermaphrodite."

In their trinity, humans are linked in the text to the grammar of Pali (though not of Northern Thai), and toward the end of chapter 3, the last in the *tamnan*, the Buddha speaks at length about the origin of language, explaining that the "consonants are combined with vowels to form words of three genders: the feminine, the masculine and the neuter. The genders," he continues, "are also determined by the final vowels."[46] In the same way that linguistic gender is a function of combinatory principles, so the gender of humans seems to permit diverse relationships. From the woman's point of view, the hermaphrodite, named Napumsaka, is a husband. From the man's perspective, Napumsaka is a wife. Coupling with each other in various ways, the "three parents" give birth to several children. Like all humans, they must eventually die. And as in so many other origin myths, the first death comes in the *Pathamamūlamūlī* as a result of violence. It is the hermaphrodite, Napumsaka, who brings this first death, murdering Pullinga, the man, after realizing that he and the woman named Itthi share real and profound affection for each other. The loss that Napumsaka experiences after this deed is, however, unbearable, and shortly thereafter, the *kathoey* dies.

There is, nonetheless, a certain ambiguity about who suffers the first death. In two consecutive and contradictory (or perhaps inverse) passages, the *tamnan* narrates both the woman's loss of her two husbands and the man's loss of his two wives. In each case, the hermaphrodite dies second, but unlike the woman or the man (depending on the passage), his corpse is left untended, a fact that is remarked with great concern by the children. When they ask their surviving parent why he or she is not leaving flowers or making offerings to the departed hermaphrodite, the survivor denies having felt any affection for it.[47] Napumsaka's death, by contrast, has been linked to the hermaphrodite's own

---

46. Ibid., 236. The discourse on the gender of the language indicates that at least this part of the text is firmly within the Buddhist tradition. There would be no comparable reference in Northern Thai, despite the ubiquity of the *kathoey* as a social category. Any attempt to read the myth as being pre-Buddhist and, hence, authentically Yuan must be eschewed.

47. Peltier, *Pathamamūlamūlī*, 207–13.

"oversensitivity" to loss and other sensuous experience.[48] Thus, the hermaphrodite's hyperreceptivity to material stimulus is inverted and even repaid by a lack of material offerings. In this manner, the text suggests an economy in which sin is recompensed in the form of its expression. The inherent insatiability of the hermaphrodite's desire becomes the experience of lack, which is to say the experience of a desire redoubled in time.

Significantly, the *Pathamamūlamūlī* not only suggests that lack and excess are twinned, but it associates this pair through the death that they bear and signify with the birth of writing. Indeed, the *Pathamamūlamūlī* makes the hermaphrodite the displaced progenitor of inscription. It is this inscription that permits the writing and the legibility of sexual difference. The triad thus not only gives way to binary opposition (the hermaphrodite does not appear again in the story) but makes this binarity possible by occasioning the mark that will represent masculinity as the other of the feminine.

The birth of writing is worth considering in some detail. When the Buddha realizes that "the customary practice of listening [the Dhamma] was not yet established," he determines to "make the letters [of the Alphabet] (Ackhararūpa) appear before their eyes, so as to enlighten their knowledge."[49] In this, he aspires to a speech that uses only sounds that occur naturally at birth, but he recognizes the difference between these cries and the speech of adults and understands that a certain regimen must be imposed in order for the sounds to be recognized as the bearers of meaning when combined with other sounds. The laws of composition will be "difficult for ignoramuses to understand,"[50] and so the Buddha inscribes the rules of writing in the script that he invents for this very (and very circular) purpose. Whence comes this script? Initially, the Buddha is perplexed about the form of that writing in which the truth will become audible, and he asks, "What shall I choose as a mark?"[51] Looking around for a sign, the Buddha is inspired by a woman "staking out the site of the cemetery of her husband."[52] The stake itself becomes the sign of the masculine gender, the letter *i*. A deconstructionist's dream text, the *Pathamamūlamūlī* makes writing the condition of possibility for hearing the truth, even as it suggests that inscription is imitative of sound and supplementary to it.

It is important to bear in mind that it is the hermaphrodite, Napamsuka, who has caused this death even as it is the fact of the hermaphrodite, a sign of

48. Ibid., 207.
49. Ibid., 236.
50. Ibid., 236.
51. Peltier, *Pathamamūlamūlī*, 236.
52. Ibid., 236.

the human, that makes death a matter of salvation when Naang Itthang Gaiya Sangkasi is threatened by her own malignant productivity. But what does *kathoey* mean here? We have no idea what it meant at the time of the myth's first telling, but there is sufficient continuity between the time of the last redaction and the present to hazard some ethnographic speculation. Recent ethnography suggests that to be *kathoey* is not, in fact, simply to be a hermaphrodite; indeed, it rarely indicates any genital ambiguity. Rather, it is to inhabit an ideal form of femininity. Although there are frequent references in historical texts of the eighteenth and nineteenth centuries to masculinized women, some of whom were soldiers and warriors, others of whom seem merely to have inhabited the bodily rhetorics of the masculine, *kathoey* is not a term that is frequently applied to them. Today, *kathoey*s are invariably men who dress and live as women and who consider this to be their natural state. Some *kathoey*s must, by virtue of their employment, comport themselves in a manner that represents ideal masculinity during the working day (government regulations implicitly prohibit cross-dressing), but others live their entire lives in the mode of hyper-femininity. A few theatricalize this femininity as stage performers at sex clubs and burlesque entertainment venues. *Kathoey*s may have sexual relations with both overtly self-identified homosexual and heterosexual men, although they are increasingly represented in popular media accounts and in advice columns as "queens," gay men who engage sexually only with other gay men, termed "kings."[53] This historical trend is, it should be noted, less a reflection of the transformation of the category of *kathoey* than it is an index of the radicalization of heterosexual masculinity and the encompassment of that masculinity by the binary logics of sexual difference now circulating via the globalized discourses of sexuality.[54]

As a mode of performance, acting *kathoey* entails the hyperbolic citation of a feminine ideal. It is a citation generally undertaken only by individuals who are identified in their childhood as boys (hence its translation as a kind of "transexualism"). In this regard, *kathoey* designates a secondary performance and one in which the fact of that secondariness is often made clear through an extravagantly and therefore visibly gestural femininity. *Kathoey* is, in this sense, a

---

53. Peter Jackson's work on the column of Uncle Go Paknaam is especially revealing of this. See *Dear Uncle Go.*

54. I have elsewhere drawn attention to the ways in which the term *kathoey* has been used in sex radical circles of the West to signify a mode of pure possibility despite the fact that historically it has constituted a pillar of patriarchal masculinity. It is my belief that the affection displayed by Westerners for the idea of the *kathoey* has been a force in the growing disavowal of effeminate gayness in Thailand itself. See Rosalind C. Morris, "Educating Desire: Thailand, Transnationalism, Transgression," *Social Text* 52–53 (1998): 53–79.

mode of camp in northern Thailand. And camp, Thai or otherwise, is nothing if not a consciousness of citation, of a writing that invokes what has already been inscribed. One might therefore say that northern Thai camp, or at least being *kathoey* in northern Thailand, is a sexualized theatricalization of writing (hence, citation). Of writing as theatricality. And certainly of the unnatural. However, the citationality of the performance does not function everywhere to dislocate maleness and femaleness from their claims to the natural. To the contrary, the idea of *kathoey* provides conservatives with the idiom for criticizing all sorts of excess, including the excess of mediumship. But also the excess of political extremism.

When, for example, General Suchinda Khraprayoon's prime ministership was opposed by democracy protestors in 1992, posters and chants of opposition frequently accused him of being *kathoey* (see chapter 6 for a full account of the movement). The same epithet-hurling critics also insinuated that Suchinda's wife was a medium (the word *maa khii*, or mount, was often used), and at some point after the general's ignominious flight from office, photographs of the Khunying dancing for the spirits appeared in local newspapers. Emasculating accusations are, of course, commonplace in many political arenas, but there is something of particular significance in this doubled slander. Suchinda was accused both of being *kathoey* and of being married to a woman whose relationships to the spirits flirted with that same position, on the grounds that he had used murderously "excessive force" against an unarmed civilian population. Suchinda and the generals of Class 5 with whom he had staged a coup in 1991 had, in fact, justified their own actions with reference to the excessive or "unnatural" wealth of the regime they deposed. Both sides thus deployed the term of excess (*maak keun paj*) in relation to each other, and both mobilized the figure of the *kathoey* in the process of accusation.

If accusations of emasculation are the currency of political insult in the current, highly heterosexualized Thai world, they are the signs of contempt in discussions about mediumship. It is frequently remarked that the vast majority of spirit mediums are women, and that the vast majority of male mediums are *kathoey*s. Not surprisingly, one finds claims about the putative domination of spirit mediumship by *kathoey*s most often in the discourses of those who espouse the complex values of Buddhist modernity in Thailand, and it is emphatically associated with a condemning imputation of sexual excess. People who are vehemently opposed to mediumship have, on occasion, whispered to me their belief that Praise Ceremonies are the sites of orgiastic sexuality, where relations between women and women, men and men, men and *kathoey*s are pursued to abandon. All manner of indecency is imagined to take place there, and mediums are thought by many to use the practice as a veil behind which they can pursue sexual fantasies, especially same-sex sexual fantasies, that would not normally be permitted them. Although there is occasionally sexual play between mediums and between mediums and their clients, and although sexual violence is not unheard of at Praise Ceremonies, this is not generally the case, and mediums uniformly deny any sexual impropriety even when they admit that some of their possessing spirits, having been robust men in previous lives, do find it necessary to act on their desire. In general, though, whenever sexual relations are publicly admitted by mediums to be a part of their ritual lives, they are construed in the terms of normative masculine desire, and this as a function of male need. That anxious claim to normativity rarely satisfies critics, however. And this is because the figure of the *kathoey* works metonymically, to stand in for all of mediumship in an economy that identifies sexual difference—or polymorphousness—with representational excess. It is an economy to which mediums themselves are subject, despite the fact that the same economy is constantly threatened by the practices of possession.

The accusation of excess is made mainly from the perspective of Buddhist scripturalists, the individuals who adhere to primary texts (especially the *tipitaka*) and who believe those texts to contain the words *spoken* by the Buddha. Many, if not most, are monks. Ironically, though, the accusations against mediumship are essentially the same as those made against writing in relation to speech: as having a secondary and derivative, even gratuitous status. And it is for this reason that I believe a reading of the *Pathamamūlamūlī* can be so relevant to an analysis of mediumship in northern Thailand.

Recall here that the paradigmatic form of receiving the *dhamma* is, in Buddhist ideology, one of listening to a speaking. For this reason, sermons are broadcast throughout the city via linked amplifiers on occasions such as the annual "Ceremony to Extend the Fate of the City," the *phithii syyb chataa müang* (see chapter 7). At other events where there is a public sermon, individuals will often link themselves, via threads of cotton, to the monk who is delivering it or, if that is not possible, to the amplifier through which his voice is being broadcast. I have even seen people bind themselves in this manner to television sets on which services are being broadcast. The idea here is that an actual transmission of truth is occurring via the voice, which has a materiality not unlike that of electric current. The *dhamma*, it is said, needs no mediation.

Mediums, unlike monks who merely incant the truth that the texts have preserved through history, are thought to be excessive not only in their sexual practices but in the very fact of their mediation. This is because they claim to be expressing, in the manner of speech, the truth of the spirit's residence within, when, for nonbelievers, they are not expressing but merely representing (falsely) that spiritual presence. Form a nonbeliever's perspective, the form of

possession is separated from its referent in a manner analogous to the autono-
mization of gesture in the sword dance of the Praise Ceremony. And its excessiveness is like the excessiveness of poetry in the wake of prose. It is fictive. It is
ornamental. It is like the sexual identity of the *kathoey*, consciously mediated,
artificially constituted.

Returning once again to the origin myth, one is compelled to recognize that
the alterity of the *kathoey* does not reside in its polymorphousness (which is
treated as natural) as much as it comes from an excessive affect, a receptivity to
sensuous experience that emerges in the citation of the feminine. Polymorphousness becomes the sign of that excess only after the fact, in time and in
history. But death enters the receptive space that the performance cites, and in
the process, the *kathoey* is made subject to northern Thailand's Buddhist patriarchy. The whole text seems in this manner to be a kind frame-up. Indeed,
the *kathoey* becomes the displaced synonym of the frame, and holds the place,
as it were, for a space (a spacing) through which alterity, and thus death, passes.
Female mediums, on the other hand, can be seen to assume the place of the
*kathoey* in their disavowals of menstruation and in their assumption of (their
being assumed by) masculine personae. In the process of disavowing the threat
of unbridled productivity that their bodies are said to hold, their own sexual
identities become unstable. Sexual "identity" then becomes something that
needs to be performed or, to use the language of speech act theory, cited.
Usually, that performed and alienated identity is ideally male, but sometimes,
as in the case of Queen Camadevi's extraordinary possession, it is female (but
female in the mode of the woman warrior). In any case, the process of assuming
the place of the frame ensures that death, in its radical difference, is domesticated and transformed into the possibility of several, serially possessing spirits.
Sex radicals in the West who want to read the *kathoey* of myth—by which I
mean the category and not any individual so identified—as being like the
Sadean libertine, flirting with the limits of representational order in a way that
unites sexual alterity with linguistic transgression and death, are probably incorrect. The imagination of *kathoey* as a sex identity is already a containment.
Indeed, if what is at stake in the *Pathamamūlamūlī* is the spacing between male
and female, then the *figuration* of that space has already domesticated the more
chaotically indeterminate (one wants to say queer) possibilities that can be
produced in sexual practice.

### *The Magic from Afar*

The performance of sexual identity occurs not only within the theatricalized
realms of mediumship, of course. Indeed, if the demand for careful citation is

born of the instability with which Praise Ceremonies and more mundane possession performances flirt, the same demand makes itself felt by mediums in their everyday lives. This is especially true for women, and indeed, many female mediums appear to be veritable paragons of normative gender. In my experience, the most exalted of mediums are the most likely to be the most meticulous in their comportment *as* women, usually after a bourgeois fashion. In part, this can be understood in class terms. Higher-status mediums are generally higher-class people, and they partake of the gendered ideologies that dominate all of Thailand. The values of domesticity, of genteel self-presentation, of closure, and of quietude—all of which are evoked in the term *suai ngaam* (elegant)—are enormously powerful in the lives of all upper-class women and are marketed in the rural peripheries as points of longing identification. The traffic in cosmetics and especially cheap shampoos is perhaps the most obvious sign of this economy, but it is lived in the anxious attention to bodily form that so many middle-class girls display. And of course, it is present in the glowing praise that attaches to the successfully domesticated female medium in Chiang Mai.

One of the most renowned of Chiang Mai's mediums, that of Ramkhamhaeng, who is also in the lineage of Mokkhalaan, is revered as much for her everyday elegance and beautiful speech as for the power of the spirit that possesses her. I have often heard people remark on her extraordinary grace, and I have observed in the eyes of less accomplished mediums a look of admiration laced ever so slightly with envy. Once, I even heard her likened to King Rama V's, Chulalongkorn's, beloved Chiang Mai consort, Dararasmri. The likeness was telling, for Ramkhamhaeng's medium was emphatic about her northern identity, despite being married to a Sino-Thai man from the south of Thailand. She spoke a mellifluous kam müang, and unlike most mediums, her dancing was indeed northern in style, with open fingers and fluid but heavier steps. There are nearly uncanny parallels between the many stories northerners tell about Rama V's love affair with Dararasmri and the affair that brought Khun Singh to Chiang Mai where he met his wife. In both, there is a fusion of the place with the woman and the rendering of each in the language of gems to be admired but never quite possessed. In his own identifications, or rather, his longing to identify with Rama V, Khun Singh himself tells the tale of his love of the north, of the enormous attraction that its beauty had for him but also of the desire to master this space through discipline and Buddhist enlightenment. Khun Singh also speaks of the strange alienation that he continues to feel from a place where only his wife is truly at home.

Ramkhamhaeng's medium was first mentioned in the introduction to this book as the woman whose husband arranged for her possession in an effort to stave off his own emasculating penetration by spirits. The two of them live an exemplary life in the minds of many mediums and clients, and they are sought widely for advice by newly possessed individuals and by those whose illnesses have not found remedy in the hospitals and clinics of biomedicine. But their exemplarity is not simply a function of their very bourgeois lifestyle, which is extremely impressive to many. It is also a consequence of their rather elaborate negotiation of the dilemmas of national belonging and sexual identity in a context of competing local affiliations and of deep personal loss. In their efforts to preserve or perhaps to constitute a relationship of sexual difference, in their simultaneous valorizations of things northern and Siamese, and in their disavowal of ethnic and communist otherness, they have achieved a kind of dream narrative of national becoming. It is worth considering the relationships among these elements of their life stories in some detail for, in many ways, their personal experience refracts the complex and conflicted history that binds the *khon müang* of Lannathai into the Thai nation-state. It is a history that has often been lived as an uneven identification with ethnicized Thainess and an equally uneven opposition (which vacillates between desire and disavowal) to things un-Tai and un-Thai.

At various points in recent history, Chiang Mai, and northern Thailand in general, have occupied the place of alterity in a Thai national imaginary. Indeed, at the turn of the century, most Bangkokians referred to Chiang Mai as a part of Laos, and they associated it with grotesque incivility: the eating of insects, a lack of proper attire, and rude ritualism.[55] For the past four decades, however, otherness has been assigned to non-Tai-speaking people, many of them refugees from the wars of Indochina's communist movements or from Burma's particular version of ethnic cleansing. Some are descendants of migrants from Yunan, others inhabit the diaspora of nations that were rent by state-building exercises in the late nineteenth and early twentieth century. Meo (Hmong), Karen, Akha, and other such groups suffer the winter of exile, to borrow Wallace Steven's phrase, and are generally confined to village encampments in the hills that rise to the north of Chiang Mai. Today, most survive by virtue of tourism, either selling crafts and the few objects of their cultural patrimony that remain, or by serving as attractions for trekkers who visit the uplands in search of authenticity and rustic adventure.[56]

It is perhaps not surprising that ethnically minoritized subjects would ap-

---

55. See Nithi Aeusriwongse's sharp account of the changes in perceptions of the north and his indictment of the ahistoricism that retrojects a picturesque aesthetic onto Chiang Mai, in his review of "Sao Khrua Faa" [Madama Butterfly], *Silapa Watthanatham* 12, no. 1 (1991): 180–185.

56. David Kisly, "Commodity Native? The Politics of Hill-tribe Tourism in Northern Thailand" (M.A. thesis, York University, 1991).

pear in the discourses of spirit mediums as the quintessential figures of un-enlightened ritualism. Themselves marginalized by doctrinal Buddhism, many mediums project their own abject status onto others, as was the case with King Ramkhamhaeng's spirit. Not long after we met, he recounted a cautionary tale about Meo magic, using the occasion to explain the limits of his own curative power. He told of a Meo man who had come seeking help after having been cursed by a compatriot. By means of magic, a piece of buffalo hide had pur-portedly been inserted into the ensorcelled man's stomach. The hide had begun to rot and bloat, soon distending the victim's stomach and causing him great pain. King Ramkhamhaeng's spirit admitted that he could not help the man and that he had told him so directly. This despite the fact that the Meo man promised to make merit at the spirit's chosen wat and to observe eight of the Buddhist precepts.[57] His death, apparently inevitable, followed shortly thereafter.

When I asked Ramkhamhaeng's spirit why the Meo magic was so powerful that not even the great king of Sukhothai could save its victim, he produced a moralizing explanation in which the Meo would constitute the mark of magic unbridled by Buddhism. Indeed, he attributed to the victim a *kam*mic vul-nerability that was the product of his very ethnicity and, more particularly, of an identity that remains definitionally marginal to Thainess. This ethnicized *kam* was, for Ramkhamhaeng's spirit and for Khun Singh, powerful by virtue of its antiquity, and malignant because that same antiquity had not been inserted into a narrative of progression toward Buddhism. It was instead a stubbornly residual and unrecuperable primitiveness. As Ramkhamhaeng put it: "These wild people [literally, 'people of the forest' (*khon paa*)] have very powerful teachers, and their traditions are very old [*kaokae*]. They know how to put things inside of people and cause them to die from within. And besides, this man . . . was not good. He was involved in the heroin trade, so he was constantly exposed to evil. His heart was not pure and his *kam* was bad. If it is a matter of *kam*, there is nothing that can be done."

Every instance of Meo magic described to me involved the appearance of some foreign substance within the body of the victim, usually nails or buffalo hides. The former seems to have been associated with internal hemorrhaging and the latter with bloating and distortion. Perhaps these metaphors bespeak the agonies of what Western biomedicine metaphorizes as colitis or cancer. Perhaps they simply designate the myriad ailments that remain beyond bio-medicine's vocabulary. But whatever their referent, they are also made to speak

57. Eight precepts are generally considered a high level of commitment; most mediums observe only five.

of the problems of the state, of its feared penetration by otherness and the secret opening of its skin to foreign substances that could rot, push, or tear at the boundaries and then drain the body politic of its lifeblood.

Walter Irvine suggests that spirit mediumship has, in fact, been structured by a fear of boundary penetration since the 1960s, when it was overwhelmed by state-sponsored discourses in which the fear of communist insurgency was cast in the idiom of infectivity.[58] By Irvine's account, hegemonic political discourse and popular Buddhist conceptions of the relations between persons and spirits came to overlap in their assumption that the integrity and thus wellness of either can be protected only by "ensuring the balanced inter-relation of interior constituents, while the threatening agents are attacked."[59] The proposition is not without its merits, and the rhetorical parallels between official propaganda and the embodied discourses of spirit mediums are striking. So is the material evidence. In the proliferation of Praise Ceremonies and in the increasing use of state iconography, such as flags and images of Chakkri monarchs, mediums seem to have allied themselves at least momentarily with nationalist discourse. But perhaps more than the theatrical displays, it is the rhetorical doubling between nationalist discourse and mediumship's practice that grounds Irvine's notion of a "replicating image." Yet, because nationalist discourse posited alterity as localizable, as a foreignness out there (one that would be subject to the indexical gesture of military cartography), does not mean that the state did not also cultivate its own internal instability as well. Indeed, we will want to return to the problem of the foreign and the inscription of it as infectivity following further consideration of the anticommunist rhetoric within which the Meo medium signified doubly.

During the 1960s, the idea of "communal solidarity" (*saamakhii*) became the watchword of conservative politics, a banner beneath which anticommunist policies could demand everything from the censorship of the media to the arrest, detainment, and execution of suspected insurgents. Individual failures to maintain a visibly disciplined state of subjection to the state could be, and often were, construed as a weakening of the national body before communism, itself imagined in viral metaphors. Citizenship therefore came to require and to revalorize submission to one's teachers, parents, monks, and bureaucratic functionaries in a manner that was believed to solidify the necessary hierarchy within which the monarchy could continue to operate and, indeed, to be renewed. In pageantry and in populist right-wing movements such as the Village Scouts, elaborate displays of devotion were coupled with procedures that stripped

58. Irvine, "The Thai-Yuan 'Madman.'"
59. Ibid., 255.

individuals of their status before reinterpellating them as ideal citizens—often with uniforms and insignia marking a privileged affiliation to the triumvirate of "Nation, Religion, and King" which King Vajiravudh had made the pillar of Thai nationalism earlier in the century.[60] It is for this reason that the politics of that era have been termed a form of "despotic paternalism,"[61] and it is for the same reason that "excess" of any kind came to be reinscribed as a site of criminality.

Representational "excess" had assumed that status of the criminal in the nineteenth century, when, for the first time, charges of lèse-majesté were brought against the author of a poem, *Nirat Nongkhai*, on the basis that he had used a language in excess of its function within the parameters of the *nirat* genre.[62] Then, as a century later, in the 1960s, representational excess would be policed most rigorously in relation to the representation of the state. But in the sixties, it was not simply the use of improper language but performances premised on the literalization of metaphor (the illusions mistaken for spirits) that constituted such excess. Strangely enough, it was the very sharing of terms that incited the disavowal of mediumship by Buddhist and bureaucratic officials and that led to accusations of excess on the part of mediums. Mediums and all undisciplined meditators who risked a confrontation with external forces—be they spirits or merely the illusions that educated meditators claim are mistaken for spirits—began to assume the aura of the illegitimate despite their often vociferous professions and patently visible displays of loyalty to the state. But mediums were a religious rather than a political threat and, because the discourses of criminality were so imbricated with those of psychiatry at the time, possession came to be constituted merely as a kind of madness, the kind of madness that befalls a religious person who fails in the quest for truth.[63] Again, dominant ideology enmeshed itself with local knowledge in uncannily synchronous ways. For madness is often spoken of, colloquially, as a kind of possession called *phii paa* (literally, "crazy spirits").

Readers may recall that it was the fear of this madness, the fear that an encounter with his own bad *kam* had made him vulnerable to his own delirious desire and thus to uncontrollable possession, that led Khun Singh to make his Faustian bargain and to give his wife over to spirits. From his conservative

60. See Katherine Bowie's excellent history of the Village Scout Movement and the political conflict from which it emerged in *Rituals of National Loyalty: An Anthropology of the State and the Village Scout Movement in Thailand* (New York: Columbia University Press, 1997).

61. Thak Chaloemtiarana, *Thailand: The Politics of Despotic Paternalism* (Bangkok: Social Science Association of Thailand and Thai Khadi Institute of Thammasat University, 1979).

62. Craig J. Reynolds, "Sedition in Thai History: A Nineteenth Century Poem and Its Critics," in *Thai Conceptions of Knowledge*, 15–36.

63. Irvine, "The Thai-Yuan 'Madman.' "

Buddhalogical perspective, she was the rightful vehicle, being a woman whose natural fecundity simultaneously gave her power and made her unstable. Were he to have been possessed himself, he would have experienced a disintegration of the psyche whose feminizing consequences would have been unbearable for him. So, he agreed to act as the framer of an instability that could be neutralized by being kept in its rightful, which is to say feminine, place. And he made himself eligible for that role by intensifying his meditation and achieving his own emasculation through a renunciation of sexual activity, fasting, and long, devoted meditation.

It was, perhaps, the best that a man of those violently paranoid times could do to be a good Thai citizen when confronted by visions that bespoke powers beyond the state. And, in the context of such paranoia, it is perhaps inevitable that he would not only have demanded the submission of his wife but that he would also come to espouse xenophobic notions about the *kam*mic inferiority of the Meo patients who sought his wife's help in times of need. It was, after all, a time in which conservative Buddhist monks like Kitthivuddho could incite the murder of communists on the ground that those who opposed the "King," who threatened the "Nation," or who did not share the "Religion" could be killed without generating demerit for the executioner. Even in 1991, long after the dissipation of communist insurgency in Indochina and long after it had become fashionable for students to cite the "historical Marx" in the belated belief that communism, and even history, was dead, Khun Singh could attribute to the Meo victim an irredeemable alterity. Nor was he alone. In fact, the capacity of the Meo to signify oppositional otherness for Thais remains powerful. In the late 1990s, the Meo have again been accused. This time, they are suspected simultaneously of stealing jobs from Thais, engaging in prostitution and narcotics trafficking, waging a right-wing conspiracy to destabilize the regime in Vientiane, and opposing state officials in the manner of communists, with whom they are directly linked.[64]

The capacity of the Meo to represent such monstrous and aggressive otherness—for both Khun Singh and the National Security Force, both of whom insinuate linkages between communism and narcotics—has a long history, of course. It is best understood with reference to the discourses in which the risk of political infection came to be located in the hills, and in this respect, we will do well to remember the fact that Khun Singh's first experience of penetration

64. Supamart Kasem, "Anti-Drug Team Warned about Attacks: Hmongs Hire Gunmen to Kill Them," *The Bangkok Post*, 27 July 1998, Internet ed.; Matchima Chanswangpuwana, "Facing a Mountain of Obstacles," *Bangkok Post*, 5 February 1997, Internet ed.; and Bhanravee Tansubhapol, "Hmong Blamed for Local Woes," *Bangkok Post*, 25 December 1996, Internet ed.

by spirits took place at a forest monastery in the mountains east of Chiang Mai. In a space that cosmology identifies as the margin, in the wilderness on a hill, Khun Singh was attempting to confront his own demons, as indeed is the mandate of every meditator, but in doing so, he found himself overwhelmed by that which he sought to transcend. Seeking to shore up a Buddhist masculinity, he discovered a weakness in his own heart, and he identified this as femininity. But being from the south and identifying so emphatically as a Sino-Thai man, Khun Singh was not about to assume the posture of that womb that will be penetrated for the purpose of bearing the dead. He was not about to betray his "birthright," as is often said of *kathoeys* and other men who display what are recognized as feminine traits. He therefore demanded that his wife assume the role of the passage and in this way came to frame her possession. Each time he translates the utterance of the spirit and each time he provides a Buddhist gloss on the spirit's pronouncements, each time he organizes donations to temples and each time he gathers the offerings for a Praise Ceremony, he asserts this framing function. Indeed, I have often thought of Khun Singh's speech as being rather like hermeneutic marginalia in a text that he is circumscribing through the discipline of negative space. Only by rewriting his own relationship to a text that he did not want to read *him* could Khun Singh fortify himself in a gesture of projection. He did so in a manner not unlike that of the Thai state that was attempting to defend itself against a power whose threat to the masculinized body of the nation-state was being metaphorized in rumors about the penis-shrinking medicines of the communists who came from the mountains.[65]

### The Wilderness of Ethnicity

In 1965, Lieutenant General Saiyud Kerdphol, a key architect and spokesman for Thai policy toward the mountain populations, described the communist threat in terms that are uncannily reminiscent of Ramkhamhaeng's spirit's exposition on sorcery. Speaking to an American delegation in Bangkok, he

65. Stories about the penis-shrinking poisons the communists supposedly dropped in the water along the Thai-Lao border were rampant throughout the sixties and seventies. They have an interesting contemporary analogue in the phenomenon of *phii mae maaj* or "widow ghosts," which are thought to be the rapacious spirits of women who died untimely deaths. These ghosts are held responsible for the sudden deaths of migrant laborers and are imagined to be in pursuit of a husband. Hence, they are said to lie with men and to drain them not only of semen but of life. See Mary Beth Mills's account of the *phii mae maaj* in "Attack of the Widow Ghosts: Gender, Death, and Modernity in Northern Thailand," in *Bewitching Women, Pious Men: Gender and Body Politics in Southeast Asia*, ed. Aihwa Ong and Michael G. Peletz (Berkeley: University of California Press, 1995), 244–73.

asserted that "the only effective way to counter this subversion is to gain a maximum of cooperation from the local population in the *infected* villages or provinces."[66] Isolating "hill tribes," or *chao khao*, as they are known locally, to prevent them from becoming transitional vectors between the lowland Thai and what he felt were the more serious threats of Chinese communists became an obsession for Saiyud Kerdphol and for many loyal Thai officials.[67] Under his leadership, Thai strategy ranged from the recruitment of *chao khao* security teams to the bombing of villages (sometimes with napalm). Such violence contradicted the more benevolent strategies of economic enrichment espoused in King Bhumipol Adulyadej's demand that the Thai state "take prosperity to the hill-tribes, not bring them to prosperity."[68] But in both cases, the *chao khao* were to remain marginal, constituting a human buffer between the capitalized Buddhist Thai state and what was perceived to be the barbaric incivility of the communist peripheries. Eventually, touristification would form the technique through which development and marginalization could be simultaneously achieved,[69] but until then, open military suppression of border communities was the tactic of preference for the militarily dominated regimes that held sway until 1973 and after 1976.

The Meo, whose homes tended to straddle the Thai-Laos border, were especially vulnerable and specifically targeted by military raids. The fact that the Meo did not always recognize the laws of inheritance laid down by the Thai state made them even more suspect in the eyes of the military, who branded them as inherently communist and who used the ethnic epithet "Meo Daeng," meaning Red Meo, to great rhetorical effect. Civilian anticommunist groups such as the Village Scouts figured political evil in what were, locally, more exotic and archetypically Other forms. In the initiation rites recounted by Katherine Bowie, for example, they dramatized a fantasized peace process through the reenactment of Baden-Powell's treaty with the Zulus rather than through the granting of citizenship to the Meo.[70] This despite the fact that, at some initiation camps, Meo people constituted a sizable minority of recruits.[71] Although the Village Scouts were to become potent and violent defenders of a militarized state, and although they had been established by the CIA-backed Border Patrol

---

66. Saiyud Kerdphol, *Addresses of Lieutenant General Saiyud Kerdphol, 1968–1971*, Bangkok Historical Division, SCHQ [no additional data on publication source; microfilm by Library of Congress dated 1975], 10, my emphasis.

67. Ibid., 23.

68. Ibid., 70.

69. Kisly, "Commodity Native?"

70. Katherine Bowie has provided an unparalleled account of such initiation rites in *Rituals of National Loyalty*, esp. 183–219.

71. In the initiation rite attended by Bowie, 20 percent of new recruits were Meo. See ibid., 172.

Police as part of a massive counterinsurgency campaign, they were initially perceived as an alternative to military suppression, working through forms of incorporation rather than expulsion. They were, in fact, intended to provide innoculation against communism by virtue of a mimetic, verily viral logic. Through cell formations based on those of communist organizations, outsiders would be ingested and neutralized through education programs facilitated by sensory deprivation. Then they would be converted into detectors of transgression. Many Meo responded, but the military did not desist. The Meo continued to signify dangerous and volatile alterity. Even the king, who defended the Meo, worried that they were vulnerable to a politics of vindictive, self-othering transformation. In 1973, His Majesty remarked, "If we make mistakes, the whole Meo tribe will turn red and cause incessant trouble for us later."[72] The putative instability of Meo political affiliation was compulsively remarked, rendering them the objects of a fetishistic discourse that could only reassert the risk of betrayal with every effort at conversion.

Times have changed, of course. If communism was represented as the primary threat to boundedness in the 1960s and 1970s, narcotics and corruption now share the role of invisible enemy, of invisible poison.[73] Indeed, the imbrication of the two—narcotics and corruption—is so thorough that they provide each other with metaphors. The Border Patrol Police that once carried out the anticommunist raids in the mountains and joined forces with the army to suppress overt resistance in the capital city now polices drugs in the northern provinces. Aided by U.S. advisors and United Nations funding, it carries out a broad range of policies and programs in an effort to stanch poppy cultivation and heroin production. Crop substitution is one strategy for effecting this change. Tourism is another. And often, the Border Patrol Police bring "prosperity" to the people by bringing "hill tribe" people to the Chiang Mai Cultural Center, where they are forcibly detoxified and employed as "ethnic dancers" in exchange for access to education for their children.[74]

At the Chiang Mai Cultural Center, tourists and conference-goers can enjoy

---

72. Ibid., 92; Jeffrey Race, "The War in Northern Thailand," *Modern Asian Studies* 8, no. 1 (1974): 105.

73. Kavi Chongkittavorn, "Amphetamine Metaphors and the Abuse of Power," *The Nation*, 2 January 1997, Internet ed. Kavi claims that the popular hysteria about drugs and corruption is akin to that which surrounded communism, and suggests that the problems, though significant, are being inflated to legitimate extrajudicial practices, including the execution without trial of suspects. As in the past, it is the Interior Ministry (under whose auspices the Border Patrol Police were formed) that is being named as the site of unjust and distinctly uncivil practices.

74. Michael Vatikiotis, "Ethnic Pluralism in the Northern Thai City of Chiang Mai" (Ph.D. diss., Oxford University, 1984), 146; also Charles F. Keyes, *Thailand: Buddhist Kingdom as Nation-State* (Boulder, CO: Westview, 1987), 129.

elaborate *khantok* dinners followed by dance performances in two parts. The first features formal classical dance, including Siamese court dance and a few putatively local specialties, such as the "Finger Nail Dance" and the "Umbrella Dance," which claim to have northern origins but feature the tight fingers and more delicate steps of the Siamese tradition. These are followed by "hill tribe" performances in which ethnically minoritized individuals appear in "tribal costume" and shuffle listlessly around an outdoor fire, displaying not technique but costume. Among such performers, the "medium" is a favorite figure for both Thai and non-Thai audiences, invariably eliciting sighs and remarks of delight when he enters the framed space of the performance. He appears with his empty opium pipe and a sac of herbs, as a disembodied voice broadcasts his importance in the indigenous culture from which he has been pried. Aware of his own ridiculousness, the dancing medium is a sign not only of his own alterity, but of his domestication.

And yet, the domestication is incomplete here. The presence of the Meo medium constitutes something of an abrasion in this falsely picturesque context, where surfaces are valorized and things primitive are attributed the quaint beauty of the vanishing. He is, to a certain extent, the limiting point of authenticity, and his appearance as the opium smoker bespeaks what is implicitly a notion of his immunity to salvation. Oddly enough, this is both because he is what he seems to be—that is, he is not so much possessed by otherness as he is the very body of otherness—and because he will not display the secret of his identity in a manner that can be rationalized or reconciled with the other logics of appearance that mark the modern in northern Thailand.

The choreography that demands the opium pipe makes of it a fetish and imputes to it a metonymic function. The pipe is the sign of being Meo, and being Meo is inextricable from drug dependency and, thus, criminality. He is always already addicted, always susceptible to his need, which inhabits him totally. In short, he is thought to submit himself to a foreign law, and more, to the law of the foreign. Recall the Meo suspicion of the judiciary apparatus and state-mandated laws of inheritance, which are contrary to Meo tradition. What is important in this rendering of the Meo is the degree to which it distinguishes him from all other mediums (and all other Thais). To submit oneself to the foreign is not the same as being overtaken by a foreign law, and here, we will need to distinguish between mediums and shamans.

For mediums, the Meo man is the threshold of magical potency, the point where it can become wild, escaping the constraints of Buddhism and, thus, of Thainess as well. I am, of course, no longer speaking of the impotent dancer on the floor of the Chiang Mai Cultural Center, but of those Meo magicians feared by Ramkhamhaeng and the others who inhabit the periphery of Chiang Mai's community of mediums. There is, for example, a particularly famous medium, especially beloved of local journalists, who resides in a resettlement community some fifteen to twenty kilometers outside of Chiang Mai. The suburb, a grotesque grid of cement lanes and tin-roofed houses, was constructed to house dislocated residents after a dam was built (such prefabricated villages were also used to house Meo who were relocated after bombing raids). However, no provisions were ever made for the kinds of social relations that had informed the old communities: no public meeting sites, no central buildings, just raw, dusty roads and sharp corners at the driveways that led to tin-roofed houses. Here, in the newly rational space of the resettlement camp, minority individuals often suffer acute isolation and depression, reverting to rather than escaping from opium and heroin addictions or patterns of domestic violence.

Such was the milieu of the Meo medium who appeared on the periphery of Chiang Mai in the early 1990s when I met him. He appears to be a vehicle for a generic "hill tribe" spirit, one who remains nameless for him and visually indistinguishable from the medium, who is himself something of an interloper in Chiang Mai's community of mediums. The medium himself does not speak Thai. Nor is he particularly conversant with the forms of the ceremonial tradition, and he is often the recipient of stern-voiced directions and pushy instruction by other possessed mediums at annual Praise Ceremonies. At his own Praise Ceremony, he had to be told to initiate the proceedings and to commence the *wai*-ing of the tutelary spirits. Even then, there were few visible signs to suggest possession after he did so: no vomiting, no vocal transformations, no reorientation of posture or bearing. Nor did he display any *khan* dishes for other spirits to visit, and in this he marked his exteriority to the lineages that constitute legitimate mediumship. On the occasion of his own ceremony, most mediums ignored him while paying tribute to each other.

Those who publicly turn away in contempt or ridicule nonetheless privately express awe at the petite man with the decorative opium pipe and they claim that he controls extremely powerful magic. They are loathe to expel him altogether from a scene at which he is otherwise socially incompetent, for fear of a knowledge they do not know how to thwart. As long as he can be framed within the discourse of public ritual propriety, they assume that his magic will not be directed at other mediums. In fact, the Meo "medium" is a shaman, and he has acquired his knowledge through inherited techniques of ecstasy that do not leave him vacated, and that permit him a heroic kind of subjectivity that can recall what is learned through communion with others. Hence the poverty of his possession performances. Hence also the fear and suspicion with which Chiang Mai mediums greet him. For he is other to them in the ontological tenacity of the selfhood that he inhabits, and in the fact that it is he, the medium, and not the spirit of another, who possesses knowledge. The distinctions between mediums and shamans, so well rehearsed in anthropological and religious studies literatures, is never absolute, of course, but in this case, they have some salience. For mediums, the identificatory claims that ground a shaman's power constitute the boundary between properly Buddhist practice and a barbarism that was supposed to have been banished centuries ago. In Theravada Buddhism, humans can know only by surrendering their selves and coming to terms with the fact that, though there is causation, time, and space, there is no subject who endures, no being or soul in whom these principles are comprehended beyond momentariness.[75] By the same token, however, the belief in spirit possession today offends scripturally oriented Buddhists, who see in the claims to spiritual presencing precisely that same ontologizing gesture that is prohibited in the Buddha's teachings of impermanence. Ritualism is the epithet given to an overidentification with appearances, to the mistaking of form for reality, and even more, to the attribution of reality to form. And it circulates widely: hurled at Mahannikai Buddhists by Thammayut monks, and at mediums by Mahannikai monks, at shamans by mediums, at northerners by southerners, and at women by men. I am, however, less interested here in the philosophical arguments within which different discourses legitimate the particular lines they draw between themselves and others, than in the history and logic of that line or, more precisely, that drawing of the line that frames difference.

Let us then reconsider that moment of the Village Scout initiation rite at which the staging of national "reconciliation" was conducted following the dramaturgy of British colonial subordination. The unnamed referent of the Zulu character, one might imagine, was precisely the Meo. Bowie has already remarked that many of the individuals acting as stage managers for this false

75. Needless to say, few mediums and even fewer laypeople could expound on the texts and philosophical arguments within which the debate about impermanence, momentariness, and causation have been explored. The refined discourses on such topics are the purview only of learned monks. Nonetheless, they have informed official policies on ritualism and, in translated form, are often invoked in the condemnations of those whose practices and beliefs are thought to be inadequate by scriptural standards. For an account of Buddhist philosophies of nonself, see Th. Stcherabatsky, *Buddhist Logic*, 2 vols. (1930; New York: Dover, 1963). Although Stcherabatsky's work focuses on Mahayana and Central Asian Buddhism and in particular on the school of Dignaga, his explication of "dependent origination" and its implications for concepts of will and causality is extremely useful. It also has relevance for the study of Thai Theravada Buddhism, which has a relatively direct linkage to the Indian school via Sri Lanka. On the relationships between Thai and Sri Lankan Theravada Buddhism, see Richard Gombrich, *Theravada Buddhism: A Social History from Ancient Benares to Modern Colombo* (London: Routledge and Kegan Paul, 1988).

theatrical substitution were themselves Meo. Indeed, one is startled by the "foreignness" of the Zulu warrior in this milieu, and one therefore wonders at the logic that informed this oblique referentiality. Neither the indigenousness of the Zulu nor the colonial context of South Africa seem to map themselves onto the Thai scene. In the end, such efforts to find a hermeneutic solution to the enigma of the Village Scout only obscure what the initiation spectacle actually reveals about the logics of signification within which the Meo (and the *kathoey*) signify.

In Katherine Bowie's rich ethnography, there appears a description of the culminating moment in the Scout initiation rite. One could have expected oaths of loyalty, pledges of fealty (such as were sworn at the well in Chiang Mai), or professions of belief. One could have anticipated deeply committed expressions of nationalist subjectivity. Yet, that is not what occurs in this moment. To the contrary, the reinterpellated participants of the rite promise only to perform in the manner desired by the bearers of power. Bowie quotes them: "I will do good things, things that the government wants."[76] What the rite requires, then, is less a national subjectivity than the appearance or the performance of ideally nationalist behavior. It requires that one conform oneself to the ideals of the nation, and it makes performance the criterion of proper citizenship. But in making appearance the index of national belonging it opens two possibilities. The first is that appearance will produce the subjectivity that it is supposed to signify, thereby inverting the directionality of reference. The second is that appearance will conceal a divergent intention, a potentially subversive subjectivity, and that there will be no guarantee of national sentiment provided by the appearance of national propriety.

If the Zulu is the sign that both evokes and refuses to be conflated with the Meo, it is also the character around whom a new suspicion enters. How can a nation that demands only proper performance ever be sure about the commitment of its citizens? And if it cannot be so sure, if the rite itself has introduced doubt in the most emphatically national of institutions, has it not also generated the conditions of its own failure—and necessary repetition? Compulsive efforts to perform national propriety stave off the doubt that might enter in a context where no one can be sure of the real intention behind performance. But they only defer that doubt to resummon it later, in a more virulent, a more violent manner. When the king expressed his concern that the Meo would become red, he was speaking in a manner that seems to be a pun, affirming the logic by which the Meo, always already the "Red Meo," might be made to stand for the possibility of everyone's becoming red. This possibility, which the Meo

76. Bowie, *Rituals of National Loyalty*, 209.

represent and which Meo magic theatricalizes, is that of a foreignness within. It is for this reason that the Meo themselves will never be stabilized by being named in the rite. It is for this reason that the Meo are translated into the Zulu. For in that gesture, which is a gesture of false translation (in what sense can one people ever really be equivalent to another people?), something foreign enters (as that which is residual, which is untranslatable). One could say, then, that the degree to which the state and conservative mediumship metaphorized their own practices as being "about" border preservation and the risk of penetration, they masked something deeper, something more dangerous, something less placatable. They masked the impossibility of their own unicity. They repressed the degree to which Siam/Thailand, like all nations, is a nation only to the extent that it is haunted by all other nations, and to the extent that it represses its own spectral status, its own submission to the fantasy of universality.[77]

There is, nonetheless, a more particular question about the Meo and their relationship to both mediumship and more doctrinally legitimate Buddhism: How is it that a Meo shaman comes to figure Buddhism's other? And in what does this otherness consist? What histories have permitted mediums, once the very index of ritualist excess, to make such adjudications, to be the bearers of such discretion? Within what parameters does such judgment hold sway? Or, to put the matter in more general terms, when is ritual the proper expression of truth, and when is it a gratuitously, parasitically symbolic decoration? Two things are clear. The first is that mediumship has a history and that this history is inextricable from the history of ritualism in Thailand. The second is that ritual—as discourse—is a mode of enframement, a process of judgment that attributes to the figure it delineates the values that come from without and that make such delineation possible in the first instance.[78] A frame does not simply outline something; it produces the limits of that thing and makes it visible as such—even when the content that is framed is simply space itself. The frame constitutes the difference between figure and ground. But there are many frames in this story, none entirely independent of the other. The frame of ritual

77. Readers will find this passage reminiscent of the arguments made by Benedict Anderson in both *Imagined Communities: Reflections on the Origin and Spread of Nationalism* (London: Verso, 1983), and in *The Specter of Comparison: Nationalism, Southeast Asia, and the World* (New York: Verso, 1998). The resonance is intentional.

78. In making this argument, I am following the path traveled by Jacques Derrida in *Truth in Painting*, trans. Geoff Bennington and Ian McLeod (Chicago: University of Chicago Press, 1987). See especially the discussion of the *parergon*, 37–82. My understanding has been greatly assisted by Samuel Weber's excellent explanatory essay on the *parergon*, "The Unraveling of Form," in *Mass Mediauras: Form, Technics, Media*, ed. Alan Cholodenki (Stanford: Stanford University Press, 1996), 9–35.

discourse gathers up practices and ideas, mythic stories, commitments, and fears, and attributes to them an underlying unity that is driven to reproduce itself in endless circles of self-citation. It does so through the processes of representation and through the imagination of representation as the function of ritual. But representation has its own fantastic productivity; it gives birth to its referent. And this is how I understand the history of mediumship in Chiang Mai. Hypostatized and rendered as representational practices, indeed, as the signs of cultural authenticity, mediumship has enjoyed an extraordinary renaissance in recent decades. To be sure, its loss of magicality has been the condition of possibility for that revival, but then the revival itself has entailed the risk of a renewed belief in magic. So proliferation has also entailed difference.

There is still much to be said about the histories of ritual and ritualism in northern Thailand. What I hope to have accomplished here, in the chapter that now closes, is some understanding of the contours within which the drive for order (to which the discourse of ritual is always a handmaid) has both incited difference and then summoned the recuperative narratives of sexual and national identification, often in ways that implicate the one in the other: masculinity and Thainess, Buddhism and anticommunism. Yet, it should be clear that no political ideology exists independent of the workings of language and that no representation can be understood merely as a matter of content. Hence the doubled attention to architectural metaphorics and to the principles of spacing in language. In the idioms of households and differently sexed bodies, in the narrations of nations and of nationally focused mediumship, we encounter the figures of an alterity that must be incorporated, but only insofar as it can be made to mark a limit. These figures are on the peripheries of the normative in northern Thailand, even though that normative space is itself in contest. A *kathoey*, a Meo magician, a rumor of poison. All threaten to leak into a world that otherwise seems to want order. The order of descent, of hierarchy, of nation, and of monarchy. Now then, it remains to be seen: What is the lineage of this order? And what secrets does it contain? If the presence of the *kathoey* and the Meo has already suggested that spatialized and territorialized order contains a potential for rupture, then perhaps the logic of descent also conceals its own unstable thread.

# 5 THE SECRET OF THE DISH

Not all antiquity converts itself into authenticity, as the case of the Meo shaman on the periphery of Chiang Mai's community of mediums makes clear. Some histories reach into a past so deep and so opaque to the narratives of progress that no effort at domestication can finally contain the possibility that they represent something other than the antecedent of the present. And it is the narrative of arrival in the present, spun backward from the moment in which pastness is imagined, that determines whether or not the primordial moment is one of origin or of departure. In the period of Chiang Mai's full membership in the Thai nation-state, after the encompassment by Siam through treaties and nationalized institutions of law and education and after the boundary consolidations of the anticommunist years, ethnic otherness and even (but to a lesser extent) sexual otherness are increasingly read as unrecuperable abrasions in a fabric aspiring to smoothness. Virtually everywhere a sense of the nation-state as an entity bound in and through the rule of law has come to dominate Thailand—and this is as true for spirit mediums as it is for liberal democrats.

Incorporation in Thailand is the idiom in which citizenship is spoken, but it is also the idiom of governance. Prior to the modernization of the bureaucracy, politicians were said to "eat the country" (*kin müang*), a term that bespoke the financing of operations through taxes on labor or in kind. It was a practice sanctioned by law, but one that preceded legislation and the judicial apparatus. What, then, is this law that precedes the state? The production of law is widely imagined to be a process sanctioned by law, a fact nowhere more visible than in the seemingly endless constitutional revisions to which successive political regimes have devoted themselves in their efforts to appear credible. In many respects, contemporary legislative practice seems to respect the universalism first enacted in the Aśokan ideal of Buddhist monarchy, where even kings were subject to the *dhamma*. Today, politicians are subject to the same accusations of criminality that they level at common people and are considered subject to the law. If the king has once again become relatively immune to question, he is no longer the author of law, he is merely the instrument of its authorization. Mediums do not appear to observe this distinction; in most ways, they recall a time in which the very utterance of the king was invested with the power over life. Yet, in other ways, and especially in their own highly theatricalized submission to Buddhism, they partake of a similar understanding. They too have been submitted to a law. And so have their spirits. Indeed, in claiming that their returns to the human plane are motivated by the need for merit, possessing personae bespeak the anxiety that afflicts the king whose two bodies have been so rent that the one can be subject to the law of the other.

Since Aśoka's reign, all Buddhist kings have been imagined as being subject to the laws of *kam*, of course, and all kings are advised to make merit in order that they travel safely.[1] Some, like Taksin, have even suffered exile and death for having exceeded their place in the moral universe. Yet, when spirits voluntarily and profusely profess their subjection to *kam*, one detects something else and something more. None of the nineteenth-century accounts of possessed mediums record anything about confessions from spirits. They tell only of a commandment, issued from the mouth of the one possessed and infused with the power of the sovereign performative. "The spirits forbid the whiskey monopoly," asserted the royal medium's, Cao Ubon's, spirit when confronted by the illness of the reigning *cao*'s wife and the impending loss of her own lucrative concession in the mid-1880s.[2] The very force of those commandments worried the Siamese bureaucrats who were charged with implementing new national legislation.[3] Today, however, spirits can authorize their commandments only with reference to the law that bids them dance in tribute to those above them in the hierarchy of moral achievement. In this, they reveal the complex nature of that inheritance that narrates itself as a mere calling and a blind submission to the demands of the dead. Their ambiguous claims to power then direct us again to a consideration of how inheritance, particularly the inheritance of debt, is

1. An archetypical example is to be found in the *Cāmadevīvamsa*, where the sage, Subrahma, lectures Cāmadevi on the laws of codependent origination, or "compounded things," and advises her to "accumulate more merit" to be able to "go safely by the power of [her] meritorious deeds" (Donald K. Swearer and Sommai Premchit, *The Legend of Queen Cāma* [Albany: State University of New York Press, 1998], 94). On Aśokan kingship, see John Strong, *The Legend of King Aśoka* (Princeton, NJ: Princeton University Press, 1983).

2. Carl Bock, *Temples and Elephants* (1885; Bangkok: White Orchid, 1985), 340.

3. Ratanaporn Sethakul, "Political, Social, and Economic Changes in the Northern States of Thailand from the Chiang Mai Treaties of 1874 and 1883" (Ph.D. diss., University of Illinois, 1989), 272.

narrated within the stories that spirits tell of a simple journey toward the present. For it is as a journey to the present that the stories of spirits metaphorize the problematic of a relationship between past and present, and it is in their choices of who will be permitted to choose them that they dramatize what is, in effect, the question of ethical responsibility in the face of fateful circumstances.

In the pages that follow, then, I attend to the narratives of spirits' descent into the present and the ways these are mapped onto both the landscape and the standardized stories of Buddhism's arrival in northern Thailand. Such considerations seem to me to lead inevitably to an examination of how the logic of descent is reconciled with that of ethical choice—the very choice that Buddhism insists is the correlate of humanness. What emerges here is yet another tale of conflict, of a multitude threatening the idea of lineage. But something else also becomes evident, and that is the degree to which mediumship has been encompassed by the rule of law despite its valorization of personal, face-to-face power. Indeed, the very submersion of mediumship in the orders of the state and of law drives this attraction, this retrojective longing for the charismatic authority, which mediums, like many other northern Thais, now fantasize in their place of origins. What the stories told here suggest to those who would read modernity's notion of law as a form of benign universalism is that, in the process of imagining law as that which precedes legislation, something has been secreted: an origin has been forgotten or displaced, and a violence concealed. The question to be asked, then, is who inherits the law, and which law do they inherit? For mediums, the question to be asked might be: How has the question of inheritance been reconciled with a submission to a law of rights? When is a bequest of right a demand for obligation? And when does a "birthright" become a matter of ethicopolitical possibility? To answer such questions requires that one encounter the narratives of descent from and debt to the past within which mediums negotiate the multiplicity of the dead and the individuation of the living as two sides of a coin—a coin that is, and is not, the currency of an exchange.

### I Come from the First Country

I asked the spirit of every possessed medium I met to tell me where he (and occasionally she) had come from, repeating the gesture that greeted me at the beginning of every new acquaintance with a medium. The term of greeting in northern Thailand is *Paj naaj maa*, an ambiguous expression that can mean "Where have you been?", although it is usually used much like the English (not American) "How do you do?", a question not intended for response. It is a seemingly innocuous fact, this greeting that asks for the visitor's trajectory, but it is part of a complex web of directional orientation that is worked out at every level of discourse and bodily gesture. In both Northern and Central Thai, the progression of a sentence is always that of subject-verb-object, and indirect objects must always follow direct objects, so that sentence structure itself is a directional flow from the speaker or the subject. Its logic is one of causality through contiguity. One goes (*pai*) or comes (*maa*) upstairs, for example, depending on the speaker's position above or below the climbing actor. Proximity to the point of the speaker and to the point of telling also has a temporal quality, and past deeds proceed toward the present tense of the speaker, who occupies a kind of zero point on the time line, just as the future moves away from the speaker on a single continuum.

Invariably, the response to my question was a narrative of travel, in which the spirit named the cities he had inhabited in different lifetimes. Always, the teleology of the narrative was one that arrived in Chiang Mai, the "jewel on the River Ping." And how could it be otherwise, given that we were conversing in the city to which their journeys through time and space had brought them? Caopuu Phayaphrom, whose own wanderings had followed a route like that of the poet whose name he so cavalierly assumed, told me the following story: "I was born in Chiang Saen. My father was a great *cao* in Chiang Saen, but he lived in the time before recordings. You will find nothing about him in the history books. I came from Chiang Saen to Lamphun—do you know Wat Haripunchai?—that is where I lived (just yesterday I went to make merit at Wat Haripunchai). Then I came to Chiang Mai. I have lived in all the great cities and I have lived in all times. Each era has its place [*müang*]. Now, I am here in this *muu baan* [neighborhood] and I protect all of the people who live here."

One of the astonishing features of these narratives is the uniform sense of historical reigns. Naang Khao had only a third-grade education, but her spirit was at ease enumerating the rise and fall of empires in northern Thailand. Historians agree that Chiang Saen was a dominant *müang* prior to the establishment of Chiang Mai and either preceded or was contemporary with the Haripunchai empire, which was situated in the modern city of Lamphun prior to its defeat by Chiang Mai's founder, Mengrai, in the late thirteenth century.

Phayaphrom's own time travel mirrored the legendary journeys of Caoluang Kham Daeng, the mythic founder of Chiang Mai. As he narrated his peripatetic wanderings across time and space, Phayaphrom retraced and encompassed that first unknowing pilgrimage to the site of Chiang Mai's founding. He also asked me to perform similar tracings. In one of our meetings, Phayaphrom asked if I had been to Chiang Dao and seen the spectacular mountain caves a few hundred kilometers to the north of Chiang Mai. The trip is a stunning one for motorcycle enthusiasts and connoisseurs of natural phenomena, and I had made the trip for both reasons. Caopuu Phayaphrom claimed to go to Chiang Dao regularly, each *wan phra'* (day of Buddhist worship).[4] There are actually four *wan phra'* each month, which means that the spirit goes to Chiang Dao to be possessed about once a week—though not necessarily traveling in the body of his medium.

Caopuu Phayaphrom describes Chiang Dao as a place of great spiritual power (*ittharit*) and, according to most possessed mediums, it is also a place where all great northern spirits originate. The caves actually stretch more than a kilometer into the mountain and are divided into chambers. Their stalactite formations are said to represent various mythic creatures, so that the caves contain a "natural" bestiary. There are also several Buddha statues and shrines within the temple and a large wat outside. Tourists who want to pay a few baht are given guided tours into the caves, which are lit by the wheezing handheld gas lanterns carried by guides. These guides have been well trained in the art of terror, invariably allowing the lantern to go out during the descent, but they are also consummate storytellers and provide careful descriptions that transform the rocky outcrops and protrusions into marvelous beasts inhabiting the rock. For these reasons, Chiang Dao is one of northern Thailand's favorite tourist attractions. It is also a revered site among mediums, both as a destination of ritual pilgrimage and as a point of origin in their own narratives of historical becoming. Most of them claim to have particular places in the caves that belong exclusively to them. Caopuu Phayaphrom, for example, keeps his tobacco on a shelf just inside the first gate (*pratuu*) of the first cave, or so he told me (I was never able to locate the shelf or the tobacco). This is, he says, his own place, and other spirits have other places in the caves.

In instructing me to go to the caves to find his shelf, and in carrying out the ritual pilgrimage himself each *wan phra'*, Caopuu Phayaphrom maps his own history onto the trajectory of Cao Luang Kham Daeng's life, which provides one

4. The northern Thai calender is divided into a series of twelve lunar months of twenty-nine and thirty days in alternation; these are further divided into the waxing and waning stages of the moon. Every day is considered more or less auspicious for ritual purposes, according to Indian *narayana* calculations that are based on the movement of the sun, the moon, the five visible planets, and two nodes. Many mediums know by heart these calculations and the means of determining the auspiciousness of a moment, but others rely on Siamese texts to determine the particular days of ritual propitiation for each spirit. The *jok khruu* rites, when mediums and lower spirits acknowledge the tutelary spirits with tributary dances (*forn phii*), are scheduled on this basis and change from year to year accordingly. The northern Thai calendar also acknowledges the seven-day week, which it attributes to Mon origins (the categorical term for the seven days is *wan meng* or Mon day). Over and above this is the Siamese calendar, which is now rationalized with the international annual calendar.

of the archetypical narratives of northern Thailand's progress from darkness to Buddhist enlightenment.[5] In the many versions of this myth that mediums recite, and in those disseminated in folkloric studies, Cao Luang Kham Daeng is said to have been seduced by a golden deer while out hunting. He chased the deer from Chiang Dao to Chiang Mai and its mountain citadel, Doi Suthep, unable to kill it but entranced by its grace. Along the way he met a beautiful woman whom he took as his bride, as well as a *rysii* (hermit) who informed him that the deer was actually a deity who had promised Indra to lead Cao Luang Kham Daeng and his people to Buddhism. The great man apparently converted and resided in Chiang Mai for some time before returning to Chiang Dao, where he died and became a guardian spirit of the mountain there.[6]

Points such as Chiang Dao that are the sites of originary events are considered by mediums to have particular localized but materially transmissible power. They are often referred to in the idiom of electricity, as batteries (an English borrowing), and spirits are said to go there to charge themselves, as it were, with spiritual power. The material transmissibility of the power is crucial in these stories, as is its limitless capacity for renewal. People do not exhaust the power of a place by partaking of it; they merely tap into something that radiates outward in time and space. In this manner, the value of place finds a material metaphor. Indeed, it is quite literalized, and its literality is of the same kind that allows popular Buddhists to believe that *stupa*s, the architectural edifices in which Buddha relics are often kept, house the presence of the Buddha himself. Orthodox Theravada interpretation prohibits such understandings, of course, and argues that the monuments that memorialize the travel and teachings of Buddha are just that: mnemotechnical devices intended to provoke contemplation rather than actual traces of the Enlightened One. Nonetheless, the valorization of place expressed in these beliefs continues to exercise a potent influence in the lives of many northern Thais, and although I intend to argue that the very nature of place has changed and that a global dialectic has effected the abstraction and hence delocalization of place, it is still the idiom within which me-

5. The oral versions of Caoluang Kham Daeng's journey to Chiang Mai occupy a territory somewhere between *tamnaan* and *phongsawadan* historiography, including elements of universal Buddhist history, and the genealogical or dynastic histories of particular historical cities. As David Wyatt has argued, the line between these genres is often blurred, and narratives are often classifiable only as being more like one than the other, a standard that would lead us to categorize the story of Caoluang Kham Daeng more in the *tamnaan* camp. For a discussion of historiographical genres, see David Wyatt, "Chronicle Traditions in Thai Historiography," in *Studies in Thai History* (Chiang Mai: Silkworm, 1994), 1–21.

6. Santi Chantasawon, "The Spirit Cults and Superstition in Thai Habitation: A Case Study in the Northern Region" (Ph.D. diss., University of Michigan, 1987), 33–34.

diums narrate their relationship to originary power. Few did not tell me of their sojourns to Chiang Dao, and most repeated the story of Cao Luang Kham Daeng in their own narratives of return. The return itself is spatial only insofar as it permits a movement in time. Indeed, the value of place is precisely identified with the value of origination, and it is for this reason that power, though transmissible, is also seen to dissipate as one moves away from its locus. Hence the very common proliferation of secondary shrines in the vicinity of an important primary shrine, or of miniature imitative *stupas* around larger ones where actual relics are housed. The baroque elaboration of the place of origins is experienced as the multiplication of traces in the present.

Here, indeed, is the paradox: The closer one gets to the present, which is to say the point from which one speaks, the more traces of the past does one encounter. In northern Thailand, the closer one gets to Chiang Mai City, the more encrusted with signs is the narratable landscape. Some of these signs, such as the shrines at the city's corners, actually refer inward. It has been explained to me, for example, that the spirits residing at peripheral shrines serve as intermediaries between the living and the most potent founding spirits of the central *lak müang*, who generally do not possess individual mediums. Still others are simply testimony to the proliferation of events that are deemed relevant to the city in the cultural imaginary that is inscribed there. It is as though the relative plenitude of recent memory had been translated into a landscape architecture of increasingly baroque folding. The past bunches around the present, gathering itself until it approaches full presence, the zero point of representation. A full presence would be impossible, of course. Or at least, it would be unavailable to sight. In the end, this is why the *lak müang* cannot be looked upon; it is so proximate to full presence that it is ideally invisible. The traces and signs of the past activate memory precisely to the extent that the past is not present in its entirety. Just as one sees figures by virtue of a purposeful blindness to the ground, so one recalls by virtue of a forgetting that serves to hierarchize events according to a value that comes from without. Perhaps this is what Maurice Halbwachs meant when he wrote:

> We ask how recollections are to be located. And we answer: with the help of landmarks that we always carry within ourselves, for it suffices to look around ourselves, to think about others, and to locate ourselves within the social framework in order to retrieve them. We find, in addition, that these landmarks become multiplied in proportion as our memory explores regions closer to our present, to the point that we can recall all the objects and all the faces on which yesterday our attention was even slightly focused. . . .

Why does society establish landmarks in time that are placed closer together—and usually in a very irregular manner, since for certain periods they are almost lacking—whereas around such salient events sometimes many other equally salient events seem to gather, just as street signs and other signposts multiply as a tourist attraction approaches?[7]

Attending to the stories of descent that mediums tell, one is struck both by the fact that the present is cluttered by traces of the past and by the implication that these traces are hollow in the manner of wombs (like the *dhatu gabbha*). Such semiotic vacuity is not surprising if we accept Roland Barthes's claim that signs are evacuated of their utilitarian and communicative content in the process of mythification.[8] Such an understanding would permit one to comprehend how an outcropping, a tobacco pipe, or a cave can become the place of a spirit. But traces demand narration, demand to be expanded outward and backward in the (always incomplete) moment that they are pried open and invested with story. The trace itself, this hollow thing that initially greets the viewer in its mere visuality, this resistance to the eye asks as much as it tells. The trace is what facilitates inheritance while, at the same time, making the content of that inheritance a matter of historical, political, and ethical decision: of *af*filiation rather than simple filiation.

### The One and the Many: Inheritance and Historical Knowledge

Every possession entails an encrypted narrative of historical descent, one that is mapped onto the storied landscape as a series of marks with mnemotechnical and even magical power. The journeys lead inexorably toward Chiang Mai's present, leaving behind them a landscape filled with signposts for those who can read them. Caopuu Phayaphrom, for example, tells of lifetimes moving between Chiang Saeng, Lamphun, and Chiang Mai, noting the wats at which he has made merit when recounting the story of his pilgrimlike progress. The spirit of Sukhothai's Ramkhamhaeng, to be discussed below, tells of his journey northward in stories that pit Buddhism against the primitive sorcery of ethnic others such as the Meo and the Karen, reiterating nationalist historiography in a personalized mode. Cao Saen Müangma, the possessing spirit of a medium we shall meet in the next chapter, is associated with a point in the River Ping where a Buddha relic is said to have emitted great shafts of light. Because that burst of

7. Maurice Halbwachs, *On Collective Memory*, trans. Lewis A. Coser (Chicago: University of Chicago Press, 1992), 175–76.

8. Roland Barthes, "Myth Today," in *Mythologies*, trans. Annette Lavers (New York: Hill and Wang, 1986), 122.

luminosity was thought to evidence the need and the receptivity of the city to the enlightening effect of Buddhism, there is now a wat to mark the spot of the miracle. The wat is not only the product of the relic's arrival, but commemorates the event in a multilingual plaque, and each time the spirit possesses his medium, the story demands to be retold. Caoluang Kham Daeng's site of arrival in Chiang Mai, which is said to lie behind the forest monastery called Wat Umong, receives offerings that mark the place in an imaginary landscape pregnant with historical signification. The list is nearly endless, and its extension is witnessed by the innumerable shrines that surround the city and are said to be the residences of spirits.

To this extent, the discourse of mediums seems to be aligned with that of classical cosmology, including the *Traiphum* cosmology and the more specifically northern *Pathamamūlamūlī*. There is no space without time, no distance that is not already traveled or known as the line that constitutes a relationship, no commensuration between journeys. The *Traiphum* consists in a descriptive account of all the realms in the universe, from the lowliest hell to the most ethereal heaven. But these are not locations so much as moral spaces, the domains in which particular kinds of beings reside by virtue of their store of merit. Accordingly, the traversal of these spaces is made possible by merit-producing or diminishing acts; merit itself works only in and through time. The *Traiphum* cosmology has thus been likened by many to a kind of temporal map in which an overarching principle of duration provides the frame. In this context, the relationships between places are to be comprehended in the idiom of time-bound movement. It is for this reason that scholars such as Frank Reynolds have pointed to the narrativity of temple murals, noting that the wat housing an image is often pictured and situated within the stations of the Buddha's life.[9] The murals can thus be read as maps identifying correspondences between places in this world and the "universal land of the Buddha," itself projected into a future that encompasses all time. Thongchai Winichakul has observed the parallels between such murals and the properly narrative *tamnan*, which also describe the relationships between particular places and the universal space of merit and rebirth. Both are distinctly premodern in his account, simultaneously different from the military maps of the early nineteenth century in which routes were drawn to reflect the time of travel, and from the more modern and territorialized maps in which the nation is conceptualized as a bounded entity made up of commensurable units of abstract space.[10]

9. Frank Reynolds, "Sacral Kingship and National Development: The Case of Thailand," in *Religion and Legitimation of Power in Thailand, Laos, and Burma*, ed. Bardwell Smith (Chambersburg, PA: Anima, 1978), 194.

10. Thongchai Winichakul, *Siam Mapped: A History of the Geo-Body of a Nation* (Honolulu:

The mapping of the murals, and of mediumship, is perhaps congruent with the logic of the radial polity in that it presumes a notion of distance that is experiential, a function of time traveled, and of the influence that can be exercised from one point to the other. It is certainly at odds with the logic of geography's territory and its measure of abstract and interchangeable units of ideal space (square acres, hectares, kilometers, miles, and *naa*).[11] For a map to evoke the space of travel, it must ultimately be construed as the space of experience—of walking, or practiced space, as Certeau would say—and not merely its representation. It must provoke the imagination to retrace prior activity and thereby to localize memories,[12] without, at the same time, reifying the sites of localized memory. Of course, narratives of travel do not have to be visually spatialized. They can remain at the level of language. Thus, the mapping of experience may take the form of stories about that space: stories that ask the listener to move across and through the landscape, stories that can be enacted, stories whose telling is prompted by objects and the images of objects (like *stupas* and spirit houses, or Phayaphrom's tobacco) that emerge from the very earth traversed by the tale. As Caopuu Phayaphrom says, one lives in different cities in different times because "Each era has its place."

But if, for spirit mediums, Chiang Mai of the present is the destination of time travel, then the present is also the space of an increasingly dense existence. In Chiang Mai, many hundreds of spirits now preside over the minute *müangs* that are symbolically materialized in the shrines of their mounts. In fact, the proliferation of *müangs* and the recent explosion of mediumship is homologous with the history of modernity as many people now understand it. The movement forward in time is said to run alongside the involution and crowding of cities, the massification of the marketplace, and the sense of hastening of daily existence. It is, in fact, the era of time's disappearance, in which people constantly remark that they "have no time" (*maj mii welaa*) and that tasks (*thura'*) occupy all their hours. Every medium I met spoke about this sense of time's crowding, and of its awful counterpart in the increasing numbers of bad deaths (*phii taaj hong*). The cycle is vicious, for bad deaths interrupt the possibility of higher rebirth and leave Chiang Mai vulnerable to precisely that strangulation by (represencing) beings that had so threatened Naang Itthang

University of Hawaii Press, 1994). Victor Kennedy, "An Indigenous Early Nineteenth Century Map of Central and Northeast Thailand," in *In Memoriam, Phya Anuman Rajadhon*, ed. Tej Bunnag and Michael Smithies (Bangkok: Siam Society, 1970).

11. On the discourse of geography, see Michel Foucault, "Questions on Geography," in *Power/ Knowledge: Selected Interviews and Other Writings, 1972–1977*, ed. Colin Gordon (New York: Pantheon, 1980), 63–77; also Thongchai, *Siam Mapped*, esp. 113–27.

12. Gaston Bachelard, *The Poetics of Space*, trans. Maria Jolas (Boston: Beacon, 1964), 8, 175.

Gaiya Sangkasi. This is because the *müang*, and especially its center, is understood as the destination of movement rather than the space of its occurrence.[13]

Mediumship is not the only discourse to imagine Chiang Mai as the center and the object of movement and power. There is also a specifically northern Thai system of pilgrimage sites associated with the year of one's birth in a duodenary cycle that reflects a similar logic. The sites, which are actually reliquaries, "together constitute a plotting in space of a sacred or ritual topography."[14] Ideally, pilgrims travel to these places to make merit by leaving offerings at the reliquary, although today few know of the routes, never mind travel them. Eleven of the sites are on earth; the other is in heaven (though it has an earthly stand-in). Arranging these sites on a map of South and Southeast Asia, Charles Keyes points out that more of them are within the Chiang Mai valley than anywhere else, and that the vast majority are in northern Thailand (the others being in Laos, Cambodia, Burma, and India). Swearer adds that the majority of the reliquaries were "seats of power in Northern Thailand," and he thereby infuses the idea of pilgrimage with that of geopolitical order.[15] One way to read this transnational, or rather, prenational sphere of pilgrimage destinations is as a means of "promoting a community that transcends the fragmentation of the principalities."[16] But the journeys that constitute the webbing in which destinations are bound remain singular, and there is no reason to believe that an abstract spatial domain was imagined to stretch between them. Indeed, if Thongchai Winichakul is correct in his interpretations of geography's history in Thailand, it is likely that the points were conceived as precisely that, nodes of social, political, and religious activity between which stretched an undifferentiated space of wild antisociality. Only the *Nirat Dyan Müang Nüa* (Journey through the months of the northern Thai calendar), Singkha Wannasi's nostalgic narrative poem describing a journey to all sites (including heaven), attains the totalized perspective within which the twelve reliquaries become part of a whole. Moreover, in the poem, it is time rather than space that constitutes the encompassing structure.

The implications of this fact are of singular importance to an understanding

13. It is to Nancy Munn that I owe this understanding of centralized space as terminal space. See her essay "Excluded Spaces: The Figure in Australian Aboriginal Landscape," *Critical Inquiry* 22, no. 3 (1996), 446–65.

14. Charles F. Keyes, "Buddhist Pilgrimage Centers and the Twelve Year Cycle: Northern Thai Moral Orders in Space and Time," *History of Religions* 5, no. 1 (1975): 85.

15. Donald K. Swearer, "The Northern Thai City as Sacred Center," in *The City as a Sacred Center: Essays on Six Asian Contexts*, ed. Bardwell L. Smith and Holly Baker Reynolds (Leiden: E. J. Brill, 1987), 111. Also Keyes, "Buddhist Pilgrimage Centers."

16. Keyes, "Buddhist Pilgrimage Centers," 86.

of the historical consciousness that now dominates Chiang Mai, but the differences between the kinds of spatial and temporal relation that once characterized mediumship and those that now enjoy hegemony in Chiang Mai's cultural imaginary are profound. What I hope to achieve in the present chapter is a comparative sketch of these different timespaces, one that explains how it is that a discourse of presencing in which time constitutes the primary organizing principle can be displaced by one structured by spatial logics. This pattern is a familiar one, of course, and much has already been written about the dehistoricization and the concomitant spatialization of the world under late capitalism.[17] Yet, the narrative of late capitalism's transformations is often presented too simplistically. What becomes apparent in the historical ethnography of northern Thai spirit mediumship is the ironic and seemingly contradictory dimensions to these changes. For it is not simply that the cosmological world submits space to time, or even that it assumes the primacy of locality when compared to a modernity wherein time is subsumed by a global space that has expunged the local. More complicated than that, a cosmological orientation permits practices in which presencing (in possession and other kinds of hauntings) is assumed to be possible. Thus, the world dominated by time is also one in which time can be absolutely transcended.

The relation among cosmological times is no more stable than that among places. Thus, cosmology's world is not a historical world, if by historical we mean to imply a representational consciousness of historical progression. And this is precisely the point. History is a representational discourse, and it is premised on the absolutely irremediable difference among moments. Disciplined by the logics of the clock, history is emplotted on the racinated line of commensurated time. History eschews simultaneity. The profanity of its line is potent enough to banish ghosts and spirits and all those specters who testify to the folding and the possible multiplicity of time (though it is doubtful that any society has ever come completely under its sway). There is, therefore, a difference between the spirit mediumship that is thought to have magical efficacy, that is felt to be real, and the mediumship that functions as a representation of authentic northern Thai practices, as a sign of history. In the latter case, rituals are enframed as symptoms of the past and as the objects of visual consumption. It would be fair to say that this perspective now dominates the cultural imaginary of elite Chiang Mai. Ironically enough, it has stimulated a florescence in mediumship that has, in turn, fueled a psychic and cultural reinvestment in the

17. Fredric Jameson, "Postmodernism, or the Cultural Logic of Late Capitalism," *New Left Review* no. 146 (1984): 59–92; David Harvey, *The Condition of Postmodernity: An Enquiry into the Origins of Cultural Change* (Oxford: Oxford University Press, 1989).

possibility of magical represencing on the part of those who, like their contemporaries in other parts of Asia, Africa, and North America, are seeking magic rather than visual pleasure in the modern. In northern Thailand, at least, historical discourse produces its others not merely as antecedent, but as the risk of a recurrence.

The very tokens of disappearance—monuments and plaques, commemorative performances and theatrical reenactments—can become the instruments of revival for those who believe (*chya*), although it will become apparent that even mediums now observe the disciplinary principle of sequentiality. One understands the differences between these kinds of mediumship by the kinds of questions that people ask of them. The demand to know what something signifies, rather than the demand to know how it works, marks the modern—and expels haunting.

## Substitution and Inheritance

The incitements of ritual's discourse are to be found in the increasing arrivals of spirits at the *khan* dishes of mediums. This much has already been stated, and the *khan* dish itself has already been described as a kind of key, a device for opening that space into which the dead can enter following their long journeys through time and space, and the space of time. So too has the risk of that opening been addressed. The figures of the *kathoey* and the Meo shaman may provide representational instruments for containing radical difference, but they are certainly not the only ones. If, as I have attempted to demonstrate, the Praise Ceremony marks the entry of the medium into the ritual community and if that entrance corresponds to the new medium's own disciplining of possession's chaotic potential, then the rite itself is conceivable as a "dramaturgy of disavowal," to use David Levin's evocative term.[18] Possession opens up and represents the opening up of a space in the world that language has made (and that it makes through such spacing). More than that, it thematizes the vulnerability of meaning, the possibility that it could be swallowed up by that space, as indeed is threatened every time death comes to consume the lives of the living, robbing families of children and lovers of their others. It does so in a variety of ways and in a range of idioms: architectural, representational, sexual, and national. It would be wrong, however, to imagine the Praise Ceremony as a moment of structural apotheosis. For, though the pedagogy of the Praise Ceremony acts to insert the medium and his or her volatile body into a hierarchy of patriarchal order (and this even in matrilineal contexts), it also marks the

---

18. David J. Levin, *The Dramaturgy of Disavowal: Richard Wagner, Fritz Lang, and the Nibelungen* (Princeton, NJ: Princeton University Press, 1998).

beginning of a career in which spirits will both proliferate and accumulate. In fact, it places the medium in relation to what might be called a manifold inheritance. Moreover, it is in the face of this manifold inheritance that mediums are most emphatically subjected, most completely aligned with the forces of Buddhist order, most likely to construe their choice as the response to a commandment.

Mediums acquire spirits over time, eventually being possessed by several discrete characters, most of whom are associated with a distinct epoch and a particular geographical site of origin. They are frequently of different generational status, and it is generally the case that all mediums are eventually commanded by a repertoire of spirits who inhabit all statuses and represent several geopolitical territories. Thus does the medium become the site of a nation forged through encompassment. The spirits who finally compose the miniature pantheon of one medium are all integrated with each other in an overarching hierarchy and with the spirits of other mediums in relation to whom they are also relatively positioned.

Praise Ceremonies often are understood by anthropologists in a functional idiom, as occasions that "establish the institution as a public, culturally sanctioned one, rather than some vaguely illicit, private practice."[19] Andrew Turton has made the most ambitious assessment of the northern Thai ceremonial system in his claim that it facilitates the coalescence of an "order of authority." He describes this order as a "supra-territorial organization" centered around cults of Cao Luang Kham Daeng, and he claims that such cults have been widely distributed throughout northern Thailand.[20] Wijeyewardene is far more circumspect on the issue, saying at once that he cannot discern the order of authority, but that, if there is one, it may not be that of the nested *müang*.[21] At present, these rites seem to have little significance beyond Chiang Mai, but a supraterritorial organization is indeed fantasized by mediums and permits the elaboration of a historically manifold order within and between Chiang Mai and the surrounding suburbs and towns. The multiplicity of spirits and the diversity of locations within which spiritual power is to be found are somehow knit together at the rites by a delirium of both overt and implicitly mythic narration in which stories of origin are made to encompass and overcome the breach that is threatened by competition between cults.

My first encounter with this multiplicity occurred on that first day of my

19. Gehan Wijeyewardene, *Place and Emotion in Northern Thai Ritual Behavior* (Bangkok: Pandora, 1986), 223.

20. Andrew Turton, "Matrilineal Descent Groups and Spirits Cults of the Thai Yuan in Northern Thailand," *Journal of the Siam Society* 60, no. 2 (1972): 217–56.

21. Wijeyewardene, *Place and Emotion*, 225–26.

meeting with Naang Khao. After Phayaphrom had vacated her body, the medium's head fell forward and her friend remarked quietly and nonchalantly that Caopuu had left (*ork pai*). Shortly thereafter, Naang Khao began to speak in an astonishingly different voice. She disrobed and drew from the glass cabinet a brilliant cobalt suit, which she pulled on, like the earlier white suit, over everyday clothes. With the voice of a child now speaking firmly, it became apparent that the medium had been taken over by the rambunctious and petulant spirit of a young boy. He soon identified himself, simply, as *kumaannooj*, a generic name for a youngster. As I would soon learn, Kumaannooj's high and nasal prepubescent pitch is typical of infantile spirits, all of whom are marked in this manner. Also like others, the child who regularly returns to Naang Khao is undisciplined and obnoxiously flirtatious. He adores cameras and gawdily brilliant colors, brassy sound, and indeed everything that seems at odds with the decorous regality of monarchical image. His penchant for Western things, especially Western women, simply amplifies a gluttonous fascination with the Other of northern Thai aristocracy as it is currently imagined to have been.

In general, spiritual personae are recognizable through styles of dress, qualities of voice, and specialties of spiritual power. Senior spirits are generally those of individuals who were the founders of principalities or polities, and occasionally the warrior heroes or saints of popular Buddhism. Some decades ago, these spirits tended to be specifically local characters, often associated with particular sites and events in the northern landscape. Such figures continue to enjoy popularity in Chiang Mai, but now they also compete with other kinds of spirits, especially those who have been assigned heroic roles in the emergence of the Thai state. Northern spirits of special renown are those of Cao Luang Kham Daeng, Queen Camadevi, and King Mengrai. Among the spirits associated with a more properly Siamese and indeed Thai national history are King Narasuan, King Ramkhamhaeng, King Taksin, and, most popular of them all, Rama V.[22] Some of these last are said to be under the tutelary leadership of Mokkhalaan, the Buddha's acolyte. Yet another category of possessing spirits, of more recent vintage, includes more anonymous figures of foreign nationality, often from India (but also from Iraq and Egypt). Recently, even Hindu deities such as Siva have appeared in the bodies of local mediums (see chapter 9). And on the periphery of Chiang Mai's spiritual imaginary, but deeply influenced by it, the spirits of ethnic culture heroes have recently appeared among the minority groups displaced from Burma into northern Thailand.

---

22. On the cult of King Chulalongkorn, see Nithi Aeusriwongse, "Latthipetthii Sadet Phor Rama V" [Beliefs and rituals regarding the Royal Father, King Rama V], *Silapa Wattnanatham* [Arts and Culture] 14, no. 10 (1993): 78–102.

Naang Khao's spirits are not among these towering figures of either the Lanna or the Thai cultural imaginary. But like all mediums, her spirits are of three orders: *caopuu*, or grandfather spirits at the highest level of the hierarchy; *caophor* (sometimes called *caophii*) or father spirits at the second level; and child spirits at the bottom. The logic of authority is explicitly generational, but it also echoes the political structure of the old northern states more directly. Up until the early twentieth century, northern Thai government bureaucracy was organized in three tiers. At the top were the *cao khan*, consisting of the *cao luang* or "lord of life" and the other members of the preeminent ruling family, including the *cao ratchawon, cao ratchabut*, and the *cao hor müang kaeo*. Next were the *khao sanaam luang* or state council, made up of thirty-two men from lesser aristocratic families but still retaining the tile *cao*. Finally, there were the village leaders.[23] Although very few, if any, mediums can elaborate the particulars of the northern bureaucracy, either in the past or in the present, virtually all possessing personae claim that they are members of a political universe that is pre-Siamese, and many make reference to the reign of Kawila (1781–1813) in their effort to explicate the relationships that define their participation in the community of mediums. Kawila's reign was the first in the new House of Chiang Mai following the expulsion of the Burmese in 1774, and it is always represented as the restoration of Chiang Mai. Some mediums do refer to the time before Burmese occupation, citing the reigns of Saen Müangma (1385–1401) or Phra Müang Kaeo (1495–1526), the period generally identified as the Golden Era of northern Thailand. In this way, they suggest an impossible tradition of Lanna culture, one that somehow withstood the violent expulsions of citizens and the inundations of foreigners. The detail of chronology, however, is not matched by a detail of political knowledge, and inevitably, a reduction and a flattening takes place in the efforts to describe the political economy of spirits. It is the order of three that seems most salient and that is anachronistically retrojected so that all of antiquity appears under the principle of a transcendent generational hierarchy. That hierarchy finds itself expressed not only in the generationally named levels of spiritual authority, but also in the timbre of the spirits' voices. Thus, *caopuu* have deep but often tremulous voices; *caophor* usually speak in powerful masculine voices; and the words of child spirits are both squeaky and inelegant.[24]

23. Ratanaporn, "Political, Social, and Economic Changes," 17–20.

24. Walter Irvine provides similar accounts of stereotyped status within the spectrum of possessing spirits. See "The Thai-Yuan 'Madman,' and the Modernizing, Developing Thai Nation as Bounded Entities under Threat: A Study in the Replication of a Single Image" (Ph.D. diss., University of London, 1982), 253–56.

Despite this multiplicity of hierarchically ordered spirits, mediums claim a highly personalized relationship with those who possess them, one that traverses the eras and reigns between the living and the point of origin from which the spirit supposedly comes. Such intimacy seems, at first sight, to contradict the threatening randomness of possession as well as the claims to naïve inspiration that mediums so frequently make. The story is a complicated one, however, and like the matter of sexual identification, the question of distinguishing among spirits opens onto a fraught scene of substitution, spacing, and originary instability. Nowhere is this more poignantly narrated than in the stories of nurturance by wet nurses.

When Caopuu Phayaphrom explained to me his choice of Naang Khao for a vehicle, he spoke with sympathy and generosity about a woman who had given him suck as an infant and shared her life's substance so that he would grow up a man. The kinship that they shared was not one of the matriline, but it enacted an alternative kind of affinity, one symbolic of the structural roles that women are asked to play in Thai Theravada Buddhist society.[25] Milk, rather than blood, instantiates an economic kinship in a context where feeding is a vehicle of continuity, remembrance, and social definition for women. The ideological naturalization of women's prescribed roles, this rhetoric of feeding transforms filiation into affiliation. It is described in the *Traiphum Phra Ruang* as the natural ground of society itself: "It is normal for people in this world, for the Boddhisattas, and for the animals, that once the newborn baby has left its mother's womb, her love causes the blood in her breasts to become milk, and to flow out from her breasts so that the child can suck it and be nourished. This is a characteristic of living beings."[26] One cannot help but observe that the representation of maternity's social dimensions is drawn, in both the *Traiphum Phra Ruang* and in less literary stories of the same origin, as the transformation of blood, the substance of generation, into milk, the substance of nurturance. The natural becomes social in a manner that is itself tellingly naturalized. Yet, the milk of the wet nurse is different. Her milk is not the transformation of that blood that has become the child she suckles. It has its origins elsewhere, in another birth, and in an excessive or at least residual productivity. Indeed, her breast is symbolically rent from the body in which a womb would have constituted purer beginnings.

---

25. Penny van Esterik, *Nurturance and Reciprocity in Thai Studies: A Tribute to Lucien and Jane Hanks* (Toronto: York University Thai Studies Project/Women in Development Consortium in Thailand, Working Paper no. 8, 1982).

26. Frank E. Reynolds and Mani B. Reynolds, *Three Worlds According to King Ruang: A Thai Buddhist Cosmology* (Berkeley: University of California Press, 1982), 122.

For all its evocations of maternal devotion and useful sacrifice, then, the substitutional logic of the wet nurse reiterates that other lesson of the *Pathamamūlamūlī* and of so much of mediumship's narrative: that alterity lurks in the place of origins. Not blood, not descent, not identity, but substitution and thus spacing. However, just as sexual excess is contained through thematization in the myth and in everyday discourse, so the risk of the many—which always threatens simultaneity—is disciplined in sequentiality. Thus, at the annual Praise Ceremony for Queen Camadevi in Haripunchai, when up to twenty of her mediums gather in the same place, her spirit is said to pass from one medium to the other in rapid succession. Mediums go in and out of trance accordingly, attiring themselves and stripping off their costumes as is required by her descent and departure. In this process, Camadevi's presence is sustained as a coherent principle of both unity and origin. And the line of time, which is also the basis of inheritance, is preserved. From one medium to the next, and from one generation to the next.

### Gift and Commandment: The Law of Debt

It is, in fact, the principle of this passing between generations that the Praise Ceremony serves. And it is the evasion of simultaneous claims to power that is effected in the giving of the dish and in the submission to teachers that is performed in its acceptance. The explanatory efforts by which mediums maintain their adherence to principles of priority and sequentiality, and therefore of descent, are not especially surprising in the context of broader social and ideological forces. Many ethnographers have remarked the aversion to simultaneity and equivalence as a deep and powerful force in the organization of society in both northern and central Thailand. One frequently hears of twin births in which one child is positioned as the elder and the other as the younger (seconds being adequate measures of seniority), and of social exchanges in which the relative status of each party is vigorously marked with kin-based pronominal terms such as *phii* and *norng* (meaning older and younger sibling) or bodily gestures of deference and condescension. Liberal democratic politics are quite clearly in tension with this tendency, and overt discussions of that antagonism inform a vocal debate about how new political forms and civil arrangements can be effected in a milieu where the residue of hierarchy is so deeply and even unconsciously felt. Needless to say, possession performances are not frequently the venue for such conversations, although, as chapter 7 demonstrates, even spirit possession has been rendered effective in democratic political arenas by having been rendered as ritual and as a sign of the traditional.

The dish that a medium gets at the Praise Ceremony is both the instrument of a hierarchization and a point of conversion between realms. Spirits descend there, and food, money, or mass-produced commodities are placed on the dish for the spirit's consumption. The money that clients and mediums offer to the spirits, however, is not referred to in that language, not as *ngeun* (money) or baht but as *suai* or tribute. In this it attempts to escape the general economy and become a gift. The standardization of offerings (most mediums required twelve baht in 1992) is independent of the kind of advice or the spirit being sought by a client, and thus the money is not thought to constitute an exchange. It does not pretend to evaluate and commensurate the spirit's act but simply remarks the presence of the spirit. Indeed, it rejects such a commensuration, and whenever I have asked mediums whether clients paid for their services, or suggested that the spirits were themselves indebted to the mediums (for having been nursed in previous lives, for example), I was flatly rebuffed. In this manner, mediums and their clients insist on the voluntariness of the offering and deny their own encompassment by the logic of commoditization even as the standardization of the "fee" mocks the denial of economization.

Marcel Mauss knew that the opposition between gift and economy is a tenuous one,[27] and the purity of the forgetting that would be required to render a gift as such remains an ideal that the offerings and the Praise Ceremony approach but inadequately. The fetish of the dish in the Praise Ceremony only obscures, momentarily, what is the profound violence of the patrimonial bequest. What it cannot hide in the dish, however, it conceals through the secreting of invitations.

Normally, a Praise Ceremony is jointly hosted by the spirits, the medium, and her assistants. Invitations for the event are printed on empty envelopes that always list the hosts in order of seniority, from the highest *cao* to the merely mortal attendants. Such invitations are not unique to spiritual beings or sacral occasions, but are also used for weddings, funerals, and other more mundane events. In the case of Praise Ceremonies, they always read as follows: Caopuu so-and-so, Caopho so-and-so, caonooy so-and-so (with as many titles as necessary for a given medium) are pleased to invite all the *cao*s, the mediums, the *luuk sit*, and anyone else who wishes to pay tribute to attend a *phithii jok khruu*. The date, time, and location are then given and directions provided.

These invitations are secretly printed by the medium's assistants, who not only attempt discretion for the sake of their medium but who also pretend to the miraculous appearance of the envelopes. They are distributed throughout

27. Marcel Mauss, *The Gift: Forms and Functions of Exchange in Archaic Societies* (1925), trans. Ian Cunnison (London: Routledge and Kegan Paul, 1966).

the season of Praise Ceremonies and normally at the events themselves, although they are sometimes ferried between the homes of mediums by their assistants at hours that are likely to conceal the fact. The clandestine quality of such deliveries is hard to overstate. More than any other aspect of professional mediumship, this one seems to demand the elaborate measures of concealment and indirection that produce invisibility. It is a public secret, of course, made ironic by the fact that the rites are the most publicly visible moments in the calendars of mediums. And it is made even more ironic by the fact that the envelopes will be returned publicly, when they are used for offerings that will be laid on the spirit's dish.

Perhaps because it entails the implicit demand for offerings, thereby violating the principle of the merit-producing (because unremarked) gift, mediums are enormously circumspect about discussing the organizational business of the Praise Ceremony. Were it to become apparent that invitations to the ceremonies were actually demands for tributary offering, were the gift to be recognized as payment toward an insatiable debt owed by all junior spirits to their tutelary overlords, the entire edifice of tribute-as-merit-production would fall into ruinous hypocrisy. Such structural principles, however, are not addressed overtly by spirits, who insist only that the secreting of planning activities is necessary to ensure that only believers are permitted entrance and that no spirit is exposed to the insult of ridiculing disbelief.

Though part of an elaborate, if ultimately unconvincing, deception, the point of the envelopes is not to enclose another inscription. Ironically, the form of its secrecy is one of display, and the bold print on the outside of the envelope makes this fact abundantly clear. In the first place, the envelope seems merely to act as an invitation. When it is returned by its recipient, however, it disappears into the instrumentality for which it was intended: as the bearer of money. Nor should we overlook the fact that the envelope is a historical artifact, one that bears testimony to the emergence of a kind of discourse, the technologized letter, which occupies that strange zone between public and private as an intimacy exchanged from afar. As Phayaphrom's epistolary poetry made clear, that letter differed from the messages that kings and their messengers once delivered to one another in that it imagined itself being circulated in public, passed anonymously through other hands and voices, and overheard by virtue of its personalized address rather than its material receipt. It would be too ambitious to speculate here on the relationship between letter writing and the politics of the public secret, but it is possible to observe the extent to which the Praise Ceremony shares in this logic of a publicity that is nothing but the assertion of private knowledge and intimate relation, to which only initiates have access.

When mediums arrive at Praise Ceremonies, they place the baht-filled envelope on red lacquer or silver *khan* dishes, ostensibly purifying the money in the process of giving it over to the tutelary spirits. Though it is usually the hosting spirit who receives such offerings, it falls to the attendants to gather the cash and keep careful records of the donations. For this purpose, they use elaborate columnar registers that, like Caopuu Phayaphrom's notebooks, bespeak both the rationalizing logic of commensuration and a fetishism of the documentary record. Given the care with which the amounts are observed and noted, one imagines that reputations are made and broken at such occasions, and even that there may be sanctions for failure to give appropriately. The sanctions, to the extent that they exist, are ambiguously public judgments and generally take the form of gossip. The purveyors of that loud but mercurial damnation are, in fact, mainly the attendants themselves. However, the renown that accrues to a giver is not produced in Praise Ceremonies, but at *thord phaa paa* rites at Buddhist wats, where mediums give to monks and are thereby seen to be sacrificing, through expenditure, what they have earned in their professional practice.

At *thord phaa paa* rites, powerful *caos* and their assistants organize and then preside over lavish contributions to poor temples and monasteries. On these occasions, other *caos* are invited to witness the generosity of their peers but also to contribute to the donations the senior *caos* are making. The origin of the rite is the giving of robes to monks, but the *thord phaa paa* of mediums is modeled on the extravagant gestures of donation that the king and his royal entourage make each year to the *sangha*.[28] The witnessing of the gift is, in truth, a threat to its merit-producing function, and thus mediums construe the invitation to other *caos* not as a mode of self-display but as the provision of an opportunity to make merit. In this way, they appropriate for themselves the function of the *sangha* as a field of merit, while using the *sangha* as the occasion for their own sacrificial offering. This may indeed be the point at which mediums are most overtly threatening to the *sangha*, the moment at which imitation threatens to displace its referent. Accordingly, monks at the recipient monasteries accept mediums' donations as they must, but with frequent grumbling and vehemently displayed disinterest. However, their contempt is, in my opinion, never as pronounced as on those occasions when they themselves become the recipient of a generosity that pretends to disinterest.

Once, in 1992, I joined a group of mediums whom Khun Singh and the medium of King Ramkhamhaeng had invited to a *thord phaa paa*. In two

28. See the excellent account of these rites and their relationship to monarchical politics in Christine E. Gray, "Thailand: The Soteriological State in the 1970s" (Ph.D. diss., University of Chicago, 1986).

school buses rented for the occasion, the brightly clad, bespectacled mediums and I drove for nearly three hours to a small monastery north of Chiang Mai. At the time, it seemed to be an occasion of utterly Rabelaisian abandon. The mediums smoked, ate noisily, and chatted loudly, climbing over the seats like the schoolchildren who used the bus on other days of the week, gossiping maliciously, and teasing each other about sexual preferences and desires. They stopped at the roadside and squatted to relieve themselves after drinking too much Coke, and they never once mentioned the purpose of our long hot drive through the rice fields and the condominium communities that interrupted them. However, when Khun Singh opened the door to the bus and the mediums descended, it was not as a riot of color and obscene chatter that they descended but as an entourage, orderly and abjectly submissive before King Ramkhamhaeng's spirit as he descended into Khun Singh's wife. Although some of the many tens of thousands of baht being given to the monks had come from the minor *caos* present, it was the spirit of Ramkhamhaeng who appeared there as the giver. Gloriously elevated by the magnanimity of his gesture, his renown was only enhanced by the loss that such giving demanded. He became one whose name "sounds" (*mii siang*). In verily feudal fashion, he partook of the wealth that his fame had attracted, while acting the patron of those whom he had tutored and introduced to the dish on which they received their own offerings. Nor is the idea of entourage inappropriate. All the mediums who made the trip in Caopuu Ramkhamhaeng's and Khun Singh's protective custody were members of a lineage produced under the distant authority of Mokkhalaan at the Praise Ceremonies that Khun Singh had arranged for his wife's spectacular spirit. Caopuu Ramkhamhaeng had given them their respective dishes and blessed their entry into the profession after adjudicating the authenticity of their claims to possession. The debt that obliged the mediums to give was indeed produced at the Praise Ceremonies where they received their dish.

The spirit comes down (*long maa*) for the one who holds the dish, and arrives from the past as a force that must be obeyed. So profound is the obedience to this spirit that the medium is seen by it but remains blind herself. In this sense, the possessing spirit resembles the very principle of inheritance by which individuals are made subject to law. In mediumship, as in Shakespeare's *Hamlet*, that law manifests itself as a voice.[29] If for no other reason than this, mediumship would have to entail the fetishization of vocal primacy that writing makes possible. Perhaps the most acute instance of that fetishization appears in the rumors mediums tell of a spirit in central Thailand who needs no body. This spirit is said to speak miraculously from the middle of a room,

29. Jacques Derrida, *Specters of Marx* (1993), trans. Peggy Kamuf (New York: Routledge, 1994), 7.

audible to all but independent of clothing and material signs. No one I ever met had actually been present when the disembodied voice spoke, and no one could even specify the spirit who was supposedly speaking in this manner. Yet the force of that idea was as potent as the light from the Buddha's own eye. The rumor itself replicated the logic of the disembodied voice, being transmitted invisibly from one medium to another in whispered tales of miraculous sound, one that "sounded," in the sense of being famous. Nonetheless, the legibility of the voice, its location in the middle of the room, betrayed the thrilling possibility of its pure vocality. It had a place, and in this placement, this localization, it had become legible to listeners.

The legibility of the mysteriously disembodied voice made it capable of eliciting oaths or pledges. In this, it was like any other spirit whose aid is sought by individuals and whose blessing is solicited by means of a promise of an offering (*kae bon*). All spirits can command such oaths, and it is the secret demand for such an oath that is signaled by the envelope. The demand, hiding in the gift, makes the relationship between spirits and human beings one of force and propels it in time in the guise of an inheritance. And what an inheritance. The student must give to his or her teacher, the child must give to his or her parent. Spirits are as bound by this law as are humans; indeed, it is their existential lack or demerit, their state of debt, that makes them return to the world of mere mortals.

Possessed mediums always explain the fact of possession in terms of this complex and ultimately impossible economy. Spirits who possess are but one form of spirit in a highly differentiated spectrum, but like other spectral beings who return to haunt the material plane of human existence, they are said to be in need of merit. Indeed, they come back to the future because they have committed sins in previous lives. And they acquire merit by helping mortals who are mired in a world of sensuous distractions: tempted by evil, afflicted by disease, beholden to money, and availed of opportunity. Ideologically, merit is a function of deeds, the accrued value of acts that an individual commits during his or her life. Those acts that are valorized according to the precepts of Buddhism generate merit; those that are violations of the precepts cause demerit. As Charles Keyes explains, merit is the variable that explains the distinction between *kam* (destiny) and *chataa* (fate). *Kam* is transcendent. It is given at birth and encompasses all of the lifetimes a being may be forced to inhabit before escaping the constraints of existence altogether. *Chataa*, on the other hand, is a function of one's deeds and, unlike *kam*, can be changed within a single lifetime and even extended through ritual action. Mediums generically claim that both inadequate merit and accumulated demerit can strand a being in the netherworld between incarnations and make him or her dependent on the sacrificial giving of humans or on ghostly acts that are themselves meritorious.

When I questioned mediums about the reasons for such a poor reconciliation of merit and demerit on the part of possessing spirits, spirits that were, after all, reputed to have once been great leaders, I was told that the life of a prince is necessarily soaked in blood. The man or, more rarely, woman who founds a city, who defeats an enemy in war, who defends his or her territory against intruders, and who conquers other lands to capture slaves to repopulate a reclaimed principality must inevitably shed the blood of others, must kill or be killed. But the paradox of such foundational narratives is that the one who commits such violent deeds is the founder of an order in which these same acts will become sinful. In the stories mediums tell of their possessing warrior-princes, the one who establishes the city and the law does so through an act of violence, and then acquires the mantle of the properly Buddhist king by prohibiting violence. The violence of the founder seems to come before the law while making law as such possible. However, because the law then claims to be universal, the founder becomes retroactively subject to it.[30] Thus subject, he must seek merit or suffer an eternity in the impossible space between realms, where he can have no firm residence, no proper place.

## The Order of Appearance

One could read this secretly violent economy of debt and repayment as a mark of the premodern. Inheritance, the virtue of submission to teachers, the beauty of military power, sovereign performativity: all these values reign here and seem, on the surface, to betoken a direct and unbroken chain of cultural transmission from the time of the caos. As Phayaphrom's poem makes clear, that time was already split, but this is not how most mediums perceive the matter. The personalized power that is enacted in the Praise Ceremony and extolled by mediums is one that speaks the law and is the law, that adjudicates crime and metes out punishment without reference to a standardized penal code. How, then, is this aspiration for pure, personal power reconcilable with the logic of returns and the servitude to kam that the spirits confess? Is it simply a question of the spirits having failed to make merit sufficiently to compensate for their evils? Are they merely inadequate kings by Aśokan standards? Are the spirits who descend in mediumship "thugs" (naaklaeng), as one monk put it to me? Or is there something else at work here, a sense that the caos of northern Thailand have themselves been subjected to law and subjugated by a law that came from without, instituted by a power greater than theirs? Perhaps the stories that spirits tell of their arrival in the present also have secreted within themselves this other possibility, this haunting story of an encompassment by

30. See ibid., 31.

Siam in the forging of a nation for which Chiang Mai, the jewel of Rama V's crown, was once "the past" and "another country."

The *caos* of Chiang Mai lost their power to act as both judges and executors of justice only after the first decade of this century. In fact, they had combined in their person functions that had been separate in both Indian and Siamese legal systems, where the interpretation of the *dhamma* and the implementation of or enforcement of those interpretations had been split between Brahmanic and royal persons, respectively.[31] In the adjudication of legal contests, there were four modes of procedure: "ordeal and oath, witchcraft proceedings, mediation by elders or persons of high status, and formal judicial proceedings conducted by local political rules."[32] When Siam began to consolidate its hold on the area, it not only attempted to force the *caos* to recognize the separation between interpretive and executive functions, as had been the case in Bangkok, but it brought an entirely new organization of the legal and criminal system to bear. Indeed, the transformations in Siamese justice were partly motivated by a need to establish Siamese jurisdiction in contexts where extraterritorial rights had been exercised by the English and French as well as other foreign governments through a system of international courts at which consular representation could ensure that ex-patriots were tried under their own rather than Siamese law. It was indeed in Chiang Mai, as much as any other place, that modern law was initially systematically implemented.

That law, however, was conceived elsewhere, in the interfacing relationship between Bangkok and Europe. King Rama V had hired Belgian legal advisors to assist him in reconceptualizing and restructuring the legal system in Thailand as part of a general project of modernization. Belgium's neutrality made her lawyers invaluable assets for Rama V, who was struggling to prevent the French and English dispute from turning into a war that would lead to Siam's annexation by either colonial power. Rama V chose a Benthamite and legal comparativist named Gustave Rolin-Jaequemyns to aid him in his task, and brought to Bangkok a man whose priorities were liberal in the conservative English sense of the word: the abolition of slavery, the liberty of establishment, a rationalized relationship between crime and punishment, the decriminalization of usury and the termination of monopolies, a free exchange rate between gold and national currencies, and the right to form associations.[33] Rolin-Jaequemyns

---

31. David M. Engel, *Code and Custom in a Thai Provincial Town: The Interaction of Formal and Informal Systems of Justice* (Tucson: University of Arizona Press, 1978), 23.

32. Ibid., 20. See 20–22 for a discussion of how these methods differed and on what assumptions they operated.

33. Walter E. J. Tips, *Gustave Rolin-Jaequemyns and the Making of Modern Siam: The Diaries and Letters of King Chulalongkorn's General Advisor* (Bangkok: White Lotus, 1996), 18–19.

arrived in Siam in 1892, the same year in which the new Ministry of Justice was formed. In 1893, the first Law of Evidence was approved, and within two years, a new systems of courts, consisting of two magistrate's courts, (the Borispah), a central Criminal Court, an International Court, a Court of Appeal, and a Supreme Court of Appeal, all of which were to be brought under the authority of the Ministry of Justice, was transferred there from the Ministry of the Interior under Prince Damrong.[34] In 1895, with Prince Phichit and Prince Nares, who were respectively in charge of justice and the police, Rolin-Jaequemyns began a review of the criminal justice system, using English colonial law in Singapore and India as guide.[35] The job was slow, beginning with an inspection of the prisons and a review of all pending cases for which individuals were being held. This, it was thought, would permit the commission to determine the priorities of Siamese justice and also the sources of inequity in the system, of which, it seemed, there were many. In 1902, a British official named J. G. D. Campbell recalled that, not long before Rolin-Jaequemyns began his work, dozens if not hundreds of prisoners had been waiting years for trial, sometimes incarcerated with the plaintiffs and other witnesses whom the judges feared would flee rather than testify.[36]

Only two weeks after the establishment of the commission in Bangkok, a decree was passed to initiate an inquiry into the administration of justice in the provincial courts, the point being to determine how these courts were in fact operating and how they might be reformed to bring them into line with the objectives of Rama V's program of judicial modernization. The date was 21 October 1896. And to this end, Robert Kirkpatrick, another European advisor, and Prince Rabi Bhatasakdi and Khun Luang Phra Kraisi were made special commissioners. It was, however, Prince Damrong who wrote the "Explanation of the Establishment of the Provincial Courts" in late 1895 or early 1896. In his capacity as minister of the interior, he was responsible for the northern provinces, and his desire for a separation of judicial and administrative functions, derived from his experience with English law, was unequivocal: "The customs regarding the judges of provincial courts, even to the present day, are such that administrative officials from the rank of governor downwards are compelled to examine and decide legal disputes in addition to their other administrative responsibilities. Nearly every person has his duties mixed together in this way. Because we have established the *thesaphiban* system to improve our country through discipline and strength, it is now necessary to separate these functions. That is, one unit will now be established for political administration while a

34. Ibid., 248.
35. Ibid., 237–38.
36. Ibid., 249.

separate judicial unit will handle lawsuits."[37] Damrong was especially worried about cases in which a plaintiff could act as the judge.[38] This had been the case to an extreme degree some twenty years earlier, in the reign of Cao Kawilorot (r.1856–1870), who had absolute power over life and was indeed titled the *cao chiwit ao* (Lord of Life). Under Kawilorot, crimes that were not crimes against the property of another person were, by definition, crimes against the *cao*'s person. And he apparently exercised this power with great relish.

Strangely enough, it was just after Kawilorot's reign, under the auspices of the newly signed Anglo-Siamese treaty, that the *caos* suffered their most devastating loss of performative judicial authority. In 1874, following a series of disputes on the border between British Burma and the northern provinces, the Chiang Mai Treaty was signed with the objectives of "promoting commercial intercourse between British Burmah [*sic*] and adjoining the territories" of Chiang Mai, Lakhon, and Lomphun, "and of preventing dacoity—and other heinous crimes."[39] The treaty established a permanent commissioner, or *khaa luang*, to be appointed by Bangkok but resident in Chiang Mai for the purposes of mediating disputes between British Burma and Siam, although it allowed British subjects to be tried by an English officer in Yoongzaleen District or by the British consul in Bangkok if satisfaction was not obtained. The problems with the first few *khaa luang* were legion. Phra Narin, the first commissioner, spoke no Northern Thai, and translation was slow and inaccurate. But perhaps more significant, he was said to lack a sense of standardization and treated his job instead as one of mediation in which compromise rather than punishment was the goal.[40] Phra Narin was nonetheless a brilliant political administrator, and he not only managed to resettle Chiang Saen but succeeded in persuading the Chiang Mai *cao*, Inthawichayanon, to share taxes with Bangkok and even to institute new taxes on guns and ammunition, pork, spirits, tobacco, siri leaf, horns and hides, ivory, and kingfisher feathers.[41] For this, Rama V awarded him the honorific title of Phraya Thep Prachun. But local residents were overwhelmed and greatly oppressed by the taxes. Thus began the resentment toward Bangkok-appointed officials in Chiang Mai, a resentment that was to grow as

37. Sutcharit Thawonsuk, *Kaan chat san huamüang khrang raek* [Establishment of the first provincial courts] (Bangkok: Ministry of Justice, 1964), 40; cited in Engel, *Code and Custom*, 26.

38. Sutcharit, *Kaan chat san huamüang khrang raek*, 45; cited in Engel, *Code and Custom*, 26.

39. Treaty and Legal Department (Thailand), *Bilateral Treaties and Agreements between Thailand and Foreign Countries and International Organizations* (Bangkok: Prachrandra, 1969), 39, cited in Ratanaporn, "Political, Social, and Economic Changes," 181.

40. Ratanaporn, "Political, Social, and Economic Changes," 189.

41. Ibid., 192.

the conversion to monetary taxation spread and the commercialization of production intensified after the 1870s.[42]

Ironically, the presence of the *khaa luang* contributed to the autocratic tendencies of the most powerful *cao* in Chiang Mai, Cao Luang Inthawichayanon. They became indispensible to each other, in part because Inthawichayanon brought back from Bangkok many of his predecessor's most bitter enemies, giving them exalted positions and thereby buttressing himself against potential competition from other, lesser *caos* who had acquired power under Kawilorot. When, in 1974, the Bangkok government laid claim to the mineral, forest, land, and water resources of the area through the Act for Thai Governors Making Contracts with Foreigners, the *cao luang* suffered a mortal blow. Compounded by the effect of tax farming, which permitted ethnic Chinese tax farmers to consolidate relatively large amounts of capital at precisely the same time as aristocratic control over resources was being replaced by state-sanctioned monopolies, thus depriving the older families of the *caos* of their income, local royalty was irrevocably destabilized. Their diminished powers were increasingly confined to ideological functions, and they held power as much because of their access to spiritual power as to wealth. When a conflict emerged between the Christian missionaries and the *caos* in 1878 and resulted in the Siamese government's Proclamation of Religious Toleration, the *caos* stood to lose even this last slender support.

The demand for such a proclamation came after a Christian convert refused to pay bride price to the spirits of a woman's matriline, a practice the missionaries dismissed as blasphemous and fetishist in nature. The lesser *cao hor naa* had wanted the converts to delay the wedding until the payment was made, but the *cao luang*, who was at the time embroiled in conflict with him, advised that the missionaries petition the king. What they received was not only a guarantee of religious tolerance, but indeed an exemption from the feudal economy in which *phrai* (commoners) were subject to the *cao*. In effect, the Proclamation of Religious Toleration put limits on the juridical authority of the *cao* in his own territory: "From this time forward, if any person wishes to worship any religion, that person can do so. No Lao *chaonai* [*sic*], prince, other high ranking rulers or commoners who are related and friends of those who worship the religion of Jesus Christ shall be obstructive. Anything the religion of Jesus Christ objects to or forbids, such as spirit propitiation or working on Sundays,

---

42. James Ansil Ramsey, "The Development of a Bureaucratic Polity: The Case of Northern Siam" (Ph.D. diss., Cornell University, 1971), 88. On the history of commercialization in rice agriculture, see Anan Ganjanapan, "The Partial Commercialization of Rice Production in Northern Thailand (1900–1981)" (Ph.D. diss., Cornell University, 1984).

no one can force such things to be done except when in times of war when it is essential to make use of those people."[43] The king was perhaps more calculating with the edict than even the missionaries imagined, for the propitiation of spirits had been associated in Lannathai practice with the recognition of spirits of place. In suggesting that the practices need not be recognized, the proclamation implicitly undermined affiliation to local power.

The matter became even more complicated when the Christian missionaries attempted to intervene in witchcraft accusations, which were common at the time and frequently leveled against new converts. In a particularly significant episode, the reverend Daniel McGilvary agreed to shelter a family accused of witchcraft when the reigning *cao* asked him to do so, but the community of Chiang Mai revolted and demanded that the witches undergo exorcism or exile when a fever broke out and claimed the lives of local residents. Under such pressure, the *cao* recanted and asked McGilvary to turn the witches over, but under the new treaty, the missionary could demand legal appeal. And he did: "I replied that I was perfectly willing that the case be tried; but it should not be tried before a *lao* [Lannathai] court, but before the Commissioner. If they could convince him that the sickness in the village was caused by a malicious spirit resident in that family, they should be sent off immediately."[44] The catch was that McGilvary insisted that the plaintiffs would themselves be exiled if they failed to make their case. Fearing an inability to make the new court listen to the evidence, which was to be obtained partly through a medium's divination, the plaintiffs dropped their case. As a result, McGilvary won one of his few devoted families of converts, and although waves of witchcraft accusation were yet to plague northern Thailand, the legal authority of the *cao*s would never again be the same.

It is not insignificant that the *cao*s' loss of performative authority should occur here, in a battle with the religion of the logos, the book that is also the law, or that they should lose such power in a contest over witchcraft accusations in a court that was soon to be subject to the principles of habeas corpus. The Laws of the Provincial Courts were enacted in 1896, although King Rama V was still expressing his hope for the establishment of those courts throughout his domain in 1898[45] and a penal code would not be passed until 1908. Even then,

---

43. The translation was made by Ratanaporn Sethakul from a photograph of the edict in George Bradley McFarland, *Historical Sketch of Protestant Missions in Siam 1828–1928* (Bangkok: Bangkok Times, 1928), 124. See Ratanaporn, "Political, Social, and Economic Changes," 209.

44. Daniel McGilvary, *A Half Century among the Siamese and the Lao: An Autobiography* (New York: Fleming H. Revell, 1912), 206.

45. Tips, *Gustave Rolin-Jacquemyns and Modern Siam*, 255.

the distinctions between modernized and traditional courts were as evident in the fact of chairs or their absence and in the wearing of socks and shoes as in the application of any principle of universal access to the judicial process.[46] Yet, as the new laws began to be felt in Chiang Mai, spirits in mediums gave voice to anger, speaking out against precisely the bans on privileged corporations that Rolin-Jaequemyns had set among his priorities for the modernization of Siam. Carl Bock mentions Cao Ubon's explanation of illness in a woman of the court as having been caused by the whiskey monopoly, which in fact was established by the new state in place of local concessions owned by the royal house. And Khrom Mun Phichit gave vent to exasperation over the mediums, whom he claimed attributed every evil and every affliction experienced in Chiang Mai to the legislating efforts of the Siamese: "Propitiating spirits and having mediums throughout the entire city, the spirit of Chaofa Chaikaeo (Kawila's father) came to reside in Chao [sic] Mahawong. He called on the Chao Nakhon Chiang Mai [chao luang] to force abolishment of the swine tax and spirits tax. The Phra-chao Chiang Mai consented. [When] that spirit demanded that or wanted this, [he] complied. Finally a rumour surfaced that this was because the southerners were doing that and this."[47] The spirits seem to have articulated a sense of outrage at the encroachments of Siamese bureaucracy, despite the fact that the cao luang was often siding with the Bangkok regime in opposition to his own people.

In this context, it is interesting to observe that in his accounts of possessed mediums, Bock describes women dancing with "frantic movements . . . pulling their hair, and shouting at the top of their voice." The image is undoubtedly colored by the Englishman's blander sensibility, but Cao Ubon, the medium of whom he wrote, was a close friend, and if Bock was dismissive of spirit beliefs, he was not dismissive of mediums. So one cannot help but be shocked by the

46. Émile Jottrand, who replaced Rolin-Jacquemyns in 1898, remarked repeatedly on the new appearance of the courts, and it is worth quoting him at length here: "Some years ago, the judges were seated on the ground, the parties made a circle around them, discussed, disputed, and sometimes grabbed one another by the throat. Now, under the presidency of a distinguished magistrate, Phya Kraisee, a doctor in law from Oxford University, where he has obtained all his degrees, things have singularly changed. A gilded rostrum occupies the whole back of the hall and two punkahs attached above the magistrates provide them fresh air. Above his white tunic, the president wears a small black toga, typical of Oxford law students, which gives him a bizarre look. Seated on an elevated chair, he dominates the judges English fashion. The employees wear socks and shoes—a remarkable thing" (97). It was 1899. See Mr. and Mrs. Émile Jottrand, In Siam: The Diary of a Legal Adviser of King Chulalongkorn's Government, trans. Walter E. J. Tips (Bangkok: White Lotus Press, 1996).

47. Ratanaporn, "Political, Social, and Economic Changes," 272.

contrast between what Bock describes and what one now sees in Chiang Mai. His accounts depict a much less decorous aesthetic than that which mediums now display in their efforts to evoke the courtly world of Bock's own era.[48] Although capital was just beginning to form in northern Thailand at the time of the last *caos*, contemporary mediums imagine that moment in terms that are singularly bourgeois, colored by a distressing nostalgia that makes monuments of decay and by a vision of power as that which is always already orderly. For this reason, the performances of contemporary mediums often seem to neutralize the past in the very moment that they attempt to invoke it. In efforts to summon a personal power that can command life or death, they become home to spirits who must confess their sins and admit their submission to the law of *kam*. In attempts to pay tribute to the value of antiquity, they make a fetish of it in a generalized form. In their valorization of the local, they equate all localities. In seeking to discipline possession, they are overwhelmed by the logic of substitution and commensuration. And in their insistence on proper gifting, they convert debt into an economy. It is as though they are summoning spirits who really did inhabit Chiang Mai at the time of the last *caos*, but by then, these *caos* were already mute as corpses, incapable of transforming their worlds through speech in any way (despotic or benevolent) that could resist the engines of commodity capitalism and legal universalism. The past that comes back in this cadaverous form can perhaps only provoke a recollection of the profundity of structural change that overtook Chiang Mai at the turn of the century. But then, if the medium's body can be reanimated, so too can the corpse's. And it is in the confrontation with loss that contemporary mediums and their clients now find themselves so desirous of magic. Theatrical representations of an antiquated world, which made mere images of that which could speak the world into being, now call the specter of transmission back from the dead. As we shall see in the following chapter, the technologies of mass reproduction play the role of magician in this process, intensifying and complicating that paradoxical relation instituted by law in which loss makes desire possible and history emerges in the present.

48. Bock, *Temples and Elephants*, 340–41.

# 6   TRANSMISSIONS,
## OR, THE APPEARANCE OF CULTURE

The performances of mediums in the contemporary era are characterized by a profound concern with decorum, a love of the disciplined surface, and even a certain historical "fashionability" (marked by the emergence of what can only be called the period costume of generic pastness). Perhaps this is predictable given the degree to which mediums are now objects of fascination in a mass media that devotes itself to, among other things, the preservation and exaltation of "culture." Nonetheless, it is difficult to overstate the recentness of this concern to perform order through the cultivation of appearances. Indeed, it is probably not unfair to say that, in the long century that stretches between Bock's account and the present, there has been a radical revaluation of appearances. The simultaneous enormity and relative historical shallowness of that transformation is evident when one considers how Bock's descriptions of mediums "tripping the light fantastic toe" in an orgy of "great excitement" were to be amended several decades later, when W. A. R. Wood, the British consul in Chiang Mai, turned again to the description of a medium's possession. Although Wood would continue to inscribe mediumship under the rubric of the exotic in a chapter titled "Oddities," his portrayal reflects a matter-of-factness rather removed from the spectacle of Cao Ubon's more fabulous antics. Yet, it is less the banality that Wood accords mediumship than the combination of moralism and modernity that makes his narrative interesting.

Wood remarks retrospectively that the spirits who possessed mediums in the early decades of the century were often "dreadfully narrow and puritanical" in their moral standards. However, when he recounts the possession itself, he comments, in a tone that approaches sarcasm, that the medium "would hurriedly put on a pair of trousers, because that particular sort of spirit dislikes women and will only communicate with a man or else with a woman who has diddled it into mistaking her for a man by the simple expedient of putting on trousers."[1]

Bock made no reference to such dress, and one can be forgiven for being surprised, more than half a century after Wood's described encounter, by the assumption of such modern attire at a site now so invested with tradition's aura. From the vantage point of the present, such dress can only seem foreign to, and even at odds with, the aesthetic of contemporary mediums' performances and the values of traditionalism they so ostentatiously display. After all, it was still necessary for Luang Wichit Wathakan, the culturalist architect of Thai nationalism, to defend trousers as being authentically Thai when the government's mid-century publication of cultural mandates regulating dress and requiring trousers (for men) elicited criticism in the middle of this century precisely for betraying Thai custom. Even in the 1940s, trousers could be construed locally as a symptomatic abandoning of the local, and Wichit's defense of them was matched and ironically negated by Prince Wan Waithayakon's claim that their propriety in relation to modernity resided precisely in their newness. In any case, appearing modern was not a problem for mediums in Wood's time, no more so than appearing traditional was a necessity. It is only in the aftermath of a cultural revolution—of what will come to appear as the revolution of "culture"—that mediumship has come to require traditionalism and, more particularly, the costume of the traditional.

At the moment that one recognizes the traditionalism of today's mediums as something new, one enters the terrain in which the idea of history as progress loses itself in the flurry of an angel's wings. It is Benjamin's angel who hovers there, looking backward and yet moving forward: propelled less by the past or the storm of progress than by its own retrospective glance.[2] The bearer of that glance is thoroughly mass-mediatized and, as Benjamin well knew, it is the mediatization of that glance that redirects its look and makes of the modern the experience of both newness *and* loss. It is, moreover, the process of mass mediatization in Thailand that makes mediums the object of traditionalism's desire. If, forty years ago, mediums were largely ignored by a media industry self-defined as an instrument of modernity and national integration, they are now the stars of a grand pageant in which ritual and tradition are the signifiers of an authenticity on which the nation now grounds itself.

The signs of this transformation are legion, but perhaps most visible in the

1. W. A. R. Wood, *Consul in Paradise: Sixty-Nine Years in Siam* (London: Souvenir, 1965; rpt. Bangkok: Suriwong Books, 1991), 95.

2. Walter Benjamin, "Theses on the Philosophy of History" (1950), in *Illuminations*, trans. Harry Zohn, ed. Hannah Arendt (London: Fontana, 1973), 257–58.

mass media. Recently, for example, the mediums of Lamphun received into their midst a television star named Duangchiwan Komonsen. Duangchiwan is now one of several vehicles for Queen Camadevi and she enjoys widespread renown among mediums in both northern and central Thailand. Appearing for photographers at the annual rites devoted to the founding monarch, she is almost as visible in the press as a *raang song* as she was as a media personality.[3] But Duangchiwan is not the only medium to receive the inquisitive and covetous look of the print and televisual media and their audiences. Other mediums frequently adorn the personal interest segments of national newspapers and magazines devoted to the miraculous. In the 1990s, they are not entirely uncommon guests on television talk shows, where they suffer accusations of greed and dishonesty as often as they are questioned about the extraordinary feats they perform. In Chiang Mai as in Bangkok, they are not infrequently the subject of gossip and innuendo and even of newspaper exposés on their own violations of tradition. Some keep elaborately archived video libraries of their own possession performances and virtually all have photographs of themselves prominently displayed along with those of twentieth-century monarchs and heroic Buddhist teachers.

Perhaps neither Weberian prophecies of modernity's inevitable secularization nor Benjaminian anticipations of revolutionary materialism could have anticipated the full encompassment of mediumship by the technologies of mass reproduction. For, as a field that has more typically been represented in terms of "cult value," mediumship would seem likely to resist the circulation of mass-reproduced images. And yet, in northern Thailand, mass mediatization seems not to have entailed de-auraticization so much as it has incited a reformed magicality. Or rather, these two have been entwined in a dual and mutually productive trajectory. One could even go so far as to say that the case of northern Thailand's spirit mediums calls into question the very oppositions on which so much theory of modernity and the mass media rests, suggesting not the displacement of a primordial sacrality by profane technology but the very splitting of the modern into the sacred and the profane in the process of mass mediatization.[4] As this has occurred, local understandings of signification have

---

3. Donald K. Swearer and Sommai Premchit, *The Legend of Queen Cāma* (Albany: State University of New York Press, 1998), 27–28.

4. By splitting I mean something other than the disappearance of the sacred, something other than mere secularization in the Weberian sense. Of course, the division of the world into sacred and profane domains is part of the bifurcation of the political into civil and private domains. We see the first recognition of the difference between these two modes of secularization (that which demands secularity even in the private, and that which guarantees a right to privacy precisely to prevent the

been revalued, and the power of appearances has assumed rather new dimensions. Mediumship, once opposed to the possibility of fixation and serialization in photography, now finds in it the excitement of an uncanny mirroring: a risk and a possibility for renewal. And a second risk: of encompassment by representation.

It may be best to begin here with the lesson of a photograph, told to me by the medium of Phayaphrom. This is not because the camera has a uniquely or simply causal status in the transformations to be discussed here but because the lesson of the photograph is what first seemed to me to demand explication through recourse to a history of appearances and, consequently, through reference to the history of mechanical reproduction. That history is one of doubling and splitting in a narrative of culture, anticipated in the moment of photography's arrival in the north and apotheosized in the moment of its fetishization a century later. Of course, photography is not independent of more general discourses of loss—some economic, some political—within which it promises the only access to an unrepresentable and vanishing present.[5] It is, indeed, their instrument and their locus, their philosophical toy and their secret source of power.

In an effort to anticipate somewhat the movement of this chapter, I want to note that the camera arrived in Thailand as one of many scientific instruments and that it was initially cast in the idiom of a substitutional eye, but one perfected in its objectivity. With microscopes and telescopes, many of which arrived as gifts with diplomatic envoys, the camera summoned in Thailand, as elsewhere, the fantasy of an ideal vision unlimited by subjectivity: the promise of a documentary totality and a truly prosthetic vision machine.[6] Initially, then, photography seemed at odds with the occult practices of mediumship or

demand for absolute secularism) in Marx's (troubling) writings on the anachrony of Judaism in Germany. There, he states that the preservation of a right to religious belief in the private domain and a restriction of the political to the public domain is an a priori abrogation of revolutionary possibility. Since Marx, the division of the world into the private and the public has come to stand as the hallmark of modernity, but we might well map that division on the one in which religion is itself posited as an institutional domain separable from the public. That this division is, in a profound sense, a protestant division, is only proof of how close Weber was to comprehending the logic of the modern.

5. On the relationship between photographic technique and the problem of storing memory of a present unknowable in itself, see Mary Ann Doane, "Temporality, Storage, Legibility: Freud, Marey and the Cinema," *Critical Inquiry* 22, no. 2 (1996): 171–74.

6. I use the term "vision machine" in Virilio's sense to denote a prosthesis that, in its most advanced form, would not only substitute for the human eye but substitute also for memory. It would produce images for which no witness would be required. See Paul Virilio, *The Vision Machine* (London: British Film Institute, 1994).

monks' magic; it was an instrument for making the visible permanent and for drawing a line between the seen and the unseen, not for testifying to the presences or the spaces that exceeded vision. For nearly a century, photographs of possession performance seem to have been at least implicitly forbidden. Then, beginning about three decades ago, they were not only entertained but became implicated in the proliferation of mediumship itself. Indeed, it is my sense that photography and its apparati were ultimately appropriated as metaphors by and for mediums when the saturation of the Thai world by mechanically reproduced images had induced not only that mindless historicism about which Kracauer warned his German readers,[7] but also the appearance of a historical death against which mortals had to be protected. The newness of photography thereby came to be imagined as a kind of indemnification against the pastness to which it relegated the world. In the process, photography's total vision came to be figured, I suggest, as a flirtation with death, one for which mediums are especially well prepared. Ironically, mediums now assume the function of the camera in a discourse that attributes aura to the human. But they do so from within the logic of mechanical reproduction, by disseminating images of mediumship that can be recognized as the signs of history. In this self-conscious modernization, then, both the newness of the new and the newness of the past come to be foregrounded as effects of a world transformed by and into a "picture."

These are admittedly ambitious claims and ones that merit more than a little defense. I want to turn therefore to the lesson of the photograph before proceeding to the history of appearances and finally to the linkages between the two that were forged in the discourses of tradition that emerged in the middle of this century and disseminated via the mass media. The progress of this argument is recursive, taking a spiral form in which the historical trajectories of three distinct but mutually entwined domains are traced in relation to each other, namely, those of photography, fashion and appearance, and "culture," the latter opening onto a discussion of ethnographic self-fashioning. First, however, the story of an eye. Or rather, of a lens.

### In Camera: An Eye for an Eye

On my second meeting with Caopuu Phayaphrom, he pulled a framed photograph of a group of possessed mediums from one of the shelves next to his throne. He handed me the portrait and, smiling slightly, asked me to look and tell him what I saw. By now, it was clear that the exchange was to be a tutelary

---

7. Siegfried Kracauer, "Photography," in *The Mass Ornament*, trans. Thomas Y. Levin (Cambridge, MA: Harvard University Press, 1995), esp. 49–51.

one, marked by a severely asymmetrical dialogicity in which learning was to take the form of questions to which a human being's failed responses would serve as the ground for the spirit's own exposition. And so I took the picture, and looked. In the grain and the matte surface I could see that all of the mediums were attired in similar clothes, though each was draped in a different color and each had a particular mark of distinction: a uniquely embroidered scarf, a specially framed pair of sunglasses, a piece of gaudy costume jewelry unlike that worn by any other. And quite unmistakably, each had a different look for the camera: a face that had been composed in the anticipation of being seen again, as an image. Here was regal sobriety, here childish joking; here demure and coquettish reticence, here sovereign severity.

Not yet having learned that the costumes were absolutely commensurate with identity, I thought I recognized the figure in the middle of the group as Naang Khao, although she wore the cobalt blue satin and dark sunglasses that Kumaannooj had worn the first time I visited. Yet, as we spoke, and as Caopuu Phayaphrom prodded me, the photograph also seemed to give up the old monarch's image. At the time, mere dress did not seem adequate to the task of differentiating among these personae. Undoubtedly, the biases of a realist (or a protestant) refusal to grant truth-value to mere appearances obstructed my seeing anything but the same being metamorphosed on a formal level but alike in a crucial and even essential way. It was therefore unclear which of the three personae was supposed to be seen there. So, when I pointed to the body of Naang Khao dressed in Kumaannooj's garb and tentatively identified her as Caopuu Phayaphrom, the spiritual persona snatched the picture and dismissed me as a fool. This was, he proclaimed with a mocking insistence on the ob- viousness of what I could not apprehend, a picture of Kumaannooj, the child spirit who was both a son to Caopuu Phayaphrom and one of Naang Khao's possessing spirits. It was emphatically not Phayaphrom. And Naang Khao had left her body long ago.

To confuse a boy with his fatherly spirit in a context that prizes age as the locus of authority is a deep offense against patriarchal principles. Caopuu, spitting miang juice on the floor next to his throne, was more than irritated. Yet, despite the noisy performance of insult, it was, I think, less the offense against generational authority that translated itself into such demonstrative contempt than frustration at the enormous epistemic chasm that separated our two radically different understandings of the photograph. Nonetheless, the chasm demanded traversal and Phayaphrom sighed but also moved on to continue with the lesson. This time, however, he delivered a lecture on the necessity of cultivating indifference to the material world.

Mediums are not usually regarded as great meditators, and they are generally thought to be lax in their own self-discipline. Nonetheless, they often claim for themselves considerable expertise in the practice of sitting, and they frequently represent their meditation as a process of preparation for the spirits. Spirits that are self-identified as Buddhist also make reference to the virtues of meditation, but in their encouragement of such practice in mortals they represent meditation as a source of immunity to possession. Thus, Phayaphrom advised me to sit and cultivate closure in a process that would protect me, he said, from being overwhelmed by the spirits of the dead whom I would encounter in my work: "You have to sit [meditate] like this, keep your knees together, your palms up-turned. Close your eyes and empty your mind. It will be hard at first. You will get tired. Your back will ache and your head will hurt. But after a while, you will forget it completely. You won't know your body/self at all. The ants will crawl all over you, into your ears and nostrils. All kinds of insects will run over your body, eating you up, and you won't even notice it."

Odd, I thought, that the refusal of spirits would produce an oblivion so like that into which the spirits would have rushed were mine to be the body of a medium. But then, the medium is and is not like other people. And the oblivion of meditation is not, Phayaphrom reminded me, a kind of receptivity. It is, instead, a closure of the senses that permits the focalization of the mind. That focalization is supposed to permit a recognition of the impermanence of things material and of the unreality of phenomenal experience. The oblivion of mediums, in contrast, is more akin to that of the camera in which a total receptivity to phenomenal experience induces a nearly lunatic mindlessness.

There were many instances in which a likeness between mediums and cameras was drawn for me by mediums and their audiences: in imitative performances, in overt comparisons, and in more implicit analogies. But it was Phayaphrom who first suggested to me the profound affinity between mediumship and photography, and who made it possible to consider that relation as a symptom of the modernity that they share. In the process, he gave to be thought once more the rhetorics of batteries and electricity within which mediums speak of spiritual energy, and made possible the association between the fantasized tunnels linking Chiang Dao and Chiang Mai with the railways through which Chiang Mai became fully incorporated into the geo-body of the Thai nation. "The medium is like a photograph of the spirit," he said. "It is not the spirit you see, but the image [phaab] in the medium. The spirit agrees to be seen, so that people can understand and hear the dhamma [which the spirit imparts]." People are in need of the Buddha's teachings precisely because they have come to confuse appearances with truth, but to receive the dhamma, truth must find its ideal appearance. In the lesson that Phayaphrom was to give me, it would become clear that through the play of identification with a device of absolute receptivity, the more radical difference between human perception and mechanical attention is made the subject of the spirit's lesson. For those who can listen, then, mediumship provides an account of how it is that appearances operate in the world of mechanical reproduction.

Perhaps because I remained so stupefied by Phayaphrom's initial efforts to have me read the photograph, he disappeared. Kumaannooj descended to continue the lesson in the cruder but no less revealing theater of mimesis. Kumaannooj always associated me with cameras, though I rarely carried one in my visits to the homes of spirit mediums and never had one in his presence. In this encounter, he startled me with a manic performance of/with a camera, which Phayaphrom's assistants explained to me in terms of his assumption that all Westerners always carry cameras and that the camera is an essential part of their identity. He had few means of communicating other than imitation, being a child with poor language skills (linguistic infancy was performed as the absence of tonality in a language defined by tones). So, he parodied the image of me that I had attempted to resist, rushing around the room while sputtering guttural sounds to evoke the camera. Finally, in exasperation, he asked me to take his picture: "Take a picture," Kumaannooj gestured with his hands in the manner of photographer.

"I can't. I don't have a camera."

"Don't you want a picture?"

"Yes. Yes, I'd love to have a picture of you."

"Take a picture."

"I didn't bring my camera with me, but if you like, I can bring it next time."

"Why?"

"Why didn't I bring a camera?"

"Why?"

"Well, I didn't know whether you'd like to have a picture taken."

"Do you want a picture?"

"I promise to bring my camera next time."

"I like cameras."

"I do too."

"Did Caopuu show you his picture?"

"Ah, yes, yes, I think so."

"No he didn't."

Kumaannooj leered. Then he rushed, gesturing with his camera, gesturing *as* a camera, until he all but fell on top of me as Naang Khao's assistants laughed. His noisy parody of both the camera and the shutter-clicking tourist suggested all of the violence of a device whose most common metaphorics (in English) are those of the gun and whose associations (in Thai) are often of loss or transformation. Nonetheless, when the assistants translated Kumaannooj's gestures as an act "like taking pictures" (*baeb kaan thaaj ruub*), they somehow lost what had been present in his own performance, namely, the resonance of a word, *thaaj*, which is also used to mean "change" or "discharge" or even "cast off," and whose associations include those of defecation and urination, wastage, and emptying. Perhaps only a child from another time, still in the process of acquiring a modern vocabulary, could return to a word the etymological associations forgotten by habit and repressed or separated out by linguistic propriety. Kumaannooj's speech, which was invariably sexualized and infused with scatological reference, suggested something both more and less than mere imagistic reproduction. It seemed, uncannily, to resurrect the fears of photography that Balzac had once expressed to Nadar, namely, that photography would lead to the absolute diminution of the one whose spectral skin had peeled off and left itself in the trace on a daguerreotype's surface.[8] A loss not unlike a rotting. Photography as detritus. Or rather, photography as that which makes detritus of the world.

In the rush toward his spectator, Kumaannooj's aggressive antics were also suggestive of the grotesque proximity normally reserved for telephoto lenses, and he found the shocking effect of that nearness wildly hilarious. "I want you. I love you," he often said, in a childish recitation of tawdry come-ons. "Do you want to play?" Then the gesture of a violation. "Kik. Kik." And laughter unredeemed by joy. Kumaannooj's rushing mimicry was as aggressive as a joke, but one with an equally aggressive object. It took aim at the violent economy that would convert people into images, places into tokens of "having-been-there." In its sight was the ruin that photography leaves in its wake.

As Walter Benjamin suggests, mimicry is never more oppositional than transformative. The intimacy between a thing and its copy and, more important, that between a copyist and his or her object can never leave the original intact.[9] And so there can be no absolute demarcation between the world of the camera and that of the medium in a milieu where the medium has posed *for* the camera and posed *as* the camera. Kumaannooj's performance concretized what Phayaphrom had merely verbalized, namely, that mediumship's modernity finds its (new) form in photography. After Kumaannooj made this point in

8. Rosalind Krauss provides an excellent account of this anxiety and the ways it reflected other, more general apprehensions of the dangers inherent in photographic uncanniness in Western contexts. See "Tracing Nadar," in *Illuminations: Women Writing on Photography from the 1850s to the Present*, ed. Liz Heron and Val Williams (Durham, NC: Duke University Press, 1996), esp. 39–40.

9. Walter Benjamin, "On the Mimetic Faculty," in *One-Way Street*, 160–63; also Michael Taussig, *Mimesis and Alterity: A Particular History of the Senses* (New York: Routledge, 1993).

rudely physical terms, Phayaphrom could take up the photograph again and turn me back to a contemplation of seeing and the manifold dimensions of blindness in order that I comprehend why I had not seen what was there for me to see and why I had sought in the photograph's invisible recesses a truth that was not one. The child exited. And the grandfather returned.

It might seem, on the surface of things, that the spirit who demands that a viewer recognize spirits in the photograph is warning her away from an overinvestment in appearances. What appears to be the medium is, in fact, the spirit. The cobalt blue–clad woman is neither Naang Khao nor Phayaphrom but Kumaannooj. But in this case, the risk of the photograph is not that one will be seduced by mere appearances and thus remain ignorant of the truer picture. Instead, it is that one will immediately distrust appearances and, in the effort to see beyond them, err. The power of the photograph, which is also the power of mediumship in the age of photography, is that it assumes the truth of appearances. And it assumes them because photography has generated the conditions in which truth will be understood as the conformity between one's image and one's origin, or rather, the image of one's original form—imagined as the anticipation of one's future recall *as* image. The cobalt blue attire is the sign of Kumaannooj and none other. Looking on it plainly one confronts this fact: that dress does make the spirit. Appearances can be everything.

How is this possible? How is it that a practice whose condition of possibility is the existence of otherwise invisible beings can turn out, at the end of the twentieth century, to be allied with the instruments of mere appearance? What lay at the heart of Phayaphrom's insistence that I look again was a distinction between my look and the look of the camera. The camera had seen everything, had captured every fleeting detail, and even given to the innocuous tatters of fabric and the crooked placement of glasses on the bridge of the nose an autonomy. And as every historian of photography well knows, it was precisely this access to the minutiae of the world that made it the favorite new toy of science and theater alike.[10] The camera made it possible to look at the image

---

10. The idea of an optical unconscious and the corollary interest in the revelation of the previously unregistered detail is generally attributed to Walter Benjamin in the "Art Work" essay. But the issue had already been identified in 1839, when the first daguerreotypes were being circulated in public. As Philip Hone wrote on 4 December 1839, "The reflection of surrounding images created by a camera, obscured upon a plate of copper, plated with silver, and prepared with some chemical substances, is not only distinctly delineated, but left upon the plate so prepared, and there remains forever. Every object, however minute, is a perfect transcript of the thing itself; the hair of the human head, the gravel on the road-side, the texture of a silk curtain, or the shadow of the smaller leaf reflected upon the wall, are all imprinted as carefully as nature or art has created them in the objects transferred; and those things which are invisible to the naked eye are rendered apparent by

again and again, linger over one detail or another, measure the distances be-tween bodies or calculate the time of day according to the shadows that fell on shoulders. Phayaphrom did this. And Kumaannooj asked me to do this. Nor could the fact of framing, by which the portrait artist had assembled these brilliantly clad bodies, mitigate the stubbornness of this "fugitive testimony," as Barthes would perhaps have called it.[11] All that was left to me was to disappear the traces that could not signify. My looking became, in relation to the photo-graph, a kind of unseeing when the virtue of the photograph was precisely its extraordinarily indiscriminate seeingness. But then, this is the case with all photographs, as Barthes well knew. Indeed, when one is confronted by the disjuncture in his thought about photography, which vacillates between claim-ing that we must read images in a manner analogous to the way we read texts and suggesting that photographs are precisely indexical traces of a past that they have wrenched from context, it is not because of any contradiction on Barthes's part. It is simply a function of Barthes's recognition, which is also Phaya-phrom's recognition, of a difference between what spectators do and what cameras do. That the residue of the Real can leave its shocking mark in the typified (what Barthes calls "unary") surface of the image, in the form of the *punctum* can only confirm the fact that photographic meaning is achieved in the process of composition and semiotic stabilization whose goal is both a testimony to and an overcoming of the Real.

My encounter with the photograph of Kumaannooj was maddening because I did not understand it, but the photograph also represented a certain kind of madness. That madness took the form of total receptivity to the world, includ-ing the world of spirits. It is the madness that is "false on the level of perception, true on the level of time," the "shared hallucination" that is nonetheless "chafed by reality."[12] If one were to imagine a state in which all materiality would imprint itself on us, on our eyes and our bodies' other sensory organs, it would be a state of absolute unboundedness and of porous imbrication with the world. One would erupt outward as the world penetrated one's being. Flesh would dissolve, and what is an always already socialized identity—"social skin," as Turner called it[13]—would become utterly unsustainable. In short, one would have become a medium.

---

the help of a magnifying glass" (excerpted in Merry A. Foresta and John Wood, *Secrets of the Dark Chamber: The Art of the American Daguerreotype* [Washington, DC: National Museum of American Art and Smithsonian Institution Press, 1995]), 233.

11. Roland Barthes, *Camera Lucida*, trans. Richard Howard (New York: Hill and Wang, 1981).

12. Ibid., 115.

13. Terence S. Turner, "The Social Skin," in *Not Work Alone*, ed. J. Cherfas and R. Lewsin (London: Temple Smith, 1980).

Let me reiterate. In the 1990s, every medium (at least all that I have met) has one or more photographs of himself or herself in a possessed state. These are invariably framed and hold a certain pride of place among the other icons and images that clutter the medium's shrine. Sometimes they are juxtaposed with illustrations of the celestial city or of Angkor Wat, implying through their proximity a common origin in Buddhist cosmology's paradisical urbanity. The photographs of northern Thai spirits are not quite like the ghost images that were so beloved of American spiritualists and mediums in the nineteenth century, although such phenomena as blurring and doubles are also remarked by northern Thai mediums for their uncanniness.[14] They are, rather, more like family portraits and often include all of the possessed mediums who share a single tutelary overlord, such as Luang Kham Daeng or Mokkhalaan.

Photographs of this sort, it seems, are always objects of explanatory rationalizations, and they are potentially sites of awkwardness. For, technically speaking, spirits are not supposed to be amenable to photography. This at least is what mediums say when they trot out their pictures and accord to them miraculous status. Many people (mediums and their clients, as well as ethnographers) remark that, until recently, say about three or four decades ago, mediums refused to have themselves photographed and considered cameras to be a threat. Now, however, they narrate these ubiquitous images as evidence of the spirit's willingness to be photographed and indeed as an index of magical agency. The spirits, it is said, have imprinted the photograph so that their existence will be visible to humans. They are, in effect, translated by the photograph to resemble the performance of the possession itself, and the possession is represented as that which resembles the spirit. Always, the spirits are depicted as those who wish to become visible and audible to humans, who otherwise could not perceive them. Thus, the receptivity of the film, like that of the medium, has been effected by the spirit. The spirit is therefore not "captured there," and no soul is risked as a result. If Kumaannooj momentarily returned the fear of material waste to the term *thaaj*, it is once again repressed in the habituated discourse of those senior spirits who are accustomed to photography. For them, photography translates what cannot be directly transferred. The problem is that the translation may not be recognized as such. The spirits may be confused with their instruments, and one may see mediums instead— as I did.

14. I am indebted here to Tom Gunning's excellent account of the relationship between photography and spiritualism in "Phantom Images and Modern Manifestations: Spirit Photography, Magic Theater, Trick Films, and Photography's Uncanny," in *Fugitive Images: From Photography to Video*, ed. Patrice Petro (Bloomington: Indiana University Press, 1994), 42–71.

The wise person, the one who has comprehended the instructions of spirits, has learned to recognize such translations. He or she has learned that it is the custom of human beings to screen out what cannot be made meaningful and to seek unambiguous significance in the invisible. He or she knows that, in this process, humans become blind to much that is visible, and to the logic of specularization itself. This is a modern wisdom, however, one that Edgar Allan Poe recognized in his tale of the purloined letter that becomes most invisible in its display, and one that Siegfried Kracauer enacted in his analysis of that grotesque and occulting artificial light in which the salaried masses of modern Germany worked, oblivious to the system that made them as instrumental as mediums.[15] In Thailand, the wise person has understood that mediums, unlike other people, do something different, indeed quite opposite in nature. What mediums do, and what normal mortals cannot do, is substitute the maddening blindness of indiscriminate seeing for the meaning-producing blindness that is the effect of vision—a vision that seeks figures against grounds and sees only what has been seen before. In this regard, through a negative mimesis, vision shows up the nature of seeing in a realm where appearances have indeed come to be magically invested with the power to make the world. It is for this reason, because mediums have been likened to cameras and because true perception and insight require something other than receptivity, that the discourse of spirits is always preceded by the assumption of vision's alienating fetish, namely, spectacles. Spirits, it seems, must also see in the manner of humans to claim the moral authority that makes their words meaningful.

Possessed mediums make ostentatious display out of the donning and shedding of spectacles, whether these are reading spectacles or darkly tinted lenses. Often, they are the most carefully assumed object in the repertoire of fashion accessories. Indeed, one may surmise that possessed mediums insistently remark the fact of seeing and the deficiency thereof with eyeglasses because the same glasses are somehow implicated in the distinction between medium and spirit and between photography and seeing. It is admittedly possible that these glasses are irrelevant, nonsigns in the language of style: mere fashion, in Simmel's sense. Possibly, they are longings toward erudition and the sagacity that comes with age, imitations of monks and others whose eyes have tired with reading. The ubiquity and banality of spectacles, however, should not be taken

---

15. Edgar Allan Poe, "The Purloined Letter" (1845), in *The Norton Anthology of American Literature*, 3d ed., ed. Nina Baym et al. (New York: Norton, 1979), 1:1425–37; Siegfried Kracauer, *The Salaried Masses: Duty and Distraction in Weimar Germany* (1930), trans. Quintin Hoare (London: Verso, 1998). Kracauer makes specific reference to Poe's story in his own discussion of the economy of display and ideological distraction.

as grounds for dismissing their significance. As Peter Stallybrass has shown, the prostheses of everyday life form bodies and selves in powerful ways.[16] Whether one is speaking of shoes or of jackets, of corsettes or of spectacles, it is hard to avoid the recognition that these mundane accoutrements are endowed to the point that one can hardly imagine being what one believes oneself to be without them. One's feet become tender by wearing shoes, and thus come to require them. And a short-sighted person squints in the absence of spectacles and relates to the world as though a stranger to it without them. The nearly universal presence of glasses in mediums' attire, and the fact that they are almost always the spirits' only admitted condescension to modernity, therefore suggests that they betoken something more than stylishness or a longing for scholarly citizenship or even some resemblance to the reigning monarch, King Bhumipol (whose portraits always feature him in dark-rimmed spectacles).

A provocation of contemporaneity (?): glasses permit the spirits to see. They do so either through the normal compensatory mechanisms that make spectacles what they are, or they screen out the glare of too much light in order that clarity be achieved in a narrow spectrum. Either they magnify or they screen out, but in both cases, they permit a focalization to take place. The question is why this would be necessary when the medium has already been established as an instrument of total receptivity and of absolute seeingness. And the answer, I think, is that neither spirits nor mortals can afford the kind of failure to limit vision or "to unsee" that mediums suffer. That way lies oblivion and thus the impossibility of ethical action. In possession, vision has been alienated. Glasses, by remarking and indeed producing an intensive gaze, make judgment possible. In this manner, at a time when spirit possession can be denounced as absurd atavism, they facilitate the spirit's renewed claims to see into the heart of things. Those who live in the world of cameras need glasses. Technologized, an eye for an eye has become a lens for a lens.

This ethicizing performance has as its corollary, however, the insinuation that mediums are somehow allied with inhuman technologies. Indeed, the medium who has found a doppelgänger in the camera has become something of an automaton, an enlivened doll whose still and maniacally open eye sees everything and nothing at the same time. The camera, we might say, gives the uncanny back to the medium and restores what the age of de-auraticizing mechanical reproduction both produced and threatened to undermine. One of the most common sources of uncanny feelings, says Freud, is the uncertainty one experiences about whether a seeming person is actually alive or is, in fact,

16. Peter Stallybrass, lecture delivered at the Ficto-Criticism Conference, Columbia University, New York, April 1996.

merely an automaton.[17] In this context, characters who seem to have risen from the dead, ghosts of all sorts, and self-directing machines can incite enormous uneasiness. Northern Thailand has its quotient of tales in which one cannot be sure of the nature of a person. In the dreadfully beloved ghost stories that fill books of myths, movie theaters, and pulp novels, the most common instance of this uncanniness occurs when a beautiful woman turns out to be a monstrous succubus, a half-dead spirit whose malevolent intentions cannot be recognized by desirous men. In these stories, the inability to tell a spirit from a living person is always fatal. And, in my assessment, the possibility of mistaking a dead being for a live one constitutes a major and renewed trope of contemporary popular culture. The recent spate of stories about Widow Ghosts, who are widely held to have caused the deaths of migrant laborers, is but one example.[18] In this regard, mediumship would seem to be the archetypical instance of a technology of the uncanny, newly enhanced and indeed revivified by technology itself. Not only do the spirits descend into a body that appears, to all intents and purposes, to be dead—the vomiting and groans having marked a death of sorts—but the medium herself is invariably alive by virtue of the spirit's miraculous interventions. She should have died, one might say. Were it not for the spirits, she would be dead.

If spirits were commonplace inhabitants of the premodern Thai world, photography has made them the bearers of strange new powers. Before photography, spirits had to be placated and honored, but they were not surprising presences, save in instances when they caused illness, and in that case, they could be exorcized. After the advent and naturalization of that technology, they have become either ridiculous or terrifying, and sometimes both at the same time. But illness is now rarely attributable to spirits even when its cure is sought through the intervention of mediums. Indeed, the uncanniness of spirits, which is instituted by the reciprocal and metaphoric doubling of photography and mediumship, is perhaps only thinkable in a place where disease has been naturalized and accidents have become conceivable as such, displacing the notion that catastrophe is the sign of malevolence on the part of a spirit or a witch. When people describe modernity in Thailand as the era of "bad deaths," as they so frequently do, and when they explain the rise in mediumship as a symptom of the proliferation of spirits rendered placeless by accident (*phii taaj*

17. Sigmund Freud, "The Uncanny," in *Writings on Art and Literature*, trans. James Strachey (Stanford: Stanford University Press, 1997), 202.

18. See Mary Beth Mills, "Attack of the Widow Ghosts," in *Bewitching Women, Pious Men: Gender and Body Politics in Southeast Asia*, ed. Aihwa Ong and Michael G. Peletz (Berkeley: University of California Press, 1995), 244–73.

*hong*), they speak to this fact: that the uncanniness of ghosts is a function of the naturalization of death. This is an entirely different economy than that in which spirits could be conceived as things to be expelled. This is why one can say that dread rather than fear characterizes the response to spirits today, a fact that is perhaps most neatly crystallized in the title of the most popular contemporary magazine devoted to miraculous and mysterious phenomena, *Plaek* (Strange). This is also why the clichéd refrain with which audience members addressed me after every possession performance was, almost without exception, "Strange, eh?" ( *Plaek na?*). In part, the remark was intended to elicit those statements of disbelief that I had evaded in the more directly pointed interrogations, "*Chya ry plao?*" (Do you believe or not?). But in this latter form they seemed to suggest something else, namely, that doubt is the condition in which spirits acquire their full mysteriousness. It is this doubt that photography incited with its claims to reveal all that could be seen, and it is in the context of this doubt that photography unleashes its other, magical capacity. So, from the rationalization of the world, the phoenix of the uncanny rises, again. Today, the recurrence of spirits is sought, but their expulsion is not and need not be. All that is required is that the spirit conform to an image that, when materialized, makes the present seem like an echo of the past.

In fact, the repetition of formalized, standardized costume gives to the successful possession performance a sense of déjà vu in the sense that Benjamin gives that term. As in Benjamin's description, it is sound that becomes the transmitter of uncanniness, but here too sound acquires its potency by virtue of having been expelled by the visualization and spatialization of the world. So, the standardization of costume permits the voice "to be endowed with the magic power to transport us into the cool tomb of long ago, from the vault of which the present seems to return only as an echo."[19]

Of course, one could also read this phenomenon in Lacanian terms. In his essay on the anamorphosis, Lacan argues that individuals become subjects through a process of scopic misrecognition (or *méconnaisance*) in which they are both expelled from and seduced into delirious identification with the Gaze—that place from which the visual field is organized. Lacan lays out his notion of the Gaze as something other than the intersubjective look of the Other (as in Sartre's work), and something distinct from the "unnamed substance . . . the irridescence of which" the subject "as eye" emerges in "the function of seeingness" (as claimed by Merleau-Ponty).[20] Nonetheless, he

19. Walter Benjamin, "Berlin Chronicle," in *One-Way Street* (1932), trans. Edmund Jephcott and Kingsley Shorter (London: Verso, 1979), 345. See Jacques Lacan, "Anamorphosis" (1973), in *The Four Fundamental Concepts of Psycho-Analysis*, trans. Alan Sheridan (London: Penguin, 1977), 79–90.
20. Lacan, "Anamorphosis," 82.

makes much of Sartre's famous account of a boy being discovered in the act of peeping through a keyhole, whereupon he is rendered immediately abject.

Though Lacan attributes to Sartre an error in his conflation of the look that surprises the boy with the originary Gaze in which desire is organized, the attention given to sound in the moment of expulsion from the position of visual sovereignty repays rereading. In this scenario, the child hears the rustling of leaves and a footfall, and must therefore turn away from what lies through the keyhole. We can perhaps surmise that, in all circumstances where desire operates in the "domain of seeing"—circumstances that are, it must be said, historically and locationally specific—the prioritization of vision is precisely what makes (some) sound the source of a trauma and inevitably of a repetition in which the delirium of misrecognition is pursued again. In such circumstances, the dramaturgy of absolute subjection necessarily looks like an effacement of vision and a responsibleness to voice, itself the instantiation but also the elision of language. Insofar as a subject must vacillate between the position of subject and that of the Gaze, and insofar as he or she must entertain misrecognition as the condition of being a subject, total subjectification and total annihilation begin to resemble each other. A dramaturgy of radical subjectification would therefore entail a disappearance of the one who looks in favor of a principle of the gaze that nonetheless dissimulates and appears as a powerful bearer of the look, one that seems, at the same time, to call out audibly to those who will yet be found wanting in vision. And such a dramaturgy is precisely what informs the performances of spirit mediums in a world overtaken by images.

What calls attention here is the observation that the organization of perceptual consciousness within a domain of seeing is what makes sound the source of a traumatic awakening. The emergent hegemony of vision, so belabored in theories of the modern, is not the displacement of an auditorily oriented sensibility (which attends the proliferation of images) but rather that which gives to sound, and in the case of northern Thai spirit mediumship, voice in particular, its new potency, its capacity to disorient the hearer from the space of attention. It is, in short, the hegemony of vision, in a pictorializing mode, that makes mediumship's faithful capable of being called and of experiencing that call as something that comes both from the past and from the future.

In the present of successful mediumship, like the impossibly stilled and dislocated present of photography, one is witness to a past that already anticipates its recall and in which the present feels like the repetition that was awaited long ago. Accordingly, the successful self-translating spirit makes himself legible by projecting an image that appears to be nothing but the repetition of a previous image. This is the point where photography appears not merely to have transformed the way people see but the way they anticipate being seen. In the uncanniness of photography's mediumship, one recognizes that the successful photograph works only to the extent that the one photographed is capable of assuming a recognizable face. Even so, this legibility of spirits has two dimensions. On the one hand, the face that allows itself to be pictured asserts the identity of a particular historical figure; on the other, it asserts the generic values of a type whose meaning emerges in relation to a generic pastness. Not just King Ramkhamhaeng nor Queen Camadevi, but personalized power and monarchism in general are seen in the images of possessed mediums. Not just a person, but a type, one might say. This is the doubled operation of Phayaphrom's photograph. If, in the end, Naang Khao is not altogether successful as a medium, it is as much because she fails to look like one being or another as because of her poverty, though the two are, finally, inextricable. And if Ramkhamhaeng's medium is renowned, it is as much because she performs the ideal image of that ideal king in a recognizable form as it is because she is wealthy, though here too, means and the means of (self-)representation are not separable. Ultimately, it is this knowing capacity to look like an image, to be legible as a copy, that constitutes the radical newness of mediumship in the age of mechanical reproduction. Accordingly, it is the history of the acquisition of this capacity that now calls us.

### The Naked and the Dead: A Period of Costume

As already stated, the "becoming-picture" of the spirit is a question of appearances, or rather, of posing: of the anticipation of one's own future recall as an image. The dialogue on photography with Phayaphrom suggested that one needs to learn how to make distinctions between photographic attention and ethical perception, between mediums and persons (spiritual or mortal), but it also begged the question of whether one also needs to learn how to be pictured. If the history of perception can be written in relation to photography, cannot the history of self-presentation for the purposes of being perceptible in the photograph also be written? Spirits translate themselves, make themselves visible, audible, and otherwise perceptible. So do people. But they make themselves visible in different ways, in ways that assert their individuality and in ways that assert their own typification. What interests me here is how spirits in northern Thailand have come to demand figuration in the mode of the traditional and how traditionalism has come to be imagined as a matter of costume. In other words, I want to consider the histories within which northern Thailand has emerged as the sign of pastness in a national imaginary wherein the representation of culture has, over the past century, come to mean the culture of representation. It has been said that Thailand is defined by the "transformability of surfaces."[21] Here, I want to consider the historical emergence of the *performativity* of surfaces. I want to explore the circumstances under which attire can be made to express an identity, and more than this, a cultural identity. In considering the history of mediumship in northern Thailand, one is struck by the fact that the rapprochement between mediums and photography has been accompanied by an explosion in the number of mediums and by the fact that this proliferation has been virtually simultaneous with the efflorescence of literatures on northern Thai culture and tradition, as well as documentary projects in which photo- and videography are pursued in an effort to stave off disappearance. The conditions (one might call them prehistories) that make this linkage appear to be more than mere coincidence are those in which photography was accompanied by a growing concern with appearances and by an emergent and normativizing discourse on culture that sought to render appearance the sign of identity.

Histories of the regulation of appearance in Thailand often begin and end with the administration of Phibul Songkhram, prime minister of Thailand from 1938 to 1944 and between 1948 and 1957. This is not surprising given that it was Phibul's government that took the regulation of cultural form to the most elaborate lengths, producing legislation that not only required particular attire but also the forms in which it could be inhabited. The wearing of trousers or skirts, the doffing of caps, and the kissing of husbands and wives came under the purview of his "cultural mandates" or, to use Prince Wan Waithayakon's term, "state conventions" (*rathaniyom*). Coming as they did, as part of a deeply nationalist program of racialization and regulation, Phibul's interventions merit considerable attention, but if the legislation of appearance assumed its most hyperbolic extreme in the middle years of this century, it had already become a concern at the middle of the previous one, and we will begin this inquiry there.

In 1851, just after he assumed the throne and as he was about to become the most photographed man in Thailand, King Rama IV formally expressed his anxiety about the appearances of individuals who visited the palace. The early date of the proclamation indicates that improprieties of form had already begun to suggest a kind of incivility to Mongkut, and he was desperately concerned that failures in etiquette would be read by Westerners as legitimating grounds for what the latter would term a "civilizing colonization." Thus, he stated: "People who wear no upper garments seem naked; the upper torso looks unclean, especially if the person has a skin disease, or if he is sweating. Other

21. Penny van Esterik, Keynote address, Conference on Gender and Sexuality in Thailand, Australian National University, Canberra, August 1995.

peoples of civilized countries wear upper garments with the exception of the *lawaa* and the Laos people who are forest dwellers and uncivilized and do not use clothing. But since Siam is a civilized country and understands civilized ways, we should not cling to the ancient ways of our forefathers who were forest people. Let everyone, therefore, wear upper garments when coming to royal audience."[22]

Rama IV's remarks are notable for a number of reasons, not least of which is their strange status as a kind of decree without legal sanction but nonetheless bearing the aura of law. As Prince Wan Waithayakon observed in his 1944 essay, "Thai Culture," decrees of this sort (including the *rathaniyom*) occupy a transitional status in the legal history of the country.[23] They facilitated the transition from a kind of sovereign performativity, in which the king's word is always already law, to one in which law is understood as the expression and representation of a collective will and need. On its own, Mongkut's edict is interesting for the way it construed attire in relation to historical difference. First, it singles out the people of Laos and, by extension, the people of Chiang Mai as being incapable of proper decorum and moreover of occupying a temporal domain of wild antiquity that was, in some important regards, antecedent to the nation. The association of the terms Lao and *lawaa*, the latter referring to a relatively marginal and tribal community makes it clear that Mongkut's intention here was to mark a threshold beyond which Thainess could not be recognized, in any sense of that term. Chiang Mai's rudeness had often been assumed by Bangkokians, but in Mongkut's proclamation, it is specifically the appearance of northerners that is read as a sign of their pastness and not simply of their foreignness. The words about dress are remarkable in their lack of differentiation between men and women, only part of which can be accounted for by the relative absence of female visitors to the palace. But there is another issue here, namely, that the regulation of attire made sense in this early formulation only in terms of the king's gaze, which occupied the center of the visual field even when that field included Western spectators. Rama IV expressed a sense that the palace was the proper space of cultural self-representation, assuming his own centrality in the view of his visitors. He made no mention of the spaces beyond his palace walls.

22. Thipakhorawang (Chaophraya), *The Dynastic Chronicles: Bangkok Era for Fourth Reign*, trans. Chadin Flood (Tokyo: Centre for East Asian Cultural Studies, 1965), 1:5.

23. Prince Wan Waithayakon, "Thai Culture: Lecture Delivered before the Thailand Research Society [formerly the Royal Siam Society], 27 February 1944," in *The Centennial of His Royal Highness Prince Wan Waithayakon Krommun Naradhop Bonsprabandh* (Bangkok: Office of the National Culture Commission, 1991, 33–34. Originally published in *Journal of the Thailand Research Society* 35, no. 2 (1944): 135–45.

That lack of differentiation between men and women and the inattention to attire in public space was to be overwhelmed in 1899, however, when an anxious anticipation of state visits from abroad generated legislation on proper attire for the public domain as well. Émile Jottrand noted in his diaries that a decree had been passed concerning dress that could be worn in public and observed with a combination of amusement and pity that the police had begun enforcing it five days before it was actually to have come into effect. The decree of 1899 made the sumptuary display of gendered differences a matter of law and no longer restricted itself to the space commanded by the regal gaze. Moreover, it suggested a displacement of the palace as the site of ideally representative performance. In its stead, the space of everyday life would assume the role of theatrical stage on which local identity would have to be displayed. As will become apparent, the turn away from the palace and the emergence of a normativized public domain, defined as typically Thai, had everything to do with the ways photography was mobilized in the production and maintenance of racial, ethnic, and class difference. By the time of the 1899 decree, proprietary attire had become a matter of cultural signification not only for foreigners but for Thais, who were beginning not only to anticipate but to internalize foreigners' perceptions. To a considerable degree, the decree's extension of Rama IV's concern expressed the impact of Christian missionary anxieties about the inherent capacity of the body to signify within a moral code, and it suggests that pressure was already being placed on the more contextual logic of the earlier prohibition. Clothing was no longer merely what one wore on particular occasions; it was beginning to signify the moral nature of Thai being.

According to Jottrand, the "innovations" of the 1899 proclamation were as follows:

1. In the streets men may only wear a *phanung* or a *sarong* which descends lower than the knee (exception is made for those who bathe in the *klong* [*sic*] or return from it);
2. Women can show themselves in public only if their bust is covered by a *phahom* (no exceptions);
3. Children must wear clothes and can no longer walk around the streets naked (exception is made for a bath). The parents are held responsible for their naked children until the age of fifteen years. Breach of obedience results in a fine of one *tical* first, for recidivists four *ticals* and, at the second relapse in the offense, twelve *ticals*.[24]

24. Mr. and Mrs. Émile Jottrand, *In Siam*, trans. Walter E. J. Tips (Bangkok: White Lotus Press, 1996), 96.

The measures were, as Jottrand said, "rigorous," the fines severe. At the time, one *tical* was worth nearly sixty U.S. cents, a considerable sum for an average worker. Fifty *ticals* would have been the fine paid in lieu of a six-month jail sentence,[25] and would have purchased several dozen kilos of rice. But the enforcement of the law was equally rigorous. In one day alone, the police arrested fifteen people for allowing their children to run naked; among these had been an eight-month-old infant.[26] The reason for this extraordinary dedication to the maintenance of public decorum, otherwise rather absent in Bangkok and even more so elsewhere, was the impending visit of Prince Henry of Belgium. At a time when King Rama V was traveling widely in Europe and posing for cameras in the attire of his hosts, cultural self-representation was assuming extraordinary importance as a technique in international affairs. But it was not without its ironies, and these were not lost on Jottrand, who exclaimed, "Poor princes who go traveling! By their arrival everything becomes a lie."[27]

Without disingenuousness, one can wonder about precisely which aspect of the decree struck Jottrand as being the most hypocritical. In all probability, he was simply observing the fact that the modesty being demanded in legislation was not normally part of everyday life in Siam, that bathing in public and the nudity of children were commonplace. But he could as easily have been astonished by the fact that women were being allowed to "show" themselves only by not showing themselves. Indeed, there was a strange logic embedded in the decree—the very logic of Christian modesty—that made a virtue of concealment at the same time that it demanded an ethics of transparency. Yet, if he found this particular decree bizarre, Jottrand seems to have been less perplexed by the rigor with which the courts enforced other laws concerning clothing, including that which prohibited the then very fashionable theft of hats. In his writings, there is no discomfort expressed over the general notion that law should concern itself with appearance, and in this regard, he departed little from colonial officers everywhere who were policing social difference and access to metropolitan citizenship by insisting on the display of colonial status in dress. If access to such citizenship was irrelevant in Thailand, where an enforced free trade had done the work of colonialism, attire could nonetheless provide a site at which the defacement of class prerogative and Western identification could yet have meaning and suggest a dangerous instability. Hence the waves of "hat snatching" to which Bangkok fell subject at century's end.

In the logs of commissioners who were involved in the reform of Siamese

25. Walter E. J. Tips, *Crime and Punishment in King Chulalongkorn's Kingdom* (Bangkok: Bua Luang, 1998), 275.

26. Jottrand, *In Siam*, 97.

27. Ibid.

law, hat snatching generated considerable anxiety and was noted as a serious crime, punishable by prison sentences of two to three years. This was an inordinately lengthy sentence for the time, even for the crime of stealing a buffalo, and similar sentences were meted out by the Special Commission of 1896 for offenses such as robbery with assault and even, on at least one occasion, murder.[28] In part, this seeming disproportion between crime and punishment—Rolin-Jaequemyns's gravest concern in the reform of Siamese law—is explicable in terms of *sakdi naa*, which remained operative in the courts through the differential assignment of punishments according to the status of the victim offended. In the Ayutthian period, when it was instituted by King Borommatrailokanat (r. 1448–1488) in a piece of legislation called the Law of Civil Hierarchy, *sakdi naa* had been a minutely differentiated and heritable status measured in terms of land but referring more directly to labor controlled.[29] The term actually means "field of power" or "power over the field," but even those without land possessed some *sakdi naa*.[30] Although Chaophraya Thipakhorawong would remark, in his annotations to *The Dynastic Chronicles* of the fourth reign, that the system was "purely honorary" by the nineteenth century, Jot-

28. Ibid., 63. In the table of findings from the Special Commission's report of 1896, the sentence of three years was also given for jewelry theft with assault, and murder. The table is reprinted in Tips's *Crime and Punishment*, 259–75.

29. On the system of *sakdina* or *sakdi naa*, see Quaritch H. G. Wales, *Ancient Siamese Government and Administration* (1934; New York: Paragon, 1965), and Akin Rabibhadana, *The Organization of Thai Society in the Early Bangkok Period, 1782–1873* (Ithaca, NY: Cornell University, Southeast Asia Program, 1969). David Wyatt's explication of the earlier history of *sakdi naa* in the early Ayutthyan period stresses its ideological function as that which would "regulate natural human inequality for the sake of the proper functioning of the social order." But the critique of *sakdi naa* was most forcefully articulated by communist writer Cit Poumisak. See Craig J. Reynolds, *Thai Radical Discourse, The Real Face of Thai Feudalism Today* (Ithaca, NY: Cornell University Southeast Asia Program, 1987).

30. In his annotations to the *Dynastic Chronicles*, Chaophraya Thipakhorawong notes that under Borommatrailokanat, the *sakdi naa* varied from 25 *rai* of land for commoners to 20,000 *rai* for members of the royal family, each referring to the amount of land that one could cultivate or have cultivated on one's behalf. The more power and status one had, the more remote one was from the actual process of cultivation. The titles were not technically hereditary, but they were nonetheless categorically transmitted and to that extent remained more or less fixed for commoners, save those men who were promoted for military service or the like. Thipakhorawong claims that, by the nineteenth century, *sakdi naa* was a "purely honorary" institution, but this seems to be an ideological fantasy of modernity and can perhaps be understood in terms of the function that the memorial volumes of the *Dynastic Chronicles* were intended to perform. That is, they were part of a nearly hagiographic representation of King Rama IV as the father of the modern, and this seems to have demanded a claim to having recognized the equality of nonroyal persons. See, in particular, 3:54–55.

trand and the administrators of the new legal system found it everywhere implicit in the assignation of penalties. In all probability, the residue of *sakdi naa* was the greatest single obstacle to the establishment of a rule by law in which all subjects would have equal rights to the judicial process. Indeed, left-wing radicals such as Cit Poumisak would later claim as much in their insistence on a persistent feudalism in Thailand.[31] In 1899, however, Jottrand described it as a rather exclusively juridical measure: "Everyone has a number of *saknas* [*sic*] or if you like, points which represent his or her judicial value."[32] In the calculus of the time, a commoner ranked 5 *saknas* [*sic*] and a prince 15,000, not far removed from the spectrum of 25 to 20,000 that had been operative in Borommatrailokanat's time. Which is to say, crime was not yet crime sui generis but crime against a particular kind of person whose value determined the nature of the transgression and its punishment.

The point of all this is that the consequences of the *sakdi naa* system's residual presence informed response to the hat-snatching craze. Those who wore the hats were generally either foreigners or wealthier Siamese citizens with exposure to the West and perhaps even some experience in universities or administrative service there. Although any assault on a person's head is accorded more seriousness than other bodily crimes in the somatic economy of Buddhism (which, like Brahmanism, values the head over all else), hat snatching was rendered serious mainly by virtue of the category of persons against whom it was committed. The seriousness of the crime then translated itself and fed back into a penal system where crimes against appearance could assume even greater significance. Eventually, defacing bourgeois fashion could be interpreted by the courts as being as heinous a crime as robbing a peasant of his livelihood and even, in some cases, his life. Fashion became "valuable" in proportion and was indeed inserted into the new economy of monetized exchange values, for unlike the premodern courts, the new legal system demanded payment in cash for such transgressions.

Hats are not everything, of course. Or at least, they are not adequate explanations of fashion's transformation. There were many other sites at which the reciprocal relations among new consumer practices, new forms of wealth, and new processes of criminalization came together to make fashion the mark against which crime would measure itself. Moreover, the discursive circuits within which new notions of criminality and new forms of fashionability came together were refracted further by the phenomenon of photography, which, although it had arrived some fifty years earlier, acquired its popular potential only

---

31. Cit, *The Real Face of Thai Feudalism Today*.
32. Jottrand, *In Siam*, 70.

after the century's turn, when both Rama V and Prince Damrong Rajanubhab took it up and became enamored of the idea of cultural tableaux. It is indeed through photography that fashion assumed its capacity to represent culture.

## Photographic Legacies

By the time Prince Damrong began collecting photographs and imagining them as part of a museological project to which the collection of costume would also contribute, there were some twenty professional photographers in Thailand and several dozen amateurs.[33] In Rama IV's reign, however, it was still an extraordinary process and one for which foreigners could be called to the palace. In 1855, Rama IV expressed his gratitude to President Franklin Peirce of the United States for a gift that had been sent with Townsend Harris, the envoy plenipotentiary for treaty negotiations. Included with mirrors, glass chimneys, dissecting instruments, microscopes, and guns was a "camera lucida, by which an accurate drawing of any object viewed in the microscope may be taken."[34] Also mentioned were several "colored views" of American cities and one of an express railway train. In all likelihood, these "views" were daguerreotypes; it had become common, by this point, for daguerreotypes to be included in the diplomatic gifts exchanged by national governments. Thus, in 1857, Rama IV sent to Queen Victoria two daguerreotypes of himself, "one of which is a likeness of His Majesty the First King of Siam dress [sic] in full royal robes and decorations sealed on his throne. The Other is the Daguerreotype of His Majesty with the Royal consort and two Royal children seated in [sic] Their Majesties knees."[35] A subsequent letter to Queen Victoria, dated 1861, nonetheless suggests that the images Rama IV was sending abroad may have been made by foreigners. Certainly, the new photographic processes of wet-plating were not being undertaken locally, for in his letter, Rama IV mentions that some of the objects sent by the English monarch had not been usable because their operation had been mysterious to the recipients. Among these had been a coining mint and a camera. The letter follows (reproduced here verbatim, with original errors):

33. Anake Nawigamune, *Thaaj ruub müang thai samai raek* [Early photography in Thailand] (Bangkok: SaengDaed, 1987), 16.

34. S.P.P. Mongkut (Rama IV), "Proclamation About the Letter and Presents Received from Franklin Peirce, President of the U.S.A," in *A King of Siam Speaks*, by M.R. Seni Pramoj and M.R. Kukrit Pramoj (Bangkok: Siam Society, 1987), 114–17 [original in English].

35. S.P.P. Mongkut (Rama IV), "Letter to Queen Victoria," in Seni and Kukrit, *A King of Siam Speaks*, 131 [original in English].

The Hydro press of cotton can be understood and worked bery well in facility by Siamese workers immediately on arrival of the instrument, without enquiry for direction from European visitor, but the coining mint was postponed several months, when there was an English engineer called to Siam. . . . But the photographic cammera was to postpone very long because Siamese have no facility to work. Afterward however we have met with a Swedish photographer being visitor here, and the other gentleman, who was a person of good understanding of photographic work introduced to us by your Majesty's consul Sir Robery Schomburgh, who both have given some instruction and assistant to our native worked who become now in some facility in the photographic work. Wherefore we on this occasion have liberty to let our native photographers take the likeness of ourselves, when we adorned with the watch decked with diamonds and the double edged sword which were honorary royal gracious gifts from your Majesty, received by us a few years ago, and seated ourselves by the tables containing the gift silver inkstand and desk together with the revolving pistol and rifle, wholly being royal gracious gift from your Majesty, in a framed piece of paper, have caused another photographic likeness of our royal affectionate Queen consort to be done in another framed paper, and let the painter paint both according to their ability, and got the said two photographic portraits, with a lump of pressed cotton in the Hydro press, and a set of silver coins made up here by the native worker is the coining mint, so that there are three articles in number entrusted to the care of the present Siamese Embassy in accompany here with—designed to be offered to your Majesty by them for inspection, hoping that your Majesty will see the effects of your Majesty's gracious present bestowed on us.[36]

One cannot but be charmed by the juxtapositions in the letter: the guns and cameras, the sword and pen, the priceless watch and the technology for coining the measure of value. The gifts were sparkling toys of a phantasmagoric commodity parade, and they withheld their darker sides from the Siamese king even when he could not comprehend their workings. And, when the strangeness of the technology threatened to exclude Rama IV from membership in the community of modern subjects, he responded with knowingness, so much so, indeed, that he was able to play on the desires of his foreign portraitists and seduce them with the promise of a picture from behind the scenes.

There is a particularly curious and provocative story about such a seduction related by John Thomson, a Scottish photographer who traveled to Siam three

36. Ibid., 134.

years before Rama IV's death in 1865. Requests to photograph the king were increasingly common through his reign, but only that of the governor of Singapore finally made it into *The Dynastic Chronicles*.[37] Nonetheless, all such events were attended with much ceremony. Thomson's permission to photograph the king was granted through the British consul, and on 6 October he was received by the court astrologer into a room that had been prepared for the occasion with canopy and carpet. King Rama IV entered in a white floor-length robe, in a fashion rather typical for the aristocracy and certainly without any obvious marks of royal rank. According to Thomson, the king requested that he be photographed while in prayer. It would have been a usual image, to say the least, for it would have pictured the king in a manner that did not permit his gaze to command the camera. At the time, one did not look upon the king without his gaze structuring the entire circuit of looks, and had Thomson shot His Majesty in prayer, it would not have been the king's look that was pictured. He would have appeared merely as one who had been seen: caught, as it were, in the act, even if that act was a devotional one. Thomson, somewhat surprised, "accordingly adjusted his instrument" in preparation for the shot, but was robbed of the opportunity when Rama IV suddenly and "without a word to anyone passed out of the sight."[38] Advised that any question might be reproved with violence, Thomson waited for some hours, and Rama IV eventually returned to reward his patience. This time, however, he was "dressed in a sort of French Field Marshall's uniform."[39] No explanation for the delay or the French clothing was offered, save that the king was said to do "everything which is right."

Thomson's perplexity at the disappearance was equaled by his astonishment at the foreign attire in which Rama IV returned, though on entry to the room he had remarked its pastiche of furniture from Europe and China and the portraits of Napoleon III and the French empress that hung on the walls. It seemed odd to Thomson that the king would have appeared there, in so foreign a guise, unconcerned that he appear as a representative of Siam through the vehicle of costume. But the Supreme King had no need to perform his Siamese-

---

37. Mention of the governor's request appears in the account of the king's journey to observe a solar eclipse: "at some time after nine o'clock, the Governor of Singapore asked to take a photograph of King." The actual taking of the photograph is not described, however. Thipakhorawong, *The Dynastic Chronicles*, 2: 538.

38. J. Thomson, *The Straits of Malacca, Indo-China and China, or Ten Years' Travel, Adventures, and Residence Abroad* (London: Simpson, Low, Marston, Low, and Searl, 1875), excerpted in *Descriptions of Old Siam*, compiled by Michael Smithies (Kuala Lumpur: Oxford University Press, 1995), 198.

39. Ibid., 199.

ness; he was, after all, in Siam, and unlike many of the portraits he had sent as part of diplomatic communications to Europe, Thomson's was intended for local consumption. On other occasions, Rama IV did pose in Siamese regalia, but from the start, portrait photography was associated for the upper echelons of Siamese society with the possibility of charade, with the virtual mobility of costume, and it was as much like the fantastical magic of the theater as the faux empiricism of the travelogue. The staging Rama IV had both promised and withdrawn in the scene with Thomson was indeed exceptional in its promise of a look behind the scene, but it also suggests the degree to which the "private" realm of the king was already a matter of public theatricality. The staginess of portrait photography was mitigated as little in Siam as it was elsewhere, in Europe and the Americas, at the time. That the privacy of the palace would be an already publicized domain is perhaps less surprising than that public space should soon come to demand performances in which one's private identity is also performed, and yet the latter would come to pass via the camera and the new economies within which portraits would circulate alongside ethnographic postcards.

Initially, portraiture was largely the preserve of the wealthy. And for this very reason, it was little encumbered by a desire to signify Siameseness. Costume in portrait photography was a sign of a virtual mobility, if not actual mobility in the newly transnationalized space within which the technology circulated. For the aristocracy in general, costume was part of a luxurious pastime of make-believe and the pursuit of entertainment. Thus, when Rama IV wrote to Phya Montri Suriwongse, the ambassador to the Court of Queen Victoria, he lamented that the diplomat would not be able to buy English-women and suggested that "it might be a good idea to buy some of their costumes and bring them back home to dress up some of our earthly beauties here [in Siam] for the sake of variety."[40] Rama V (Chulalongkorn) would later have himself photographed in everything from English suits to Russian uniforms, and wealthy nobles often posed in the bourgeois country fashions of Europe. Costume was correlated with ethnic identity, was read as an expression of a culturalized being (though the word for culture, *watthanatham*, would wait another half-century for coinage) only in the photography of the poor, for whom there was not so much portraiture as ethnographic inscription. Unlike in England or the United States, there was not at this time a large middle class whose members could conceive of photography as a democratic "art" or who

40. S.P.P. Mongkut (Rama IV), "Letter to Phya Montri Suriwongse, the King's Ambassador to the Court of Queen Victoria, and Chao Mun Sarapethbhakid, Vice-Ambassador, 1857," in Seni and Kukrit, *A King of Siam Speaks*, 214.

could cast themselves in the place of imaginary sojourners. Instead, the photography of the masses was the photography of documentation and idealized typification. Moreover, it was associated with the very constitution of the masses as an ethnicized, if split, category in a renewed opposition between rurality and urbanity that was not only not overcome through the railway, but actually enhanced by it. Northernness and northeasternness, as well as tribalness, came to be read as what Barthes called the "universal signifieds" in ethnographic photographs of farmers, rural musicians, and elephant trainers, among others.

It is no accident that the American president would send an image of a railway along with views of New York and Philadelphia, or that the railways in Thailand were well-photographed sites in a country that was becoming nothing but sites to be visited by the train. Yet, the ironic interest of the railway photographs is often that the train is absent and that the scene, if not the mise-en-scène of the station, provides the occasion for an ethnographic image of "local people." The railway in Thailand, as elsewhere, was associated with the compression of spatial distance, but the transcendence of space was coupled with a new sense of locality's value and in fact produced that value as its effect. It was therefore almost inevitable that the train station would become the stage for local culture's photographic inscription. And here, one cannot overlook the fact that the founder of the ethnographic costume collection that was to become the centerpiece of new museological efforts in the 1930s, Major Erik Seidenfaden, was also the author of the Royal State Railway Department of Siam's *Guide to Bangkok with Notes on Siam*.[41] Railways and ethnographic inscription, transportation and locality, were mutually entailed from very early on.

In the photographs of Siam that were taken for the World Transportation Commission (WTC) between 1894 and 1896 and preserved at the Smithsonian Institution archives, images tend to coalesce into three categories. Those in which the railway features are yet few, but much more abundant than any other scenes of technology. Those featuring Bangkok's religious and monarchical monuments dominate the collection and exhibit all the hallmarks of postcard aesthetics. But in addition, a sizable portion of the images are focused on unnamed representatives of the Siamese or Lao people. In these, the nakedness of any person in the frame is remarked in the caption, often in contrast to the other barely specified category, namely, "person of rank." The WTC, of course, was aided by local guides, and the clumsy illustrative captioning of the images

41. Erik Seidenfaden, *Guide to Bangkok, with Notes on Siam* (Bangkok: Royal State Railway Department of Siam, 1927).

reproduced what was emerging as a more generalized ethos in Siam. That ethos was one in which the periphery, especially the northern and northeastern regions, was becoming an object of visual consumption for Bangkokians. In this process, nakedness was to become a sign of peripherality, of premodernity, and of pre-Thainess. Without clothing, there would be no name. Without a name, there would be no national identity. As though clothing were the prerequisite for that hailing by which subjects could be summoned into the national collective.[42] The conflation of nakedness and national exteriority that had first manifest itself in Rama IV's edict thus came to be the axis on which appearances were made to signify. As peripheral communities and populations were incorporated into the state, it became necessary for them to appear in a manner that represented their acquiescence to the state, and it is in this moment that the demand for ethnic costume begins to be made. In effect, costumes come to work as the signs of a double status, evoking both anteriority vis-à-vis the nation and encompassment by the state. The one who wears ethnic costume is not so much a subject-citizen as a sign of difference abstracted.

The irony of this relationship was both potent and violent: ethnographic photography could only alienate locality from its place, and costume could only suggest the dislocation of what was supposed to be an expression of primitive identity. Nonetheless, it would be a mistake to assume that ethnography had interest only for foreigners. For the agency of urban Siamese subjects was best enacted in relation to national tableaux over which they could exercise authority, and it is for this reason, or at least in this context, that the photography of local people came to be so very popular among the most elite of Siam's new bureaucratic modernists.

At his floating studio in the Chao Phraya River, the first in Siam, Francis Chit (Khun Sunthorn Satitsalak) offered portrait services to foreigners and advertised the sale of "Photographs of Palaces, Temples, buildings, scenery and public men of Siam."[43] His card announced his appointment as photographer to "H.M. the Supreme King of Siam," and he had among his subjects not only King IV and his court but also the literary luminaries of the day as well as economic power brokers, religious leaders, and the architect of modern history and judicial reform as well as the first collector of photographs, Prince Dam-

42. It is interesting to note in this regard that the registration of second or family names came into practice only in 1913. The Personal and Family Names Act provided a list of names to choose from and was so associated in the minds of commoners with the notion of title that "lists of forbidden names had to be compiled and disseminated." See Walter Vella, *Chaiyo! King Vajiravudh and the Development of Thai Nationalism* (Honolulu: University of Hawaii Press, 1978), 134.

43. The advertisement appeared in *The Bangkok Recorder*, 14 January 1865. It is reproduced in Anake, *Thaaj ruub müang thai*, 103.

rong.[44] Like all photographers of his time, Chit also undertook the photography of curiosities and medical anomalies, picturing victims of elephantiasis, tumors, and other deforming diseases in what was becoming a generically disseminated style of medical and criminological documentation. The style was of a piece with a broader collecting aesthetic (full frontal shots paired with profiles) and was not clearly distinguishable from the ethnographic work that Chit also performed at his studio in his series of images of common and unnamed men and women, many of whom were pictured wearing fine silk "models" of clothing that more often would have been woven from cotton and cheaper fabric.

Later, both Rama V and Prince Damrong became aficionados of ethnographic photography in this mode, not only as consumers but as photographers in their own right. Rama V spent a great deal of time posing his wives and consorts in regionally ethnicized costume, but Damrong had occasion to travel widely and frequently in his capacity as Minister of the Interior responsible for the northern provinces, and his work tended to be more properly ethnographic, being devoted to "local scenes" and "common people." In producing these images, Damrong seems to have found the possibility for a playful identification. Nonetheless, it was an identification without risk and perhaps without desire. Certainly, it was one that remained subordinate to his drive to modernize the rural peripheries.

One sees the resistance to a more total identification with the "primitive" in the images that Damrong permitted to be taken of himself. One of the more interesting portraits features the prince standing before a camera in peasant attire augmented by a distinctly European hat and glasses. In the picture, Damrong is posing with his camera in front of a neutral draped background, which hangs as a blockage in the frame: the threshold of location and condition of possibility for a certain claim to universality. Indeed, the aspiration to authenticity via costume assumes a rather ludicrously alienated quality in this context.[45] Damrong's self-consciousness in the pose heightens this sense and implicitly asks the viewer to recognize the fact that what makes the farmer is what he does and what he does is determined by where he is. Thus attired as a farmer but without land or even the props that would produce the mise-en-scène of rurality, Damrong in his costume does not so much resemble a farmer

---

44. The modernity of Damrong's notion of history derived at least in part from the fact that he was an avid reader of German historian Leopold von Ranke and shared the latter's commitment to the notion of universal progress. See Scot Barmé, *Luang Wichit Wathakan and the Creation of a Thai Identity* (Singapore: Institute of Southeast Asian Studies, 1993), 47.

45. Anake, *Thaaj ruub müang thai*, 178.

as he resembles one for whom such a resemblance is a matter of choice rather than being. Indeed, the image that emerges from the photograph is precisely not that of a farmer but of an aristocrat in the position of playful masquerade. In its improbable juxtapositions, in the spaces where the signs of rurality and urbanity abut, he appropriates for himself the promise of modern magic.[46]

In this context, it becomes especially important to understand why the images that Damrong and his contemporaries produced of regional "others" effaced the hybridity of such juxtaposition at every turn. In part, this can be understood as the different relationship that rural nonaristocratic subjects were permitted to have to photography. For them, the camera demanded a conformity to the image of an identity, then conceived in essentialized and even ontologized (racialized or ethnicized) regional terms. The demand for a culturally representational purity is perhaps nowhere more clearly exhibited than in the likenesses made of "local" people from the outlying provinces, who were photographed while in Bangkok in costumes that were supposed to stage their local identity. Musicians or dancers from Chiang Mai were especially desired subjects in studio photography and were often posed in performance. However, it was their appearance more than their art that was staged there.[47] What strikes the viewer, therefore, when comparing these studio scenes to those seemingly more candid images produced in situ is that the latter reveal faces unprepared for the lens, faces that have not yet anticipated their own future recalling via the photograph *as image* and, more important, as a metonym of local culture.[48] If one traces the looks of these faces in the frame, there is not only no center, but the reciprocal Archimedean point that we commonly accept as the mark of portraiture in photography seems absent. The looks emanate from a variety of points, and nothing in their eyes suggests a consciousness in which the photographer could himself be conceived as part of a picture. There is no behindness to these eyes, no retrospectively antecedent look. In short, the subjects of these images do not seem to fantasize for themselves that kind of subjectivity that Lacan would say rests on the desire to see oneself seeing oneself. And as

46. Such juxtaposition was more literally realized in the New Year's cards that featured images of the king, Buddhist monks, and scenes of Bangkok with traces of leaves and inscriptions of well wishers. See Anake Nawigamune, *Phaab kao lao tamnan* [Old pictures and the stories they tell] (Bangkok: Matichon, 1997), 84.

47. Ibid., esp. 34–36.

48. There are innumerable examples of such not-yet-composed faces in the cartes de visite that circulated in the early decades of the century. Some of these have been reproduced in *Post Cards of Old Siam*. A particularly exemplary instance is to be seen in the image taken by Rama V in Kamphaengphet in 1904, where four young women wait with baskets of flowers and seem utterly without sense of where the look of the camera comes from (Anake, *Thaaj ruub müang thai*, 171).

Lacan observes, such a structure of subjectivity is premised on the organization of desire in the domain of "seeing,"[49] in a world of visual hegemony. Or, to put the matter in terms that we have already encountered in discussions of Heidegger's work, the "objects" of these photographs do not appear to enframe the world in response to their own enframement. So, a disjuncture: between the urban demand for an ethnicized rurality that would transparently display itself through the signs of costume, and a consciousness in rural areas that did not yet comprehend and could not yet anticipate the demand for such metonymic self-composure.

The irony of that disjuncture becomes much poignant when one recognizes the degree to which the photographic project of those early years, in what we might call the second stage of photography in Thailand, was informed by a sense of impending loss. In fact, the loss was doubled. Not only was a way of life deemed to be on the threshold of demise, but the photographs themselves were thought vulnerable to this fate. Thus, by 1899, Prince Damrong had already begun gathering up photographs and putting them into a book, even pursuing the owners of closed studios for negatives and castoff images. Initially, Damrong undertook his compilation in secret. One cannot help but speculate on that secrecy, but there is little to explain it, save Sthirakoses's recollection that the need for secrecy had to do with Damrong's fear that the need for collection would not be self-evident.[50] Perhaps he worried that his attachment to these images would seem improper, itself indicative of something occult. Equally plausible is the simple fear of seeming ridiculous, for it was not yet clear how many shared his own anticipation of disappearance.

Later, Sthirakoses, the prolific author who wrote famously under the pen name Phya Anuman Rajadhon, would express his gratitude for these pictures, for their capacity to stir his memory of vanished places. Thinking back on Damrong's secretly compiled album, he remarks explicitly on the images' prosthetic memory: "The pictures would jog my memory. . . . From those pictures you could see how Ratchadamnoen Avenue, which had just been completed at that time, was different from the Ratchadamnoen Avenue of today. You could see how the people were dressed and how the Chinese still wore long pig tails. The pictures give me a warm feeling of nostalgia, and I have to thank Prince Damrong for compiling those of this event [the celebration of Rama V's return from Europe]; otherwise following generations would not have a chance to see it. It is equivalent to passing down a cultural heritage to the new generation;

49. Lacan, "Anamorphosis."
50. Sthirakoses (Phya Anuman Rajadhon), *Looking Back: Book One* (Bangkok: Translation Center, Chulalongkorn University Press, 1992), 271.

without it we would be a nation with only a present and no past to speak of."[51] Though a boy at the time of the celebration, Anuman was to become the father of Thai folklore studies and the foremost authority on Thai traditions. What is therefore notable in this brief passage is the linkage among three distinct elements: photography's mnemonic function, the significance that appearances acquire in that context, and the sense of a national purpose attaching to the collection of imagery that will become patrimonial in the museological context.

The national value of photography was explicitly recognized when, during World War I, the German-owned Robert Lenz studio in Charoen Krung Road went out of business and was taken over by the Bureau of the Palace Ministry (later to be called the Royal Household). It lasted about twenty years under the name Norasingh Photo Studio and was run by two men, one of whom was from the family that had previously owned the famous Chit and Sons Photo Studio on the Chao Phraya River.[52] Not incidentally, many of the images generated by these studios ended up in the National Museum for which Major Siedenfaden was collecting regional costumes in the hopes of establishing a "Folk Museum or an ethnographical branch."[53]

Siedenfaden, an indefatigable ethnologist and central member of the Siam Society, "got the idea of collecting, as far as possible, all the national costumes of the various branches of the Thai people" in the early 1930s, and with the assistance of Prince Wan Wathaiyakon, the inventor of the Thai word for "culture" (*watthanatham*), proceeded to collect seventy-two samples. These were displayed in 1937 at the Society's hall and donated to the National Museum in 1938. The motivation for the project was belatedness. As Siedenfaden put the matter:

> During my frequent travels in the provinces in these latter years I have noticed to my sorrow how the picturesque and time-honored national and

51. Ibid.

52. Ibid., 272–73.

53. Erik Siedenfaden, "Siam's Tribal Dresses," *Journal of the Siam Society* 31, no. 2 (1939): 169. Siedenfaden had originally been appointed inspector general of the Royal Siamese Provincial Gendarmerie between 1908 and 1919. He arrived in Thailand just four years after the founding of the Royal Siam Society by a motley group of expatriate and local intellectuals, bureaucratic officials, and visiting academics. Siedenfaden took Francis Giles's position as president of the Siam Society in 1938, during the period of Phibul's ascendant nationalism. Giles himself had been borrowed by Thailand for the purposes of overseeing revenue collection in 1897 and had worked closely with Prince Damrong in the capacity of director of the Exterior Revenue Department, which was placed under Damrong's ministry as part of the reform of the judiciary and the administrative apparatus (for which Rolin-Jacquaemyns had also been hired). See Peter Cuasay, "Siamese Montage" (M.A. thesis, University of Washington, 1995), for an account of Siedenfaden's ethnological writings.

regional costumes, nearly all over the land, are fast disappearing, to be replaced by dresses of a more or less international fashion. It has rightly been said that the honk of the motor lorry with its load of cheap foreign textiles sounds the death knell of the national costumes, while the radio and the cinematograph are rapidly exterminating provincial dialects and ancient manners and customs.

Therefore if future generations are not to be kept in ignorance as to how their ancestors clothed themselves, it is high time now to collect all the various dresses still worn by inhabitants of this picturesque and beautiful land, and to keep them carefully preserved in our museums for future information and study.[54]

Things were more complicated than that, of course. Radio would become the site of the first vernacular movements, and central government agencies would soon require individuals to wear putatively regional costume as evidence of its local representativeness. In penning the Royal State Railway Department's *Guide to Bangkok*, Seidenfaden himself was contributing to the process by which foreignness would penetrate those recesses of the country that electricity and railway transport had only recently begun to illuminate.[55] Nonetheless, the combination of lamentation and anticipatory grieving make Seidenfaden's otherwise facile remarks exemplary. Indeed, there is a profound congruity between his sentiment and that of Anuman Rajadhon and other folklorists, including those in the North, who were soon to be conducting ethnographic surveys, photographing "local people," and buying from them the "costumes" that they otherwise continued to wear.

In one of myriad asides on the virtues of museology in the project of national culture, Anuman leaves his autobiographical narrative to state (with surprising lack of irony) that if "something can be kept for future generations to study in terms of cultural development, then keep it in a museum as a relic in order to create constant self-awareness. Then you can be called highly civilized. If it is something that has lost its utility, but if kept, does not harm or impede progress, then it should be kept as a tradition. This is to make us feel proud that we

---

54. Seidenfaden, "Siam's Tribal Dresses," 170.

55. Interestingly, Seidenfaden's account of Bangkok attends to the fact of electric light in great detail; his narratives of the Chinese district in 1927 describe it as being "brilliantly lighted up by tens of thousands of electrical lamps, and the towering scraper-like Chinese hotels are ablaze with illumination" (*Guide to Bangkok*, 76–79). The association of Chinatown with light and noise nonetheless contrasts with that of the rest of Bangkok and Thailand, where such facts of life are seen as part of a process of cultural disturbance, save where inscribed within the heroic narrative of the Chakkri dynasty at the book's end (305–8).

have a past, and are not just recently born with only a present."[56] He would be echoed, more than twenty years later, in the national culture policy of the National Culture Commission, which included among its tasks the "conservation, preservation and restoration of culture to safeguard our cultural heritage, be it of actual use or not."[57]

The point, then, is not merely that local traditions are thought to be vanishing, but that a sense of history itself is on the verge of demise. The storage of local tradition therefore promises a kind of apotropaic effect, promises to mitigate a loss of historical consciousness—if only by substituting the prosthetic memory of museums and photography for the organic memory of one's parents. To this end, the local can be pressed into service of a national memory but only if it produces tokens and images of itself. Whence originates the demand for individuals on the periphery to pose as signs of the local and to compose themselves in and as the images of pastness. By the 1930s, as the modernity of the nation passed out of question, folkloric writings about the periphery became what can only be termed the discursive memory machine of the nation. Lannathai in particular came to signify an anterior history that was both pre-Thai and proto-Thai. Its alterity was to be neutralized by teleology.

It is, one speculates, horribly appropriate that Anuman should worry about the loss of his own memory and take solace in Damrong's photo album while failing to recall the names of the photographers—one of them a colleague of his in the Department of Fine Arts—who ran the Norasingh Photo Studio.[58] As Virilio would have it, the technologized archive is not so much an aide-mémoire as it is a memory substitute whose capacity expands in direct proportion to the diminution of individual, personal memory. This is because photography is so indiscriminate and because the fantasy of photography as a device of memory aspires to totality without recognizing what mediums know, namely, that the camera never sees what people see. One might even say that the camera can capture everything *but* what people see. So it gives to the forgetful subject what would not otherwise have been his or her own. This is, I think, the deeper origin of Anuman's anxiety over the loss of both memory and history. The consciousness articulated in his autobiography is perhaps one, the radicality of which is best addressed by Heidegger. In his essay "The Age of the World Picture," Heidegger describes the effect of technologization as the emer-

---

56. Sthirakoses, *Looking Back*, 194.

57. Office of the National Culture Commission, Ministry of Education (Thailand), *The National Culture Policy and Guidelines for Preservation, Promotion and Development of Culture 2529 [1986]* (Bangkok, 1987), 10.

58. Sthirakoses, *Looking Back*, 272.

gence of a new sensibility in which the world is construed as a systematicity representable by the subject. The newness of this perceptual and conceptual event is coupled for Heidegger with the emergence of the "new" as such. In Anuman's writings, this sense of newness, marked by the fear of residing in an eternal present, has as its corollary a fetishism of the past, but one that can be gathered up as an image whose meaning is immediately available. For this to be true, the occupants of this space would also have to signify transparently, would have to be made immediately legible. This was the work of costume. It was to be a cartographic key for ethnographic recognition, an archive of image types. With it, bureaucrats and tourists could move through the country and know, if only from the train's window, that the person in the field or at the station or even in the mountains was of one ethnic or tribal group or another. And with such recognition, they could then turn for meaning to the accounts in the Siam Society journals, where standardized ethnological surveys had produced standard cultural types. Perhaps they could even imagine themselves to be seeing something for the last time. Sthirakoses's sense of newness as the site of loss saturated the ethnological project and the tourist industry that attached itself, like a tick, to the back of anthropology and to history. And everywhere, the power of the new was experienced as a capacity to delineate the figure of disappearance.

In the end, it is with history, as much as anything else, that Prince Damrong is associated, his prolific writings on the subject constituting an utterly central edifice in the discipline as practiced in Thailand. Damrong, prince of modernity, bequeathed to his era an extraordinary array of accomplishments, but the modernized discourses of history, photography, and museology gravitate around a single, absent center of loss. His own portraits circulate there, and one cannot look at them without seeing in them a quintessentially modern subject. He looks back, claiming for himself the capacity to dissimulate but demanding of all others a kind of legibility that could be captured with cameras and signified in standardized costumes. One sees the turn of an era and the emergence of a politics that effected the containment of difference in and by historical representation. Soon, this incipient politics would become the formalized program of a state apparatus. And soon, mediums would be asked to represent the pastness of the periphery itself by becoming photogenic in costumes that date to the moment of photography's arrival in Thailand. That they would also become the sites for a critical commentary on the mindlessness of photography's historicism and that they would offer their clients oblique lessons on the transformation of representational consciousness in the very moment that they assumed the function of representation testifies, as will become clear, to the ironies of a history that is not simply the narrative of progressive development.

Before returning to the latter issue, however, it is necessary to understand how the emergent fetishism of appearances came to inform national cultural policy and, through it, the new discourses on local tradition.

## The Culture of Modernity

It is clear that, by the second and third decades of the century, modernity seemed to demand the assumption of Western attire—along with technological progress and the ideological development of notions of citizenship and public morality.[59] The precursor of that demand had, of course, been evident in Rama IV's demand for upper garments in the palace and in the decree that required women to cover their breasts and men to cover their legs. Nonetheless, it achieved a more radical form in the years of Luang Wichit Wathakan's bourgeois cultural nationalism. Indeed, in his address on what constituted civilization (*aryatham*), Wichit exhorted his audience to dress the part of modern subjects to appear worthy of a modern nation: "Fifty years ago people would have probably walked from Uthai to Bangkok . . . but if I told you I had walked here from the capital you would probably think I was mad. We have trains so why not use them? Similarly, . . . if I wore a loin cloth (*phakhawma*) you would say I was most definitely insane. I have to wear shoes and socks, a shirt and coat. It's the same for all of you . . . we are all hot, but we have to deport ourselves in a modern way."[60]

Wichit did not yet appreciate just how modern his audience was becoming—or that such modernity would refuse to remain a matter of surfaces. The still absolute monarchy was under increasing pressure as a result of the depression and the state's inability to cope with it. Rice exports had begun to decline in 1929, and indebtedness among farmers was growing enormously as a result.[61] Unemployment in Bangkok was also growing, and the demand for land and area taxes was creating unbearable burdens for salaried workers both in the cities and in the rural areas, where increasing numbers of agriculturalists had become contract laborers. When the government of King Prajadhipok, Rama VII, enacted a "bureaucratic assistance tax" of 5 percent on the salaries of government employees, opposition coalesced enough to sustain a coup.[62] It was

59. Luang Wichit Wathakan itemized the qualities of civilization as knowledge (including technological knowledge), moral uprightness, proper behavior, and a sense of public duty. See Barmé, *Luang Wichit Wathakan*, 51.
60. Wichit Wathakan, "Aryatham" [Civilization], in *Pathakatha lae' kham banjai* [Lectures and talks], (Bangkok: Soemwit Bannakan, 1973), 1: 54–64, cited in Barmé, *Luang Wichit Wathakan*, 52.
61. Barmé, *Luang Wichit Wathakan*, 64–65.
62. Ibid., 66.

led by a Paris-based student of law named Pridi Phanomyong, whose People's Party of Thailand enjoyed the support of several young military officers, including Phibul Songkhram, the man who would soon become prime minister. The political history of the coup and of the period immediately following it has been well documented and elegantly interpreted by the historians of the period, and I leave readers to pursue those texts devoted to the minute chronology of events and the larger, internationally circulating discourses of revolution as they manifested themselves in Thailand.[63] What is of interest here is less the maneuverings of politicians and generals than the ways the new government of Phibul Songkhram sought, with the help of Luang Wichit (who was able to transfer his allegiance from crown to constitutional monarch), to consolidate a new order through recourse to a new notion of culture in which appearances would be revalued yet again. The necessity for that revaluation was created by the fact that the new regime needed, in some crucial way, to authorize its activities by presenting them as the expression of a public (not to say popular) will. By the people, for the people. This would require, first and foremost, the drafting of a constitution that would explain the state and its bureaucracy as representative bodies, thereby guaranteeing its future actions as having come from the people. It would also require a general popularization of cultural discourse, such that the dissemination of governmental legislation could be undertaken and a certain discursive saturation of public discourse by hegemonic ideologies achieved. Vernacularization of both print and radio would become the means of fulfilling these objectives; thus did the popular become the means to an end, the instrument for producing a deliriously unified public.

The promulgation of a new constitution provided the new regime with its first challenge and lay the groundwork for the first turn to the ritualization of national culture in the new order. Outside of Bangkok, few Siamese people shared the rationalized conceptions of personhood as a rights-bearing status, and thus the principles on which the coup had ostensibly been staged were inadequate to make the desacralization of the monarchy a truly popular event. Attacks from both right and left led to the formation of the Association of the Constitution, with Wichit as secretary. And, in what would become a hallmark of his production under the new regime, Wichit literally staged the sacralization of the constitution by presenting miniature versions of it to *changwad* (district)

---

63. In addition to Barmé's excellent account of Wichit Wathakan and Thai nationalism, useful studies of the political economy of the period are provided by Chatthip Nartsupha, Suthy Prasartset, and Montri Chenvidyakan, eds., *The Political Economy of Siam, 1910–1932* (Bangkok: Social Science Association of Thailand, 1978), and Benjamin Batson, *The End of Absolute Monarchy in Siam* (Singapore: Oxford University Press and the Asian Studies Association of Australia, 1984).

representatives at an official ceremony consecrating a Buddha image.[64] The presentation of the miniature copy, especially in the context of historical pageant, could not help but be haunted by the miniature constitution of Vajiravudh's earlier Dusit Thani and just as Dusit Thani sought to make the miniature a site of order's dissemination, so Wichit's state theater sought to effect change through the performative power of the exemplary center.

Dusit Thani appeared to be a fabulous, indeed a fabular, miniature of the kingdom, complete with palaces, Buddhist wats, and representative housing from the various regions of the nation. King Vajiravudh's closest aides and relations were permitted to entertain themselves by fantasizing the operation of the country in what can only be described as a delirium of scale and proportional implosion. But Dusit Thani was less a philosophical toy of administration and administrative transformation than the instrument of heroic self-imagining. This despite the fact that the endowment of Dusit Thani with a constitution has led some historians to speculate about the King's possible intentions to submit his own monarchy to the principles of representative government. Given Vajiravudh's rather extreme autocratic tendencies, such a theatrical exploration of revolution seems unlikely. What is interesting about the theme park is the degree to which it enacts the crisis of representation that was beginning to emerge as the fantasies of realism reached their limit. These would not become visible for another half century when, ironically, the principle of the miniature would be reborn and with it the fantasies of absolute mastery, even divinity (see chapter 8). However, Vajiravudh's miniature theme park was, in its own time, less a representation of the real than a fantastic substitute for it, even though it shared that fantasy of unity that was driving the more ambivalent projects of vernacularization. For, in the place of a popular solidarity, it produced the charade a divine oversight that effectively neutralized any performative effects and made of constitutionalism a null spectacle rather than a model for transformation. One recognizes here that miniatures are not always models for something. Referentiality is not intrinsic to them, and may indeed be the other of their logic. But occasionally the principle of miniaturization is mobilized with an aim to transformation, in the mode of a more rational, but still sympathetic, magic. And spectacle can generate a desire for mimesis. This was the logic that motivated Luang Wichit and that propelled his cultural production. This time, however, the exemplary center was attired in popular garb.

The force of that center was not left to chance, and Wichit was tireless in the production of cultural artifacts through which the policies of the new government could be inculcated in Thai subjects. His composition of nationalist plays

---

64. Barmé, *Luang Wichit Wathakan*, 111–12.

and his promotion of courtly aesthetics through the new (1933) Department of Fine Arts under the Ministry of Education knew few bounds. A new School of Dramatic Arts provided tutorial instruction in classical dance, elocution, and etiquette, as well as both Thai and Western dramatic traditions, and its students became performers in the historical operettas that Wichit favored as the vehicles of the new ideological agenda. In this manner, Wichit attempted to expel popular aesthetic forms from the domain of art.[65] Yet, because the dissemination of these highly bourgeois narratives and values took place via the newly inaugurated medium of mass transmission, the radio (broadcasting commenced in 1930), Wichit also commanded the creation of a popularized, but still bourgeois, national culture. Through the dramatization of cultural values and the structuring of political didacticism in the mode of entertainment, the new regime sought an unprecedented standardization of national fantasy, albeit one that had been anticipated by the educational reforms of Rama V's reign. One of the most overt demands for such standard conformity appeared in the State Conventions (*rathaniyom*) that Wichit and Phibul developed in pursuit of a total transformation of the relationship between appearance and identity. These decrees concerning attitude and the performance of national identity were not only disseminated in the form of pseudo-legal commandments but were also incorporated into radio plays and other dramatic presentations. Like the edicts of Rama IV and Rama V concerning proper attire, these reflected an enormous concern about the possible failure of Thailand to assume an internationally legible form of modernity.

The State Conventions were described by Phibul as being "similar to the proper type of etiquette to be observed by all people."[66] Their purpose was to remedy the "flaws" of Thai society, particularly those that conflicted with the drive to modernity.[67] They regulated the name of the nation, which changed from Siam to Thailand via the first *rathaniyom* in 1939, demanded public deference to national symbols, mandated both work and the consumption of national products, and regulated almost every aspect of daily life, personal hygiene, and dress.[68] Regarding the last, men were called on to wear hats, shoes

65. Ibid., 114–17.

66. *Bangkok Times Weekly Mail*, 26 June 1939.

67. Thamsook Numnonda, "Phibulsongkram's Thai Nation-Building Programme during the Japanese Military Presence, 1941–1945," *Journal of Southeast Asian Studies* 9, no. 2 (1978): 234–47; Chai-Anan Samudavanija, "State-Identity Creation, State-Building and Civil Society, 1939–1989," in *National Identity and Its Defenders: Thailand, 1939–89*, ed. Craig J. Reynolds (Chiang Mai: Silkworm, 1991), 59–86; Barmé, *Luang Wichit Wathakan*, 144–60.

68. Many writers have observed the affinity between Wichit's and Phibul's nationalism and the cultural politics of National Socialism in Germany. Barmé echoes British Minister Cosby, who

and socks, jackets, and long trousers; women: hats, skirts, blouses (covering the shoulders), skirts, gloves, and high-heeled shoes; stockings remained optional. What had been so unusual thirty years before (recall Jottrand's astonishment at shoes and socks in the courtroom) became the mandatory display of nationalized modernity. The motivation behind the policies was, in large part, a matter of avoiding embarrassment in the face of Westerners who were thought likely to frown on improper dress.[69] Nonetheless, the State Convention on dress was not without critics. Strangely enough, the dress codes elicited more negative response than nearly any other State Convention, and Wichit was forced to address the inordinately vocal outcry via radio addresses that found what were perceived to be authentic local precedents or analogues for the practices and forms being commanded in the Conventions. Prince Wan himself used the criticism of the edict requiring men to wear trousers as the occasion for a brief discourse on culture:

> The function of culture is two-fold: it is calculated to bring about, among the people, a mode of life, which can meet the requirements of the times, while at the same time upholding the spirit of the nation. It is a fact that modern civilisation in the form of the Industrial System has pervaded the world. Each nation, in order to achieve progress or even merely to survive, must so organize the life of its people as to be able to make an adequate response to the challenge thus put forward by the prevailing world economic system. Some time ago, I asked a Japanese friend of mine why Japanese men had taken to trousers. He replied that he put on trousers in order to go to the office, because he felt more business-like than if he wore the kimono, which he preferred to wear at home. I have been struck by his remark; and, from the psychological point of view, I think there is a great

termed Wichit a "pocket Goebbels," when he says, "Whichit, like Goebbels, provided a new conceptual framework for the way society was to be conceived and governed" (*Luang Wichit Wathakan*, 180–81). In an essay titled "The Crisis of Siamese Identity," Sulak Sivaraksa referred to Phibul's program as an "imitation of Nazi Germany" and remarked that Wichit and Phibul both admired Mussolini and Hitler (in *National Identity and Its Defenders: Thailand, 1939–89*, ed. Craig J. Reynolds [Chiang Mai: Silkworm, 1991], esp. 47–49). Although both Wichit and Phibul were imprisoned on charges of war crimes following Thailand's alliance with Japan in World War II, it should be noted that the systematic murder of ethnic others was not a part of their program, and I would therefore hesitate to draw parallels of this sort. This is not to belittle the fascist tendencies implicit in the program that emerged, so ironically, from the proto-socialism of Pridi's People's Party, but to suggest that in matters as grave as genocide, precision is too important to sacrifice to rhetoric.

69. Thamsook, "Philbulsongkram's Thai Nation-Building Programme," 238.

deal to be said for it. An English journalist once said that the Thai played at work and worked at play. In order to meet the requirements of the times, we must work at work and play at play.[70]

Can there be any wonder that critics have remarked (only slightly excessively) that the transformations in dress were among the Phibul administration's most "enduring successes"?[71] As Prince Wan's remarks make clear, appearance was inseparable from the very concept of culture, and it was the idea of culture that constituted the second most powerful (perhaps the most powerful) invention of the Phibul era.

The Thai neologism *watthanatham* had, ironically, been invented on the basis of Pali-Sanskrit roots as a result of Vajiravudh's anti-Western linguistic policy, but it was put into effect by Wichit in an effort to render Thai culture comparable—and therefore commensurable—with other cultures, especially those of Western Europe. In Wichit's pen, the term came to refer not only to newly typified forms of architecture, art, and attire but also to a code of morality. Thus, behavior that promoted "national progress and stability" was always already Thai by Wichit's standards, and cultured people could be recognized by virtue of their industriousness, their penchant for precision, their affection for beauty, and their tenacity.[72]

Prince Wan was aware that the Thai concept of culture placed a certain emphasis on detail, especially on the detail of appearance, and that this emphasis seemed at odds with the more overtly anthropological definitions being used by ethnographers. He cited Wissler's definition, with its list of language, material forms (in which dress was but a single subcategory), arts, mythologies and scientific knowledges, religion, family and social system, forms of property, modes of government, and kinds of warfare. And he explained the difference between the two in terms of a process of development, such that "those matters are regulated first, in which the need for regulation becomes apparent to the competent authorities concerned."[73] Attention to etiquette therefore rested on the assumption that etiquette was the point at which cultural failure had first made itself visible in Thailand. More than this, cultural failure was seen to turn on a failure of appropriate visibility, on the very possibility of masquerade when the prerogative of dissimulation and multiple dissemination was no longer restricted to the self-representation of the upper classes.

In truth, this failure was entailed within the very idea of national cultural

70. Prince Wan Waithayakon, "Thai Culture," 36.

71. Barmé, *Luang Wichit Wathakan*, 158.

72. Ibid., 161.

73. Prince Wan Waithayakon, "Thai Culture," 35.

policy. Wichit's program had demanded only visible signs, and it therefore opened the possibility of a dissimulation, of a performance in excess of the modernity of its actor. One could appear modern but harbor primitive sentiments. Hence, a certain paranoia came to afflict the consciousness of culture in Thailand, a paranoia that is nowhere more evident than in the exponential growth of activities devoted to the documentation of culture that sprang from those very policies and Conventions. If Phibul's and Wichit's policies made it necessary to promote culture, the demand for a culturing of the masses could elicit only doubt as to the status of those peripheral subjects whose national identifications had not yet taken the *form* of modern display. It was, undoubtedly, in the double construal of culture as a principle of order and the nationally cultured person as one capable of displaying such order that the new nationalism of the 1930s converged with the ethnographic discourses within which otherness was to be both regionalized and, by extension, ethnicized. For nation and culture had become virtually synonymous. Everything else would be rendered as historical "matter-out-of-place."

So potent was this identification and so central had the value of order become that, in 1944, when Prince Wan summed up the matters to be regulated by royal decrees under the National Cultural Development Act of 1940, and then the National Culture Acts (Nos. 1 and 2) of 1942 and 1943, they almost all reduced to a question of "orderliness": "1. Orderliness in dress, behaviour and etiquette in public places or in places visible to the public, 2. orderliness in personal care and care of the home, 3. orderliness in personal behaviour looking to the honour of the nation and the Buddhist religion, 4. efficiency and etiquette in occupational pursuits, 5. spiritual and moral development of the people, 6. progress in literary and artistic works, and 7. appreciation of things Thai."[74] The National Institute of Culture, which was established to promote these principles, consisted of five bureaus: those of spiritual culture, customary culture, artistic culture, literary culture, and women's culture. Not surprisingly, it was in the area of customary culture that the ambitions of a state apparatus that imagined its object as one in which it would "control and instill the national culture into the spirit of the people" began to converge on anthropology.

### *"Culture": The Return of the Repressed*

From the beginning there existed a tension between a cultivation of representational diversity and the demand for identification with the idea of nation. In 1940, the National Cultural Maintenance Act was passed; it was followed shortly

---

74. Ibid.

thereafter by two subsequent acts and the establishment of the National Culture Council under the prime minister's office.[75] In the 1960s, a magazine entitled *Warasan Watthanatham Thai* (The journal of Thai culture) appeared, its pages including everything from stories about folk belief and regional food to national rituals and Buddhist traditions.[76] Like the more scholarly publications of the Royal Siam Society, *Thai Culture* was a pastiche of the local under the rubric of the national. It would be followed in 1976 by the more ideologically right-wing magazine, *Ekkalak Thai* (Thai identity), whose raison d'être was the reestablishment of national unity in the aftermath of the military's bloody suppression of student activists at Thammasat University.[77] Indeed, when the drive for national unity reached its apogee and even its apotheosis in the coup of 6 October 1976, the idea of *ekkalak thai* was converted into a banner under which the militarist tendencies of Wichit's cultural policy assumed their defensive function. The magazine was to be associated not only with the documentation of local cultural forms but with the exclusion of certain political and ethnic affiliations from Thailand's national body, among these the communist and, as already discussed, minoritized non-Tai-speaking groups such as the Meo.[78]

75. Craig J. Reynolds, introduction to *National Identity and Its Defenders*, 12. Also, Prince Wan Waithayakon, "Thai Culture," 34–35.

76. Reynolds, introduction, 12.

77. Ibid., 13. On the movement, see Benedict Anderson, "Withdrawal Symptoms: Social and Cultural Aspects of the October 6 Coup," *Bulletin of Concerned Asian Scholars* 9, no. 3 (1977): 13–30. Also see the new collection, published on the occasion of the twenty-fifth anniversary of the coup and edited by Thanet Aphisuwan, *Rao maj lyym hok thula* [We haven't forgotten October 6] (Bangkok: Committee to Commemorate the 20th Anniversary of October 6, 1976, 1995).

78. Charles F. Keyes has indicated the degree to which the communists were denied membership in the national body in a discussion of the then popular monk Kittivuddho. Kittivuddho advocated the murder of communists and informed his audiences that this would not result in demerit, as communists are not human and so their killing was to be thought of as no more significant than the killing of an animal for food. Many were shocked by this outright incitement of murder, but Kittivuddho retained enormous influence. See Keyes, "Millennialism, Theravada Buddhism and Thai Society," *Journal of Asian Studies* 36, no. 2 (1977): 283–302. Kittivuddho's outrages are not only symptomatic of the hysteria that afflicted Southeast Asia during the years of the Vietnam War, however. One is somewhat chastened in the rush to optimism about a more democratic present when one considers that, in 1998, monks can still call for the murder of undesirables. Thus, for example, Luang Pho Khun Parisuto, a popular abbot working out of Wat Banrai in Nakhon Ratchasima, has recently advocated the extrajudicial killing of drug dealers. In a climate that associates the Meo with drug dealing, this amounts to an advocation of genocide. In a confrontation with Prime Minister Chuan Leekpai in August 1998, Parisuto is reported to have said, "You don't have a decisive measure. The nation will not last. If you put them (drug dealers) in jail, people

Between the invention of "culture" and the coining of "national identity," then, there stretched the history of a rupture. The fear of displacement that drives all ontopological movements made itself felt in Thailand, as in so many places, through the discourse of communist insurgency.

Communism betokened many things to the cultural and ideological conservatives who would dominate Thailand after 1976, just as it betokened many things to the U.S.-backed military during the late fifties and throughout the sixties. The possibilities of socialized production and wealth, of class warfare and the elimination of aristocratic privilege, of the monarchy's displacement, and of religion's effacement: these are the promises whose actualization the right could not abide. Their vilification of the communists and their attribution to them of monstrous inhumanity were certainly not mitigated when news of Cambodia made it back to Thailand; but long before revolution was converted into reactionary totalitarianism, communists had assumed the mantle of the demonic in Thai political discourse. These developments have been well documented and well studied by political scientists and social theorists in Thailand and outside, but what I would like to remark here is the logic that made it possible for communism to assume the burden of signifying alterity. For, as already discussed, communism was not merely a threat from without, as the ideologues of the moment would like us to believe. Indeed, it behooves us to think about the history of communism's repression from a position that is not spoken in the language of the oppressor. Communism was also a threat, was indeed inscribed as a threat, because it did not conform to the logics of representational transparency that Thailand's modernity needed and produced. Anyone could be a communist, despite all appearances to the contrary, despite professions of national devotion, filial piety, or monarchical adoration. One could never be sure that one's neighbor was not a communist and one could never be sure that one's children would not join the Party secretly. This very possibility was cultivated in institutions like the Village Scouts, who asked their initiates to promise proper appearance but not subjective commitment. Yet it was communism that represented the threat of the secret without the possibility of its elimination through disclosure. A century of efforts and less intentional developments to make people the signs of their own identities, to make culture a mode of display, and to ensure the purity of the nation would

---

have to feed them and they will get the wrong idea. Do you want to keep them or the country? Once they are out of jail they will do the same thing. You need a decisive measure. . . . You can do whatever with them. We have a population of 61 million, 30 million should be sufficient. Do a vasectomy!" ("Monk Meets His Match in Showdown with Chuan," *Bangkok Post*, 10 August 1998, Internet ed.).

fall impotently before the specter of communism, before communism as the technology of spectrality.

Soon after the National Culture Commission was established in 1979 to coordinate the proliferating institutions associated with the promotion of national culture, English-language publications replicating the content of both *Warasan Watthanatham Thai* and *Ekkalak Thai* began to appear. As Craig Reynolds has observed, the English publications addressed themselves to the now explosive tourist industry, and in so doing confirmed the mutual imbrication of Thai nationalism with foreign gazes that had been first articulated in Rama IV's edict on palace attire.[79] However, the drive toward more centralized control could not mitigate the fact that, in the documentation of local ethnic traditions, the culture industry had also incited local affiliation and a production of local culture.

The tension between an aspiration to national integration and an encouragement of local tradition marks virtually every official publication of the Commission, and its hyperbolic rhetoric of preservation, promotion, and harmonization is unambiguously conservative in tone. The National Cultural Policy of 1986, for example, begins by describing Thai culture as that which "symbolizes the identity of the Thai nation," and proceeds to define the mandates of the Commission as the promotion of cultural preservation: "to protect culture and religion from being destroyed, and to preserve and maintain the purity of religion as a force in the spiritual development of the people's mind." Secondarily, the Commission is charged with an advertising mission: "to publicize the application of all facets of Thai culture to the Thai people . . . and to promote understanding among the people within our nation and with other countries." The third item of the policy directly addresses the problem of the popular in relation to official nationalism, when it states that the Commission is "to promote folk culture and culture of the indigenous community with the hope that, with better understanding of each other's culture, people will acknowledge and accept its value; hence it will result in a homogeneous cultural transformation."[80] Similarly, in section 4 of the *Guidelines*, entitled "What to Develop in Thai Culture," the Commission lists its priorities as, among other things, "national religion, religions established in Thailand, philosophy, customs and traditions, concept, and the essence of being Thai."[81] Customary practice and national identity are no longer seen as mutually exclusive. Indeed, the former can be promoted as a means of ensuring the latter, thanks to a long

79. Reynolds, introduction, 15.
80. Office of the National Culture Commission, *The National Culture Policy*, 2–3.
81. Ibid., 9.

history in which the nation has been construed as an immanent and tele-ologically overdetermined entity. That such a notion was largely moot by 1987, when the policy was published, cannot have escaped the attention of the authors who penned it. Thus, in a section entitled "How to Preserve, Promote and Develop Culture," they seem to both recognize and evade the historical facts of the previous decades, pledging the Commission to establish "cultural freedom by allowing the public to express its opinion" and advocating both education and community development. Here too, the "fostering of understanding of cultural differences" is intended to mitigate "cultural conflict." As though haunted by the moment that it disavows, namely, the military repression of democracy in 1976, the Commission writers insist that "opportunity will be open to the public to freely choose proper cultural conduct of their own on the condition that it will not harm or affect the security of the Thai society as a whole."[82] It goes without saying that the concept of national security is precisely that which permits the state to negate the promise of freedom, of representa-tiveness, and of claims to locality uncontained by nationalist teleologies. Its invocation in the policy is nonetheless increasingly inadequate to the task of threshold maintenance and increasingly hollow as a justification for the containment of difference. Nothing can intervene to retrospectively undo the fact of populism or the history in which vernacularization programs promoted difference in an effort to contain more radical alterity. All that can be said is that such policy succeeds in its objectives only to the degree that it renders (local) culture a matter of representation, of proper presentation. The risk of all repre-sentation, however, is that it has the capacity to incite a commitment to its referent, to proliferate its own object in the delirium of its own claim to simple transparency. Sometimes the assumption of costume can produce a new sub-jectivity, and sometimes historical pageantry can be experienced as the return of the past. Nowhere is this more apparent than in Chiang Mai, where dis-courses on local supernaturalism, sometimes cast in the idiom of "popular Buddhism," seem to have been accompanied by, and indeed to have stimulated, new and ambivalent modes of ritualism.

The context for this discursive circuit of representation and proliferation was the ambivalent relations between the north and the central administration during the years of counterinsurgency on the part of the central government. In the north, the consequences of military campaigns against Laos had been acutely felt, and disaffection with the military regime in Bangkok, powerfully articulated by the Farmers' Association, was redoubled when northerners per-ceived the manner in which the regime treated those Thai citizens among whom they had so recently come to count themselves. By this time, Bangkok-

82. Ibid., 11.

based capital had come to so dominate the area that rates of landlessness exceeded those of landed agriculturalists. What was perhaps merely residual and latent resentment against the powers that had usurped the *caos* a century earlier became in the 1970s the catalyst for a new regionalist movement. Testifying to the power of the transformations emanating from Bangkok, this new movement has been conceived primarily in culturalist terms and as a matter of appearances. To this day, revival has been contained mainly within the aesthetic domain, and unlike so many other movements of local identification, that in northern Thailand has not generated nationalism proper, has not devolved into separatism, and has been relatively exempt from the kinds of violent antistatism that have bloodied assertions of autonomy elsewhere. The Lannathai Movement, as I shall refer to it here, has been as entwined with self-touristification as were national identity programs in Bangkok. Like them, it has also acquired an unexpected power to incite what it claims to represent. In this manner, it has also been part of the process by which the disappeared have been summoned from the dead. It is a child of rationality, but it is also a medium of magic. Let us turn then to the specifically northern experience of those historical transformations whose histories we have thus far been tracing from the perspective of the center.

In the five decades following Camille Notton's arrival in Chiang Mai as French consul (1925) and Georges Coedès's appointment first as curator of the National Library of Siam (1918) and then secretary-general of the Royal Institute of Siam (1927), little attention was devoted to the histories and literatures of northern Thailand.[83] However, under the auspices of the Siam Society, attention turned back to the histories and literatures of Lannathai in the 1970s. Beginning with a survey of palm leaf manuscripts under the direction of Singkha Wannasai and the establishment (with Toyota Foundation monies) of a project at Chiang Mai University (led by Sommai Premchit) to survey northern Thai manuscripts, a small culture industry began to emerge.[84] The manuscript collection now forms part of the archive of the university's Social Research Institute, and a separate Center for the Promotion of Northern Thai Arts and Cultures is also housed at the university. With the institutional structures pro-

---

83. Charles Notton undertook the first translations of the chronicles of Lamphun, *Chronique de La:p'un: Histoire de la Dynastie de Chamt'evi*, vol. 2 of *Annales du Siam*, 3 vols. (Paris: Charles-Lavauzelle, 1930), and of the Singh Buddha relic *P'ra Buddha Sihing* (Bangkok: Bangkok Times Press, 1933). Georges Coedès authored the monumental *Indianized States of Southeast Asia*, trans. Susan Brown Cowing (Honolulu: East-West Center, University of Hawaii Press, 1968), and also the *Documents sur l'Histoire Politique et Religieuse du Laos Occidental*, vol. 25 of *Bulletin de l'École Française d'Extrême Orient* (Paris: École Française d'Extrême Orient, 1925), and *Prachun Silājāroek Phak Thī 2* [*Recueil des Inscriptions du Siam Deuxième Partie*] (Bangkok: Siamese Society, 1961).

84. Swearer and Sommai, *The Legend of Queen Cāma*, xxiv.

vided by these two entities, the Siam Society's initiative has since generated dozens of articles and books on Lanna customary practice, a number of academic journals devoted to Lanna history, and more than one popular magazine that occupies the genre initiated by *Warasan Watthanatham Thai* and extended most recently in the more elite publication *Silapa Watthanatham* (Arts and culture). *Lanna Syksaa* (Lanna studies) and *Lannathai Khadii* (Lannathai research) are but two of the academic venues for such localist studies. *Panna*, subtitled (in English) *What Happened in Chiang Mai*, is a nonacademic but still elite venue typically devoted to stories about current cultural events, environmental issues, and the histories of local practices and arts.

The journals are an important gauge of the ubiquity of discourse on Lannathai history and culture, but they are by no means the only venues in which such discussion occurs. Indeed, there has been a veritable efflorescence of publication on customary ceremonies and traditional belief in a field that is perhaps more folklorist than anthropological. Nonetheless, a great deal of this literature has taken the form and ethos of salvage ethnography and is imbued with a sense of urgency, a hastiness born of the deep conviction that any residual authenticity in Chiang Mai is lying helpless before modernity's pulverizing engines. Much of the work devoted to northern Thailand has been addressed, not surprisingly, to the histories of Buddhism there, but the rubric of Buddhism has not exhausted the subject of ritual. In Lannathai studies, ritual is no longer understood merely as a popular mode of Buddhism, as it was in the writings of Phya Anuman Rajadhon, but has indeed assumed a kind of autonomy. Such autonomy has been manifest in the hyperbolic elaboration of formal procedures that characterizes this literature rather than the hermeneutic interpretation of belief and its affinities with or departures from cosmological or more scripturalist versions of Theravada Buddhism that tended to defend analyses of ritual in earlier times. The term *phithii* is usually used in this context to designate ritual and has largely displaced the more colloquial word for ceremony, *ngaan*. But custom and/or tradition (*prapheenii*) has gripped the imagination of ethnographers and autoethnographers alike. To wit, in his bibliography *Religious Traditions among Tai Ethnic Groups*, Shigeharu Tanabe lists more than 150 books and articles on the subjects of "Buddhist rituals," "calendrical rituals," "spirit cults and society," "*khwan* theory and practice," "rites of passage," "magic and spells," "traditional medicine," "architectural rites and spatial symbolism," "agricultural rites," "divination, astrology and calendars," "theatrical performance and music," and "myths, legends and folk literature."[85] This does not yet include the category of chronicles, among which scores of publica-

---

85. Shigeharu Tanabe, ed., *Religious Traditions among Tai Ethnic Groups: A Selected Bibliography* (Ayutthaya: Ayutthaya Historical Society, 1991).

tions can also be counted, many of them having been produced under the initiatives of the Siam Society and the Social Research Institute. What is so striking about the list is not simply its extent, or the fact that nearly half of the pieces have been written in Thai in a process of grand autoethnography, but that the vast majority have appeared since 1970. Kraisi Nimmanhaeminda can perhaps be credited with the first wave in Lannathai studies, but the most prolific and influential of the more contemporary authors in this proto-genre are Manii Phayomyong and Sanguan Chotisukarat.[86] Sanguan's work, in particular, bears the mark of an ideological shift, the publications prior to 1970 generally bearing the term *phaak nüa* (northern Thailand), and those after 1970 the proper name, Lannathai. No longer requiring insertion into the narrative of the nation-state, for which the north is merely a region, the literature on Lannathai quietly testifies to the resurgence of an alter-history that is thought to have run parallel rather than prior to that of the Thai nation.

Most of the new discourse on Lannathai ritual and popular culture (*watthanatham phyyn baan*) has been descriptive in nature, consisting of the cataloguing of the forms and procedures used in the rites that it defines as traditional. A few notable exceptions are to be found in the more properly anthropological literature addressed to the same issues; here, the writings of Shalardchai Ramitanondh and Anan Ganjanapan deserve special mention for the critical vocabulary within which they cast the question of tradition (although Shalardchai's more functional interpretations of spirit mediumship differ considerably from Anan's historically oriented materialism). In general, the folkloric studies of Lannathai seek to isolate the forms and practices that its authors deem to have survived relatively unchanged, even in the face of depopulation and colonial encompassment. Here, ritual constitutes a site of reproduction and continuity, even an obstacle to modernity. Only recently has the historicity of customary practice become an issue to address and this only to the extent that recent historical transformations are read as contaminations of a tradition whose integrity is thought to have remained otherwise intact. A case in point is to be found in Sommai Premchit and Pierre Doré's *The Lan-Na Twelve Month Traditions*, which follows Manii's delineation of calendrical traditions and includes a brief essay on historical change. At the conclusion of

86. A small sample of the most important works in the Lannathai movement would have to include Sanguan Chotisukarat, *Phrapheenii thai phaak nüa* [Thai Traditions of the northern Region], 2d ed. (Phranakhon: Odeon, 1969), *Phrapheenii Lannathai lae' phithii kam taang taang* [traditions and ceremonies of Lannathai] (Chiang Mai: Prathyang Withayaa, 1971); Manii Phayomyong, *Prapheenii sipsong dyan Lannathai* [Lanna traditions of the 12 month calendar] (Chiang Mai: Sapkaanphim, 1989), *Phithiikam Lannathai* [Lannathai ceremonies] (Chiang Mai: Sapkaanphim, 1986), *Prawat lae' wannakhadii Lanna* [Lanna history and literature] (Chiang Mai: Mitron Raakaan, 1973).

their text, Sommai and Doré make the startling claim that the influence of central Thailand on northern Thai custom has a history of only thirty-five to forty years' duration.[87] After all that has been said here, such a claim must come as a shock and a seemingly flagrant refusal of history. Yet, it would be wrong to think that Sommai and Doré have simply erred or submitted themselves to the attractions of a willful naïveté. For the kinds of change to which Chiang Mai has been subject in the past four decades are truly qualitatively different.

Something has changed when, for example, those early photographs of Chiang Mai taken at century's end begin to reappear, reprinted as postcards and posters on which the bare breasts of Chiang Mai's not-yet-modern women can offer an eroticized view of the past rather than a sign of a barbarity stubbornly resisting the modern. Or when government bureaucrats are not only not prohibited from wearing clothing other than trousers and skirts but are actually mandated to wear the indigo-dyed clothing of the peasant (*chao naa*) each Friday. Or when, at a political rally demanding more democratic political representation, an exhibition of sorcery can be staged to submit the actual return of autocracy to the force of a theatrical politics in which personal power is retrieved from the mere representation of personal power. As Nithi Aeusriwongse has remarked, something has changed when Chiang Mai is no longer the site at which the imagination of primitiveness invested its disgust, but rather is an object of such powerful romantic desire that *Madama Butterfly* can be staged as a play in which a Bangkok soldier falls in love with a Chiang Mai maiden, whose love for him ends (as it must in such tales) with a suicide.[88] Chiang Mai has become a fetish of the picturesque. And, like all fetishes of a "colonial" imagination, however "internal," it operates through mechanisms of displacement and projection, disavowal, and compulsive repetition. It is, in short, imagined as the place from which fetishism itself emanates, as the place where people overinvest in appearances and where that overinvestment creates the space of ensorcellment.

### Northern Thai Supernaturalism and the Dialectic of Fetishism

The trope of fetishism is so common in colonial discourse that it is often difficult to know how to specify it. Nonetheless, few officials have given voice to it in more patronizingly stereotypical terms than did W. A. R. Wood, whose

87. Sommai Premchit and Pierre Doré, *The Lan Na Twelve Month Traditions: An Ethno-Historic and Comparative Approach* (Chiang Mai: Faculty of Social Sciences and cnrs, France, 1991), 198. The authors claim thirty years, but seem to identify 1960 as the turning point.

88. Nithi Aeusriwongse, "Sao Khrua Faa," *Silapa Wattanatham* [Arts and Culture] 12, no. 1 (1991): 180–85.

descriptions of mediums first provoked this discussion of appearance and its histories. Wood arrived in Bangkok in 1896 along with scores of European aides and officials of the new regime and became British consul in Chiang Mai in 1913. In 1965, he published his rather romantic memoir of "sixty-nine years in Siam" under the tellingly sentimental title *Consul in Paradise*.[89] Wood's recollections of dealings with spirits and with spirit belief constitute a brief but central passage in the book, one that begins with the observation, "My readers will have seen that there is a very plentiful supply of spirits and ghosts in northern Siam, and that they intrude at every turn into the lives of the people."[90] On at least two occasions, Wood was himself called on to exorcize spirits that had become intransigent in the face of local remedy. In the first, the spirit of a tree that had been cut at the cemetery for which Wood held responsibility was said to have caused the injury of the two men who had been hired to trim it. Several years later, when yet another gardener fell ill while attempting to prune the tree, Wood offered his own "witchcraft," having determined by this time that the belief in spirits could only be met with the performance of a similar belief. To that end, he had the son of the afflicted man go to the cemetery, light candles, and plant a rosebush, whereupon he intoned a "magical" sermon and placed a talisman on the earth. The talisman itself was a "lump of sugar" in a box wrapped with red tape: "When I had gone, I prepared my little box containing the magic talisman. The box was wrapped up in white paper tied with red tape, and sealed. The talisman was a lump of sugar. At first I thought of putting in a pebble, but this seemed rather like sharp practice, so I used a lump of sugar. I also prepared a bottle of magic medicine. This was composed of water, with a little alum to taste nasty, and a little washing blue to look pretty. As in more orthodox medical practice, spirit medicine must look nice and taste beastly."[91]

Wood found the pretense to magical knowledge a source of enormous power, and he used it (wittily but also meanly) both to buttress his local authority and to link himself to the power of Imperial England. On one occasion, he even claimed to be the nephew of the "Chief Sorcerer and Court Magician to the late Queen Victoria."[92] To his northern Thai interlocutors, Wood declared that his uncle had bequeathed him his book of spells. So, when an irritable spirit threatened the rice bin of a village headman, the consul could offer his assistance by firing different colored cartridges from his gun and reading the magical words of Rudyard Kipling: "The walrus and the carpenter/Were walking

89. Wood, *Consul in Paradise*.
90. Ibid., 105.
91. Ibid., 109–10.
92. Ibid., 111.

hand in hand . . ."[93] There is nothing like the literature of coloniality to produce the image of a subject in need of colonization by modernity. Indeed, the story is so akin to that of Conrad's "Karain" (where an Indonesian man is saved from madness by a fake amulet) that one wonders whether Wood had not in fact read it.[94] Of course, Conrad was more cynical and more literarily gifted than Wood, but the point is perhaps moot, insofar as the trope of a subject incapable of distinguishing actuality from mere performance is a generalized one, as common in colonial literature as in the pages of ethnography.

By Wood's account, northern Thai people are vulnerable to witchcraft and spiritual forces because they believe in the power of what they see, because they assign surfaces a performative function. In this, he suggests, they differ from proper modern subjects, for whom the fantasy of transparency has been so naturalized that surfaces can only signify and are denied efficacy. Wood basically accuses his northern Thai companions of indulging in an impotent mimesis, and he attributes the efficacy of his own rite to their belief in it. Magical agency is thereby transferred to the psyche of the one who suffers its effects. Consequently, the critical subject (in this case, Wood himself) can enter into the performance of magic without risking his own status as a rational subject of the modern. Such is the power of bourgeois ideology, which conceals itself, like poison, in everything it sees elsewhere.

One wants to respond to Wood by remarking that the very possibility of this masquerade rests on that investment in appearances that is the product of the modern, the same investment that led to a belief that dressing in socks and shoes, to say nothing of trousers, could transform a peasant into (the image of) a legal clerk. The assumption that formal procedure and surface appearances alone will suffice to persuade the primitive mind is nothing if not a projective naturalization of those policies in which the proper display of modernity was considered the first and necessary step in the development of modern sensibility. The last "flaws" in Thailand were, for Wichit and Phibul, matters of etiquette. It is therefore far from coincidental that the majority of new literature on northern Thai custom takes the form of an etiquette on matters magical. They are minutely descriptive accounts of the "how to's" in rites of location, tribute, and fateful renewal.

Appearances can be transparent to truth only for the modern subject, or so the modern claims. As Peter Cuasay has observed, there was an intimate relation between the collection of artifacts and the imagination of ethnology's

---

93. Ibid., 112.

94. Joseph Conrad, "Karain: A Memory," in *Eastern Skies, Western Skies* (New York: Carroll and Graf, 1990), 129–60. My thanks to Chris Gogwilt for drawing my attention to this novella.

function as a decoding and transmission of otherwise secreted knowledges.[95] By the standards set within the anthropological modern, the primitive becomes precisely that which secrets knowledge beneath a veil of illusion only to render itself ignorant of the real. The task that ethnographic etiquettes then produce for themselves is the explication of beliefs and knowledges that magical form presumes and hides. In essence, this kind of hermeneutic nullifies magic by attributing it to a fallacious reading of surfaces and a misrecognition of power's origin. Nor is this all. For, in telling the secrets of custom, the treatises on northern Thai ritual become the means for a conversion of the primitive into the modern, through the representation of such practices as mechanical imitations of tradition. This is why, along with the cataloguing of practices in folkloric texts, one invariably finds an explanation of the putative "supernaturalism" of the northern Thais and an account of how it is that animist practice and Brahmanic ritual continued to suffuse a consciousness that professed its commitment to Buddhism at every turn.

In many ways, the dilemma that emerges here is that of the religious reforms initiated in the nineteenth century, for in their implicit denigration of ritualism (by which is meant a commitment to form unenlightened by the scriptural truths of Theravada Buddhism or of more secular modernism), the ethnographic inscriptions, like the religious reforms, cannot help but render inscription the site of a renewed ritualism. Here, everything becomes procedure. Procedure becomes, in fact, its own end. By formalizing the techniques for rites such as the *syyb chataa müang*, the *riak khwan*, and *jok khruu*—rites previously presided over and guarded by knowledgeable individuals and technical specialists—the authors fetishize fetishism, substitute their own logics for those of the people they have already excluded from the category of modernity. The crucial moment in this process, however, is the publication of magical etiquettes. Not only do these texts assume the nonefficacy of magical technique, but they produce that impotence in the moment that they convert practice into a matter of representational knowledge. The etiquettes are not intended for use so much as they are intended to reveal a worldview in which such use would be possible. They construct a space of action, seen from on high, from the perspective of the one who could see everything. As Heidegger might have said, they produce a worldview through a pictorializing gesture that gathers the world up for instrumental purposes and sets it before a newly coherent and demanding subject, whose archetypical embodiment is the anthropologist.[96] What is left, then, is

95. Cuasay, "Siamese Montage," 19.

96. Martin Heidegger, "The Age of the World Picture," in *The Question Concerning Technology and Other Essays* (1936), trans. William Lovitt (New York: Harper & Row, 1977). Heidegger himself

the gossip of science. For, at bottom, magic requires secrets. If everyone can know how to perform magic, then no one can believe in its miraculous operations. This is knowledge production in its most objectivist mode. Ethnography has become a kind of defacement or overinscription, a nullification: the betrayal of secrets.

How then, does one explain the growth in mediumship, the rise in public gestures of ensorcellment? In the 1990s, more and more people go daily to consult the mediums of Chiang Mai, seeking advice on how to cope with catastrophe and illness, but more often than not, asking for some prophetic knowledge that will give them advantage in a newly entrepreneurial economy where risk is both the source and the limit of value. In the 1990s, mediums can curse politicians in public and leave the bones of the dead on the stairways of government buildings, then offer spiritual protection for those who would be affected by the power of the spirits who have been summoned from other dimensions. Prime ministers and generals seek the guardianship of powerful mediums, and environmental activists mobilize other mediums in contests with them. Plane crashes and earthquakes are once again explained as the effects of spiritual discontent, and "witchcraft" can again be written on the front pages of the national newspapers. The fact of the matter is that the objectivism of folkloric and ethnographic studies, and of national culturalist promotions of an instrumentalized local culture, has not had a singular effect. It has not simply produced rationalist treatises and rationalist readers. To the contrary, it has been associated with the veritable explosion of magical practices, among which mediumship must be counted as the most spectacularly resurgent instance. Twenty years ago, Walter Irvine estimated that there were about three hundred mediums practicing in Chiang Mai, an increase of about 600 percent over a period of twenty years.[97] In the early 1990s, when I asked both mediums and monks to estimate the number of active practitioners, they guessed there were between eight hundred and eleven hundred, although Shigeharu Tanabe's informants led him to believe that the number is closer to five hundred.[98] My own surveys suggest that Tanabe's more modest estimate is probably closer to the truth. Even at the most conservative estimate, however, the growth has been phenomenal, ridiculing the Weberian visions of so many

---

makes specific reference to anthropology as a symptom of this particular structure of consciousness (133). Nonetheless, he is speaking of something beyond disciplinary formation.

97. Walter Irvine, "Decline of Village Spirit Cults and Growth of Urban Spirit Mediumship: The Persistence of Beliefs, the Position of Women and Modernization," *Mankind* 4 (1984): 315.

98. Shigeharu Tanabe, "The Person in Transformation: Body, Mind and Cultural Appropriation," special lecture, Sixth International Thai Studies Conference, Chiang Mai, 15 October 1996.

Thai scholars and students of Thai culture who feared that modernity would be a site of secularization and self-interested rationalism.

It seems to me that the only way to comprehend this fact is to recognize the degree to which Chiang Mai has indeed been subjected to a discourse of culture premised on the fetishism of appearances. Certainly, the recent resurgence is inexplicable in terms of deprivation theory. Although Cao Ubon did indeed articulate the anxieties of an increasingly displaced aristocracy during her possession performances, the current revival has no straightforward relationship to the earlier spasms of spiritualist critique. And though the conditions in which women now live are ones in which a vast new set of structural pressures are coming to bear on daily existence, mediumship is becoming increasingly attractive to wealthier and more middle-class women and also to men. One might even say that to the extent that mediumship acquires force as a representation of tradition in an economy that values pastness, it has become the site of masculinist investment and appropriation. So then, to repeat the question: How are we to understand the recent resurgence of mediumship?

Phayaphrom had already answered this question before I could begin to ask it. Mediumship discovered its double in photography and found its value in culture. What is meant by such a formula is not simply that a new metaphorics came into the hands of cultural bricoleurs. Rather, northern Thai subjects, including mediums, became subject to, became subjects of, modernity. In a history that seems in retrospect to be both wildly improbable and eminently predictable, northerners were transformed from the objects of a scopic desire in which they were looked on and photographed by relatively mobile cosmopolitan subjects, then asked to signify both locality and tradition in a standardized code, until they finally assumed the position of citizen-subjects. Inevitably, this meant enacting the same economies of desire and visual consumption in relation to yet other, ethnicized peripheries (recall here the story of the Meo). But it also meant that northerners would come to inhabit the delirium of the nation and to take on the function of signifying pastness. This is palpably discernible in the world of mediumship, where the assumption of self-consciously "traditional" postures and costumes is the hallmark and the instrument of successful performance. It is also present in the compulsive self-documentation and self-portraiture in which mediums now indulge. Mediums are successful to the extent that they are legible as mediums, to the extent that they can anticipate their recall *as* images. And become images they will. Everywhere, everyone is photographing themselves in the pursuit of future memory. Thus do they become their own signifiers of pastness. Thus do they assign to cameras the function of seeing themselves seeing.

One cannot overlook the fact that the rise in folklore and autoethnographic practice, cultural promotion, and institutional preservation in northern Thailand corresponds precisely to an explosion in the importation and sale of instant cameras, and to the decision on the part of the Thai government to make transport the takeoff point to modernization. The 1970s were both a repetition and a farcical failure to repeat what had been achieved during the period of early modernization that began with King Rama IV and ended in the massacre of 6 October. If, during the earlier period, the relationships between center and periphery provided the conditions within which a relative mobility of the center was matched by a demand for a relative stability of the periphery— if time travel and ethnographic morbidity were the two poles of an axis on which self-representation moved—then more recent history is both the inversion and the overcoming of that binarity. In Thailand, modernity rests on the fetishism of appearances, on the demand for a signifying surface, and on a representational politics in which the processes of enframement are repressed. Yet, modernist Bangkokians accuse northern Thais of fetishism and offered them access to the modern only through the renunciation of a belief in hidden forces. To be sure, this has happened to a large extent and many, if not most, people now publicly disavow a belief in spirits even when they make offerings to local shrines. For a few, however, modernity has meant something else and something more: a reinvestment in the power of appearances. This is where magic returns. This is where technique converts itself back into the instrument of performativity.

Phayaphrom can exist and Kumannooy can be distinguishable from him—as spirits and as voices—largely because appearances have acquired a capacity to produce what they claim merely to signify. It does not matter that spirits possessed mediums before the arrival of cameras and before ethnographers made of them the culture heroes of survival. It matters only that the logic of appearances has changed. We can recall here that Phayaphrom advocates a distinction between the kind of vision that grants appearances their power and that which understands the dramaturgy of costume as a response to the demand for legibility. That he casts this lesson in ontologized terms does not negate its profundity. That he makes of ontology an ethics says much about the stakes in a world saturated by mechanical reproduction—although none of this makes magic a politically adequate response to the violations of modernity. Indeed, the violence of Kumannooy's antics resurfaces and reminds us that there is also wastage, or at least excess, in photography as in ethnographic representation. In literal terms, this excess may be a double in the image, an inexplicable mark, the disorderly aspect of a photograph that undoes the representational movement that would obliterate the real. The photograph is always subject to some eruption. Call these what one will: an indexicality that will not signify or a magicality that will not be explained away. In the age of mechanical reproduction, every empiricist project, every attempt to render the world a mere object of representation, seems to be haunted by its opposite. And this is equally true for every other discourse that fantasizes transparency and denies its own practices. The forms that such a dialectic have taken in Thailand require still sharper contours, however. Accordingly, the next chapter considers the place of mediumship and sorcery during the democracy movement of 1992. In that context, we will have occasion to explore the particular forms that a renewed magicality can take in a context where tradition has become the fetish of a newly new city and where the value of locality has made of its landscapes a labyrinth of sites, the mise-en-scènes for the transnational politics of representation. There, in the shadows of an electric light where everyone anticipates being seen from afar, a telephone is "shrilling."[99]

99. Walter Benjamin uses the term "shrilling" to describe the telephone of his childhood, affixed to the shadowed hall of his father's house. It is the sign of a technology that has the capacity to shock precisely because everything else has been rendered in terms of the visual. See "Berlin Chronicle," 326.

# 7 REPRESENTATIONS: LOCALITY AND THE SPIRIT OF DEMOCRACY

Chiang Mai, this newly new city, the center of a periphery and the periphery of another center, recently celebrated the seven hundredth anniversary of its founding by King Mengrai. The celebrations conducted under the auspices of the municipal government were grandly theatrical, and the centrality of historical pageant on this occasion would surely have warmed even Luang Wichit Wathakan's heart. On the festive evenings of the event, women and men clad in Lanna costume mounted the ruins with candles in hand and stood in the light, as happens for many rites associated with the city. There, they served as icons of a past whose ruin had underlain their own arrival in modernity. The fact of that modernity was evident in the banners and billboards around the city, surfaces on which almost any commodity could be pictured as heir to a triumphal local history. Local shops and branches of national corporations testified to their membership in or patronage of the local scene with tributary advertisements in which they, like mediums, paid homage to the founding monarch. In the center of the city, the statue of the three kings enjoyed renewed popularity as a site of offerings, their bronze forms more lavishly wreathed in jasmine than usual. In short, the occasion enveloped virtually every aspect of metropolitan existence.

Long after the official events had come to an end, festive lights remained to bathe the ruins and the moats that form their encircling frame in electrical light. Each site of entry and exit to the old fortress had become a glowing stage, one on which the theatricality of the ruins themselves became apparent. What the city wanted to project in the illumination of the ruins seems clear: antiquity, continuity with ancient monarchical power, locality. Perhaps less clear is the unintended sentiment that it conjured there: namely, a collective sense of loss of the sort that the crowd experiences in the aftermath of a theatrical performance, when it disperses because the object of attention has vanished. And, like the dissipation that occurs after the fantasy of the theater dissolves, it rests on the experience of untransformable anonymity before a specularized scene. In contemporary Chiang Mai, the juxtapositions that give rise to such locally particular experiences of loss are redoubled because the people are so constantly vacillating between a distracted participation in an eternal movement of dispersion, and an absorption in and by the pageantry of renewed monarchical sacrality. As the previous chapter attempted to demonstrate, this vacillation is generated by the logics of mass mediation, logics in which space and time, proximity and distance, presence and absence have been entirely reformed.

## The Age of Accidents: Traffic, Crowds, and the Solace of Thainess

Simmel has described the affect of the metropolitan masses under the rubric of the "*blasé* attitude," by which he means the "faithful subjective reflection of the completely internalized money economy."[1] In a context where total exchangeability has become the norm, where quality has been transposed into quantity, says Simmel (and, I would add, again following Heidegger, where quantity itself has assumed an incalculable value),[2] there is only the monotony of an "evenly flat and grey tone. . . . Things themselves appear insubstantial." Simmel was writing of Germany in 1900, of course, a place and time far removed from Thailand in the 1990s. Nonetheless, there is a strong resonance between his words and those of Thai scholar Kasian Tejapira. In 1996, Kasian delivered a paper at the Sixth International Thai Studies Conference, which was held in Chiang Mai on the occasion of its seven hundredth anniversary celebration, and described Thainess as that which has become insubstantial:

Pseudo-chemically sublimated Thainess is returned to us in a solid but useless, irrelevant and fossilized or mummified form right from a temple,

1. Georg Simmel, "The Metropolis and Modern Life" (1900), in *The Sociology of Georg Simmel,* trans. Kurt H. Wolff (New York: Free Press, 1950), 413–14.

2. This is the argument that Heidegger makes in "The Age of the World Picture," in *The Question Concerning Technology and Other Essays* (1936), trans. William Lovitt (New York: Harper & Row, 1977): "Everywhere and in the most varied forms and disguises, the gigantic is making its appearance. . . . The gigantic is rather that through which the quantitative becomes a special quality and thus remarkable kind of greatness . . . this becoming incalculable remains the invisible shadow that is cast around all things everywhere when man has been transformed into *subiectum* and the world into picture" (35). It is worth noting in this context that Thailand has witnessed a spate of contests devoted to "the largest," and many commentators have observed this trend in entertainment spectacles of grandiosity as being a symptom of Americanization.

theater or museum. And this is as it should be for now that Thainess has been ripped away from its traditional, historical, theatrical or religious context and deprived of its aura, it becomes an empty shell, a neutral terrain, a free-floating signifier which can be entered in and "exited" at will by commodities of whatever nationality or ethnicity. Thus, apart from *Coke*—the promoter of the value of Thainess, we have, in this official Year to Campaign for Thai Culture [1994], such Thai-Thai advertising campaigns as "Singha Beer—the pride of the nation," "Thai Life Insurance— the life insurance company of, by and for the Thais," "Central Department Store—the Thai Store," etc.

No matter how spurious their claims to Thainess may be under scrutiny, the fact that these commodities have indeed been turned into signs of Thainess has changed Thainess willy-nilly into one identity option among many others in the free market of a limitless plurality of commodities and/or brand names.[3]

Much of this book has been devoted to an argument against the postulation of a unified Thai authenticity as anything but the product of national culturalist politics. I have also attempted to show that even the local "tradition" of Lannathai, whose very locality the policies of national culture attempted to neutralize, was split and hybrid prior to the advent of the modern. In this context, Kasian's (admittedly sardonic) reference to an auratic moment that antedates the postmodernization of Thailand requires some skepticism. Yet, he is correct to point out the fact that "Thainess" acquires its value in the very process of its encompassment by commodity logics and, more important, that the only "Thainess" so valued is increasingly that which has utility in the global market. Indeed, it is the process of instrumentalizing purification that he identifies with the term "pseudo-chemical sublimation."

For whom is this purification being undertaken? Toward the end of his essay, Kasian refers to the "seemingly endless and meaningless collective suffering of nameless, faceless and powerless drivers in Bangkok's world-notorious suffocating traffic jams."[4] And he notes that it is to these psychically impoverished masses that the value of Thainess is offered as an almost narcotic kind of solace. In Chiang Mai, the specter of Bangkokian traffic jams constitutes the point of most ardent disidentification with the capital city and with the idea of modernity. Indeed, the growth in traffic "problems," referred to in the all-encompassing

3. Kasian Tejapira, "The Postmodernization of Thainess," in *Proceedings of the 6th International Conference on Thai Studies, Theme II: Cultural Crisis and the Thai Capitalist Transformation* (Chiang Mai: 14–17 October 1996), 397.

4. Ibid., 400.

term "jams" (*rot tid*), is compulsively remarked by residents as the sign of Chiang Mai's impending loss of authenticity. "These days, we have more problems," remarked one taxi driver. He continued, "We have more traffic jams. We need to progress. We need more democracy." It is not easy to imagine what logics might link accidents and democracy, nor what explains the assumption that more adequate representation before a rule of law will nullify the forces of contingency. Yet, these linkages are often made by people in northern Thailand.

In Chiang Mai, traffic has become the symbol for the mass in the manner that fire was Canetti's symbol for the crowd.[5] It substitutes for metropolitan sociality and specifies its volatile nature as one stretched between commencement and dissipation. Indeed, if, for Canetti, the "slow crowd has the form of the train," the anxiously modern crowd of northern Thailand has the shape of the highway at rush hour.[6] Everywhere, the specter of a mobility exhausted by its own excess is invoked through reference to the accumulation of cars and, either directly or indirectly, to the accumulation of dead bodies on the sides of highways. These "heaps" of dead bodies, to remain within Canetti's idiom, and the sites of their accidental demise, are often memorialized with small spirit shrines and offerings of flowers. Nonetheless, accidental deaths are said to produce chaotic spiritual presences, which mirror and index the accidental universe of the highway while haunting the modern with everything that it cannot explain. The cars, and the bodies that are their effect and their double, constitute what might be called the "traffic crowd." It is my impression that the compulsive conversations about them bespeak an anxiety about the possibility that social intercourse will be, or perhaps has already been, absorbed by the forces of massification. Indeed, the iconic status of white-gloved traffic cops and kerchief-masked motorcyclists, which appear in apocalyptic newspaper stories about the costs of modernity, are the signs that this process has already come to pass.

The passing that occurs here is manifold. Seven hundred years after its founding, Chiang Mai has come to inhabit a state of permanent passage, both in the sense of movement and in the sense of disappearance. It is afflicted by accidents. And many of its residents are conscious that this affliction is merely one measure of a total social fact. They speak of broken familial relations, diminishing religious commitment, and dwindling contributions to temples. They speak of doubt about employment, fear for the future, and instability in the world beyond Thailand's borders. Over and against its increasingly faceless subjects and their increasing concerns about temporal dislocation and genera-

---

5. Elias Canetti, *Crowds and Power* (1960), trans. Carol Stewart (New York: Noonday, 1996), 20.
6. Ibid., 39.

tional rupture, the monarchy and the military attempt constantly to cast the long shadow of the Thai nation and, by extension, Thai national culture.

"Shadow" is my term and not Kasian's. Or rather, I have imported it from Heidegger's and Benjamin's writings, where it is used by both, but in different ways, to suggest the relationship between subjects and the objects of their sacralizing investments. In Heidegger's writing, the shadow refers to the wreath of a "becoming incalculable" that surrounds the quantified thing of value in the modern era. It identifies the threshold to which knowledge aspires in its bid to contain a world where technology promises to render everything representable. In Benjamin's works, it refers to the force of absorption within which the subject of cult value is held.[7] Here, I use the notion of shadow to suggest that what has been at stake in twentieth-century efforts to re-auraticize the Thai monarchy and the value of "tradition" is the absorption of subject-citizens in and by an institution that claims to express local interests in the mere act of representing locality.

In making this statement I mean to suggest that, in Thailand, what Benedict Anderson calls the monarchy's "resacralization" has occurred not merely because the institution has appeared increasingly modern, but because its modernity has manifested itself as a renewed and deepened devotion to local tradition. Thus, for example, the increasing prominence of community development in the stated agenda of the monarchy has been accompanied by devotion to the support of revivalist activities, for example, the rejuvenation of such arts as silk double-ikat weaving, and to theatricalized rituals of place, such as the Rite to Renew the City [*syyb chataa müang*]. However, if the monarchy's renewed power of absorption is seemingly contradicted by the state of mobile dispersion in which the "faceless" masses of the traffic-crowded streets exist, it is our task to understand that the latter dispersion is precisely what makes such absorption possible. In the end, the masses return their energies to the center of power and are subjected to what comes from them because they have come to see the state apparatus, including the kingship, the constitution, and the military, as a representational force and because they believe that representation has itself become a source of political efficacy. In this economy, locality is both that which demands to be represented and that which is nullified in the moment of being represented.

The seemingly ironic fact that the theatricalization of Chiang Mai's history

7. Heidegger, "The Age of the World Picture," 35; Walter Benjamin, "The Work of Art in the Age of Mechanical Reproduction" (1936), in *Illuminations*, trans. Harry Zohn, ed. Hannah Arendt (London, Fontana, 1973), 222–23. See Sam Weber's excellent comparative essay on these authors, "Mass Mediauras, or: Art, Aura, and Medium in the Work of Walter Benjamin," in *Mass Mediauras Form, Technics, Media*, ed. Alan Cholodenki (Stanford: Stanford University Press, 1996), 76–107.

has occurred just as anthropologists observe a diminution in the role that the discourses and powers of place enjoy in northern Thai society is, in the end, not ironic at all. When anthropologists remark that people in northern Thailand are no longer beholden to the spirits of place and that they are now less likely to pay respects to local shrines, when they argue that place has given way to a more abstract spatial sense, they recognize that a new conceptual universe is operative. But they often err in discerning a total displacement of place by spatial and semiotic indeterminacy. Place has its value in contemporary northern Thailand. Indeed, I would argue that it has had that value returned to it, but in the alienated form that the dialectic of history gives to repetition. As Adorno has already taught us, locality acquires its value in a dialectic with universality. It appears after its loss and seems to have been at the place of origins from the start. The seven hundredth anniversary celebrations were nothing if not the confirmation of this actuality.

In this context, however, it is worth noting that many cultural activists found the municipality's formal activities inadequate to the task they set for themselves. In a parallel set of festivities, the activists organized an alternative commemoration of Chiang Mai's founding. In doing so, they aimed to assert both the autonomy and the organic continuity of local history, one they claimed could never be properly overseen by a governmental office that is, after all, an extension of Bangkok's national government. Chiang Mai's cultural activists identified the mere theatricality of the government-sponsored events as the mark of their exteriority to local tradition. The celebration was "all show," they said. It was "intended for Bangkokians, rather than northerners." Hence, in opposition to a merely performative celebration, the same critics sponsored a tributary dance before the *lak müang* and a possession performance by a prominent Chiang Mai medium. The medium who performed at this alter-event is a talented dancer, artist, architect, and dreamer whose historical association with the *lak müang* is matched by his credentials as a participant in the national democracy movements of 1973 and 1992. During the latter, the medium helped to orchestrate a ceremonial cursing of the usurping General Suchinda Khraprayoon by invoking the spirits of the mountains and of a local, pre-Thai monarchical past. The rite, which took place at Thapae Gate, was intended to injure Suchinda, but also to curtail the resurgent power of the military in the interest of more democratic representation. One might say that, during the performance, representation gave way to an earlier mode of enunciation—that of the sovereign performative—only to restore representation in the image and the service of a more widely distributed sovereignty. But it achieved its effect by mobilizing the fact that "tradition" had been revalued precisely in the process of becoming representational. The mountains that had been transformed into the mere horizon of a city imagined *as* view became, once again, the sites of power. This was the power of a city whose northernness has become inextricable from its image as the mountain fortress. It was the power of a commodified locality in a world where consumption is taken to be a crucial index, if not the sole register, of political agency.

This chapter devotes itself to an account of the moment and the context in which this medium, whom I shall call Saeng Suang (meaning light), rose to prominence. It continues with the story of his implication in a restructuring of the mediatized relationships between Bangkok and Chiang Mai. And it concludes with an exploration of the limits of locality's value in the representational economy of contemporary northern Thailand. Considering the farcically repetitious relationships between 1976 and 1992, I hope to make clear that the media in Thailand have both enhanced and extended the auratic power of the monarchy even as they have produced its apotheosis in the form of a demand for locally representational democracy. To make such an argument, I begin at Thapae Gate to consider what the relationships between crowds and power might be in Chiang Mai. From there, I shall have occasion to consider the many (ironic) sites at which a newly valorized locality is produced and, in that context, to ponder the political dimension of a moment in which new forms of immediacy emerge via new techniques of mass mediation.

### Emptiness at Thapae Gate

It will be remembered that Thapae Gate is at the center of several intersecting historic, economic, and aesthetic zones. At the head of Thapae Road, which extends out to the train station and provides the main thoroughfare for visitors entering the city, the gate opens at the eastern side of the old city and faces the Ping River. It dominates an interstitial space that was originally sheltered by a second wall and a second moat, a market zone that has been the site of translocal trade for centuries and is now geared to the most translocal of consumer activities, tourism. The gate itself has been restored so that the perpetually crumbling brick walls around the huge door constantly remark the city's antiquity, thrusting its modernity into ironically chiaroscuro contrast. Extending around it is a cement plane, about half the size of a football field, where food vendors hawk snacks of iced colas and coffees, cut pineapple, dried and pressed squid, barbequed pork, and steamed dumplings. On summer evenings, young men set up nets and play the balletic football game called *takraw*, while elderly men sit and visit or drink whiskey.[8] Often, young women can be seen saunter-

---

8. *Takraw*, an almost exclusively male pastime, is something like a cross between volleyball and soccer. A hollow bamboo ball is kicked over a net tied at eye's height, the object being to have the ball touch the ground in the opponent team's court, while keeping it airborne in one's own court.

ing past on the arms of foreign men, en route to the nightclubs and sex bars just behind the gate on Moon Muang Road. Other women (older women and schoolgirls) are relatively infrequent visitors to this space, except on the occasion of special events. Between such occasions, however, male travel agents and trekking guides wander in cliques of three and four, accosting foreigners with picture books depicting "pristine" mountain villages where authentic "hill tribe" people can be seen in authentic "costumes" and authentic opium can be smoked to enhance an experience of "untouched" Asian beauty—all for a few hundred baht and a large dose of Orientalist desire.

Thapae Gate is the site of major cultural events, including fairs and fashion shows associated with the annual renewal of Songkhran (usually in mid-April), major Buddhist celebrations, public displays and theatrical events associated with civic holidays, as well as political rallies. Of all the gates in the old city— there are five—Thapae Gate is deemed the most important, both by virtue of its historical positioning in the heart of the market district and because of its remembered sacrality in the cosmological order. Its situation at the center of the eastern wall, where it greets the sun as it rises above the city, is frequently referenced by older ritual specialists (spirit mediums and *luang phor*) in Chiang Mai. They also remark that Thapae Gate would occupy the place of the *sao mongkon* were the city to be imagined as a house. It is therefore a place of origination, albeit one that differs from the purer productivity that is figured in the city pillar (kept at Wat Cheddi Luang). Hence, the gate is described as being in a complementary relationship with the city pillar, where the violent founding power of the city's guardian spirits is localized and symbolized.

As a public space in Chiang Mai's cityscape, Thapae Gate is less a place than a site. It is a frame in which events occur, one defined mainly by its emptiness and by the fact that, despite the fact that or even because events take the form of momentary coalescences there, its normalized state is that of abandonment. After the shops close and the sun goes down, it is as deserted as a crime scene.[9] People imagine and speak of it as the point for chance meetings or accidental encounters and, above all else, for waiting. One can be bored (*bya*) at Thapae Gate, can spend time simply attending the passage of time. In the shade of a few trees to one side of the doors drunken men sleeping off their whiskey, brothel

---

Any part of the body other than hands and forearms can be used, but the game is famed for the spectacular acrobatic smashes by which the ball is kicked from heights of about eight feet into the opponent's court. The game is a national pastime for young men and a source of considerable masculine prestige.

9. It was Walter Benjamin who identified the logics of modernity, and of mechanical reproduction, as manifested in the crime scene photograph rather than portraiture, and who singled out desertion as the definitive quality of the crime scene. See "The Work of Art," 226.

owners not yet ready to open shop, and solitary elderly people without family members to converse with can often be seen. They appear to be waiting; normally, they are simply "spending time" (*sia weelaa*).[10]

Others know Thapae Gate only as the entry point to a labyrinth whose every route leads to the place of possible purchasing.[11] Religious sermons, which are held at Thapae Gate on marked Buddhist occasions or municipal celebrations, do not succeed in making it a sacral space; they merely arrive there to borrow and then to fill its emptiness. The emptiness of the space and the state of dispersal that defines the constant flow of traffic around Thapae Gate are the flip sides of each other. Indeed, if automobile traffic is the sign of the mass in Chiang Mai (and in Thailand), then Thapae Gate is the crime scene where the forensic photographer documents its effects. Permanence (and presence) is as absent from the space of the gate as it is from the fluctuating streams of cars.

It is the very emptiness of Thapae Gate's cement plane that makes it the appropriate site for the theater of memory in which the value of an abstracted locality is invoked. Presence would have obstructed historical representation; absence demands it. It was because Thapae Gate existed as an emptied stage whose material backdrop was an already theatricalized history that the 1992 democracy protests in Chiang Mai were staged there despite the fact that such a location made protestors exceedingly vulnerable to military action and police oversight. There were practical considerations for this location, of course. The gate's position at the intersection of three main traffic arteries provided a means of distributing printed leaflets to passing motorists and of catching the attention of passersby, people whose very state of passing was facilitated and symbolized by the gate. But the political protest staged at Thapae Gate during May 1992 also partook of its form and its status as site, as a point at which people would randomly coalesce and then discover new social relations. The protest was undertaken in the mode of media spectacle, and in the elaborate discourses of mediation and center-periphery tension that were enacted there, the gate loomed as both backdrop and icon. Its tense position as a center on the periphery of both its own cityscape and the nation-state could not have been more viscerally evident than when local protestors set up video monitors and fax machines there, describing themselves as the "media" while receiving transmissions from Bangkok and staging a local rite (a rite of locality) intended to affect

---

10. The expression for spending time, *sia weelaa*, contains within itself an etymological linkage between expenditure and wastage. The same word, *sia*, is used to identify rot (as in fruit) and purchase (as in shopping, where one can spend money, or *sia ngeun*).

11. Walter Benjamin also describes Berlin as a "theatre of purchases" in "Berlin Chronicle" (1932), in *One-Way Street*, trans. Edmund Jephcott and Kingsley Shorter (London: Verso, 1979), 327.

the activities of a city several hundred miles to the south. Before describing the particular relationship of media and medium at that rally, however, it is necessary to delineate the contours of the democracy movement itself.

### Histories of Repetition: The Democracy Movement of 1992

In February 1991, a group of generals from Class 5 of the national military academy staged a bloodless coup d'état and removed Prime Minister Chatichai Choonhaven from his post, establishing themselves as a junta with the title National Peace-Keeping Committee (NPKC). Chatichai's regime, which had presided over some of the strongest economic growth of any nation in Asia, was notoriously corrupt and generally disliked by agricultural laborers, urban factory workers, and Bangkok entrepreneurs for its failure to distribute the fruits of Thailand's phenomenal economic growth beyond a small clique of elite and entrenched interests.[12] Following the February coup, there was an initial outcry in the elite press about the generals' violation of democratic principles, principles that were, in fact, just emerging from the legacy of the resurgent anticommunist militarism of the late 1970s and 1980s. Nonetheless, most people were initially prepared to accept the military's intervention as a necessary gesture to restore moral order. In Chiang Mai, and in most of the north, the sentiment on the street was generally phrased as one of willful disinterest: "No problem. There will be stability. This is Thailand, and Thai people will not abandon order." Similar comments circulated with almost liturgical rhythm.

The idea of military intervention in the interest of moral order is certainly not new in Thailand, but the NPKC gave its activities a veneer of ethical modernity by appropriating the formalism of electoral politics and claiming the need

---

12. The military made much of Chatichai's corruption, but it should be noted that the rates of corruption during his regime were not statistically higher than those of military regimes in the past. In fact, Pasuk Phongpaichit and Sungsidh Piriyarangsan have undertaken a systematic survey of the records kept by the Counter Corruption Commission since its establishment and have observed that there has been a general attenuation of corruption since Sarit's regime, which, they say, constituted the apogee of governmental failure in this regard. Sarit's personal wealth was "equivalent to 42% of the government budget" when he died, most of the monies having been obtained through "income diversion, cuts on expenditure, fees for services, [and] asset seizures." Chatichai's improprieties appear to have taken the form of fees for services and cuts on expenditures, even by the reckoning of the NPKC. Although not attempting to excuse the corruption of Chatichai's government, Pasuk and Sungsidh nonetheless point out that the accusation of corruption has been used by the military to generate the appearance of their own moral rectitude and that such accusations have effectively obscured the relative criminality of the military in this regard. See *Corruption and Democracy in Thailand* (Chiang Mai: Silkworm, 1994), esp. 52–53.

for a new constitution that could safeguard the principle of local representation. The generals (including Air Force Commander General Kaset Rojanil, Army Commander General Suchinda Khraprayoon, Army General Issaparong Noonpakdee, and Armed Forces Supreme Commander General Sunthorn Kongsomong) followed the coup with an immediate promise to rewrite the constitution and to facilitate fair elections within the year, emphasizing that these elections would permit a restitution of the order that Chatichai's government had betrayed. They did appoint a committee to redraft the constitution, but its status as an appointed body rendered the draft suspect in many people's eyes. There were other sources of doubt that would come back to haunt the NPKC when it fell to the pressures that its own rhetoric invoked. For example, the trials of Chatichai's ministers on charges of being "unusually rich," a euphemism for corruption, acquired the aura of the absurd as various pressures were brought to bear on behalf of those parliamentarians who remained in power even after Chatichai's ouster.

When, following the election and the establishment of a coalition government, the most visible general of the coup, Suchinda Khraprayoon, took the position of prime minister for himself (but with the blessing and explicit orders of the NPKC's nominal head, General Sunthorn Kongsompong), a popular resistance began. Suchinda defended his betrayal of an earlier promise for an elected prime minister in the interest of the nation: "Sia sat phya chat [I break my promise for the nation (national good)]."[13] But after the military's suppression of students in 1976, the idea of nation had already been so destabilized that the only domain in which it held relative sway, namely, that of the transnational mediascape, was not likely to smile on a general's masquerade as the defender of democracy. National newspapers and the conversations of political moderates were anxiously occupied by the specter of international repudiation and fretted publicly about how the general's prime ministership would be perceived abroad. Almost without exception, these accounts—in articles, editorials, and letters—were infused by a sense of humiliation, of lost face (*naa taek*).

Initially, there was dissent from the university community and from the most articulate members of the new entrepreneurial bourgeoisie. National business magazines such as *Phucadkaan* (The manager) provided some of the most acerbic and uncompromising critiques of the coup and its politics, and in so doing asserted the bourgeois nature of electoral democracy in Thailand. Almost every commentator on the matter read the democracy movements as a

13. Peter A. Jackson, "Summary of Political Events in Thailand, 1991 and 1992," in *The May 1992 Crisis in Thailand: Background and Aftermath: Selected Papers from the 1992 Thailand Update Conference, University of Sydney, 16 October 1992*, ed. Peter Jackson (Canberra: National Thai Studies Centre, Australian National University, 1992), 2.

sign that a new middle class had arrived. Benedict Anderson had already observed this emergence when he interpreted the rise in political murder in modern Siam as a symptom of the rising investments in electoral representation, but few shared his perspicacity and most have read the murders, which had been common accompaniments to electoral campaigns, as departures from rather than instantiations of the emergence of a more representationally oriented political consciousness.[14]

Following the initial outcry, the deeply respected parliamentarian from the city of Trad, Chalard Vorachat, began a hunger strike and galvanized a broader movement, which finally congealed under the leadership of the charismatic and ascetic Bangkok governor (and founder of the Phalang Tham [Dhammic force] party), Chamlong Srimuang.[15] Although he articulated a kind of antimilitarism for the bourgeois protestors of 1992, Chamlong was himself a general, the head of Class 7 of the Chulachomklao Military Academy, and a key member of a group of military men who are widely known in Thailand as the "young turks." Chamlong's previous history as an antileftist and his rumored complicity in the massacres of students at Thammasat University during the assault of 6 October 1976 made him an unlikely candidate for revolutionary leadership.[16] But, like many details of the government suppression of students and other radicals during that earlier period, Chamlong's own involvement has been largely contained by the doubt that he continually casts over his own history. By 1992, most people had forgotten or no longer knew enough to associate him with the more overtly violent elements of the right, including the Border Patrol Police and the more clandestine paramilitary organizations such as Nawaphol and the Red Gaurs (who are generally thought to have precipitated and perpetrated most of the violence). His previous right-wing extremism had been discarded along

14. Benedict Anderson, "Murder and Progress in Modern Siam," *New Left Review* 181 (1990): 33–48, and "Notes on the Changing Implications of Political Killings in Thailand," in *Proceedings of the International Conference on Thai Studies*, compiled by Ann Buller (Canberra: Australian National University, 1987), 255–62.

15. Chamlong's significance in Bangkok politics and his refashioning of the politician's image has been the subject of considerable attention. His adherence to an ascetic Buddhism called Santi Asoke, which has more in keeping with the tradition of the forest monks than urban Buddhism, has earned him the opprobrium of the national Buddhist hierarchy but given him extraordinary legitimacy in the eyes of Bangkok citizens, particularly its middle classes. For a history of the tensions among various forms of new urban Buddhism in Bangkok, see Peter A. Jackson, *Buddhism, Legitimation, and Conflict* (Canberra: Institute of Southeast Asian Studies, 1989); and Charles Keyes, "Buddhist Politics and Their Revolutionary Origins in Thailand," *International Political Science Review* 10, no. 2 (1989): 121–42.

16. An excellent account of Chamlong's political history can be founding Duncan McCargo, *Chamlong Srimuang and the New Thai Politics* (New York: St. Martin's Press, 1997), esp. 33–40.

with his uniforms, eclipsed by the image of a disciplined meditator and ardently puritanical politician who had campaigned on a platform of moral and material cleanliness. That Chamlong could have emerged as the figurehead of a new—and newly bourgeois—antimilitarism says much about the degree to which the particular histories of the more radical movement of the seventies had been forgotten or silenced. But it also marks the distance between earlier demands for the representation of working-class interests and more contemporary calls for the representation of individual interests.

Perhaps, in the end, only his pseudo-monastic existence saved Chamlong from denunciation on the left, which, in its newly moderate form, now prizes asceticism and environmentalism above class interests. But then it was monasticism, or at least the appearance of monasticism, that permitted General Sarit to return from exile in 1976, when he used the pretense of being ordained at the royalist temple, Wat Boworniwes, to return to Thailand before he seized power again. Chamlong's own affiliation with the renegade Buddhist sect, Santi Asoke, whose leader Phra Photirak had been repeatedly denounced by the Supreme Patriarch and finally ejected from the monkhood, made him something of a religious outcast from the perspective of the conservative orthodoxy. Thus, if his asceticism made him a possible hero in the eyes of nonmilitary Bangkokians, he was a suspect character in the eyes of the dominant and still militarist members and supporters of Class 5. Ironically, then, it was his previous role as an intelligence officer with the Armed Forces Supreme Command (which held distant responsibility for the Border Patrol Police's murderous activities on 6 October) that partly insulated Chamlong from being completely tarred with the epithet "communist."

For his part, Chamlong continues to disavow knowledge of the right-wing extremism to which his own actions contributed in 1976 by claiming that his intentions had been pure, guided only by a concern for the national good. In a crucial passage of his autobiography, Chamlong reflects on the catastrophe of 1976 and attributes his decision to oppose students to his viewing of a photograph that depicted the Crown Prince being hanged in effigy.[17] This photograph is now widely believed to have been retouched, and the deaths to which students were put on the basis of its putative referent continue to haunt what Thongchai Winichakul calls the traumatized consciousness of that moment.[18]

17. Chamlong Srimuang, *Chiwit Chamlong* [The life of Chamlong] (Bangkok: HJK AV Publishing, 1990), 112–13.

18. I mean to invoke the sense of the term "trauma" as it is used by Thongchai Winichakul in his discussion of *hok tula*. In his treatment of the issue, Thongchai claims that the traumatic nature of those events prohibits efforts to cover over the silences of official narratives with a compensatory

Indeed, the occult power of photography has rarely had such potent and maca-bre effects. However, the movement that Chamlong himself attempted to head in 1992 rested on a horribly ironic reinvestment in the truth-value of photogra-phy and the simultaneous commitment to the imaginal transformations that photographs can effect. In this regard, it was haunted by the ghosts of that first traumatic moment, subjected to the violently uncanny photographic effects that otherwise had been largely suppressed in official representations of Thai history. The traumatic moment, the moment that has been so missed in official historiographic accounts of *hok tula*, (6 October) would be recovered, retro-spectively, in a repetition that would seem both inevitable and unpredictable to those who experienced it.

By early May, the streets of Bangkok were full of crowds whose numbers swelled to the tens of thousands in the evenings and on weekends. Military and police forces (including the Border Patrol Police) responded with shows of force and oblique references to the bloody and successful suppression of popu-list dissent in 1976. On 4 May, Chamlong joined Chalard in a hunger strike and prophesied his own death within seven days, an act that immediately redefined the political landscape—although Chamlong later abandoned the strike at the request of his supporters when it became apparent that the military would not bow to his demands. On 16 May, when crowds of protestors attempted to move from their site at Sanam Luang to the Democracy Monument across the Phaan Fa bridge, the army and Border Patrol Police opened fire under the all too obvious code name Parii phinaad (Operation crush the enemy). Official counts put the three-day death toll at fifty-three, but several hundred people remained unaccounted for during the months that followed and rumors continued to circulate for years about the possible fate of the bodies.[19]

---

and seamless speech. He calls instead for a theatricalization of that silence as a part of nearly Brechtian politics aimed at the exposure of official discourse as that which silences the subjects of historical trauma. See his essay, "Remembering/Silencing the Traumatic Past: The Ambivalence Narratives of the October 1976 Massacre in Bangkok," in *Proceedings of the 6th International Thai Conference on Thai Studies, Theme II: Cultural Crisis and the Thai Capitalist Transformation* (Chiang Mai), 473–93. Also see "*Ramleuk 6 tula: thammai lae' yangrai*" [The massacre of Octo-ber 6: Why and how?], in *Rao maj lyym hok thula* [We haven't forgotten October 6] (Bangkok: 20th Anniversary Memorial Publication, 1995), 13–22.

19. There were suggestions and some photographic evidence to indicate that bodies were removed by military transport vehicles and possibly dropped from the air over forested areas of Cambodia. Initial searches of Thai army sites within Thailand did not turn up any bodies. Just as the number of dead during the October coup of 1976 remains uncertain, so it seems inevitable that the tally of the dead from May 1992 will be forever shrouded in doubt.

*The View from Afar*

In Chiang Mai City, support rallies at Thapae Gate, which were organized mainly by students and faculty from Chiang Mai University and the Teacher's College, had been relatively sedate and modest in size, attracting a few dozen people each day, until Chamlong Srimuang initiated his hunger strike. Thereupon, the number of nightly auditors grew to several hundred and even thousands. Each evening, students, politicians, and university professors took the stage and railed against the return of military dictatorship to Thailand. Although initial outcries were directed primarily at the issue of military visibility and were constructed as critiques of Suchinda's betrayal of electoral process, the democracy movement eventually stirred a critique of military governance on more general levels. In the months that followed, the military control over state monopolies, particularly those under the Ministry of Transport and Communications, was questioned and then broken up in response to pressures by newly politicized coalitions of business organizations such as the Business Management Service Co., the Business Club for Democracy, and the Democracy Development Fund, all of which were formed in the aftermath of the shootings.[20]

In the early stages of the movement, however, attention focused on the symbolic fact of Suchinda's appointment and what it signified for Thailand's democracy as a political form. One of the speakers at the Chiang Mai rally summed up the issues when he spoke to the protestors and accused the NPKC of dictatorship. The severity of that accusation, and its seeming anachronism in Thailand, was intended to provoke outrage, even as the speaker withdrew into the politesse of the impersonal:

> At this time, I must emphasize that a dictatorship has come to power in our country. Various groups disagree. The manner in which General Suchinda came to power is such a cunning one that many people think he is legitimate [has legitimately ascended to the prime ministership]. Many people believed that Suchinda has come to power according to a democratic system under the rule of the constitution. We should recall what Suchinda said on the 23rd of February [the date of the 1991 coup]. Even though he established a "legitimate" body to draft a new constitution, a number of items have remained in the constitution that further his power in the long term. We have not come to attack General Suchinda personally,

20. The subject of entrepreneurial politics was addressed in the local press in generally laudatory terms. See, for example, Vatchara and Jaruwan's article, "BMS Enters Political Arena," and Vatchara and Duangkamol's commentary, "Business and Politics Do Mix," both in *The Nation*, 16 June 1992.

but Suchinda is a person who does not match his words with actions. We come to protest the "democratic" system that Suchinda has created. For Suchinda has used the constitution to create a dictatorship.[21]

Such addresses, though not always so formal, were repeated hourly at the media station set up in Chiang Mai. Some were more trenchant than others, some more fearful.

In almost all cases, however, the issues that received critical attention were those of representational form: procedural questions, electoral processes, and proper relationships between local need and national appearance. Failures and blockages of access to knowledge and power and betrayals of formal process substituted here for the class-based analysis of the 1970s. In 1992, almost no one spoke of poverty. Nor did they speak of rural disenfranchisement. They lamented a proximity to power that had been interrupted. And they expressed their rage in terms of moral failures (betrayal, broken promises, unfair practices) rather than structural political inadequacies (such as the concentration of capital and the dislocation of rural subjects). For this reason, if no other, the editors of *Phucadkaan* were correct to ridicule the military's invocation of communism's specter. It was not because of the Soviet Union's demise (which commentators adduced as an "explanation" for the noncommunism of the 1990s) but because class analysis had become an unspeakability for bourgeois subjects that the Democracy Movement of 1992 achieved such widespread legitimacy. This was as true in Chiang Mai as it was in Bangkok.[22]

At the rally in Chiang Mai, organizers interspersed explanations of procedure and its betrayals with announcements of how many people were gathered in Bangkok. In this manner, political discourse was punctuated by a staged facticity. The truth value of the latter acted, in some ways, to guarantee the validity of the interpretation, but as much as the work of rhetorical persuasion, the numbers were intended to generate the sense of a collectivity so enormous that it could encompass even the people in Chiang Mai. And this it did. As the reported numbers of protestors in Bangkok grew from 25,000 to 100,000 to 200,000, cheers rose in Chiang Mai. A din of demands for Suchinda's resignation subdued even the traffic noise that accompanied the growing knots of automobiles at the intersection: "*Laa ork, laa ork, laa ork*" (Resign, resign, resign). And more people gathered.

In many regards, the rallies in Chiang Mai resembled those in Bangkok,

21. Field notes of rally address, my translation.
22. One wants to recall here the other "revolutions" of Southeast Asia in the 1980s and 1990s, revolutions in the Philippines and in Indonesia, for example, where the rhetoric of transparent representation displaced that of class to make the memory of the 1960s a matter of forgetfulness.

although the northern protests were less dominated by celebrity and more modest in size. Similar references to 1973, when the coalition politics of students and agricultural laborers had managed to bring down Sarit's military government, marked both rallies. The same strains of Caravan, the radical folk singers whose phlaeng chiwit (Music for life) had so defined an era, drifted through the audiences. The same rhetorical practices and the same populist theatricality defined events at either end of the country.

Nonetheless, the self-conscious mirroring strategies of the protest organizers in Chiang Mai were endlessly punctuated by glances into the events in Bangkok, generating both a sense of simultaneity and the demand for a belated identification with an alter-national community. The vacillation between these two sensations—that of simultaneity and immersion, and that of belated and peripheral distance from which identification could be demanded—was present in virtually every aspect of the rallies at Chiang Mai. Nowhere was this more apparent than in the code switching of speakers on the floodlit stages of the flatbeds from which the rally organizers spoke. Attempts to claim political partnership and to refuse peripheral status were generally made in the language of the center and from a decidedly centrist perspective. Rally speeches were carried out in elegant Central Thai, and though many of the university professors who chaperoned the town hall–style discussions were originally from Chiang Mai, their language (with its well-rolled rs and pronomial propriety) identified them with the cultural center. They were, indeed, deeply conscious of this fact. To parochialize the discourse and make "real northerners feel that this is their struggle too," as one organizer told me, "common northerners" were invited onto the stage as token spokespeople for local sentiment. These men and women were rather condescendingly introduced as khon thamadaa (ordinary people), an impolite term in most contexts but one that was supposed to prove the class ubiquity and hence the legitimacy of dissent. Carefully chosen farmers, merchants, and "people on the street" (but not street people) were asked up onto the stage to express their feelings about the events in Bangkok. Their speech, though peppered with occasional kam müang markers such as cao (a gender-neutral affirmative, like the English "yeah" and the Central Thai kha for women or khrap for men), could not stabilize the boundary between Northern and Central Thai. And when, on rare occasions, Northern Thai was actually spoken by uneducated commoners, it was prefaced by profuse apologies for 'uu kam müang ("speaking Northern Thai").

At the rallies, northernness was a citation, marked off by quotation marks in a discourse of the Siamified nation-state. And like all citations, it worked to produce an authenticity effect by claiming to insert the really real into the space of discourse. Most of the "common folk" who were staged at the rallies commented on Chamlong's discipline, his righteousness, and his legitimacy as a leader, while making only oblique reference to Suchinda and the NPKC. Often, they expressly refused to criticize the general, and in their silences they enacted the abjection that had been produced in them by an educational apparatus that demanded submission to status seniors.

Offstage (and out of view), Suchinda was more frequently the subject of vitriolic assault. For many, he was the personification of Bangkok itself. In this case, people elaborated their own peripherality to claim moral authenticity vis-à-vis a city, Bangkok, that is often described as the scene of moral failure in the form of excess: gluttonous consumerism, ceaseless sexual traffic, and proliferating dissimulations by individuals who no longer feel obligated by truth.[23] In the conversations that rippled through the crowds, rally speakers were typed as being from Bangkok or from Chiang Mai. Self-styled northerners often attempted to distinguish between Chamlong and Suchinda on the grounds of either man's status as a citizen of Bangkok. Thus, one woman remarked, "Chamlong is from Bangkok. *But* he's a good man. Suchinda, now he's really from Bangkok. He's bad, absolutely mad with power." Many others revered Chamlong precisely because he claimed to be a man of the entire country (*pen khon thang prathet*) and not of Bangkok, despite his position as governor of the capital. Not all people took this position, of course, and many northerners, particularly those with sons or brothers in the army, supported Suchinda. But the military was also adjudicated on the basis of its northernness. The strong support of the armed forces in the north, where it provides one of few avenues to economic mobility for lower-class men, was deeply threatened by the eventual bloodshed in Bangkok, and not a few families and friendships came to grief over the events and the need to hold someone responsible for the deaths. However, the local division's seeming reticence to move on the Chiang Mai protests was cheered, cultivated, and strategically praised by protest organizers as evidence that even the northern military was morally superior to its southern counterpart.[24]

23. In some ways, then, the people of Chiang Mai and the peripheries of Thailand acted like Meratus Batak, as Tsing describes them: they remarked and constituted their own marginality as part of an ironic self-empowerment. See Anna Lowenhaupt Tsing, *In the Realm of the Diamond Queen: Marginality in an Out-of-the-Way Place* (Princeton, NJ: Princeton University Press, 1993).

24. There were no shots fired in Chiang Mai and the military was largely invisible, although police were virtually omnipresent. On two occasions, soldiers are reported to have been ready to march on the gathering at Thapae Gate, but organizers obliged them by dispersing (and deserting the gate) rather than confront a possible repetition of the assault in Bangkok. Eventually, to accommodate the growing numbers and avoid the vulnerability of Thapae Gate, which could be approached

## Mediations

Mediating the tension between Bangkok and Chiang Mai while forging an alterior national community became the task of northern academics and media experts. This was an especially acute problem in the context of a military ban on television coverage of the protests. On 7 May, just after Chamlong had upped the ante in his confrontation with the soldiers, an elated professor from Chiang Mai University announced to the crowds that the protestors had obtained a fax machine, a video monitor, and a computer. "We will be your TV, your radio, your mass media. The truth will come out here," he declared, using the English words for "fax" and "media" in linguistic deference to the original foreignness of these technologies. During the week that followed the professor's optimistic announcement, rally organizers showed video compilations of the events in Bangkok. These had been pirated from CNN and the BBC and then smuggled north by journalists, students, and sympathetic tourists to fill the gap generated by local censorship. Rally organizers also broadcast incoming telephone calls and faxes; in so doing, they provided a virtually constant relay of information. Government- and military-owned television and radio stations responded by warning people away from demonstrations and demanding that they ignore the rumors being spread by media "terrorists."

The media station was nothing if not a monster of technological prosthesis. The protest organizers stood before their audiences as men embedded in webs of information, and made of themselves the mere amplifiers of messages that were coming from elsewhere. The telephone transmissions in particular were absurdly intimate and absurdly distanced at the same time. No one ever heard that voice whose origin we supposed was Bangkok. We heard only the citations of that voice, the repetitions of its utterances, and the false promise of a pure content, one uninflected by regional accent or technological form. With a telephone in one hand and a microphone in the other, Chiang Mai's radicals repeated what they heard and performed as people on call, as people ready to accept a call even before knowing what the demand of that call would be. In this manner, their political positions were staked as ethical positions, as a general state of readiness rather than a commitment to particular action. Indeed, the performances took place at the threshold of agency, for, as the transmitters of

---

on all sides, the rally moved to Chiang Mai University. The organizers' praise of the northern armed forces was intentionally solicitous and appeared to some as obsequiously anticonfrontational. There was, in fact, considerable explicit strategizing about how to ensure the army's sense of kinship with protestors. It was assumed (and it may have been the case) that young men would not be able to fire on their friends and relatives if the fact of kinship was maintained in the forefront of their minds.

messages, the media men were effaced in the very moment of their political participation. They had indeed become media—one almost wants to say mediums. And this is inevitable given that the entire scene was itself staged in the anticipation of being seen from afar, by the auditors of world politics in London, New York, and Sydney. There would, in fact, be mediums at the Chiang Mai rallies. Or at least there would be a medium. Ironically, he would be the man of agency. And he would be the least visible figure in this theater of democracy.

The threat of rumors spread by media terrorists also galvanized an oppositional force in Chiang Mai. Rumors themselves spread like fire and consumed the attention of activists and less interested residents. But the image that finally cemented kinship between Chiang Mai and Bangkok was conveyed by neither telephone nor television, nor any technology of instantaneous telecommunicated information. It was a front-page photograph from *The Nation* newspaper, which featured five soldiers beating an unarmed protestor to death. This was the first image of bloodshed to get out of Bangkok, and protest organizers photocopied it by the thousands, then handed it out to passing motorcyclists and pedestrians on the morning of 17 May. Upon its circulation, the crowds at Thapae Gate grew to between ten thousand and twenty thousand.

The photograph, with the grotesque luminosity of the beaten man's shirt blotting out the shadow of military cult power, arrived like a ghost. It was an apparition, it haunted its beholders, and it threatened, constantly, to return. It was, indeed, already a return: the kind of return in which the past seems to come from the future.

The photograph instantly became a focal point for the Chiang Mai movement. Perhaps it was the fact that the image was distributed by hand and accompanied by face-to-face persuasion that made it so powerful. Perhaps it was the horrible power of being the first image, or the brutal particularity of the subject (most later images were of mass shootings). Perhaps it was all of these together, but the rallies at Chiang Mai were profoundly transformed in the moment that the image circulated, multiplying in size and intensifying in affective force.

The arrival of the photograph, with its powers of capture, can be said to have transformed the rallies in ways that exceed the question of magnitude. For the earlier rallies had been marked by a fantasy of simultaneity and those that followed the arrival of this haunting and haunted image were defined by a sense of belatedness. The extraordinary spectacles of connection, in which the telephone could appear to be the repository of national presence, were displaced by the kind of contemplation that photographs permit, a contemplation made possible by temporal disjuncture. As this occurred, Chiang Mai protestors assumed the slightly different externality of witnesses. Here, the belatedness of their relationship to both Bangkokian power and the traumatic events of the military's crackdown in Ratchadamnoen Avenue was converted into a commandment: to repeat, to retell, to return in memory to the space of a transformation whose coming had been at once inevitable and impossible to predict.

It was into this space of shocked and oddly disconnected observation that the mobile telephones and fax machines inserted their promise of a new immediacy. And the relationships that emerged between Chiang Mai and Bangkok were therefore torn between alienation and simultaneity. In Chiang Mai, this very ambivalence made it possible to discern the absurdity of the nonevent that was being disseminated throughout the country via the military media networks. As soldiers were firing on crowds, television viewers were being told that nothing was happening in Bangkok. In fact, they were not shown official footage of the shootings until five days after the event. However, many northerners read the claim to nothingness as a declaration, through a strangely marked silence, that something was indeed occurring. They heard this theatricalized, all but deafening silence, and were drawn by it to the void the military networks offered as solace in the place of truth: placatory images of relatively bloodless shootings and a final conciliatory meeting between the leaders of the conflict's opposed parties after they were apparently brought together at the king's behest.

Chiang Mai was never as subject to the contrived invisibility of the nonevent to the same degree that Bangkok was. Perhaps for the first time in Thai history, people on this periphery believed themselves to be in command of a greater, a more objective vision of what was happening in Bangkok than did its residents, whose immersion in the events made them incapable of that oversight that the international news media promised in their summary coverage and perfunctory analyses. Cast in the role of spectators in relation to the excision of their own representational future, many of Chiang Mai's residents responded with an assertion of northern moral authority. As the media stations became sites for the grief-struck recognition of the impossibility of Thainess, northerners indulged in a kind of moral distancing. Indeed, the more immediate access to the events in Bangkok that people in Chiang Mai seemed to have, the more problematic became the notion of Thainess and the more vociferous became northern assertions of moral authenticity and superiority.

I spent numerous hours on many evenings with one tea vendor in particular who provided a running commentary on the entire spectacle in precisely these terms. "That person is from Bangkok," or "That person is a real northerner," she would say with a nudge as someone got up onto the stage. While she poured heavily milked and sugared tea into tiny plastic bags and whipped elastic bands around them, I asked her how long she intended to keep coming to the rallies. Laughingly, she responded, "Until Suchinda resigns." When I asked again if she really thought he would be forced out, the tea vendor could only shrug: "Who knows? These are matters of Bangkok. I know nothing of tomorrow, only of today."

For the tea vendor, and many others in Chiang Mai, northernness entails a position of belatedness in relation to Bangkok. Events and decisions of the central government, including the appointment of officials who serve in Chiang Mai, seem to arrive in this peripheral city only after their completion. The fact of democratic representation only redoubles this relationship, insofar as it entails the ceding and transference of decision-making authority to one who will represent the political will of Chiang Mai's residents in a retrospective manner. Indeed, electoral representation introduces both a temporal and a structural gap into the political process and, for this reason, needs to be distinguished from the sovereign performativity of the absolute monarch. In democratic contexts, political will is mediated. In mass-mediated contexts, the process of that mediation is dispersed along teletechnic routes whose vectors move among cities and spaces that exceed the nation in every sense. For this reason, electoral politics are no longer (if ever they were) a question of transparently expressing the will of a constituency, its diversity, or even its majority. They are, rather, refracted and triangulated by the gazes and the anticipated auditing of others. Indeed, it is in this moment that the possibility of revolution is converted into the appearance, perhaps even the rumor, of revolution. A certain lack of foresight, manifesting itself as an incapacity to imagine alternative political futures, accompanied the critical retrospection of the events at Thapae Gate. For all the talk about failures of procedure, there were almost no proscriptive utterances. No one, it seemed, imagined themselves to be in the place of political origins, to be capable of articulating a shared performativity. At best, they could ask for better representation. In the end, one could not but notice the degree to which the calls to action were, in some profound respect, calls to mere appearance, just as Scouts were called to appear like good national subjects in another time. The revolution existed there as mise-en-scène, as the condition of a possibility that would remain not only headless but bodiless: in a word, spectral. The crowd waited, already discharged, but lacking in direction.

### The Other Medium: Northern Locality and the Power of Place

Direction came, momentarily, in flamboyant fashion, and in the guise of a return to origins. Even before the shootings, the values of northernness were being mobilized by protest organizers, many of whom were from Bangkok and who believed that northernness provided the only idiom within which Chiang Mai's residents could conceive of their own stakes in local representation and hence electoral politics. In the interests of inciting precisely that identification, they staged a "traditional" northern rite of cursing, a *phithii saab chaeng*, against General Suchinda. On 10 May, following Suchinda's accusations that protestors had been paid by the opposition to betray Thailand, the rally in Chiang Mai became visibly angry.[25] The accusation effectively suggested that northerners had sided with Chatichai, who was accused of having bought votes and of operating his government, inappropriately, as a business. In Thailand, as elsewhere, there is a sense in which proper political representation is supposed to take the form of a nearly Kantian aesthetic engagement: it is to be disinterested. That such representation can never be disinterested does not, of course, mitigate the degree to which democratic politics operate on the basis of their putative transparency. Voluntarism, the condition of possibility for "free voting," requires such disinterest as its ground, and it would not be too extreme to suggest that the transnational discourse of electoral democracy represents the delayed and distant triumph of a Kantian position. But that is an issue too grand for serious contemplation here. In Chiang Mai, the more immediate consequence of these accusations was simply outrage. Thus, speakers vehemently denied Suchinda's insinuations and insisted that they had come "on their own" and were "not stupid northerners." The repetition of Suchinda's insults could only impel a negative identification: a valorization of that which Suchinda had denounced.

The protestors, most of them men, continued to speak with venom into the

---

25. Suchinda also denounced General Chawalit (one of Suchinda's major critics) as a communist and suggested that Chamlong's Buddhism was illegitimate. The charge against Chawalit was that he wanted to install a "presidium-style government." In the context of Thailand's violent anticommunism, this charge was as damning as any could be, but it reflected a military completely out of touch with its own reality. In fact, the democracy movement was a largely bourgeois affair, and it was the entrepreneurial classes who provided it with its power. Somewhat ironically, Suchinda was instantly ridiculed for his accusation of presidium politics. However, this was not because of the blatant capitalism of Chawalit and his supporters. Rather, he was mocked on logical grounds because, it was said, no one could legitimately invoke a presidium-style government in the aftermath of the Soviet Union's demise (*Phucadkaan*, 7 May 1992, 1). Francis Fukuyama's "The End of History?" *The National Interest* 16 (1989):3–18, was trotted out in some editorial columns as further evidence that Suchinda's charges could not be valid! Communism had become, quite simply, the very threshold of the thinkable, the limit of political possibility. Chawalit himself would become prime minister four years later and hold power in the moment that economic catastrophe struck. His resignation from office in 1997 did not lead to his exit from politics, however, and he remains a significant player on the national scene as the head of a potent new party.

hot night, and as they did so, an altar was set up in front of the media stage. This consisted of a two-tiered table, at the back of which was a head-and-shoulders portrait of General Suchinda framed with dead and withered banyan tree leaves. On the upper level were three monks' alms bowls as well as a *khan* dish in which fifty-nine one-baht coins (one for each year of Suchinda's life) were placed. A bouquet of jasmine, several bundles of joss sticks, and a plate full of fresh fruit, raw meat, sweets, and flowers wrapped in banana leaves with tiny green and red flags embedded therein completed the display. Around the table were votive candles and in front, a placard reading *phithii saab chaeng* ("cursing ritual"). The placard was intended for Bangkokians, in the hope that they would understand the event as a deployment of northern power and the power of northernness when they saw it in the newspapers.

A young man and woman mounted the stage above the altar and announced that an important ritual was about to be performed. They described the rite as an ancient tradition (*prapheenii boraan*) of the Lanna people, to be performed only in extreme circumstances. With theatrical gravity in their voices, they itemized the contents of the *khan* and introduced a widow and a widower who would perform the actual rite, the master and mistress of ceremonies explaining that the words of the widowed would be sacred (*saksit*) by virtue of their intimacy with death. The widowed twosome took over from there, approaching the altar and planting tiny black flags on either side, then lighting joss sticks and all of the candles surrounding it, so that the altar glowed even under the intense brilliance of the floodlights above. The woman ground dried hot red chili peppers and salt from the bowl atop the altar and then dropped them in each of the three alms bowls. Then she and her male companion turned the joss sticks upside down and planted them in the alms bowls, sprinkling more salt and more peppers as the smoke clouded Suchinda's portrait and filled the air with rank, eye-stinging potency. Tall cylindrical rice steamers were then placed upside down over the joss sticks and allowed to ignite, their coals falling into the bowls and their smoke adding to the thickening clouds.

The two officiants knelt before Suchinda's image, *wai*-ing and muttering the words of the crowd's desire in a stream of barely audible kam müang. People from the crowd pressed forward as the young master of ceremonies bounded on stage and asked them to speak with him and send the message of their hearts to the spirits. Together they (we) called upon the "spirits of the *lak müang* and the *süa müang*, and all of the spirits from the highest points of the world, from atop the mountain and from heaven itself to come into this world and to rid Thailand of General Suchinda and his wife, and all of the five governing generals who have hurt the Thai people."

Men and women cheered, and a few drunken protestors rushed forward to tear Suchinda's portrait from its place and set it afire, screaming "Death to Suchinda!" with thrilling vehemence. The crowd itself was ignited and partook of this fire, moving rapidly and purposefully toward the altar and holding up for the cameras the burning image of the reviled general.

## Forms of Alterity and Terror

The forms of the *phithii saab chaeng* are those of ancestor worship turned upside down. Invoking the powers of the spirits to carry out a deed of such violence involves the penetration of all that is other, and the inversion of forms is a poetic enactment of this encounter with alterior power. A local specialist in the arts of benevolent sorcery described it to me as a complete inversion of the remembering rites normally carried out for loved ones. Thus, instead of the image of a revered deceased relative, there is the image of the intended victim. Instead of construing him as part of a lineal tree, his image is covered with dead and withered leaves, which burn and separate him from the living. Rather than white flags of purity and rebirth for the dead, there are black ones signifying evil and continuous death. Instead of feeding the victim, chili and salt are burned to create a caustic, bowel-ripping meal whose consequences are described as being much like those of witchcraft (*phii ka'*): a feeling of being devoured from within. In keeping with this inversion of consumptive logic, the rice steamers are turned upside down to underscore that this rite is the very antithesis of the forms of remembrance termed *liang phii* (feeding the spirits).

Witchcraft is always a kind of "negative value production," as Nancy Munn would have it.[26] But in Thailand, its imbrication in the history of modernity's inversions and displacements is well remembered. Witchcraft accusations, as already stated, exploded at the turn of the century when liquid capital and currency moved in with the missionaries and the teak companies. They seem to have been targeted mainly at individuals who were thought to have inappropriately abandoned their own lineages (because the Christian missionaries forbade the worship of ancestral spirits) and to have profited as a result. The accusations, if accepted, were followed by exorcism or exile for the witches and the confiscation and burning of their property. Compared to spirit possession, such as that of Cao Ubon, which lay blame at the feet of foreigners, witchcraft accusations tended to attribute crisis to the actions of local people.[27] Witch-

26. Nancy Munn, *The Fame of Gawa: A Symbolic Study of Value Transformation in a Massim (Papua New Guinea) Society* (1986; Durham, NC: Duke University Press, 1992), esp. 215–66.

27. Anan Ganjanapan, "The Idiom of *Phii Ka'*: Peasant Conception of Class Differentiation in Northern Thailand," *Mankind* 14, no. 4 (1984): 325–29.

craft accusations, therefore, accused local individuals of identifying with the foreign, while possession named the desire of the foreigner for local objects and power as the origin of catastrophe. It was therefore significant that Suchinda's greatest sin was given the name of betraying Thainess, even when the accusation was being made by northerners in the moment that they themselves laid claim to exteriority vis-à-vis the nation. The poison of the other is insinuated in the body of the victim because he himself has ingested that poison (recall here the case of the Meo victim, whose heroin addiction makes him vulnerable to ensorcellment).

In the cursing rite, the food that is placed on the *khan* is actually intended for the spirits who will assist the cursing and is not offered to the object of the curse. The invocation of the highest spirits (*phii sung doi*) is, I was told, an explicit attempt to garner the assistance of the most exalted powers in an act whose violence has *kam*mic implications. Yet, the acts of cursing are not necessarily acts of demerit. If the intended victim is evil and a source of pain for others, then his or her injury can be considered just because it will correct an imbalance in the moral order. Spirits who are brought into play through the invocations of the widow and the widower are actually said to acquire merit by causing suffering in the cursed person and by aiding his or her victims. The risks are immense, however, and only those who are sure of their hearts and the purity of their intentions dare to ask the spirits to intervene. For if a person is ensorcelled for the sake of personal gain or petty vindictiveness, then the perpetrator will suffer in the next life, perhaps being born into the body of a starving shade or a hell-being who endures ceaseless hunger.

The images of the cursing ritual partake of the most extravagant Buddhist phantasmagoria. At the time, I wondered whether anyone could or would take the ritual seriously in any literal sense. Within days, however, rumors were circulating in the national gossip columns that Suchinda, whose own wife was infamous for propitiating spirits and dancing in tribute, had sought protection from other spirit mediums. At least one general is said to have made the trip north to obtain protective amulets. Publicly, however, most people dismissed the idea of actual efficacy and described the rite in purely cathartic terms even when they admitted that they would be happy if Suchinda did experience the ravages of burnt chilies and salt.

Beyond this drama of a supposedly peculiar northern imagination and a modality of belief that fits perfectly with Bangkok's condemning image of northern "supernaturalism," there was another terror in whose terms the images of the curse operated. These are the images of the terror that swept across Thailand in the 1970s when the country's U.S.-backed army was pursuing communist students into the jungle and when U.S. forces were napalming Vietnam and Laos with the help of the Thai air force. These are the images carefully spread along the paths of gossip: of communists torturing Thai men and destroying them with penis-shrinking medicines. They are the images disseminated by the charismatic monk Khittivuddho Bikkhu, who argued that communists were not human and could be hunted down like animals without risk of demerit. They are the images of bullet-ridden bodies in a society where political execution is a not uncommon fact of electoral campaigning. They are, in effect, the imaginal currency of violent order, of a modern military culture that rules through the promise and the anticipation of force. Since 6 October, the future of force in Thailand will always be the return of a force already deployed.

One sweltering postrally evening, some student colleagues and I received a phone call from a "family friend" (in the military) who warned us away from the rallies with news that military officials had been talking about necklacing some protestors. When he informed us that this had also been the fate of the disappeared students twenty years previously, the idea of a body burning from within no longer seemed ridiculous. In all likelihood, there were never any discussions of necklacing, except perhaps among some drunken young soldiers who were themselves terrified by the shape of events in Bangkok and who had been fed tales of the 1970s to fuel their imagination. Yet, the rumor worked, as did the curse. Its effect arrived before the deed was done. Indeed, as one of the rite's officiants later told me, the point was to kill Suchinda with fear, to make his bowels turn over with anxiety so that he would die of dread; then it would work only to the extent that Suchinda was responsive to the particular call of this force. When we answered our telephone, we acted too as ones "on call," not only to technology but to power. We never thought to ask what demand would be made of us before responding. And it fell to everyone to act (with avoidance of the rallies or persistence, with disagreement or disclosure) after receiving this call. Apotropaic medicines, such as those that the generals sought, were absurdly and desperately belated in this context. A refusal to answer would have been the most powerful response. But in the teletechnically mediated world, such refusal is impossible. Subjects of mass-mediated orders are, by definition, subjects permanently on call.

### Northernness for Northerners?

If the effect of the *phithii saab chaeng* can be understood within this logic of teletechnically mediated rumors, and of anticipatory consciousness, it was nonetheless presented to observers as uniquely northern. In this context, it is necessary to ask, Who presided over this rite that was so carefully staged as the articulation of local sentiment? Who, in effect, was its medium? Behind the stage, in a throng of excited students and journalists, the young woman who had announced the rite introduced herself in perfect Central Thai spoken in the accent of the capital. A Bangkok-born student at Chiang Mai University, she had been in Chiang Mai for only three years, although when I jokingly suggested that she had become northern already, she quickly asserted that she was interested in the local traditions of belief (*phrapheenii khwaam chya*) only from an ethnographic perspective (she used the term for anthropology, *manut saya whitthaya*): "This ritual is important to the locals. It has appeal for the people of Chiang Mai and it helps us to make the events of Bangkok immediate to them. You might say it helps them to participate in national events without losing a sense of who they are." As for whether she believed in the potential efficacy of the curse, the young woman remained silent. "Do you believe?" I asked. "My belief is not important," she responded.

It would be easy to read this entire staging of northern authenticity as merely cynical theatricality on the part of Bangkok residents. But such a conclusion would be premature and would neglect the degree to which Chiang Mai residents were themselves drawn into the reification of their own northernness and the imagination of that identity as a source of power. The cursing itself was orchestrated by a local spirit medium, Saeng Suang, one of the most politically powerful mediums in Chiang Mai. As the widow and widower whispered to the spirits, he sat behind the fax machines and the television screens under a tarpaulin eave with a distant eye on the events, making sure that all went properly.

Saeng Suang is a muscular but petite man in his early middle age, who at various points in his life has lived as a dancer, a choreographer, an architectural design artist, a jeweler, a bricklayer, and a favorite consort of powerful men. Born into an extremely poor family, with a father who rode a bicycle rickshaw and a mother who died in his infancy, Saeng Suang has led a miraculously charmed life. He is the medium of Phra Cao Saen Müangma, a heroic Buddhist prince who, according to Saeng Suang, saved Chiang Mai from assault when just a teenager. A placard at Wat Faharm on the eastern bank of the Ping River corroborates his story, telling of how Phra Cao Saen Müangma had built the wat in response to an auspicious event. According to the legend inscribed there, King Phayao was transporting the revered Phra Singh relic to Chiang Rai on the Ping River when a beam of light emerged from the icon and shot out toward the shore (a not uncommon event in the life of a Buddha relic). At this moment, "darkness became lightness," and the beam was like a rainbow stretching two hundred yards to the east. The young prince interpreted this as an auspicious sign and built the temple, which is now part of the older Mahannikai sect.

Sometime later, after repulsing attacking forces from the south and the east, his humiliated opponent, Chiang Rai's Cao Phraam, acknowledged the greatness of Phra Cao Saen Müangma and gave the Phra Singh relic as tribute.

For longer than he can remember, Saeng Suang's father has been a central figure in the extramonastic community at Wat Faharm, which occupies an interestingly peripheral position in Chiang Mai's landscape. On the eastern bank of the Ping River, it was beyond the pale of old Chiang Mai's world, in a malarial forest so marginal to the city's political life that it was virtually handed over to the Presbyterian missionaries and Chinese immigrants when they moved into the area in the 1860s. Today, it is in the heart of a residential district that is beginning to see the effects of new real estate development and tourist activities. At least three major condominium construction projects were being undertaken in the area during the first years of the decade, much to the chagrin of local residents.

As for Saeng Suang, he is unlike most other mediums, who claim to have no previous knowledge of their spirits. Saeng Suang's intimacy with the image of Phra Cao Saen Müangma is woven into his earliest childhood memories, for his father, though not a monk himself, supported Wat Faharm with offerings and voluntary services and extolled the virtues of the young prince, whom he seems to have likened to his talented son. Saeng Suang claims not to have sought the role of medium and even to have avoided it. As far as I know, he is unique in his relationship to his spirit in that he has entered a bargain that will spare him daily possessions until he decides he is ready to assume the role of a professional medium. Where other mediums speak of their early years as a period of trial and complete vulnerability to the spirits—who test them and slowly reveal an identity—Saeng Suang has taken a position of extraordinary authority, negotiating his possession with a knowingness that threatens to undermine the very claim to inspiration. His reputation is secure, however, by virtue of the spectacular nature of his possessions and their occurrences in public spaces.

Mediumship, as far as Saeng Suang is concerned, is a role to be accepted only after one has ceased committing the errors of youth (especially sexual errors). It is a calling that, he believes, should not generate income. Indeed, he understands mediumship to be a submission not only to the spirits but also to the collectivity, and he is adamant that the powers of the spirits should be available to all without charge. The meritoriousness of the spirits' deeds will, he says, be enhanced by being severed from the realm of economic exchange. There is an implicit critique of other mediums in this statement, one shared by many monks and laypeople, who see a frankly entrepreneurial spirit in the recent growth of mediumship. Saeng Suang, though acknowledging and paying respect to many of the wealthiest and most powerful mediums in Chiang Mai, nonetheless indicates that his own calling is purer despite the fact—or rather, because of the fact—of his contractual negotiation, for he will enter into a "professional" capacity only when he no longer needs to work to support himself. One can read this aspiration in the terms that Weber described for the charismatically inspired religious figure, but it is also legible in terms of the entrepreneurial economy to which Saeng Suang, like everyone else in Chiang Mai, is so thoroughly subject. In either world, work (what Kracauer would have called enterprise) and service have assumed a value that surpasses utility, that calls one for its own sake and produces satisfaction not in the satiation of need but in mere performance of duty.[28] Thus is Saeng Suang's fantasy of a future life contained by the logic that it wants to escape. In his conversations, Saeng Suang never describes the content of his future labors, never specifies the services that he will perform for his community. One can say for him what Kracauer said of the salaried worker in Weimar Germany, namely, that "work is a concept without content, which precisely through its emptiness proves that it merely reflects the entrepreneur's sovereignty in the objective sphere, without subordinating his sovereignty to anything higher."[29] In this case, Saeng Suang imagines himself as a man opposed to the logics of entrepreneurial capital, especially in its Bangkokian form, and so he invokes a kind of sovereignty that precedes that of the entrepreneur in a war against its immanent hegemony.

Nor can Saeng Suang evade the fact that the resistance to a calling has its own costs. In return for the reprieve he has apparently been granted by Phra Cao Saen Müangma, he makes generous donations to Wat Faharm and has begun building a major shrine on its grounds. He is paying for the construction himself with odd jobs, and devotes his days to designing its minutest details, arranging for mural paintings, soliciting donations, and even sculpting the bas-relief *thewadas* on its exterior walls. Until it is finished, Saeng Suang will abstain from dancing in tribute at Praise Ceremonies devoted to his own spirits. Nor will he attend any other medium's Praise Ceremony, although he has danced at them in the past.

In Saeng Suang's poignant discussions about his deprived childhood and in his loving descriptions of a poor father who worked himself to pained exhaustion for the sake of his son's education—ultimately failing to scrape together enough to send him beyond sixth grade—one glimpses a complex psychology

28. In his analysis of the value of "enterprise" in Weimar Germany, Siegfried Kracauer draws a similar conclusion to comprehend how workers could become beholden to the values that served not themselves but the entrepreneurial capitalists who depended on them. See *The Salaried Masses* (1930), trans. Quinton Hoare (London: Verso, 1998), 99.

29. Ibid.

of desire and identification. Listening to him speak of his father, I often thought it was gratitude itself that inspired Saeng Suang. When I met the old man, whose pride led him to pull shoebox after shoebox of pictures and local newspaper stories about his son from a hidden cupboard, I thought I understood why. It is impossible to dismiss the likelihood that Saeng Suang's possession is at least partly (if unconsciously) motivated by a longing to give his father what fate had deprived him of: the majestic history that was painted into the murals at Wat Faharm. I tried to ask Saeng Suang about this, about whether he wanted to be possessed by Phra Cao Saen Müangma, or even if his father had wanted him to be possessed, and he denied it emphatically. The topic could never be broached so directly again. In some senses, it did not need to be, for psychological explanations do not, in the end, explain the social world in which desires are given form and meaning. And, as far as Saeng Suang was concerned, the commandment that bid him receive spirits came from elsewhere, from the dark defile in which his own unconscious and that of his milieu spoke inaudibly but forcefully in associative patterns that were, for him, illegible. If he needed to give his father something, to mitigate his own sense of dependency or simply to express a profound love, there was nothing that dictated mediumship as the vehicle through which he would do so. Nor could he have determined the full extent of his very extraordinary mediumship. For Saeng Suang has become a medium not only of Buddhist heroes but of Chiang Mai's new locality. The representational logic that made of the north a sign of pastness has made of him the body of a new sending, of a return to the past that is also the return of the past. Representation has found its ironic effects in him.

### The Fame of the Other

In a tradition of royal mediumship that links him more to Cao Ubon than to the rural matrilineal cults favored by ethnographers, Saeng Suang is renowned for his public possessions. If he has managed to put off the onerous daily possessions that attend professional mediumship, he remains the vehicle of his spirit's theatrically strategic and occasionally despotic political will. A few years ago, at the annual festival of the Inthakin, a rite in which people from Chiang Mai and the surrounding towns acknowledge and feed the spirits of the *lak müang*, Saeng Suang was possessed in a particularly dramatic way. Unprepared and without the attire of his spirit—for he has not yet accepted the *khan* and the costume—he shocked attending crowds with a voice that prophesied Chiang Mai's destruction. According to observers who were there at the time, the spirit of Phra Cao Saen Müangma entered Saeng Suang and warned all in attendance that the city was in an extremely precarious position, that development had been allowed to proceed in violation of all moral laws, and that disaster would befall the city if something was not done to stop the defiling of the Ping River and the heavens above Chiang Mai. But Phra Cao Saen Müangma went further. He specifically charged the then-ruling governor with responsibility for the deterioration of the city and warned him to take action or suffer the consequences.

It is interesting to note in this context that the chronicles of Chiang Mai, which were last redacted in the nineteenth century, also attribute Chiang Mai's conquest by the Burmese to residents' failure to maintain the sacred geography of the cityscape. The building of temples in the southeast corner, an area deemed profane in the Indic quadrilateral cosmology, and the cremation of corpses near the life-giving Ping River were considered to have been particularly polluting gestures.[30] Whether these acts occurred prior to the Burmese takeover or reflected the anxieties of the nineteenth-century redactors (who were also faced with massive urban growth), as Sommai speculates,[31] the association of urban disintegration with a violation of the city's moral topography resonates powerfully with the debate that now engages Chiang Mai's cultural elite and that speaks through the body of Saeng Suang.

The opposition to condominium development in Chiang Mai is the point of coalescence for several "neotraditionalist" forces in the city. Prohibited within the walls of the ancient city, buildings of more than four stories are bursting through the skyline around Chiang Mai at an astonishing rate. During the period of my fieldwork, there were an average of fifty new multistoried buildings under construction at any one time. Most were never filled to capacity, having been built on speculation with an eye to middle-class immigration from Bangkok, and the crash of 1997 only exacerbated that situation of partial tenancy. Opponents to the construction have charged that licensing has been granted without adequate inspection (for an illegal fee) and with no infrastructural provisions. In a language reminiscent of witchcraft accusations, the towering condominiums are said to suck (*kin*) the water that otherwise would go to single-family homes. Indeed, each summer in Chiang Mai brings more and more acute water shortages, waste disposal problems, and traffic jams.

The fact that the condominiums are associated with in-migration from Bangkok and that they are taxing the city's already strapped infrastructure makes them easy symbolic targets of local resentment. However, this regionally inflected but basically pragmatic opposition is also interwoven with the resurgent discourses of sacral space, and the two issues most frequently remarked

---

30. Michael Vatikiotis, "Ethnic Pluralism in the Northern Thai City of Chiang Mai" (Ph.D. diss., Oxford University, 1984), 44.
31. Cited in ibid.

about the condominiums are their verticality and their location on the Ping River. Condominiums are said—by people ranging from abbots of wats to street vendors—to violate the heavens by surpassing the spires in which Buddha relics are held. They are said to insult the spirits with their audacious height and to threaten an inversion of moral order. In the cosmography of urban Buddhism, where moral and spatiotemporal proximity to the heavens is focused in the city, the threat of condominiums is felt most keenly at its center. Most people, including even the abbot of Wat Cet Yod, agree that condominiums are not in and of themselves evil (they do not violate any laws of human contact and order) so long as they are kept outside of the city. Even for those who eschew the spiritualist idioms of such critique, the height of the condominiums is often opposed on aesthetic grounds because it violates traditional architectural principles. There is a substantial web of legislation (promoted by the same elite community) that buttresses such claims and protects the ancient city through prohibitions against the destruction of any buildings with the *kalae* on the roof or the masculinist lintel above the door. Of course, in a market of escalating residential real estate values and population pressures, such questions of architectural taste are, as Bourdieu points out, also part of the aesthetic repertoire with which class interests are marked and maintained.[32] In fact, the discourse of northern architectural form is often a veil for exclusive class interests. Many opponents of condominium development resent the influx of the new middle classes, whom they quietly accuse of being *saleu* (a slang term for "tacky"), and there is a certain aura of almost sordid, transient success that adheres to condominium dwellers, not least because many are part-time residents from Bangkok. Condominiums themselves are often perceived as physical manifestations of the intrusion of Bangkok-based capital into Chiang Mai. Not only is most recent development being underwritten by Bangkok-based banks and industrial capital, but the aesthetic modernism of the condominium form itself is associated with Bangkok.[33]

32. Pierre Bourdieu, *Distinction: A Social Critique of the Judgment of Taste*, trans. Richard Nice (Cambridge, MA: Harvard University Press, 1984).

33. What Kevin Hewison says of Thailand in general is true of the north as well, namely, that (legitimate) capital is "under the hegemony of banking capital." See *Bankers and Bureaucrats: Capital and the Role of the State in Southeast Asia* (New Haven: Yale University Press, 1989), 214; also Rudiger Korff, *Bangkok and Modernity* (Bangkok: Chulalongkorn University, Social Research Institute, 1989), 41. In 1988, there were 328 commercial banks in northern Thailand, with loan-to-deposit ratios of 76.6 percent. Although most loans have gone into commerce, a shift can be seen in the past ten years, with increasing numbers and dollar values of loans going to the manufacturing and construction sectors; see Joan Adis, *The Value of Loans in Various Economic Sectors.* Interna-

There are a number of ironies here, not least of which is the fact that some of the strongest champions of Lanna aesthetics are themselves of non-Tai, especially Chinese ethnicity and are descendants of the last major wave of in-migration prior to the entrenchment of Siamese authority over the northern states. Since the late 1860s, when Chinese immigrants moved into Chiang Mai under the patronage of Cao Inthawicharinon, who granted them tax monopolies on opium, alcohol, and gambling, the Chinese have been dedicated defenders of northern autonomy, particularly in relation to Bangkok, which eventually usurped the local *caos'* right to collect any taxes at the local level. This defense of Lanna custom, though attractive to the local ruling families, was not always successful, however. No matter how much the Chinese tax collectors attempted to overcome prejudice and ingratiate themselves with the local aristocracy, they earned resentment and the wrath of would-be competitors and of the peasants and artisans whom they taxed to fill the *caos'* coffers. The results were diverse, ranging from outright revolt to the thinly masked opposition articulated by Cao Ubon's spirit.[34] Nonetheless, they maintained at least the appearance of a strategic affinity with northern culture. As Vatikiotis says, they often adopted a "pro-Northern cultural and political stance—almost Lanna nationalism," which endeared them to northern Thais who were waging their own opposition to the colonizing reforms of the newly bureaucratized Siamese state.[35] Many of the most powerful economic families in Chiang Mai—including Chinawatra, Nimmanhaeminda, Anusarn, and Tantraporn—are of Chinese descent, and although they are linked to a national Sino-Thai community, they have proven themselves extremely adept at mastering the politics of particular placement. Currently, this means supporting architectural preservation. It is not insignificant that the most powerful voice in local architectural circles is that of a Sino-Thai immigrant from Bangkok.

---

tional Labor Organization, report on Thailand, 1990, 20–21. However, Vatikiotis ("Ethnic Pluralism," 150) plausibly notes that the largest source of new capital in the north comes from illicit activities, including narcotics, contraband teak, and arms trade with Burma. It is, of course, precisely this high loan-to-deposit ratio that made Thailand so vulnerable to economic collapse at decade's end.

34. On northern Thai peasant uprisings, see Andrew Turton, "Limits of Ideological Domination and the Formation of Social Consciousness," in *History and Peasant Consciousness in South East Asia*, ed. Andrew Turton and Shigeharu Tanabe *Senri Ethnological Studies* 13 (1984): 19–74. Also Daniel McGilvary's autobiography, which provides considerable insight into the tensions and competitions that were dividing Chiang Mai in the latter half of the nineteenth century: *A Half Century among the Siamese and the Lao: An Autobiography* (New York: Fleming H. Revell, 1912).

35. Vatikiotis, "Ethnic Pluralism," 89.

Historically, local affiliations have often been naturalized by explaining social crisis in the idiom of natural catastrophe. The disruption of locality can be figured as a literal destabilization of the ground on which shared identity might be construed as shared residence. In this manner, the question of alterity is displaced and the problem of affiliation becomes one of shared commitment to the value of locality. In Chiang Mai, this process finds its metaphorics and its iconicity in earthquakes, those literal signs in which fissures and social instability are inscribed as material dislocation. But here affiliation and filiation collide, and personal biography recapitulates social history. Saeng Suang's power as an oracular figure derives partly from the fact that his father was implicated in the earthquakes that shook Chiang Mai in 1989. He has become heir to his father's power, but only in an anticipatory fashion. He waits and is instrumentalized by a force that he does not command, that was commanded in the past but that now merely commands the desire of moderns.

### Shaken: Condominiums, Earthquakes, and Spiritual Revenge

In late September 1989, Chiang Mai was stricken by a series of earthquakes that caused damage to the two temple complexes, Wat Suan Dork and Wat Phra That Doi Suthep, at which Buddha relics are kept. The local press remarked that a *phithii hae phii* (a form of ensorcelling rite) had been performed by a group of protestors opposed to condominium development and noted that these people were claiming responsibility for having brought down the wrath of the *phii sya müang*. In a series of articles, *Khaosiam* (Siam News) followed the stories of the protests and noted that local residents were attributing the earthquake to a violation of the cityscape (*kheut baan kheut müang*): "People suspect that the spirits have caused the earthquake in response to the ritual request for spirits to deliver punishment."[36] One story cited an unidentified text that recounts a history of earthquakes in the north and documents the complete destruction of the city-state of Phayao by three consecutive earthquakes several centuries ago. *Thainews* also reported that "people" believed the earthquake resulted from a violation of taboos (*kheut*), and even cited a fortune-teller who attributed Chiang Mai's bad fate (*duang maj dii*) to the construction of tall buildings.[37] The nation's premier English-language paper, *Bangkok Post*, cited a spokesperson for a local conservationist group, For Chiang Mai (Phüa Chiang Mai) as having said that the earthquakes were caused by a supernatural power following a *phithii hae phii*. The story noted that the rite had been performed by a group

---

36. *Khaosiam*, 2 October 1989, 1, 20.

37. *Chiang Mai News* [in Thai], 1 October 1989, 16.

of students, academics, and residents of Tambon Faharm (the site of Wat Faharm), and that the rite had been intended to protect the city against the growth of condominium projects.[38]

Phüa Chiang Mai is perhaps the most articulate, politically astute, and creative pressure group in Chiang Mai. A coalition of conservationist intellectuals, including numerous members of the Chiang Mai University faculty, the organization advocates a greening of Chiang Mai, the preservation of local architectural forms, and the cultivation of Lanna traditions. Members come mainly from the upper and upper-middle classes, and some even trace their lineage to the lesser *caos* of the old northern states. Yet, if they are the shrewdest orchestrators of ritual drama and if their interests are emphatically bourgeois (many are avid collectors of antiquities and northern arts), their aspirations and their anti-Bangkok, antidevelopment sentiment is widely shared by less well-placed members of the community, and especially of the suburb known as Tambon Faharm. It was, in fact, Saeng Suang's father who presided over the sorcery described in the newspapers as the possible source of Chiang Mai's earthquake. Following the prophesy of Saeng Suang's spirit, Phra Cao Saeng Müangma, in 1991, the elder ritual specialist oversaw another ensorcelling rite, this time directed at the governor himself. He described the ritual for me in minutest detail, with pride in his devotion to the "traditional way of doing things."

The *phithii hae phii* shares much with the *phithii saab chaeng* in that it engages the powers of the dead and the violent possibilities of the netherworld to effect its goals. Officiants go to the cemetery and offer fruit, rice, water, sweets, and whiskey to the spirits, then ask them to come with them. The best spirits for such things are those who have suffered bad deaths because they will earn merit by enforcing retributive justice. The spirits of bad deaths are thought to be present in this world to an unusual degree, vulnerable and in need of merit to move out of the limbo that their accidental ends both presaged and induced. Like the *phithii saab chaeng*, the *phithii hae phii* requires widows and widowers to utter the words of invitation over incense. Then, the remains of the body (which usually include a few bones even after cremation) are exhumed and placed in a new coffin, and a kind of inverse funeral procession is carried out. In the case of the rite that followed Saeng Suang's possession, the coffin was marched through the streets and taken to the governor's mansion, where the governor was publicly threatened with the wrath of the spirits of the *sya müang*, mediated by those of the bad deaths, if he did not act to prevent the destruction of Chiang Mai's beauty.

38. *Bangkok Post*, 4 October 1989, 12.

It should be noted that most members of Phüa Chiang Mai or Tambon Faharm would not acknowledge that any real exhumation took place but claimed that their funeral had been purely and merely symbolic. However, Saeng Suang's father insisted that the rite had been carried out in full and that only the reality of the performance could have guaranteed its consequentiality. The 1989 earthquake resulted, he said, from the influence (*phon*) of an earlier version of this ritual. Whether the scholar-activists were simply reticent to admit the full extent of their involvement in a rite that could be deemed "barbaric" by more cosmopolitan colleagues or were unaware of the degree to which Saeng Suang's father had enacted this theater of intimidation is unclear. Certainly, none of them imagined what events would follow the *phithii hae phii*. None probably would have believed them possible, though they were prepared to retroactively consider the possibility of causality between rite and event.

Shortly after the rite was performed, on 28 May 1991, an Air Lauda plane crashed after taking off from Bangkok. There were thirty-eight Thais on board, more than half of them from Chiang Mai. Among the dead were the governor and his wife, the last two living *cao*s of the former ruling family in Chiang Mai, and several people at the center of the political elite. More than half of these people owned land or had owned land on the banks of the Ping River and many were involved in condominium development. Chiang Mai was devastated by the loss, whose significance was also appreciated in Bangkok. The final funeral for the *cao*s (which took place one year after the deaths) was attended by the king, the queen, and their daughter, Princess Sirindhorn, in an extraordinary display of recognition for the now passed lineage of northern power.

Many who were otherwise skeptical about the efficacy of the *phithii hae phii* were awed and a little unsettled by the confluence of events. Otherwise worldly scholars at Chiang Mai University who had participated in the rite as part of a self-conscious political theatricality confided in me that the events had discomfitted them and made them wonder if the powers of the city were perhaps even more potent than the impresarios of northern tradition had imagined. I asked Saeng Suang's father outright if the *phithii hae phii* was responsible for the disaster and he said yes. I asked him further whether he accepted his role in the deaths of these people. He said yes again. But when I asked him about the deaths of innocents, he invoked the private *kam* of each person who had died in the fireball at Suphan Buri. As for the governor, Saeng Suang's father said simply that he had allowed the heavens over Chiang Mai to be defiled, and that was explanation enough. He did not remark on the seemingly obvious symbolism of the deaths: the fall from the skies of a man who had outraged the space above Chiang Mai. These specificities, as far as I know, had not been prophesied. Nor had the sordid orgy of covetousness that led passersby to scrounge for valuables amid the wreckage of the plane. A premonition of such commodity-desire run amok had indeed been imagined in Khamsing's bitter short story about a car accident and the fate of its victims, but this profane display of want, which was as remarked in newspapers as was the tragedy that preceded it, did not fit well in the representation of catastrophe as the manifestation rather than the disruption of cosmological order.

### At the Center of the Periphery

It is not coincidental that Saeng Suang's prophetic possession should have taken place at Wat Chetiya Luang, the house of the *lak müang* and the supposed center of Chiang Mai's spiritual being. Each year toward the end of May (depending on the lunar calendar), the *wiharn* housing the *lak müang* is opened and Wat Cheddi Luang becomes the site of pilgrimages from throughout the valley. Although women are prohibited from looking upon the pillar itself, they join men in making offerings of food and flowers outside the *lak müang's wiharn* and in the wat. Often described as the most ancient and important ritual of the city, the pilgrimage to Wat Cheddi Luang is a complicated reinscription of local history. Wat Cheddi Luang is, in fact, under the authority of King Mongkut's Thammayut sect. Vociferously antiritual in nature, the Thammayut order sits uncomfortably with the responsibilities of the Inthakin rites and the protectorship of the *lak müang*. The pillar itself was originally kept at Wat Sadue Müang (*sadyy müang* meaning "navel of the city"), but during Rama V's reign, when Siam was consolidating its hold over the northern states, it was moved to the Thammayut wat and subtly reinserted into a nationalist tradition of Theravada Buddhism associated with the Chakkri dynasty. The physical removal symbolized a profound political realignment. At about the same time, the well from which lesser *cao*s drew the lustral water to pay tribute to Chiang Mai's supreme *cao* was covered. The old palace was converted into a prison.

When I asked the abbot of Wat Cheddi Luang to describe for me the forms and significance of the Inthakin rites, he said quite simply that he knew nothing of them or any other local rites and that Wat Cheddi Luang, being a Thammayut wat, was not concerned with northern tradition. He could, he said, preside over only the simplest of rites: "*Thii nii rao tham phithii ngaai ngaii thaonan* [Here, we perform only the simplest of rites]." If I wanted to learn about the "traditions of local people" (*phrapheenii phyyn baan*), I would have to go next door, to the Mahannikai wat where the fertility icon, Phra Forn Saeng Haa (The Buddha of the Thousand Showers) is kept. This icon is second only to the *lak müang* in the Inthakin ceremony, being paraded through the city at the start of the Inthakin festivities on the cusp of the monsoon.

On several levels, Wat Cheddi Luang is a profoundly ambivalent site in Chiang Mai. Home to symbols of both northern origin and to the Thammayut order of the Chakkri monarchy, its position of political centrality and its tensions with another geographically inscribed mode of centeredness redouble the history of Chiang Mai itself: the history of a displaced center. That Saeng Suang should be possessed there by a spirit who claimed to be representing the interests of the city in opposition to outside forces is especially revealing. And it is important to recall here that governorship is appointed from Bangkok and its occupant is rarely a resident of the city (although there have been recent demands that residency be a criterion of appointment). Yet, the Inthakin rite is itself now sponsored by the municipality (*thesabaan*), whose structural position within the bureaucratized state apparatus is also determined from Bangkok. One of the many local rites whose cultivation the central government pursued in the processes of national integration, this one operates in the register of representation. But, like so many others, its status as a formally derivative performance—with generic pastness as its referent—has given way to an unexpected potency as more and more people attempt to summon from such re-presentations the power that they mediated without presencing. Saeng Suang's possession indexes the moment at which the investment in representation produces its own excess, the moment at which a real power returns to haunt and to overwhelm the otherwise mute signs of a waning era.

In this context, it becomes possible to return to the question of marginality and to ask about the relationship between inspired prophesy and the ensorcelling performances of the *phithii hae phii* and the *phithii saab chaeng*. One wants here to understand how it is that northernness has come to substitute for the solace that was Thainess. How, indeed, do various kinds of marginality—of the *lak müang* at the Thammayut wat, of Wat Faharm in the district that was once so peripheral it could be given away, of the poor rickshaw driver and his homosexual son in a world beholden to consumer power—articulate with each other to ground a discourse of moral centering? In essence, one wants to understand the history of a relation between two moments separated by a space of twenty-five years, 1973–1976 and 1992. That understanding is, inevitably, an understanding of technology's effects.

Like Marx's *Eighteenth Brumaire of Louis Bonaparte*, the story of Chiang Mai's restoration and its transformation into the newly productive icon of national origins and premodern authenticity is a story of historical mimesis gone awry, of what Walter Benjamin would have called "wish images" that have become fetishes. Like the second French Revolution, the 1992 democracy movement in Thailand dressed itself in precedent. It modeled itself alternately on the Thai Marxist and left liberal student movement of the mid-1970s and the

Chinese democracy movement associated with Tiananmen Square. And as in the Chinese context, the *prachaathipataaj* movement was thoroughly dependent on and determined by mass communications technology.

The "media revolution," as it was called in the local and international press, had both emancipatory and reactionary dimensions, for though the use of cellular and microchip technologies made it possible to evade brute military silencing and to forge a surreptitious and oppositional national community, those same technologies subjected their users to reencompassment via the forces of transnational capital.[39] Yet, as much as the movement reveals the force of mass mediatization, it suggests the necessity for distinguishing among different technologies and different representational strategies. One can, I believe, understand the peculiar manner in which communities were both established and destabilized during the events of 1992 by attending to the differences between the media deployed and the temporalities they assumed. It is already clear that the movement in Chiang Mai was characterized by a certain vacillation between the apparent simultaneity that telephonic and televisual media permitted and the seeming temporal dislocation that is the mark of the photograph. In the moment that the photograph of a man being beaten to death was circulated in Chiang Mai, something changed. After that, every effort to induce that experience of euphoric alter-national community save one—that of the cursing rite—failed. And the failure opened onto, or made legible, a position of political belatedness that seemed to be a peculiar function of regional location, but that was, in actuality, the symptom of the representational logic on which electoral democracies are based. Chiang Mai was both displaced and recentered as the figure of belatedness, was represented as the origin that was not there in the first place. Thus was its own history, as a colonized margin now reinserted into the narrative of origins, specularized. Thapae Gate, the restored ruin, fulfilled its function in this moment as at no other time.

One therefore comes to appreciate the performance of a cursing ritual, which masqueraded as a return to origins, as a supplementary gesture intended to augment the inadequacies of technological simultaneity. With its promises of instantaneous effectivity and the surrounding discourses (and biographical histories) that linked it to prophesy, the cursing rite liberated reality from mediation by surrendering to the need for it. The medium acknowledged what

---

39. The Thai telecommunications giant is Shinawatra (Chinawat), but the largest portion of Thailand's telecommunications industry is in the hands of Seagate, NEC, AT&T, Siemens AG, Alcatel, and Sony. International Business Research allocated the top three positions in Thailand's "Radio, Television and Industrial Machinery" category to Seagate, NEC, and AT&T, in that order. All are American-based, as is IBM, the highest-ranked and most profitable computer company in Thailand.

the media could not. In the process, he returned some of photography's magic to itself.

Indeed, considering the uncanny resonances between the movements of 1976 and 1992, one is struck by the capacity of photographic imagery to become propulsive. A certain circumspection could have been expected following the discovery in 1976 that the photograph of young activists supposedly hanging the Crown Prince in effigy was a fake or, at best, an intentionally misidentified image.[40] This image, which had been used so morbidly to justify the assault on Thammasat University students, concentrated in itself the risk of misplaced realism. Yet, such circumspection did not emerge. To the contrary, the facticity of the image remained beyond the threshold of doubt in 1992. And the more the image became a site of facticity, the more it gathered its magical, its transformative power to itself. People passed this object among themselves as they would an amulet. Its presence accumulated with each transmission, in the manner of a story. But then, perhaps this should not have come as a surprise. For, as Walter Benjamin remarked, history dissolves into images.

Photographs are not just any images, of course. They are images that claim to partake of the real and that, in the process, induce a hallucinatory fantasy about that which exceeds the image frame. It is for this reason that Christian Metz calls them inherently fetishistic in relation to cinematic images, which latter generally attempt to satisfy those phantasmatic processes within the space of narrative.[41] A corollary of this fact, says Metz, is that the photograph is inextricably linked to death and assists the memory of the dead "*as being dead.*"[42] Photography, Barthes reminds us, is the technology of ruin. In it, one makes a commitment to destruction's eventuality, to future memory. It promises, in some far-off time, to permit the viewer to experience the impossible temporal duality in which the one pictured can be seen to be both dead and anticipating death.[43]

But let us invert this formula. Benjamin also tells us that fetishes are images that embody the "arrested form of history" and that, "in the process of commodification, wish image congeals into fetish" while the "mythic lays claim to

40. I have discussed the parallel histories of photography in 1976 and 1992 in "Surviving Pleasure at the Periphery: Chiang Mai and the Photographies of Political Trauma in Thailand, 1976–1992," *Public Culture* 10, no. 2 (1998): 341–70.

41. Christian Metz, "Photography and Fetish" (1985), in *The Critical Image*, ed. Carol Squiers (San Francisco: Bay Press, 1990), 161.

42. Ibid., 158.

43. Barthes makes this realization, famously, while contemplating the image of the condemned murderer, Lewis Henry Payne. He writes of his shock on realizing that "he is dead and he is going to die." See *Camera Lucida*, trans. Richard Howard (New York: Hill and Wang, 1981).

eternity."[44] During the era of anticommunist military autocracy, the king of Thailand emerged from the periphery of constitutional peripherality into the newly potent force field that he now occupies, partly through the circulation of his own photographic imagery. And if the spectacles of national unity have become increasingly ridiculous, as Kasian argues, as they have become increasingly linked to supernational commodity logics (in the form of Coke-sponsored Thai events and national advertising campaigns with the slogan "Thailand for Sale"), the king's imageric ubiquity has led not to an evacuation of the significance of monarchy but to its intensification. In 1992, when the king summoned the warring parties to the peace table, they came, as everyone knew they would, because the king had commanded them to do so. It is possible to say that, in the form of its fetish, its photograph, the kingship has returned to itself the power of fetishism. And, as we have already seen, it has done so by projecting fetishism onto the margins. Who could have imagined the degree to which self-consciously northern cultural activists would have reappropriated that role for themselves in a process that is both the unanticipated effect and the ironic overturning of Thailand's particular modernity?

Saeng Suang was in Bangkok during the first military suppression of democratic politics in 1976. At the rally in Chiang Mai, after the last chilies had smoldered on the altar of the *phithii saab chaeng*, he spoke longingly of having been among the students at Thammasat University—not as a student, but as one of the poor rural activists who were then integral to the movement and who were so conspicuously absent from the 1992 protests. He knew people who had disappeared or died, he claimed, but when the army fired into the crowds in Bangkok a week later, his grief and rage were not mitigated by the horrific experience of déjà vu. Indeed, at that point in time, the differences that separated the movements were as palpable as the similarities that bound them, despite popular press accounts in which the politics of electoral democracy laid claim to the moral authority of those for material equity.

Unlike the earlier movement, which was dominated by agricultural labor, especially the Farmers Federation, as well as student and communist organizations, the democracy movement of 1992 was driven by highly educated, mainly male college graduates longing for access to the fruits of Thailand's phenomenal growth. This is why, when Suchinda accused another politician, Chawalit Yongchaiyudh, of wanting to install a presidium-style government, he was uniformly ridiculed by newspaper editors and columnists. Suchinda was confusing his precedents, mistaking a patently middle-class movement for a proletarian uprising, substituting 1973 for 1992 and thereby sealing his own igno-

44. Susan Buck-Morss, *The Dialectics of Seeing* (Cambridge, MA: MIT Press, 1989), 211, 159.

minious fate (he eventually resigned in disgrace—only to be recuperated a year and a half later). He was also overestimating the degree to which the military could ensure national community by dictating the experience of simultaneous readership through the careful dissemination of false images. When the military broadcast its nothingness, and when it followed that artificial absence of events with a benignly choreographed scene of gentle conflict, it was already too late. In Chiang Mai, residents had already observed the real-time footage of catastrophe, even as they had been captured by the impossible imagery of a death missed but also foretold. And no matter how hard they tried, the military could convince almost no one that the bloodshed was in the service of national unity. They did not know that they unleashed the very forces by which bad deaths could be recruited for localist projects.

But then, Chiang Mai's activists, many of whom had come from Bangkok in any case, did not know how powerful is the tendency for local myth to be encompassed by the natural history of the nation. Within a day of Saeng Suang's orchestrated cursing, protest organizers in Bangkok, who saw pictures of the *phithii saab chaeng* in the national newspaper (*Thairat*), called Chiang Mai via cellular telephone to get the "recipe" for the curse so that they could perform it themselves in Bangkok. The medium was elusive, however, and did not respond. He was nonetheless pursued, and finally, telephones were brought to him, at which point he did with the telephone what he had done with those mysterious powers from the other place: he chose to answer. And he delivered his instructions in that manner. In the process, he became the sender of a message for which he claimed to be the mere instrument, thereby enacting the logic of information in which recording and amplification devices are said to be precisely the same thing.

At the rallies in Bangkok, a similar rite was performed, and photographs of its enactment received prominent positions in the national newspapers. Indeed, the performance in Bangkok received far more media attention than its Chiang Mai counterpart. Saeng Suang, for his part, reiterated and inverted the sentiment of the organizers in Chiang Mai when he said that the rite in the capital was unlikely to have any effect beyond that of entertaining the crowds because it was the particular power of the northern spirits who determined its ultimate efficacy. These spirits would not descend to service those with no relation to the place.

An odd kind of separation occurred in the Bangkok repetition of the Chiang Mai rite. Both parties emphasized the unique spiritual qualities of the north (if only in parody), and in so doing, they reconstituted that distance that the fax machines and the video screens seemed, so momentarily, to have circumvented. Once again, Chiang Mai was on the margins of the nation-state, providing it with a token authenticity even as that authenticity was usurped in an effort to reclaim power from the military for the Bangkokian bourgeoisie. Chiang Mai's marginality, as already indicated, was physicalized in the very location of the rite at the base of Thapae Gate. It was repeatedly elaborated in the commentaries of protestors and food vendors who constructed identities for everyone, from Chamlong to their drunken comrades, in terms of their northernness. And, in the process of invoking the logic of *müang* cosmology, northerners made themselves the object of their own nostalgic desire, rendering themselves as antecedents of an event they experienced as a belatedness.

### Flashback: Excess

What flashed up in mediumship was thus not only (perhaps not at all) the image of the past, but the sense of danger that emerges when what is being invoked is what cannot be represented at all. Such unrepresentability has been attributed to the events of 6 October 1976. But there were other excesses, other transgressions of representation that emerged in the context of the democracy movement, and it is worth considering them here, briefly, before moving to a more extended discussion of the threat and the effort to contain such excess. Indeed, there is an extent to which the entire dramaturgy of (failed) revolution in 1992 can be understood as an effort to contain the dangerous possibility of excess within the system of transparent representation. One could metaphorize this as an effort to disappear the photographic frame, lest the desire to imagine its outside prove too seductive. But such metaphoricity should not be mistaken for the use of an exterior image to explain an otherwise enframed process. Photography is internal to this process, even as it provides that process with its figure.

The word "seduction" can open this conversation to its other dimension, can permit us to understand how it is that political processes and economic processes are sexualized. During the democracy movement, banners were hung at Thapae Gate demanding an elected prime minister and denigrating Suchinda with terms of animal abuse and emasculation.[45] His face appeared on the bodies of women and *kathoeys*, on gila monsters, and with his genitalia penciled on his forehead. One poster referred to him as *khii miang*, a particularly offensive northern term meaning something rotten (with the implication of fecal wastage). The more literally banalized suggestion that Suchinda's military politics were outdated appeared in numerous caricatures depicting the general

---

45. See Gehan Wijeyewardene on the use of animal categories in insult: "Address, Abuse, and Animal Categories in Northern Thailand," *Man* 3, no. 1 (1968): 76–93.

as a dinosaur. These were rife in the national press, where cartoonists remained relatively free of military censorship. Still, the most common, and the most beloved, expressions of outrage at Suchinda were either sexual or scatological in connotation.

The references to military archaism had two dimensions. On the one hand, they suggested temporal irrelevance as well as interruption. On the other, they suggested an excess, an enormity of intervention that far surpassed the legitimate demands of political representation and that actually risked the stability of Thailand's putatively rational economy. It was frequently remarked that the generals had "gone too far" (*paj keun paj*). Among the interventions that were considered to be excessive were the charges that the NPKC were bringing against the technocrats and entrepreneurial capitalists in Chatichai's regime, charges of being "unusually rich." The insinuation of excess was, indeed, intended to turn back on the military the accusations that they themselves had directed at Chatichai's regime. The question of force was therefore being rendered as a matter of economy, albeit as the limit and the outside of economy, as the domain of illegibility and of unspeakability, of writing's threshold. If telephones and photographs promised a technology that would capture the excesses of this economy, and of the military, they did so because they claimed to be more immediate. But they worked because of their mediations. Because they inhabited the economy as total mediation.

This is why the entrepreneurial elite and the government that represents it expressed their concern about the crisis of 1992 in terms of economic stability. For the marking and remarking of excess as and at the boundary of the legitimate economy—whether that excess is thought to be manifested by Chatichai or by Suchinda—also contains the fact that it is in spending (*dépense*, in Bataille's sense) that the subjects of such an economy experience their power and value. The value-producing power of expenditure is to be found on several levels, only two of which need be mentioned here. The first concerns the ways that subjects are now made to experience their personal agency through commodity consumption. Chiang Mai's decision to make shopping the center of its development plan is abundant testimony to this development. But there is more painful evidence in the statistics that reveal how often land title is surrendered (usually by the male heads of households) for motorcycles and automobile upgrades, satellite dishes, and other luxury goods. And here, the staging of the rallies in Chiang Mai at the very entrance to the space of consumer desire acquires its fuller significance.

But there is more to be said here. For the second other in which the productivity of spending emerges is that of finance capital. Finance capital operates not through investment in more efficient production, but in the anticipation of that future consumer desire whose enactment individual subjects will experience as the form of their agency. It is for this reason, as much as any other, that the individual working consumer can identify so deeply with the entrepreneurial capitalist and fantasize himself or herself in that position. Chiang Mai's residents suffered the consequences of such an economy when, in the middle of the 1990s, the real estate market of Chiang Mai collapsed. Having been driven in the 1980s by the assumption of virtually endless growth in tourism and internal migration (from both rural areas and Bangkok), it succumbed to the dissipation of desire and value even before the fiscal crisis of 1997. But that failure, being both inevitable and unknowable in its timing, is precisely what made real estate so valuable in the first place. Everyone bought and sold in hopes of beating the market. And condominiums became valuable to the extent that they were represented as being locally situated—even when such location made them a threat to other residents. That is to say, they were valuable to the extent that they risked what they needed to ground their value. The risk was internal to value, even when it constituted the limit of value—indeed, because it constituted the limit of that value.

Can there be any wonder, then, why earthquakes would emerge as the signs of value's demise? And can there be any wonder why, under such circumstances, the betrayal of local representation (in the form of an unelected prime minister) would ultimately require inscription in the form of a displaced phallus? Let us then reconsider the graffiti depicting Suchinda with his genitals on his head or as the emasculated figure of the *kathoey*. Perhaps these otherwise typical images suggest something more than simply sexual violence. As newspapers and business organizations called for stability to prevent a crash of the local currency, and as protestors assaulted the military for its violation of the Thai people's image, it became apparent that the problem of political and economic value in Thailand had become the problem of fetishism. Suchinda, castrated by felt-pen markers on the walls of the ruined city, came to stand for the loss of value's proper signification. In usurping the place of a proper representation of the people, he produced a representational lack, and the consequence, everyone seemed to suggest, would be the spiraling loss of value in currency itself. Money and Thainess would become useless, impotent, a matter of mere appearances. As in Henry Fielding's essay lamenting the popularity of castrati in Europe when that continent was being, he said, improperly overrun by paper currency,[46] the protesting caricatures that adorned Chiang Mai implied a linkage

46. See especially Henry Fielding, *The Historical Register for the Year 1736; and, Eurydice Hissed*, ed. W. W. Appleton. (Lincoln: University of Nebraska Press, 1967). A fine analysis of these issues, including the instability of value and its relationship to the question of emasculation, appears in Jill Campbell's *Natural Masques: Gender and Identity in Fielding's Plays and Novels* (Stanford: Stanford University Press, 1995).

between a sexualized capacity to control representation and an economic logic in which the indeterminacy of value could be covered over by the fetish of national image. Newspapers became obsessed with the condition of national shame, and columns were full of efforts to reclaim the country's reputation as a maturely modern and upright democratic state. Upper-class people and intellectuals seconded the anxious expressions of fear that Thailand would become the object of ridicule in the international community, and locally affiliated activists rescued themselves from broken-faced shame by asserting their priority to the nation. From the place of origins, they could enframe a certain excess as being both the center and the periphery of a nation that is no longer *one*. It is from this place, as Karl Kraus would have said, that "origin" becomes "the goal."[47] And it is from this place that a libertine refusal of representational containment commences.

47. For a discussion of Kraus's concern with origin see Walter Benjamin, "Karl Kraus," in *One-Way Street*, trans. Edmond Jephcott and Kingsley Shorter (London and New York: Verso, 1997).

# 8 OUTSIDE, EYELESS, AND ON FIRE: THE APOTHEOSIS OF REPRESENTATION

There is a highway leading out of Chiang Mai that breaks off the ring road to the north and goes to San Saay, a sprawling district of rice fields, unnaturally green golf courses, new suburban developments, and older agricultural communities clasped by coconut palm trees. At times, the road to San Saay seems like the highway passages in Terry Gilliam's dystopic movie, *Brazil*: billboard after monumental billboard display images of a serene suburban life that aspires to aristocratic grandeur while taking the form of serial sameness. The land that appears in the signs, distorted by an anachronistic colonial aesthetic, is for sale, of course. But the "referent" is mainly invisible. The signs are so numerous that they seem, at times, to constitute a scenery, a "view." In the midst of all this, about fifteen kilometers from Chiang Mai City's center, the medium whom I shall call Khun Daeng has established what he calls the Garden of No Worries. It is a complex of buildings nestled amid paddy fields, just beyond a new, treeless strip of row houses but less than a kilometer from the old village of San Saay. Water buffalo, still used as draft animals on some farms, often can be seen in the fields next to the houses and beneath the power lines that bind San Saay to Chiang Mai, the juxtaposition of animal energy and electricity providing apt augury for what one encounters inside the Garden gates.

I first made this trip in early 1992 when visiting a medium of Queen Camadevi in Lamphun. There, in the living room of a well-kept bungalow, an extremely delicate *kathoey* was possessed by the Mon queen. The possession came unexpectedly, nowhere near the shrine and without the usual prayers and offerings. Queen Camadevi did, however, have her costume in a briefcase, and she put it on quickly before telling me that if I wanted to meet with real power, I had to visit San Saay, where Siwa himself visited a medium and carried out miraculous cures. Camadevi claimed she would instruct her medium to show me the way, and I agreed to follow on my motorbike. The drive took two hours—long by Chiang Mai standards—but covered the space of universes. The pavement became a space of transport that the diesel trucks could not possibly have traveled.

The Garden of No Worries is something of a miniature theme park of the spiritual universe. In this respect, it partakes of the masculine statist aesthetic that Vajiravudh inaugurated with Dusit Thani. It, too, produces a world over which mortals can have absolute oversight. It, too, organizes the miniature as representational substitute for the social and political reality within which it is situated. But it is interestingly at odds with that aesthetic in the uncompromised centrality that it accords Brahmanism and in the emphasis on Sino-Thai identity that its chief resident articulates, these two being the others of Vajiravudh's racialized religious nationalism. In many regards, it is a doubly antipodal space, one located on the discursive periphery of both northernness and Thainess. Its motifs are primarily Saivite, but the presence of a *bot* (Buddhist temple) in the middle of the compound suggests its indebtedness to nationally hegemonic Buddhism. Abundant references to Rattanakosin-era Buddhism can be discerned in the visual iconography of the place, and especially in the prominent placement of King Rama V's image. Moreover, Khun Daeng's possession by Siwa reiterates and appropriates, on a habitual basis, the transformations that Rama IV wrought when, for the first time in the history of the Siamese tonsure ceremony, he took for himself the part of Siwa in a ceremony that had previously been organized around the deity's merely spectral presence.

The signs and practices of the Garden are fantastically hybrid, but in ways that are not altogether new. The Garden grounds themselves cover several *rai* of sandy lands; in 1992, the architectural structures were beginning to form a rectangular enclosure. The buildings all opened inward, except for a pyramid that was set apart. Begun in October 1989, the Garden grew between January 1992 and May 1993 by two buildings, including a six-apartment "hospital" complex and a two-story residence for Khun Daeng. These joined a low, tin-roofed building of about five thousand square feet called the palace, where, in addition to a large kitchen and dining area and several small sleeping rooms for both medium and guests, the *thii deum* of Khun Daeng's spirits is located. The palace, which is now on the western end of the grounds, was the first building of the Garden, financed with the medium's own money and the contributions of several wealthy benefactors. All of the other buildings, whose value I estimate to be several million baht, have been constructed with funds contributed by disciples. There was almost constant evidence of construction during my visits, although I rarely saw anyone working. The tracks of heavy equipment could often be seen in the sand, and small mountains of cement or landfill seemed fresh each week.

Like the shrines of other mediums, the Garden maps an anachronistic spatio-temporal universe. Its every measurement and orientation is calculated within a scheme of directional value. The throne in the palace, and the pyramid—where the medium meditates—both open eastward to the rising sun. Entrance and exit occurs through an opening at the southwest corner, and all refuse must be taken out there, which is the most polluted of sites. The hospital, where illness, impurity, and rank putrefaction reside, lies along the southern border of the grounds, another relatively inauspicious space. The last time we spoke, Khun Daeng was making plans to establish a crematorium to be located to the south-west of the hospital but outside the fence that is protected by the guardian *yaksa*. This will be used for patients who die while at the Garden, but also for anyone in San Saay who cannot afford the costs normally associated with cremation. The services of monks will be paid for by Khun Daeng himself.

Placing a space of death beyond the walls of rehabilitation would perhaps discomfit those for whom illness and death are artificially and hygienically separated, but within the terms of the Garden's world it is simply part of a directional movement away from the center, from life and from its animating forces. The antithesis of the crematorium, the exalted northeast corner, is the site of the pond where Narai, standing on a tiny island, presides over an aquatic world in which the first creatures—fish, shellfish, and amphibians—can be seen emerging from the water. Thus, an axis—the longest straight line possible within this space—has been created to stretch between origination and dissipation.

Inhabiting the same timespace as Saeng Suang's newly localized world, Khun Daeng's Garden constitutes both an homage to the value of place and the apotheosis of that newly valorized locality. The theatricalization of spatial meaning in this sculptural cosmology appears, in many ways, to be a literalization of the now outmoded and largely disavowed system of the *Traiphum*. Yet, the medium uses his formidable power to bless the land title deeds of condominium developers, and he is as promiscuous with transnational capital as is any real estate magnate. His enframements of the objects signifying authentic power are oddly unstable, and in the moment that he seeks to represent the extremity of Siwa's otherwise uncontainable phallic power, he abandons himself to an almost orgiastic impulse, to the ecstasy of representation's transgression. He claims to have facilitated the most originary of powers. And he is the man in whom origination comes closest to the demand for termination, for absolute limits.

## Dreams of Displacement

The arrangement and construction of the Garden have been carefully directed by Khun Daeng, who claims to receive instructions from Siwa through dreams and during other hypnomantic states, including meditatively induced trance. As in the case of Saeng Suang, this dreaming grounds a knowledge that comes from elsewhere and that possesses the medium as much as does language itself. The medium can recall these dreams mainly in their effect; he feels beholden to the dreamed knowledge, which comes to him in the waking hours less as narratives than as disjunctive images that, like history, emanate force. These dreams, or rather, the dream images, are properly performative. Although not words per se, they are signs of a volition that is authorized by the deity, indeed by the very authority of the power that produces them as a displacement. They defy reflection to a degree that normalized knowledge does not because they are thought of as manifestations of Siwa, the one in whom signifier and signified achieve their literal unity.

Obeyesekere's suggestion that dreaming forms one part of a continuum of knowing (which in Saivism includes trance, possession, ecstasy, and concentration) is well remembered here, as is his assertion that various Asian traditions—but especially Buddhism—have attempted to control or prohibit nonratiocentric knowledge because of its inherent capacity for heterodoxy and its qualities of excess, extraordinariness, and extralegality.[1] It is, says Obeyesekere, the nature of such knowledge to resist reduction to textuality and normative speech. Khun Daeng is unable to describe his dreams of Siwa except to say that he does not behold the deity himself but, instead, sees indirect signs, such as snakes, stone linga, and assorted red objects. These embed him with an unconscious and residual "knowledge" that compels him to act without revealing itself as a purpose or goal. The associative linkages between these signs and the paths of Khun Daeng's own unconscious movement among them remain inarticulable for him. Though it is possible for him to identify the referent of redness and of the lingum as Siwa, silence always breaks over explanatory conversations, marking a place where, as Freud might have said in his own reading of the dream work, they are drawn back into that dark and fecund opacity from which dreams emanate in the first place.[2] The chains of signifiers without signifieds are, or seem, symptomatic of that displacement and conden-

1. Gananath Obeyesekere, *Medusa's Hair: An Essay on Personal Symbols and Religious Experience* (Chicago: University of Chicago Press, 1981), 180.
2. Freud refers to this place from which the dream comes through the metaphor of the mythelium, and describes this point of origin as a "net-like entanglement." As Samuel Weber remarks in his elegant reading of the Freudian conundrum of dream analysis, the dark place is both the absent locus of the dream's emergence and the resistance to analysis that occurs when the object that has to be thought in consciousness is actually unconscious. See Freud's *Interpretation of Dreams* [1915] trans. James Strachey (New York: Avon, 1965), and Samuel Weber's reading of it in "The Divaricator: Remarks on Freud's *Witz*," *Glyph* 1 (1977): 1–27.

sation that Freud described as the "essence" of dreams. They are the displacement of content by affect and they permit transference of affect from one representation to another.[3]

In this context, the role of displacement in the myths of Siwa, where self-castration leads only to the return of phallic power in the form of the lingum, takes on additional significance. Khun Daeng's dreams (the precondition of his possession) were unconscious repetitions of a mythic structure in which he was endlessly produced as the medium of his own ironic displacement as an agent. In the stories that surround the deity, many of which are illustrated in chromolithographic posters that Khun Daeng has attached to the walls of his palace, Siwa's sexual appetites are represented as enormous, his amenability to satiety almost nonexistent. His power and his fecundity always threaten to transmute into malignant and destructive forces. Thus, to both maintain and contain his power, Siwa undertakes ascetic practices, the most severe of these being his self-castration. The mythic tradition is taken up in performative mode by Saivites everywhere, who produce and obtain experiences of personal power through mimetic asceticisms and the pursuit of ecstatic experiences born of pain—sometimes with castration, but more often with incision. This asceticism is not, it must be observed, a denial of the erotic origins of Siwa's power so much as a regularization of a fundamentally sexual energy.[4]

Common explanations for Siwa's self-castration take two forms: either he cuts himself off in an attempt to evade desire, or he does so in a penal gesture after raping the wives of other mendicants. In the standard posters on the palace walls, the castration is not depicted in its actuality, but the serial images show the severed penis miraculously reappearing in the form of the lingum. Transmuted thus into the sign of the phallus (of the Law, and not merely of power), the lingum then provides the symbolic point of articulation between the ascetic and the deity.[5] It also locates power in a realm that is definitionally and spatially alterior, and it thereby sets up the terms of a contradiction in which the ascetic's relationship and access to power are premised on his refusal to enact his own originary capacities. In short, he becomes powerful in a gesture of self-instrumentalization. One is struck by the recognition that this is precisely what occurs in Khun Daeng's dreams, or at least in his narrative recountings of them. Unlike other mediums in Chiang Mai, however, his prac-

3. Jeffrey Mehlman, "Trimethylamin: Notes on Freud's Specimen Dream," *Diacritics* (spring 1976): 43.

4. Wendy Doniger O'Flaherty, *Asceticism and Eroticism in the Mythology of Siva* (Oxford: Oxford University Press, 1973).

5. Obeyesekere, *Medusa's Hair*, 40.

tice also includes prolonged periods of ascetic discipline and some relatively mundane forms of ecstatic practice, such as fire walking (although none of them take the form of severe self-mutilation that is often thought to be characteristic of Saivism elsewhere).

On the eastern extremity of the Garden, facing out over the paddy toward the rising sun, is a fenced off pyramid Khun Daeng calls his *kaanmiti*. He claims that the word is of Sanskrit derivation and he interprets it to mean "eternal duration." Although I was never permitted inside the pyramid on the grounds that my femaleness would pollute it, Khun Daeng described its interior for me in great detail. He also arranged for photographs to be taken so that I might have a clear understanding of its principles.

Its sides are twelve meters high, the number reflecting the months and the years of the Thai and Chinese cycles. The base is seven meters wide, this number having been chosen to reflect the days of the week. Khun Daeng claims that the perimeter of the pyramid was divided by 972 to produce a length of 2.88 meters, which is the width of a cement well built into the center of the pyramid. Of the digit 972, he explained that 9 is the number of planets having influence over this world, 7 is the number of days in the week, and 2 is the principle of opposition, which, according to Khun Daeng, governs all life in this world.

It would indeed be wrong to call Khun Daeng's exegesis a hermeneutical one. In explaining the numbers, Khun Daeng indirectly invokes the locally standard practices of reading portents and of numerological calculation. He refers to the many manuals that abound in Thailand for determining auspicious locations and dates, but the signs have no *meaning* in the proper sense of that term. He does not say, for example, that the appearance of a snake in a dream indicates a future encounter with a lover or that the image of the sun in a dream indicates the power to defeat one's enemies, as he might, according to formalized dream manuals.[6] For him, images in dreams are the signs of deity, which is to say that they are the signs of a force that exceeds the very question of meaning and that can be appropriated only through imitation. They are compulsions to mimesis and, thereby, to self-transformation. But they have neither content nor referent. The numerological signs determine a purely positional location. In this context, explanation is accordingly secondary for Khun Daeng and is submitted to the primary fact that a formulaic calculus produces spatiotemporal centrality.

At his center, Khun Daeng receives the energy that he claims flows throughout the spatiotemporal universe. A well is positioned beneath a hole in the roof

---

6. According to Quaritch H. G. Wales, these are standard interpretations of dream signs, though others are also to be found, particularly in more formal literary accounts, such as the romance of Khun Phaen. See *Divination in Thailand: The Hopes and Fears of a Southeast Asian People* (London: Curzon, 1983), 119–20.

through which the light of both the sun and the moon pass. Khun Daeng sits there in meditation and believes that he is transected by the energy of both day and night, the former being described as a masculine principle of strength, the latter as a transcendent and rejuvenating energy associated with both female-ness and the earth. In this depressed space, his body both below the ground and on the surface, the medium occupies a point of maximal tension and poten-tiality, one that is perhaps constantly flirting with the annihilation of too much energy—such as that which struck King Mengrai in the city center nearly seven centuries ago.

The pyramid was originally intended to be Khun Daeng's only residential abode and is equipped with the accoutrements of a minimal existence: a re-frigerator, a cot with mosquito net, and a sink. On the walls are fifty-two images from the life of Siwa, many depicting the deity with a belt and necklace of snakes. However, Khun Daeng also maintains sleeping quarters in the main palace and the new house. Except during periods of heightened ritual activity, when he may meditate in the well for up to twenty-four hours at a time, he now goes to the pyramid only at dawn, to receive the first light of the day. He sits in front, his brow streaked with red dye, his right hand outstretched to the sun, palm facing upward.

During the pyramid's construction stages, Khun Daeng dressed himself only in white. In a manner demanded by the history of costume in photography, his sartorial demeanor both signified and exteriorized the purity that he was pro-ducing through ascetic self-denial. Following its completion and on the basis of more dream instructions, Khun Daeng began to dress in red. Everything in his compound is now saturated with this color. Walls and carpets, flowers and pillows, the medium's clothes (even undergarments), and paraphernalia of domesticity in the old palace and the new church, everything but the abodes of the infirm is red, which color Khun Daeng identifies with solar power, but also rage and masculine energy (an interpretation commonly held in Thailand). Indeed, it is for this reason that I call the medium Khun Daeng, *daeng* meaning red in Thai.[7]

### Enframement and Its Excess

Khun Daeng's shrine is the most spectacular such structure I encountered in Chiang Mai, and it holds a throne of such magnificent opulence that there can

7. *Long daeng*, a slang expression for withdrawal in the sense of withdrawal from drugs or addic-tion, is intended to shadow this use of the term. For, to a significant extent, Khun Daeng's practice represents the "withdrawal" from nationalist fantasies and the embrace of a more dispersed form of deterritorialized power. The convulsions it generates are indeed the convulsions that overtook Thailand during the democracy movement of 1992.

be no doubt of his stature in this world of mediums—despite his ambivalent relationship to its community. Although it is clearly recognizable within the local tradition of shrines, this one is unique in several regards, not least in the relationships that it permits and structures between medium and clients.

One enters the door to find a large space filled with leatherette sofas and carved Chinese-style tables. This pseudo-parlor is where visiting clients sit and converse with each other or with the medium when he is not yet absorbed by performance. Behind, running the entire length of the east wall (approximately fifteen meters in length) and standing from floor to ceiling, is a display case behind whose glass plates are statues of almost every deity in the Brahmanic pantheon, with human-sized icons of Phrom (Brahma), Siwa (Shiva), and Narai (Vishnu) being most prominent. The cabinet also contains statues of several Buddhist saints, images of the Chakkri kings, Buddhas from around the world, figurines of Chinese boddisattas, and even a few stuffed animals. A sunburst of tiny flashing lights throbs constantly at one end, dramatically but in poor imitation of the light that transects the room from the main door, where it enters, and which heats the room indirectly through the tin roof on which it falls.

A veritable panorama of the spiritual universe, the display case is the overwhelming presence of the palace, and it provides a literal window onto the extraordinary power Khun Daeng claims and commands. It is rarely opened, although icons and images are brought out if a particular healing seems, to the possessing deity, to be required, or if, in the course of possession, that deity deems it necessary to consult other spirits and deities for advice. In the latter cases, the icon serves as a proxy in a dialogue whose other half is never heard by any but the possessed medium. Visitors invariably express awe at the stunning richness of the display when they first enter the palace. This is power that draws the eye, even when it demands a turning away, power that absorbs the look and holds one at a distance nonetheless. In every sense of the word, it is auratic. Not incidentally, it achieves this modern form of auraticity through enframement in a cabinet that seems, in many ways, to resemble a photograph.

One notes here that the enframement of these objects is unusual for such places in Chiang Mai. In most other shrines, icons are gathered together but are otherwise uncontained by the demand for a frontal view or for the respect of avoidance. In Khun Daeng's palace, however, they are withheld in veritably museological form. Indeed, their very sacrality seems to emerge in the cabinet by virtue of a withdrawal into the modesty of distance, beyond limits imposed by the cabinet's frame. They are behind glass, under lock and key, like the domesticity that was produced when new architectural forms arrived to displace previously open households earlier in this century. Windows and cabinets like those in Khun Daeng's parlor are the residue and the consequence of this transformation, as are locks and the discourses of domestic privacy and the possibility of the household's secrecy into which they are all inserted.

In many respects, the glass cabinet collapses the distinction between image and referent. By enclosing the icons, it makes them appear to be their own images. Moreover, the frontality of the relations imposed by the cabinet partakes of that alienated and agonistic orientation of the "world picture." Subjects look at and desire the objects here as things to be appropriated, but only in their representability.[8] Such an ethos dominates all of urban northern Thai mediumship in the present moment, manifesting itself not only in the aesthetic of display but also in the structure of the seasonal calendar of performance. The growth in the number of mediums and the consequent extension of the season for Praise Ceremonies has meant that a greater proportion of mediumship's activities take place in public and, more specifically, in spaces that are cordoned off with unspun cotton thread called *saisin*. These enframed spaces become "views" for the nonmediums, who patronize them. Unlike the private practices of mediums that are undertaken in converted domestic abodes (which become public in the moment of possession), these public ceremonies do not generally entail dialogic encounters, and even the ritual tying of the *khwan* that mediums perform for their acolytes is usually done away from the delineated space of the dance.

In this context, the domination of Khun Daeng's room by the display case would seem to be yet another instance of the "becoming-picture" of mediumship's world. We might even expect to encounter a decline of aura here as the flip side of an emergent hegemony of visual representation. Initially, that expectation would be satisfied. For, in many ways, the aesthetic organization of display at the Garden is structured by the anticipation of a viewer's perception of the scene as an image. But the diminution of sacral power so often anticipated in such circumstances does not occur. To the contrary, the cabinet separates itself from photography's logic despite the fact that it is influenced by it. It remains a theater of cult value, one that absorbs its beholders and threatens them with mortal wounding should they not observe the demands of proper, which is to say *indirect* viewing.

The false modesty of the retreat that produces auratic power is matched, however, in Khun Daeng's hyperreal Garden by something else: an excess that threatens to erupt from that abyss between the sacral object and the absorbed subject. Despite the insistent enframement of icons, the boundedness of these

---

8. Martin Heidegger, "The Age of the World Picture," in *The Question Concerning Technology, and Other Essays*. Trans. William Lovitt (New York: Harper and Row, 1977), 115–57.

spaces threatens constantly to explode. The repeated gestures by which the objects are removed and the violent transgressions that mark Khun Daeng's possession performance are the symptoms of that excess. They contradict the binary oppositions between sacrality and profanity that otherwise seem to be performed by the architecture of the glass cabinet and the cosmological layout of the theme park.

Khun Daeng's possessions are themselves loud, raging affairs. The spirit often shouts his instructions, commanding the client as he would a slave. He uses the derogatory pronoun *man* when addressing them, and in that moment he fails to distinguish between them and any other "thing." Occasionally, Siwa strikes the one who has come for his assistance, and every once in a while, the possession erupts in a madness that spills over the boundary of intelligibility altogether. Possessed, Khun Daeng may run about the compound, screaming incoherently, spitting and flailing. Or he may curse in a chain of abuse that has no object. Sometimes, his assistants explain this as rage at a malevolent spirit who has entered the Garden, perhaps the escaped spirit of a person whose illness could not be cured by Siwa (because, they say, the *kam* of the person was so corrupt). At other times, they express frustration at their own limits and the inability of human beings to conform to Siwa's commandment. Equally often, they profess befuddlement and fear.

Even tamer possessions begin with extreme convulsions and spectacular ejaculations. Khun Daeng vomits and disgorges the substance of his body, the complete evacuation of his physical self being necessary for the deity to descend. Often, his body is hurled four or five feet into the air while his legs are still crossed, before being dropped heavily onto the pillow again. The physical extremity of the possessions is the sign of an alterior power for which, people say, the medium's body is fortified by the spirit, but it takes its toll on him and leaves bruises and other lesions. Scrapes and purpling flesh are the material indices of an alterity that both exceeds the body, constituting its invisible outside, and leaves its visible trace. They find their analogue in the theater of translation that accompanies Khun Daeng's possessions.

Much is made of translation in the performance. Translators are present for all clients, whether they are speakers of Thai, kam müang, or any other language. For more important and better attended possession performances, they are present as a coterie of aides. Positioned between the possessed medium and his clients, the translators form a frame, not unlike that which encloses the auratic objects of the display case, remarking the potency of the speech that comes from elsewhere while producing it as irretrievably other. On several occasions, Khun Daeng's translators spoke directly about the difficulty of understanding the deity's speech. They noted its antiquity, its guttural quality, the lack of tonality, and a lexicon that is only partially known to them.

By theatricalizing their own function, the translators act as the gatekeepers of alterity. They stand on a perimeter and hold the line of power. And they do so by confessing their ignorance and claiming that, often, they can only approximate the meaning of Siwa's words by reference to surrounding terms. Or they say they must trust to the deity a capacity to mark their speech with his intention without, at the same time, making that intention transparent to them. In the end, such stumbling and occasionally confused explanations insert a gap between speech and language. They render Siwa's speech as the untranslatability (of the Real) that both demands their own labor and mocks it as a failure.

The translators, one might say, fantasize for Siwa a speech before the alienation of presence in language, before deferral. In doing so, however, they insert him into a mythic and timeless domain before the time of the nation and the time of national language and of its writing. A similar exteriority, though not priority, accrues to the medium. Not only does Siwa's medium inhabit a theme park whose spatiality precedes and exceeds the territoriality of the nationalized consciousness that Thongchai describes under the term of the geo-body[9] (for the space of his Garden is universal rather than local, outside rather than peripheral). But Khun Daeng also insists that, before all else, he is a Chinese man, and not a Thai subject. This is why he laughs so bitterly about the desires of bourgeois democratic protestors who want a mode of electoral politics based on the idea of correspondence between place and its representation in the "voice" of the people's representative. The logic informing Khun Daeng's practice resists both locality and representation in this mode. Indeed, he is contemptuous of the aspiration to such structurations and limitations of power. That contempt is a gendered one. Relative to the masculine universality of the violently productive Siwa, the ideal of the bourgeois nation is feminized in his conversation and in the other dimensions of his practice. Indeed, when female spirits possess the medium on Saturdays, speaking an effetely proper Central Thai, the full significance of a mediumship that returns to the place *before* national origins becomes apparent.

The word for Saturday is homonymous with that for women in Thai, which fact is well used by Khun Daeng. Khun Daeng's Saturday possessions by Siwa's consorts, especially Parvati, always conduct themselves in Central Thai (rather than the grunting impossible prelanguage that marks Siwa's possessions). Coming after the deity, and being the effect of his self-disciplining through displacement (in the sign of/as phallus), the female consorts can manifest themselves only in a more alienated speech, one that has been subject to na-

9. Thongchai Winichakul, *Siam Mapped: A History of the Geo-Body of a Nation* (Honolulu: University of Hawaii Press, 1994).

tionalist purifications. The consorts speak proper (and profane) Central Thai precisely to the extent that they are construed as secondary and not originary deities. They are belated, as is language, and their belatedness underscores Siwa's priority, his firstness. Where Siwa's language is remarked and theatricalized as untranslatable in the very moment of translation, the consorts speak a language whose intelligibility is the mark of its complete interiority to law. This, indeed, is the law of Siwa's founding. It is also the law of the nation's founding. Recall here that it is Siwa who confers power on the new Thai monarch. The law comes to the king from without, must always be seen to precede the king, even when, as in Rama V's tonsure, one king plays the part of Siwa to annoint the next man who shall occupy his place. The speech of the monarch that will be authorized in this moment will appear to be both originary and citational, but only Siwa can confer the capacity for such simultaneous presence and absence. By contrast, the melodic Central Thai language of the consorts falls far short of that pure performativity that exists in this collapsed relation between precedent and citation. The voluptuousness of their performance, remarked as such, resides here. Accordingly, they are restricted to the practice of mundane divinations. They neither effect cures nor bless land title deeds, as does Siwa.

In many ways, then, Khun Daeng's universe is both the actualization and the apotheosis of that relationship between mediumship and mass mediation that was metaphorized and enacted in the stories told by other mediums and most especially by the spirit of Phayaphrom. Other mediumship seems to have experienced a rapprochement with photography and overcome the prohibition against photographing spirits in a process by which it submitted itself to the camera's metaphor. The result was the emergence of the human as an auratic value. Here, at the Garden of No Worries, where icons are enclosed in glass and the deity's speech withdraws from translation through the frame of interlocution, Siwa's pure power emerges as the rightful site of aura: the other of the human; which is feminine and derivative.

The auratic is, of course, always that which exceeds representation. One might call it sublime in a Kantian sense, and certainly the logic of enframement and of detachment here would converge with that described in the *Third Critique*. But Kantian language mitigates the sense in which this valorized exteriority to language comes to be experienced or inscribed under the sign of "excess," rather than priority, in northern Thailand. Siwa's dramaturgy of the Real notwithstanding, such excess is perceived only from within the logic of enframement, only from within the system of representation. Indeed, it is for this reason that Saivite possession comes as such a "surprise" in Chiang Mai, where the encompassment of mediumship by the logic of representation seemed, in the case of Saeng Suang and in the more general history of mediumship's legitimization, to have been so secure. After the long history of mediumship's domestication, Siwa's possession seems to produce an outside. Let us then linger a little over this spatial economy and the limits that it produces for itself.

### The Impossibility of Domesticity

After every possession, the medium leaves the public space in which linguistic mediation is necessary and takes a vegetarian meal. Passing out of the room of the *thii deum*, it is sometimes jarring to find oneself in so unexceptional a domestic space. The adjacent rooms are replete with the same photographs and decorative objects that would adorn any bourgeois house: images of the medium's family, a picture of his wife (also a medium) with a well-groomed dog, souvenirs from trips throughout Thailand, cute ceramic figurines of animals, photo-clocks, and huge paperweight ashtrays for the pipe the medium likes to smoke despite his sense that it would be wise to quit. There is a television and a video recorder (with remote control) as well. Two dining tables, one for guests and one dedicated exclusively to the medium, occupy the other end of the room and seem perpetually laden with fragrant vegetarian dishes and pungent, ripening fruit.

Beyond the dining space and through a screen door in perpetual need of oiling is a series of small, cement-walled rooms with minimal sleeping and living facilities. These were originally used for semipermanent residents who had come for extended treatment, but with the new hospital complete, the palace rooms are generally empty. He thereby restores through consumption the self that had been displaced and literally eschewed in the dispossession and subsequent possession. Only after this meal does he engage others in conversation, this time in the antechambers of the throne. Such dialogues are an integral part of the relationships between deity and client, and in many ways they suture together divine speech and everyday discourse. Khun Daeng is as much a counselor outside of possession as his possessing deities are instructors, and he interprets the orders of the deities on request (although this requires explanation, for he claims not to know what has transpired during possession). His status as mediator is thus extended into normalcy, but the discussions between medium and client are not yet polite parlor conversation.

Khun Daeng is often imperious, perfunctory, and even dismissive of clients, especially women, who treat him with obsequious reverence nonetheless. These interactions are carried out in the language of severest hierarchy. The truly personal conversations about the deity's speech take place in the back rooms, in the kitchen, and around the dining tables, in the domestic spaces where clients and household workers split their time between gossip and the interpretation of the medium's performances. Male and female clients, residents, and assistants help here in the preparation of food and in the mundane tasks of maintaining the Garden. They speak to each other as equals, normally without formal gender markers and without *wai*-ing. Experiences are shared and recounted, comparisons made, progress charted, and mutual assistance offered. There is the predictable expression of envy directed at those who seem to be enjoying the special favors of the medium at any given time, and the accompanying vindictive dissection of personal flaws. The physical space of gossip, which is materially facilitated by the labyrinthine walls that divide this back world into tiny rooms, is also that of interpretation. Conversations bleed imperceptibly from the discussion of clients' ailments or desires to that of their clothing, and from the deity's pronouncements and the significance of dictated rituals to the amorous liaisons of neighbors. This is the domain of chatter, where hierarchies are remarked and reproduced, resented and undone. Mainly, however, it is the space wherein they become habituated as dimensions of everyday life.

What Nadia Serematakis says about lament can be said of the speech that occurs here. It is a substance passed between mouths. "Commensality," writes Seremetakis, "can be defined as the exchange of sensory memories and emotions and of substances and objects incarnating remembrance and feeling."[10] The most unfettered conversations at the Garden take place in the interior rooms where cooking and eating also take place. Here, as in most northern Thai dining rooms, meals are dished onto individual plates from common bowls, but with the spoons that people use to eat with. Thus, there is contact among the mouths of the diners, a mediated contact to be sure, but one that people often remark in comparison to the restrictive separation of plates and utensils in Western dining etiquette. The public space, where verbal interactions are not only mediated but where Khun Daeng vomits out substance as a pollutant rather than the source of mutual sustenance, provides the most profound antithesis to the space of literal and verbal commensality. It is not incidental in this context that the term for conversation, *kheuj kan*, slips easily into the obscenity for sexual intercourse, *khuaj kan* (which fact is the source of endless verbal play and taunt), or that the expression for "eating together" (*kin duaj kan*) can also mean to have sexual intercourse or to live together as lovers. Interior space is that of most literal intimacy and purest mutuality: of eating and loving.

10. Nadia Seremetakis, "The Memory of the Senses: Historical Perception, Commensal Exchange, and Modernity," in *Visualizing* THEORY: *Selected Essays from V.A.R. 1990–1994*, ed. Lucien Taylor (New York: Routledge, 1994), 225.

The zone of unencumbered dialogue in the palace, the space in which men and women drop gender markers and speak as equals, in many ways seems to constitute the social analogue to the ambivalent architecture of that "traditional" northern Thai house in which interiority is both feminized and marked by ambisexual signs as a space of intercourse. However, this seeming equality is contradicted by other practices and discourses, and the world of the Garden is engendered in deeply hierarchical terms. One of the places at which this order is most visible is at the Saturday possessions. On these days, as he is possessed by Parvati or Siwa's other consorts, Khun Daeng is surrounded by female assistants who help him dress and apply makeup. They do so with a noisy parody that contrasts starkly with the awed silence that accompanies his possession by Siwa and the *rysii*. (Male assistants never address him while he is donning the leopard skins of the *rysii* or the regal dress of the deity.) Over the bearded face, the clownish rouge and the gawdy lipstick can only seem grotesque, and Khun Daeng's clumsy assumption of dress and jewelry is close to vaudeville in its monstrosity. What is most violent, however, is the publicness of this application, the degree to which a female nudity (produced in the moment of dressing) is exposed to the public. It is as though the entire process was driven by a desire to expose the always already public nature of the private. It partakes of the public secret's logic, and in this regard it is consonant with the medium's earlier life, a life lived secretly in public.

*Mafia's Medium: A Life History of Power*

Khun Daeng moved to the north at the beginning of Chiang Mai's growth period less than two decades ago and was, in fact, a significant factor in its development. In the accounts of his followers, he was an entrepreneur of legendary success, owning construction and real estate companies and backing hotel development throughout Thailand. He promoted tourism aggressively and benefited handsomely from its growth throughout the 1970s and early 1980s. He is said to have been worth many millions of baht.

Khun Daeng speaks of his famous commercial successes with pride, even bravado, and although he claims to have left behind any managerial activity, his subsequent title of his various companies remain somewhat mysterious. Also mysterious is the degree to which his involvement with miraculously successful commercial ventures was contained by law. On many occasions during our interviews, Khun Daeng laughed about his early life as a *naaklaeng* and even as a *cao phor*, terms often applied to thugs and members of the Thai mafia. More than one of his assistants acknowledged that, prior to the possession that transformed his personality as well as his calling, Khun Daeng had sanctioned the use of violence against his business opponents. Rumors hover around the Garden about Khun Daeng's former linkage to criminal syndicates that are known to traffic in contraband and to employ hit men against unsupportive politicians and intransigent business partners. These do not seem to detract from the medium's reputation so much as they buttress his image as a radically reformed man. Indeed, insofar as they constitute the rumor of a previously secreted power, they are the transformed currency of its continued existence. A certain repression of reference, a silence surrounded by evasion, works not to efface his authority but to perpetuate the circulation of its residual signs and thereby to extend it. As clients remark the "mysterious" nature of Khun Daeng's previous financial success, or as they evade requests for explanations about the sources of his enormous wealth, they make economy a matter of magic and secrecy a locus of power.

Unlike many mediums', Khun Daeng's life history is not one of prolonged illness nor of increasing alienation from the life of worldly activities. He was at the height of his career when he was first possessed. Attending an annual Buddhist rite at Doi Suthep that enacts an ascent into heaven, Khun Daeng fell unconscious for several hours. He was taken home, where he continued to slip between catatonia and despairing wakefulness for several days, but with no recollection of what had happened. Finally, during one bout, he began to speak, at first unintelligibly and then in direct address. A neighbor familiar with such things informed him that a spirit had taken over his body.

A man who, he claims, had never had a religious thought in his life and who had acknowledged the *sangha* through donations only because it was good business etiquette (though he thought it a waste of money), Khun Daeng refused to believe his neighbor. Depressed, he withdrew from his friends and business associates. He became emotionally and physically debilitated, until a monk advised him to try meditation. Although the meditation was intended to give Khun Daeng control over and escape from the sense or the reality of possession by spirits, it only solidified his new calling. Through meditation, he recovered his strength and came to the realization that he no longer had any choice about serving as a medium. At this time, he began to dream of Siwa, who directed him to begin making certain ritual preparations and to receive those in need of healing.

The source of Khun Daeng's Saivism remains unclear. Nonetheless, his origins in Kanchanaburi, where there is a large Chinese population, and his travels throughout the country would lead one to surmise that he belongs to, or at least has been influenced by, the traditions of mediumship that dominate in the south. Not only Phuket, which is known for the forms of ritual ecstasy that are now famous as part of annual cultural festivals and advertised in tour books, but also in such cities as Bangkok and Chantaburi, Sino-Thai mediums are associated with a kind of possession that enables feats of extraordinary bodily endurance. Fire walking, body piercing, and extreme asceticism take a much more subdued form than they do in parts of India and Sri Lanka, but Saivite cults have been marked of late by an intensification of the demands for bodily transgression as the rites have become media spectacles. In Thailand, as in India, these cycles of increasingly severe ordeals and expenditures are fueled, in part, by the attraction they have for tourists. Photographs of young men bleeding and transfixed with the felt presence of divinity are not uncommon in photo shops in Chiang Mai. Of course, Khun Daeng claims to be ignorant of such practices and imageries. Like other mediums in Chiang Mai, he claims that his relationship to the deity/spirit is an inspired one, and he denies prior experience of anything that could have presaged his later mediumship.

Khun Daeng's professed exteriority to these traditions is redoubled by his alienation from the community of mediums in Chiang Mai. He is a man outside. He does not appear at most Praise Ceremonies or attend public rites of the *sya müang*. He does, however, make himself visible at the annual *phithii jok khruu* of Queen Camadevi in Lamphun, but only in the form of the *rysii*, whose leopard skin rags and indecipherable rantings make him a favorite of audiences, including journalists and photographers. The reason for the exceptions is straightforward enough. According to Khun Daeng, and many of Camadevi's mediums, the Mon queen of the Dvaravati empire that began in 660 was a disciple of the Indic deities as was the *rysii*. Along with their mediums, they are part of a transhistorical community and accordingly can acknowledge each other. By the order of this universe, it would be absurd for a deity to pay tribute to the spirit of a deceased princess, and Khun Daeng emphasized the fact that it is only the *rysii* who travels to Lamphun to *jok khruu*. Camadevi herself is subordinate to Siwa and Narai, and many of her mediums come to San Saay periodically (and independently of each other) to confirm their membership in this community by attending the possessions of Khun Daeng. They also have their own *khwan* tied by Siwa while he is possessing the medium. Claiming the supreme Indic deities as his possessing personae, Khun Daeng has taken himself out of history and into the realm of pure power. No other medium in the north can equal him except by denying the validity of his possession. This they do, of course. In their attempts to denigrate Khun Daeng, many mediums make reference to a "certain excess" in his practice: to the mysteriousness of his financial success, to the occulting of his past life, and to the rumors, which are not infrequent, that the Garden of No Worries is a chaotic place at which the bodies of plagued AIDS sufferers and piratical entrepreneurial capitalists, as well as military thugs, mingle in an orgiastic community of fire walking extremity. It is, in short, perceived from without as a space of transgression and lawlessness. As "fire," in Canetti's sense. From the Garden of No Worries, a spectral crowd is thought to be always arising. The response to it, quite simply, is often a kind of panic.

### Prehistories of the Future Perfect

More than any other medium I know, Khun Daeng's emergence as a healer of renown seemed to grow organically from his previous life and to address the structural and physical violence that it had entailed. The therapeutic practice that is central to the Garden appears, in many ways, to attempt the annulment of that violent existence and the expiation of a debt that entrepreneurial capital would otherwise like to preclude from its domain. His first patient was a former employee, a man who had been paralyzed as a result of a fall on Khun Daeng's own construction site. As with most cases in Thailand, the crippled worker lost both his physical abilities and his livelihood. He received minimal compensation and had no long-term benefits plan to cover medical or living expenses. He was being tended by family members when they heard of Khun Daeng's transformation and brought the man for treatment.

The story seems foretold, veritably apocryphal, but the facts are perhaps secondary to the necessity of the narrative and the moral progress it recounts. Khun Daeng was immediately possessed upon seeing the lame man, and through a rite of spectacular success, the patient was able to walk away on his own. In an almost Aśokan paradigm, Khun Daeng made the transition from an individual whose entire mode of being was premised on the consumption of others. He "ate" his workers as much as he "ate" his debtors. And when his appetite exceeded his own capacity to consume, he was forced to retreat from the politics of incorporation. The language of eating is not, of course, merely one of commensality and sociality. In Thailand, as already mentioned, it also references agonistic business transactions, physical conflicts, taxation, and political relationality. Thus did Khun Daeng take in and spit out the broken bodies of his workers. Even now, the medium admits that he had a tendency to rage and that he fired workers on whims—without a thought for their welfare. Siwa demanded that he submerge that rage, however, and Khun Daeng describes his final accommodation of the deity's possession as the gloriously ravishing moment when Siwa "ate" him.

Consciously, Khun Daeng refuses to associate his own person with the fact of his first patient's injury. He does not see the curative gesture as being in any way a rectification of an error for which he could be held culpable. The fact that his first client was his "own" victim is, he says, but an extraordinary coincidence, one that reflects Siwa's will but not his own responsibility. It is merely the deity's appropriation of another's *kam* and the transformation of his life history into a sign for another. Despite such protestations, the early period of his practice seems to have been almost exclusively concerned to separate Khun Daeng from his previous life and to do so through a healing of those very bodies that had been sacrificed for his personal gain. He became instantaneously famous, and the wounded flowed to his door like blood. At the same time, however, Khun Daeng moved further and further from the city, first establishing a practice near Wat Cet Yod on the northwestern periphery of the city, and then setting up the Garden at San Saay.

This tale of renunciation, moral purification, and economic decentering provides the ideal narrative of the Saivite medium, its emphasis on the submersion of consumptive desire providing the perfect counterpart to the myth of Siwa's sexual asceticism. In truth, Khun Daeng's practice is far more ambivalent, and just as Siwa's repression of his own power served ultimately to enhance and control it, so Khun Daeng's mediumship, his movement away from Chiang Mai, and his claims of disengagement from the world of entrepreneurial capitalism need to be considered critically. For it is the work of disavowal to produce its others. At the Garden, the particular economy within which healing is construed as a gift, often as a gift of food, turns out to be thoroughly enmeshed in the production of economy as a distinct domain. Yet, entrepreneurial capital works to produce value most when it is premised on risk of a total destruction, the kind of destruction that sacrificial giving entails. One realizes this when considering the complex metaphors through which disease and economy, gifting and healing are imbricated in Khun Daeng's practices. One realizes this when one encounters, in the blessing of condominiums and the expulsion of poisonous spirits, that the iconicity of the Garden has no capacity to distinguish between the ideal subject of entrepreneurial capital and the mortified subject of infectivity's most iconic disease.

### Diseases of Modernity

There are two primary kinds of activities that occur in the Garden of No Worries; these can be glossed as being of a therapeutic or an economic nature. Both take place through the manipulation of an ostensibly amoral power that is objectified and spatially organized, physically disciplined, and incarnated by Siwa through the body of the medium. Both seek to enact a miraculous transformation—through an essentially metonymic magic—by intervening into the temporal processes by which value would normally be considered to increase or dissipate. Both entail a promiscuity with each other's metaphors. Both risk the implosion of their own structures and rest on the dangerous encounter with utterly abyssal negativity. This negativity has various figures, among which the lonely deaths by AIDS and catastrophic economic crisis can be counted as absolutely central. And, in fact, it is not incidental that the one should be spoken of in the terms of the other, so that, for example, the collapse of the baht can be called a "plague" (*kaalarook*) of the nation and can, indeed, be said to travel in the manner of a virus (to other nations). The fact that infection and contact are identified in the same idiom, namely, "touching" (*kaan tid*), grounds this relation of mutual imbrication and permits the proliferation of metaphors by which capital and capitalism can be construed as infectious agents: as agents that do not obey boundaries and do not respect the lines that the nation wishes to draw around itself. The centrality of physical contact in Siwa's practice, even when it is mediated by the acolytes, bears this out.[11]

At the Garden, a constant stream of patients seek Khun Daeng's advice and then petition the spirits for assistance and therapeutic intervention. They are not required to pay anything for their visits, although they are tacitly expected to make a donation upon first meeting the deity, and most make a substantial contribution if they recover from their ailments. Contributions of several thousand baht are not unheard of, and I am aware of some that exceeded 100,000 baht (then worth about U.S.$4,000). Public therapy provides the heart of the spectacle at the Garden, not only as the object and focal point of the audience gaze during possession performances, but as a verbal image that is reproduced in the endless telling and retelling of cure stories. Most patients have already received treatment from a biomedical professional in Chiang Mai before making the trip to San Saay; this movement between therapeutic regimes is as typical in Thailand as anywhere else.[12] However, the Garden is not just a last resort; many people who are successfully recovering from illness under the supervision of physicians come to the Garden to determine the cause of their illness and to carry out preventive or compensatory rituals.

The fact of an alternative medical practice in a milieu now dominated by

11. In an interestingly parallel discussion, Linda Singer has argued that the entangling of discourses about the body and about the economy takes on particular forms in the modern era, and the degree to which each is deployed to metaphorize the other indicates much about the way persons are constituted (alienated) and represented (reified) under (late) capitalism. See *Erotic Welfare: Sexual Theory and Politics in the Age of Epidemic*, ed. and introduced by Judith Butler and Maureen MacGrogan (New York: Routledge, 1993), 34.

12. Louis Golomb, *An Anthropology of Curing in Multiethnic Thailand* (Urbana: University of Illinois Press, 1985), 162.

hospital-based biomedicine will not come as a surprise. Chiang Mai's experience with biomedicine dates to the late nineteenth century, when Presbyterian missionaries set up clinics and pharmaceutical dispensaries as part of a (largely unsuccessful) evangelical program, antimalarial drugs having provided the missionaries with their primary source of power, their white magic.[13] Despite its longevity, the relationship has not been an altogether satisfactory one. However, the tension that arose between them has developed less into an opposition between epistemological systems than into a series of multiple and shifting relationships of complementarity, and contradiction.[14] What is patently absent, although we have come to expect it in histories of medical colonialism, is an institutional opposition based on a division among disease classes or between psychosocial disease and physiological disease. "Traditional medicine," which in Thailand includes everything from herbalism to ritual treatment, is not simply the repository for those categories of illness not yet claimed by the biomedical apparatus, nor for those "fantastic" illnesses that biomedicine cannot fix with its gaze. Nor is it simply an indigenous psychotherapy, although it does tend more readily to the psychosocial dimensions of illness that are frequently ignored by Western biomedical practice.

The lack of a clear binary opposition between discourses stems partly from the fact that Western biomedicine has not simply been transplanted into Thailand with its categories intact. Disease categories in national registries continue to be conceived and represented symptomatically rather than causally, as they would be in North America. Indeed, the National Statistics Office in Bangkok maintains records for disease categories that would be unimaginable in Western biomedicine. For example, "confused body," a catch term used to describe a vast array of symptoms with unknown etiologies, is used in comparative surveys of biomedical and traditional medical systems use, the very lability of the category permitting a flow between discursive regimes. Although many ethnographers continue to hold fast to the notion of epistemic irreconcilability, speaking of modernization and displacement,[15] the interpenetration of medical discourses appears to be thoroughgoing. Thus, although foreign-produced pharmaceuticals are available without prescription in a frightening multitude of drugstores, and although most people's relationship to biomedicine remains at the level of self-prescribed chemical therapy, the distribution of "tradi-

13. Herbert R. Swanson, *Krischak Muang Nua* [The northern Thai church] (Bangkok: Chuan, 1984), 51–52.

14. Golomb, *Curing*, 180–81.

15. Ibid.; Viggo Brun, *Traditional Herbal Medicine in Northern Thailand* (Berkeley: University of California Press, 1987).

tional and herbal medicines" was, until recently, concentrated in the hands of three drugstore owners.[16]

Much critical medical history reads the hospital as the site of and stage for medicine as a spectacle—of both the epistemological structures of medicine's particular gaze and the heroism of medicine itself. Nonetheless, it occupies a somewhat different and rather more contradictory position in everyday representations in Thailand.[17] A substantial minority of people in Thailand receive treatment in hospitals, but, especially among poor people, these labyrinths of surgical intervention are often imagined less as part of the therapeutic system than as places where people go to die.[18] I often encountered expressions that bordered on terror from patients (even middle-class patients) who had been advised to go to the hospital for treatment. A piquant but largely inarticulate critique inhabits the hesitation with which people approach these institutions. Recognizing hospitals as sites of death, commonsensical perceptions also recognize them as sites of a profound reification in which physical and social selves are separated from each other. The hospital is the structure in which the sick and dying person is constituted as a (mere) body, as a commodity at risk whose restored value must be paid for. The new growth in life insurance and other indemnity plans among the middle classes surely reflects this development in which bodies have been imagined as the most profoundly alienable of entities, ones in which certain kinds of investment can pay off only in the event of a loss.

It is undoubtedly because of the debilitating reifications that the hospital effects, and not because his practice is categorically opposed to biomedical models of treatment, that Khun Daeng can recruit clients right from within hospitals themselves, and with the assistance of hospital staff. Indeed, his network of assistants and disciples includes nursing staff and several well-placed physicians. He promises not only a tactile intervention over which patients can exercise some control, but a restoration of value through a combination of sacrificial giving and what Linda Singer, in her reading of the response to the economies of epidemic, calls a "selective refusal." Siwa enacts the former only to the extent that the medium and his clients undertake the latter. Through the deity, destruction turns into value. In devotees, the refusal of a value produced in such destructive acts (propitiatory rituals) can become the source of extraordinary therapeutic power. During my many visits to the Garden, I observed two tests of Siwa's capacity to achieve a cure. One occurred when a woman suffering

16. National Statistics Office of Thailand, *The Survey of Health, Welfare and Use of Traditional Medicine* (Bangkok: National Statistics Office, 1986), 60–62.

17. Michel Foucault, *The Birth of the Clinic* (New York: Vintage, 1975).

18. Golomb, *Curing*, 167.

from advanced liver cancer came to the medium for help. The other test emerged in the treatment of AIDS patients.

Though she was admitted to the hospital with her family (a mother and father as well as a husband, who were given a tiny apartment in the newly completed structure), the woman was so severely ill, a successful cure was thought to be almost impossible. Indeed, her stomach was so distended as a result of hepatic failure that she could have been mistaken for a pregnant woman were her flesh not yellow with bile's poison. Some of the visitors to the Garden remarked that her refusal to be in the hospital was an unacceptable risk; because she refused hospital-based care, they said, she was courting death. They did not perceive that such risk could itself constitute a source of power, which, if contained, might turn into something potent and magical enough to overcome the hepatic disease. Yet, it seems likely that such a refusal of care, such a risk, is part of the mechanism by which *miraculous* healing—healing as miracle—operates in a context where biomedicine dominates, as in Thailand. The family of the woman spoke about the possibility of returning to the hospital and perceived their presence at the Garden as a risk, as a choice having danger (*antaraaj*). Yet they felt compelled to be there, to pursue the improbable deferral of a death foretold. Insofar as death is imagined as the telos of a life process, one determined by *kam* and *chataa*, then the interruption of that unfolding, the deferral of that unfolding, will be deemed miraculous. Such a reading of intervention would perhaps seem primitive or at least premodern on its surface. Yet, this is precisely the narrative of heroism biomedicine claims for itself. The possibility of the miraculous is, indeed, both the ground and the threatening usurpation of biomedical prerogative.

On the first day at the Garden, the cancer patient was carried by her family and the medium's assistants to meet with Siwa. He confirmed the doctor's diagnosis.[19] Siwa recognized instantly that he would be sorely tested by the

---

19. Outside of an archaic biomedical germ model of disease, to which virtually all Thais submit without, at the same time, relinquishing causal theories rooted in concepts of moral and physical balance, disease is thought to originate in an imbalance of bodily elements. Often, such imbalance is attributed to external environmental factors, such as rapid changes of temperature, and occasionally is imagined as the result of a psychological trauma. When bodily elements are understood in the idiom of "vital essence" or *khwan*, disease will be interpreted as the dislodging of khwan. When they are imagined as principles of universal composition—earth, wind, fire, and water— disease is said to result from an overabundance of one or more element. There are numerable methods among mediums of determining the nature of the imbalance, ranging from the divinatory reading of joss sticks to numerology and telepathy (as discussed by Brun in *Traditional Herbal Medicine* and Jean Mulholland in *Medicine, Magic, and Evil Spirits: Study of a Text on Thai*

cancer patient's illness. He spent over an hour on that first day examining her, probing her body with his hands, stroking the surface of her back and stomach, and pulling back the eyelids that shielded yellowed corneas. When he deemed it necessary for her to remove an article of clothing, assistants immediately leapt forward and provided a cloth wall for dignity and privacy, but otherwise the examination was part of the morning's public spectacle.

In this, as in all other healings, there were two pronouncements beyond that of naming the illness. The first was a list of herbal ingredients that would go into the concoction that the woman was to consume twice daily. The second was an injunction to meditate. Siwa asserted that he thought a cure possible but that the ultimate outcome of the therapy would depend on the woman's *kam*. It seemed highly unlikely that the patient would be able to fulfill any of the instructions. She could not eat at the time of her arrival and vomited whenever she tried. The possibility of sitting seemed out of the question. Yet, Khun Daeng's assistants left that afternoon for the local herbal markets in search of the thirty-two ingredients that were to constitute the medicinal concoction. These matched the number of the *khwan* and were intended to achieve a numerical balance among the essential elements through the processes of contact and mimesis, or sympathetic magic. When the assistants returned, they forced the patient from her apartment and helped her to brew her own medicine. Each ingredient was pulled from the bag and forced into her hand, and as she held each, she *wai*-ed and prayed over it before dropping it into the enormous pot where it was to be boiled. The activity was excruciating for her, though she undertook it in stoic silence.

All of the therapeutic activity at the Garden requires patients to make their own medicines, to physically touch each object that is used in treatment. The accompanying rhetoric is that of self-healing. "Everyone has the power to heal themselves," Khun Daeng would repeat in his unpossessed state. "It is a matter of discipline. Siwa instructs people how to cure themselves, but he does nothing himself. The power is in us. If Siwa touched these people, they would surely die." Of course, Siwa does touch people during the possession, but this is an interrogative touch. Were he to act on the bodies of the infirm, were he to exercise his vast and always ambivalent power, it would prove too much for mortal flesh to bear. Nonetheless, the rhetoric of self-healing and of internal power is in some ways a veil for what the spectacle of the possession therapy accomplishes, namely, the objectification of power as an entity external to the self (even if within the body).

---

*Traditional Paediatrics* [Canberra: Australian National University, 1987]), and most mediums specialize in one or another.

Three weeks after the first meeting, the patient's body had shrunken and her stomach, though still swollen, was much less severely inflated. The jaundice had begun to dissipate. She could and did sit in meditation for three or four hours each day, and her family, who went about life in the tiny apartment supporting her, encouraging her, and helping her through the grueling hours of seated meditation, had begun to prepare a return home. It was unnecessary, though, because she died suddenly, appearing miraculously but ironically healthy in the moment of her death. The body was removed quietly in the night, out of the southwestern gate. By midday, there was no sign in the apartment that she had ever been at the Garden. The following morning, Khun Daeng and his assistants seemed or attempted to seem nonplussed by the passing, and said only that *kam* is irrevocable, that deaths are an inevitable part of living, and that anyone who imagined that the Garden of No Worries could become a Garden of Immortality was silly.

Yet, in the middle of that morning's possession performance, during an otherwise commonplace consultation about a business deal—the client wanted to know when to sign a deed—the possessing deity burst into a rage, leapt from his throne, and ran from the room out into the Garden. He filled his mouth with water from the fountain and spat it on the earth, then hurled his staff at the door of the apartment where the patient had been. For several minutes, he raged in unintelligible grunts and screams, kicked the door, jumped into the air and landed on his buttocks, and then ran to the gate, again spitting and screaming before dropping silent and walking sedately back to the throne, where the attending clients and assistants sat wide-eyed. Later, an assistant told me that Siwa must have felt the presence of the woman's spirit on the grounds. He surmised that this patient had not yet accepted her death, that she perceived it to be premature (and therefore that she had become a bad spirit, or *phii taaj hong*). She was threatening to haunt the rooms of the ill, he worried. But Siwa had scared her away, and the danger of the wandering spirit had been mitigated. The assistant insisted, and Khun Daeng later corroborated his claims, that Siwa was not angry because the woman's death suggested a failure on his part. Rather, he was asserting his control over the territory within the gates. He spat the spirit out.

Khun Daeng's claims to a mediumship of supreme therapeutic power did not suffer from the death of the liver cancer patient, nor from the others that periodically occurred. There were enough recoveries—from stroke, physical disability, and vague, undiagnosed illnesses ("confused body")—to sustain his reputation. Just as biomedicine establishes its authority on the grounds of a method independently of the particular cases in which its paradigms are tested and (often) found wanting, so does Khun Daeng's therapy mobilize theories of disease as a means of protecting him from accusations of failure. In the end, however, the success of that effort depends on the degree to which it speaks to other crises of meaning and power.

Ultimately, disease is its own metaphor. But much is revealed by the elevation of particular diseases to iconic status at different moments in time. Khun Daeng's response to AIDS is legible within a wider discourse about the crises of modernity. Indeed, much of the conversation about modernity in Chiang Mai is haunted by the spectral presence of this catastrophe. In many descriptions, it is said to account for as many "heaps" of the dead as do accidents. But this catastrophe, the second to test Khun Daeng, is more commonly linked to criminality than to contingency. Increasingly since the late 1980s, AIDS has been read not merely as a horror for individuals and a threat to the national future (the disease was endemic by 1990, and the estimated number of HIV+ individuals already exceeded the number of hospital beds in the country by that time) but as a *representation* of an ethicopolitical moment. It has become the sign of an irreducible present, which is to say the sign of modernity cleft from the future. National institutions and health education bodies fear AIDS as much for its capacity to wound the image of Thailand's present in the minds of its contemporary others and the imagined future minds of its national heirs, as for the costs of treating patients now. The newspapers abound with stories of young women and men, of wives infected by promiscuous husbands and husbands infected by always already infectious prostitutes. These accounts are invariably dominated by the images of abandonment, of monks refusing to provide funeral services, of family and community members refusing to share tables, of alienated and rapidly dissipating bodies that become the vectors of a new infectivity in the moment they expire. Shame infuses the stories, both as the projected value that ought to accrue to the victim and (for journalists) as the anticipated sentiment of the future generation in the face of the national response or failure to respond.

During the period of my fieldwork, however, Khun Daeng began to recruit more and more disciples from the staff of the main government hospital, Suan Dork, and through them, he made increasing efforts to target AIDS patients. These were exclusively middle-class men. Female prostitutes were tacitly but thoroughly excluded from the recruitment drive, which began in late 1992 when Khun Daeng began to make claims about his ability to cure AIDS after successfully treating a fungal infection that commonly afflicts HIV+ individuals in Thailand. This infection, which causes massive black lesions on the skin, resembles Kaposi's sarcoma in some regards, but tends to cover larger areas and grows more rapidly, though it is not cancerous.

The treatment and removal of such lesions, which involves bathing in acid peels and the ingestion of herbal antifungal concoctions, is no less spectacular for the fact that it is fungal rather than cancerous. Several AIDS patients began to seek the medium's assistance (though often in secret) on the basis of stories about this cure and "before and after" photographs that circulated as evidence of the medium's powers over a disease that had proven intractable in the face of every other therapy.

At a time when every tragedy seems to be instantly commodified as grist for the publication mill, and when loss becomes the object of luxuriously abstract theorizations that do not wait even for grief, one can approach the topic of AIDS and its representations only with trepidation, knowing that it is impossible to be sanguine about a sociology of disease in the age of epidemic. Without wanting to suggest that AIDS or liver cancer or any other illness can be reduced to or equated with the discourses of social dis-ease within which they are situated, it is nonetheless necessary to understand that illness is metaphorized, and that it takes place within particular historical contexts whose contours and imageries infuse the experience of illness with particular form and meaning. As Michael Taussig says, "Above all else, it is with disease with its terrifying phantoms of despair and hope that my body becomes ripe as little else for encoding that which society holds to be real—only to impugn that reality. And if the body becomes this important repository for generating social meaning, then it is in therapy that we find the finely gauged tuning whereby the ratification of socially engendered categories and the fabulation of reality reaches its acme."[20] In Thailand, as in the West, "AIDS provide[s] an occasion" for the representational apparatus of late capitalism to perform certain tasks and to make explicit a number of presumptions about the role of sex and bodies in capitalist production. This does not mean that AIDS is a "capitalist disease," a product or simple mirror of the economy. Nor does it mean simply that the disease can be interpreted in the image of late capitalism. Rather, it means that AIDS is mobilized by these representational systems and by agents who are differently positioned within them—to signify different things and to very different ends.

Treatment for AIDS patients actually differs very little from that of other illnesses; it includes herbal treatments, the propitiation of deities, vegetarianism, abstention from sexual intercourse (and masturbation), and meditation practice. Yet, in relation to AIDS, Khun Daeng and his possessing personae stress the disciplinary elements beyond all else, and the requirements imposed on AIDS sufferers render them veritable mendicants. The rigorous policing of bodily boundaries and the enforced detachment from sensuousness, which is

20. Michael Taussig, "Reification and the Consciousness of the Patient," in *The Nervous System* (New York: Routledge, 1992), 86.

not immediately understandable as a detachment from pleasure, does not yet constitute a discourse of blame. Sex is not said to cause AIDS; in fact, AIDS is described by Khun Daeng in abstract terms, as the *"kam* of humanity" (*kam khong khon manut*) rather than the moral failure of individuals. Nonetheless, the demands for sexual abstention resonate well with those other discourses, widely diffused in Thai society, that see the very presence of AIDS in Thailand as a failure of boundedness originating in an excess of both sexual and international intercourse.

In the nineties, estimates ranged from 2 million to 6.7 million HIV-infected individuals; the number is undoubtedly somewhere in between. After the Thai government finally acknowledged that denial was a more dangerous policy than education, the country instituted one of the most aggressive preventive education programs in Asia. Although a considerable improvement over the simple and brutally dishonest denials of the late 1980s, there are limits to this effort. For example, the 1987 Five-Year Development Plan forbade any public education programs that would or could undermine the country's international image and inhibit tourism. Almost in spite of itself, the plan acknowledged the significance of prostitution in the national tourist economy, while at the same time pointing out the relationship between sexual and political economies of boundary maintenance. Under government supervision, a proliferating discourse of safe sex has emerged in the form of posters, print and television journalism, and national condom-distribution campaigns, as well as everyday conversation.

As in so many AIDS education programs, messages are often conflicted. The Thai materials, many of which have been modeled on American and European prototypes under the sponsorship of the Ford Foundation, simultaneously assert a universal risk (deny risk groups) and blame prostitutes and foreigners (create risk groups) for the disease's entry into the country. They thereby suggest a topography of heightened risk around points of geopolitical entry that corresponds to the bodily orifices through which the virus is transmitted. The representation of AIDS as a sexually transmitted disease, which dates to the early years of the epidemic in the United States, has continuing authority, and efforts to reassign it under the rubric of infectious disease have proven largely ineffectual in Thailand as in the United States. The entire ideological weight of a disease category freighted with the stigma of the syphilitic seems to have been imported. And with it has come also the vision of the prostitute as vector. The primary thrust of education campaigns has thus been the prevention of transmission to men and children by prostitutes.

Femaleness in Thailand has probably never been construed in the idiom of corruption, at least not in the sense that it has in Western European traditions, where it has been assigned a lower but not derivative status of being. However, its representation as a risk for the corruption of males, which has a lengthy history in Theravada Buddhism, seems to have been mobilized to great new effect under the influence of AIDS. The villain(ess) in the Thai discourses of transmission is the prostitute, who is defined as structurally female irrespective of biological sex, on the grounds that male prostitutes accept a "female" position in sexual intercourse. The status of moral culpability in the transmission of AIDS is not merely a function of the multiplicity of the prostitute's sexual encounters, however, although puritanical moralism would claim this to be so. It also reflects her status as the charged point in a system of contradictions. Opposed to the heterosexual woman in the marital contract, the prostitute is the figure that actually permits capitalism to maintain the simultaneous commodification of sexual labor and ideology of a not-yet-alienated sexual labor (the labor of love).[21]

This then is the context in which Khun Daeng began to recruit AIDS patients, excluding prostitutes (who are among the most numerous of its victims[22]). In effect, he transposes the rhetoric and the practice of prevention to the domain of therapy, reversing the time of illness. The reversal is nothing short of magical. Prevention after the fact, prevention that calls itself cure, works by casting illness into the future as that which is always coming, as that whose arrival is determined by the past. Its displacement into the future, therefore, is part of the mechanism by which AIDS comes to occupy a properly spectral status. It is always coming, it is immanent, it is what might yet happen. An accident. An explosion waiting to happen. An event that can be anticipated but cannot be known in advance. AIDS is a trauma, a crisis for representation. And medical discourses about the retroviral nature of the human immunodeficiency virus, which differentiates between the virus and its illness, opening the space of both time and hope between infection and its symptoms, only confirms what the medium performs.[23]

21. Linda Singer makes this point in her own discussion of related themes in U.S. discourse about AIDS and prostitution. See *Erotic Welfare*, 49.

22. At various points since the early 1990s, the estimation of infectivity rates among prostitutes in Chiang Mai has been set at between 50 percent and 85 percent, but the higher percentage rates are always attributed to those girls and women who service lower- and working-class men.

23. Often in Thailand and the United States, the concern with the transmission of body fluids has been directly transferred to the level of the body politic, and people with HIV have been systematically discouraged from crossing national boundaries (as of this writing, HIV+ noncitizens are legally prohibited from entering both Thailand and the United States). As discussed earlier, the dominant discourse of boundary transgression in the 1960s and 1970s was focused on communism

Khun Daeng acknowledges AIDS as a transnational phenomenon with mercurial infectivity, and his therapy entails a mode of boundary maintenance that acknowledges the impossibility of isolation. But he believes himself to be immune by virtue of discipline and Siwa's power. He claims that AIDS can be passed easily among humans, but not between humans and gods, and Siwa will protect the medium's body from meeting with the disease. There is no single term that can be translated to mean "infection" in Thai. The only expression that can be forced from the language is that of "touching" disease (*tid*). Thus, to infect someone is to "cause him or her to touch/contact disease" (*tham hai tid kap rook*). Khun Daeng claims that within the realm of the Garden, Siwa himself will ensure that there is no passage, no infection, no "touching" of disease. When they die, however, AIDS patients are invariably accused of having violated the taboos of therapy and of having succumbed to consumptive desires that then consumed them.

The containment of productive power through consumption produces its own kind of scarcity, and in some senses the asceticism required of AIDS and other patients is designed to bring about a kind of concentrated value that they themselves produce. This occurs against a backdrop in which the consumption of sex through prostitutes is a critical part of masculine subject formation, but one with increasing risk attached.[24] At the Garden of No Worries, Saivite asceticism manages to extend and transmute the relationships among masculinity, sexual desire, and power, while preserving the erotic logic of commodity aesthetics.[25] Yet, it remains a site of acquisitive activity, and the practical discourse of AIDS at the Garden metaphorizes, by reversing, the forms of profit intensification that center around it.

---

and cast in the idiom of cellular infectivity. Thus, Saiyud Kherpol developed an entire strategy of encirclement and excision. Still conceived in the idiom of infectivity, AIDS is no longer amenable to an imagery of localization. But it represents to Thailand a threat at least equal to and probably far greater than communism. Indeed, communism is occasionally spoken of as the AIDS of the political world among military people; perhaps for this reason, the Thai military apparatus agreed to permit the WHO and the U.S. medical apparatus to test AIDS vaccines on enlisted personnel in 1992 (although this plan has since been abandoned by the sponsoring organizations). In 1998, military recruits were required to undergo HIV screening at their own expense before entering the army. Although there is public debate about this policy, positive results mean exclusion from the military, and this fact of exclusion likely will not be mitigated by popular opposition because the armed forces constitute the threshold against which infection is conceived.

24. Pasuk Phongpaichit, *From Peasant Girls to Bangkok Masseuses* (Geneva: International Labour Organization, 1982); Hantrakul Sukanya, "Prostitution in Thailand," in *Development and Displacement in Southeast Asia* (Melbourne: Monash University, 1988).

25. W. F. Haug, *Critique of Commodity Aesthetics: Appearance, Sexuality and Advertising in Capitalist Society*, trans. Robert Bock (Minneapolis: University of Minnesota Press, 1986).

Here, Linda Singer's insights into the relationships between economy and sexual epidemic have unexpected comparative utility with reference to the Garden, and I therefore quote her at length:

> The sexual epidemic in which the prospect of "liberated spontaneous sexuality" is represented as no longer possible, or in the process of slipping away, provides a context in which the myth of scarcity, so central to the creation of needs and demands upon which capitalist production depends, can be rewritten and recirculated. If "free sex" is scarce, one will have to pay. Sex costs. If the cost of contact with bodies is too high in the currency of risks, one will have to pay in another currency for something else. The myth of scarcity circulating in this epidemic is not only a tale of the scarcity of bodies, it is a tale about the scarcity of time as well. The sexual epidemic temporalizes the erotic and eroticizes the temporal in the direction of profit intensification, similar in strategy and effect to the profit intensification of spatiality in the 1970s under the name of the "condominium" where space is divided into the smallest marketable units and then sold as investment.[26]

Now, if the issue in Thailand is less one of a disappearing sexual liberation than of a disappearing mode of masculine subject formation, the diminishing prospects of national income generation, the sense of vanishing time is, as already stated, omnipresent in the myriad gestures and expressions of "not having time" (*maj mii weelaa*) that one encounters in the press of the everyday in Thailand: in complaints about long working hours, themselves calculated to extract maximal labor from individual workers; in the expressed sentiment of temporal acceleration, as when people say "everything is faster these days"; and in the anticipatory longing for a vanishing future. It is present in mediums' remarks about the difficulty of remembrance "these days." And it is also present in Khun Daeng's practice of blessing condominiums for those clients who come to the Garden, learn the discipline of "selective refusal," and seek Siwa's power as they carry out the more malevolent magic of capital accumulation.

### Capital as Contagion

The curing of illness is a spectacular part of the Garden's everyday life, and it generates much of the moral authority with which the medium sustains his practice. In the end, however, it is Siwa's reputed capacity to magically invest money with the capacity to become self-reproducing capital that makes the Garden the center of occult networks among developers, mafia men, generals,

26. Singer, *Erotic Welfare*, 41.

and pettier entrepreneurs. In the early 1990s, the most common activity at the Garden was, in fact, the blessing of land title deeds and new capital ventures, especially condominium construction projects. Outside the palace, an almost endless flow of Mercedes Benzes and BMWs stopped momentarily to receive the magic of a man who was once a master of occult economies. Their occupants emerged from behind darkened windows with cellular telephones in hand and, frequently, conducted their business with the spirit while receiving calls from elsewhere. These individuals, who undertake the same ascetic regimens as do recovering patients, carry out commercial negotiations, sign deals, make pledges to the spirit in anticipation of a boon, and generally treat the Garden as a secret boardroom. On many occasions, when emerging from the palace after Siwa's departure, I would find white-clad businessmen bent over documents or making calls to Chiang Mai to check on bank accounts and cash flow problems. Snippits of overheard telephone conversations often struck me as fantastic, even though I had come to expect a lack of separation between ritual and rational economic calculation. It was not uncommon, for example, to find a businessman sitting, smoking Marlboro cigarettes, while conversing on the telephone, reporting Siwa's arrival, asking about the cost of materials for a construction project, and then demanding that land title certificates for new developments be sent to the Garden via courier before the deity's departure.

Title deeds for land that was to be used for condominium development were brought to the palace, placed on a *khan*, and handed to Siwa, who invariably asked for explanations of the deal, then commented on ways to maximize profitability, such as by adding another floor to a building or renting space to competitors. He also calculated auspicious dates to commence construction and inaugurate new buildings. However, he always demanded that the owner of the land undertake a modest period of meditative discipline, during which time he or she would don the white garb of the ascetic and refrain from sexual intercourse and the consumption of meat. Had Marx dared to anticipate the image of commodity fetishism after the end of socialism, in the teletechnic era, and had he been able to continue writing anyway, he would perhaps have dreamed up the rites of blessing at the palace. They are the perfectly literal dramas of that process by which the commodity is represented as the site of magical and laborless productivity. More particularly, they are the dramas of finance capital's emergence.

On one occasion, perhaps the most visually poetic act of economic ritual that I observed at the Garden, a woman who wanted to raise capital for a new shop in Chiang Mai brought with her a bright yellow plastic purse. It was absolutely electric, its lunatic yellow making gold appear to be an always already tarnished color. The woman—middle aged and middle class—had bought it specifically for the purpose of this rite, and laughed when she remarked that it was almost gold, laughed because it was already an excess of gold. During the morning ritual, the would-be shopowner placed the purse on a *khan* with the standard red envelope of cash donation and brought it to Siwa, *wai*-ing deeply as she explained her need for new capital. In the course of his possession, Siwa took the purse and opened it, looking at its empty interior and then spitting sompoy water into it. He then advised the woman to make offerings to a number of temples and to undertake three days of discipline. Finally, he indicated that he thought she would receive what she sought: an explosion of money.

Through an act of metonymic association, what we might well call contagion, Siwa exhaled the power born of his own controlled fertility into the purse, and as he did so, it became the receptacle of fiscal reproductivity. The potency of the sexual imagery of fertilization in this gesture should not be underestimated. Nor should it be dissociated from that other representational gesture, discussed in the previous chapter, by which a certain excess was inscribed by graffiti artists as the displacement of the sexual organ. The assertive gestures of Siwa's power invariably took the form of spitting (as in the banishment of the wandering spirit), itself a displacement of an ejaculation that, it will be remembered, was rendered impossible by castration in the analogic myth of Siwa's empowerment. Sex as metaphor for economy. We have already seen that the therapeutic discourse of the Garden defines it as a space in which a sexual economy driven by consumption is organized around an artificially induced scarcity, a scarcity produced by consumption (through "selective refusal") in the midst of overabundance. This is an economy in which waste and disposal actually buttress the value generated by selective refusal (asceticism). It is an economy in which, not incidentally, the culture of the connoisseur (the antique collector and the nostalgic, modern-day version of the flaneur) and the conservationist thrive best.

Consider, then, the fact that Siwa's sartorial self-constitution always entails the covering over of his "third eye" with a red headcloth. He blinds this organ of total seeingness, he says, because the gaze of the deity would kill all that fell in its irradiating path. On one level, the self-blinding performs that splitting by which the eye as an organ emerges in its separation from the "I" as a subject in the domain of the visible. The deity can engage humans by assuming a human form, via the medium, but to do so, he must descend into a structure of subject formation premised on "castration," on membership in a symbolic domain. That his speech never finally conforms itself to this fact (its unintelligibility being a mark of anteriority vis-à-vis the symbolic) suggests only that a tension between these realms is held open in and by the performance itself. Yet, the gesture of self-blinding also works in a more economic register. It constitutes the first moment of displacement and alienation that will then permit the deity's touch to be a vector of productivity. By covering his eye, he renders his spittle and his finger the instruments of a productivity that can move invisibly.

The power of contagious magic is, of course, that it moves as a result of contact or contiguity, and that there need be no representational intervention. When witchcraft accusations were made against new converts to Christianity in the early decades of this century, they usually accused individuals of two things: the betrayal of obligations to the ancestors and the invisible production of wealth. At Khun Daeng's palace, entrepreneurs seek both an escape from the demands of generational obligation (they want to concentrate wealth without having to disperse it among their dependents) and a capacity to make their investments multiply. Productivity and liberation from the demands of inheritance: these are the marks of what would be called in the West a libertine representational politics. As Frances Ferguson has so masterfully argued in her reading of Sade's relationship to the question of heritability, the attempt to critique, oppose, or otherwise get outside of the economy in which prerogative is naturalized as a racial, familial, or class entitlement can convert itself into one of two things. Either it can take the form of a demand for universal rights, which is to say total representation, or it becomes a demand for access to and power over all others.[27] The democracy protestors of 1992 and the poor medium who had once supported the more radical program of the communist revolutionaries in the 1970s were organized quite clearly around the possibility of the former. And this is true despite the fact that they failed, in most regards, to offer any solace or programmatic interventions on behalf of the poor. That the democracy protestors (and their allies, the environmentalists) were supported by descendants of the displaced local royalty and, in at least one case, by a grandchild of King Rama V, complicates the picture in terms of the identities of universal rights activists. But it does not mitigate the fact that all of them were contesting the distribution of power on nonrepresentational grounds.

The men and women who sought Siwa's assistance and his magical interventions were also opposed to the exclusive distribution of power and wealth among the old families of Thailand's titled elite. Many, though certainly not all, were ethnically Sino-Thai, a fact that may seem ironic given that the capitalist classes in Thailand are thought, historically, to have been dominated by Sino-Thai families, particularly in the domain of banking and finance capital. Nonetheless, the history of the twentieth century is also a history of the state's (uneven) attempts to mitigate or indeed to undercut the domination of these sectors by a marginalized ethnic minority. King Rama VI's (Vajiravudh) fa-

27. Frances Ferguson, "Sade and the Pornographic Legacy," *Representations* 36 (fall 1991): 1–21.

mously inflammatory essay, "The Jews of the East," has haunted such legislative interventions as the act of 1979, which overtly required the breakup of monopoly capital and covertly sought out the containment of Sino-Thai power. In the end, the act only succeeded in extending the power of particular and not just Sino-Thai capitalist families by permitting minority shareholders to control extended capital resources in companies that became increasingly diversified but also more fractured in ownership. It provides a magnificent instance of government interventions generating consequences that are precisely opposed to their stated intentions.[28] Yet, if they opposed their exclusion from monopolized capital, Siwa's economic clients did not fantasize full and equal economic rights for all individuals. To the contrary, they specifically sought for themselves unmitigated access to and power over everyone else. In this, they were more like Khun Daeng than were the wounded workers of his former companies. It is perhaps needless to say that such power would take place in the absence of another's capacity for refusal. Herein lies the violence and the transgressiveness of libertine politics. And also their excess. Or rather, their exteriority. For, to the extent that libertine politics do not recognize the right of another's refusal, they are outside the law. This is, I think, why there appears to be such an affinity between this new (for Chiang Mai) form of mediumship and the mafia, one that is not merely enacted in the life history of Khun Daeng, but also in the (rumored) fact that so many members of the mafia seek his assistance.

One might surmise that, to the extent that there is an affinity between the two, between new forms of mediumship and the mafia, it rests on the shared exteriority of each to the state's legal apparatus. But, then, this would suggest a domain in which capital's productivity (and especially finance capital's productivity) abides by law, takes the form of law, and operates in the mode of representation. And that, I believe, would be an incorrect analysis. For, if anything, the rites performed at the Garden of No Worries suggest that entrepreneurial and finance capital operate precisely as modes of occult practice, in which nothing can be transformed into something, in which the careful decisions of refusal can contain the fact of risk, but that, in the end, it is the risk of complete destruction and expenditure (of, for example, a condominium development project that fails to attract buyers) that leads to improbable and miraculous-seeming profit.

The rite of the purse metaphorizes this logic in gorgeously sensual terms. It is not simply that Siwa renders the purse a site of multiplying money. Rather, he transforms money into its own self-generating capital. As much as the ritual

28. Akira Suehiro, *Capital Accumulation in Thailand 1855–1985* (Tokyo: Centre for Southeast Asian Cultural Studies, 1989).

baptisms of money that Michael Taussig describes in Bolivia,[29] the blessing of the purse reveals a profound sensitivity to the distinctions Marx emphasized (and Simmel downplayed) between money as an instrument of exchange, indeed of universal equivalence, and capital as the instrument of "money making" and surplus value. In the chapter of *Capital* titled "The Transformation of Money into Capital," Marx argues that the "first form of appearance of capital is money" and that the difference between money as money and money as capital is the mode of their circulation. In its prototypical form, namely, merchant capital, money permits the capitalist to buy and sell dearer.[30] In its mature form, capital actually entails the concentration of labor as a commodity for the purposes of generating surplus value. The owner of the purse in the blessing rite was seeking capital for investment in a profit-making enterprise that would exist primarily as a retail outlet. Yet, she would purchase her materials, textiles in this case, from more properly capitalist wholesalers whose factories are organized around all the principles of coerced labor commodification that Marx describes in his own discussions of the factory. The rite demonstrated and performed a contrast between money that would be used merely in exchange for luxury consumables, and capital that would be used to generate more money.

The ideology of asceticism at the Garden directly contravenes consumerism, encouraging individuals to cultivate the skills of selective refusal and to experience their bodies and its fluids as a particular kind of economy. The tacit moral lessons of Siwa's possessions and the ethos of asceticism at the Garden are those in which the economically dispossessed are prevented from obtaining further power. The person who must spend his or her everything in this system, who has no surplus, is the least able to manage and acquire power. Moreover, unbridled consumption renders the wealthy person akin to the poor person, whereas controlled consumption both represents and enables the production of wealth. Yet, for those who transgress these rules of selective refusal, there is the possibility of a gain. Such gains are greatest, one surmises, when the rules being transgressed are also one's own.

In this context, Khun Daeng's and Siwa's activities as the ritual officiants at new condominium complexes take on heightened significance. Increasingly during the time of my fieldwork, Khun Daeng and his possessing deities were asked to bless the grounds or the foundations and also the completed edifices of new condominium and high-rise construction projects. As far as I know, he

29. Michael Taussig, *The Devil and Commodity Fetishism in Latin America* (Chapel Hill: University of North Carolina Press, 1980), 133–39.

30. Karl Marx, *Capital*, vol. 1 (1887; Moscow: Progress Publishers, 1954), 145, 163.

never refused these requests. At dawn on Sunday mornings, he left the grounds in his red Mercedes for new sites in Chiang Mai, where he would be possessed and perform a brief ceremony, casting out evil, blessing the activities that would take place in the new buildings, and calling for success for their owners. Such ritual blessings are often performed by Buddhist monks, and it is not unheard of for new retail companies and brand name launches to be conducted with the ritual endorsements of the *sangha*'s slightly heterodox members. However, Khun Daeng's blessings are sought by entrepreneurial capitalists for the raw power they command and, I suspect, because of the associations that the medium himself brings to bear on his own biography as a successful developer. He is the one who draws most from the least, who converts the diminished space of the condominium into the lunatic origin of a self-renewing wealth, but one untethered to production. He is the one whose submission to law allows his flaunting of it to become fecund.

There is, therefore, an oblique structural relationship between the logic of capitalist magic and that of magical cure at the Garden, and it is one that operates at the level of signification and of time's deferral. The risk of AIDS was, and is, both its horrible consequence and the fact that it cannot be discerned in the first place and therefore, that it is infectious before becoming manifest. It proliferates in the space between a cause (the virus) and its appearance (symptoms). In other words, it makes the body a dissimulator, a duplicitous surface where a seeming absence of signs hides the inevitability of a future and fatal event. The body of the one with HIV appears well but is not. It is capable of desires, but their enactment leads to the contamination of those with whom it satisfies itself. Or so the popular discourses on AIDS seem to suggest. In the context of northern Thailand's contemporaneity already described, a context in which the risk of dissimulation has become a primary form of modern criminality, AIDS manifests itself as a criminal disease. Its sufferers are slighted with that epithet. They are referred to, by many if not most, as people with the *kam* produced by bad deeds. In other words, they are construed as already criminal. And this is why they are treated with such opprobrium. They are exiled, ostracized, ridiculed, abandoned, and sometimes made the objects of charity— the giving that they cannot refuse. Khun Daeng can intervene here only by extending that space between a cause and its sign, only by deferring the moment of an explosion. His miracle is the overcoming of a certain scarcity: the scarcity of a time that belongs to the one infected.

Elsewhere, he converts scarcity into value by rendering it the point of time's eruption. The condominium constructions and the real estate developments all produce value by investing in diminished units whose worth will increase over time. A "miracle" will occur if the time of the "return" is shortened by the intensification of another's desire. That is, if another person (a buyer) wishes to insert himself or herself in the place of one (the owner) who is to benefit from time's extension, then the buyer creates the conditions of possibility for the owner to reap rewards "prematurely." The point for the owner will then be to make the object voluptuously tempting, to make it a dissimulator in order that its face value be taken for real value and, in the process, for face value to produce its own excessive self.

The miraculous explosion of value depends on the belief that, normally, value emerges in time as the function of a deferred consumption. This is not an economy of exchange in the simple sense, where the representations of value (both words and monetary signs) are circulated in a totalized sphere of perfect translatability. It does not assume the existence of transparent and corresponding relationships of referentiality between signifiers and their signifieds. Rather, it is the economy of transgressive productivity, of risked destruction, and of semiotic proliferation. It is the economy of Siwa's castration and its excessive return. It is also the economy of national apotheosis, the point at which the dispersed simultaneous readership of the print age is displaced by the crowd of transnational capital's deterritorialized space.

## Fire

It was always difficult to reconcile Khun Daeng's intense identification as a Chinese man with that aspect of his theme park devoted to hagiographic historiography of the Thai monarchs. But these two elements coexisted at the Garden and made stubborn demands on everyone's attention. As stated earlier, Khun Daeng defined himself as being, "above all else, Chinese. Everything I do, everything I am, my whole life is the way it is because I am Chinese." Yet, he also identifies himself as Thai and, more specifically, as a man from Kanchanaburi. Although many ethnographers have inscribed the notion of Sino-Thai ethnicity as a kind of hybridity in Thai studies,[31] Ann Maxwell Hill notes that the tension between Thainess and Chineseness is maintained within both nationalist ideology and categories of personhood.[32] These tensions and oppositions often recede into invisibility, but they are also available to be mobilized in life histories and national history, as when economic relationships are cultivated

---

31. For example, see Richard Basham, " 'False Consciousness' and the Problem of Merit and Power in Thailand," *Mankind* 19, no. 2 (1989): 125–37; and Charles F. Keyes, *Thailand: Buddhist Kingdom as Modern Nation-State* (Boulder, CO: Westview, 1987), 169.

32. Ann Maxwell Hill, "Chinese Funerals and Chinese Ethnicity in Chiang Mai, Thailand," *Ethnology* 31, no. 4 (1992): 324.

through Chinese cultural associations, or when the Chinese are dragged into xenophobic discourses as the scapegoat for economic stress and class conflict.[33] It is only within this context of an ethnic consciousness that the elaborate efforts to efface Chineseness with Lanna nationalism can be understood.[34]

The culture of immigrant supernaturalization described by Vatikiotis is still powerful in Chiang Mai. In 1992, for example, the Chinese-owned Tantraphan Group, one of the largest retail chains in Chiang Mai, undertook an advertising campaign for its new supermall that featured the slogan, "We're part of the culture." A nod to the newly self-conscious buying power of the conservationist cultural elite, it also revealed the still-tense position of Chinese economic power. Again, Khun Daeng seems to have taken the opposite route, to have simply embraced his own alterity and made a virtue of it. But this apparent ease with the position of the outsider is oddly contradicted by the etching of an explicitly nationalist history into the stone pillar that stands at the entry to the Garden.

The pillar looks every bit like the famous Sukhothai stone tablets and, in like manner, is inscribed with a history of the place. It begins by describing the reign of the present monarch, King Bumiphol Adulyadej, as an era of great "progress" and "democracy," these attributes being manifest in three areas: "the power of law," "the management of the state," and the "judgmental capacities of the king." The king's reign is described as a period of accomplished international relations, of agricultural development (in which crops are numerous and diverse, thanks to new technologies of irrigation), and of matured religion. The country is said to be home to a mainly Buddhist population, but it is also defined as a place where the king encourages all religions. Four main religions are identified in Thailand: Buddhism, with Buddha as its head; Christianity, with Jesus as its head; Islam, with Allah at its head; and Hinduism, with the trinity of Siwa, Narai, and Phrom at its head. Khun Daeng is referenced as the man responsible for the construction of the Garden and its buildings, and his name is explained as meaning "the teacher of Kanchanaburi."

The final segment of the pillar's text describes northern Thailand, using the term *phaak nüa* rather than Lannathai, the site of the palace, as a land of many mountains, forests, and important rivers. Most people here, says the pillar, are

---

33. In "Withdrawal Symptoms: Social and Cultural Aspects of the October 6 Coup," *Bulletin of Concerned Asian Scholars* 9, no. 3 (1977): 13–30, Benedict Anderson describes how this occurred during the crackdown on students in 1976. The recent collapse of the Thai economy was also construed in terms of the failure of a capitalist culture that was dominated by Chinese banking families and extended loans to familial connections without insisting on adequate collateral.

34. Michael Vatikiotis, "Ethnic Pluralism in the Northern Thai City of Chiang Mai" (Ph.D. diss., Oxford University, 1984), 89.

farmers or factory workers who practice Buddhism. Buddhism is described simply as "a faith that has been in this area since ancient times." The inscription then continues to adduce evidence of the antiquity and the ubiquity of Buddhism by describing the existence of many wats and places for monks to study the *dhamma*. Finally, the stone text asserts that the people who have built the edifices at the Garden have done so to encourage all of humanity to meditate and to seek the well-being of others, to instill in them an appreciation of knowledge and to stimulate their power to share that knowledge. Beneath the last line is a list of financial contributors to the Garden. It is an inscription of "who's who" in Thailand, and includes several highly placed military officers, one national sports hero, a number of very powerful representatives from the national banking elite, and several powerful Chinese capitalists.

In the world of northern mediumship, the text on the pillar is striking for the fact that it does not accord northern Thailand a central place in the modern polity—even as a point of origins. Northern Thailand rates only a mention; Mengrai, contemporary of Sukhothai's Ramkhamhaeng, is not referenced at all. In the manner of school textbooks, the historical trajectory of the nation represented here is stretched between Sukhothai and Bangkok, and the emphasis is on the emergence of the Chakkri monarchs. Chiang Mai is but a periphery.

There are other significant departures from the discourse of other mediums, especially in the representation of kingship, which is no longer the pure charismatic emanation of the monarchical person but a category of judicial power. Indeed, in its celebration of the law and its definition of the monarchical function as an essentially hermeneutic one, the text articulates a conceptualization of power in terms that seem starkly antithetical to those actually manifested in mediums' practices. What finally permits Khun Daeng to escape the terms of that representational order is thus his claim to Chineseness, to an ethnicity that both precedes and exceeds the nation, that which was required by it and excluded at the same time.

Chineseness in Thailand is inextricably bound up with the development of capitalism, with the prolongation of monarchical power in the face of bureaucratic opposition, and with the relatively late emergence of industrial capital. Chinese immigrant labor was a crucial part of the Thai economy from the Ayutthayan era onward, but under the *sakdi naa* system, Chinese immigrants lacked property rights and were classified as aliens. Some Chinese, but a small percentage of the total, played the role of tax farmers and, as the Thai economy monetized and taxation was transformed from in-kind to cash payment, the Chinese tax-farming community began to amass considerable cash wealth. Most of this was remitted to China. In fact, between 1890 and 1910, Chinese workers in Thailand remitted an average of 25 million baht per year to their home country. Compared to the government revenues of 61 million baht per annum, the remittance was enormous.[35]

Still, the Chinese tax farmers did accumulate a considerable amount of capital, and during the pre-1932 era, they constituted the major part of Thailand's new merchant capitalist class. Although the Chinese did not reinvest in land per se, they did invest in agriculture and in other tax-farming ventures, and especially in import-export. As Ma Xiaojun argues, the mutual dependency of the monarchy and the Chinese tax farmers created the conditions for the Chinese support of monarchy and the institutions of *sakdi naa*.[36] Between the 1932 overthrow of the absolute monarchy and 1947, Chinese capitalists enjoyed the benefits of an extremely lucrative rice industry, but also began branching outward into shipping and banking, only to elicit the reactive forces of a xenophobic Thai nationalism that reinforced notions of blood ethnicity.[37] The 1950s, 1960s, and even the early part of the 1970s saw the emergence of banking capital, largely in the form of alliances between state bureaucratic and Chinese-controlled banking capital.[38] In the late 1970s, as Thailand began to sink into debt crisis as a result of an overextended military and a heavy reliance on foreign investment as well as an international recession and rising oil prices, capital accumulation and reinvestment remained almost exclusively urban, where it supported the emergence of a middle class (which matured as a political force in the early 1990s) but at a cost to agriculturalists and urban laborers.[39] Of course, this bias was less a function of planning by Sino-Thai capitalists than it was the result of international monetary and development policy. The Sino-Thais were merely held responsible for the failures of the moment. Only in the late 1980s did the country emerge from its stagnation, largely through the development of industrial capital and the service sector, and then at a rate that promised to send it to the top of the ASEAN NICS.[40]

35. Ma Xiaojun, "The Agrarian Change and Reform in Thailand (1850–1910): A Comparative Study with Meiji Restoration in Japan," in *Proceedings of the 4th International Conference on Thai Studies* (Kunming: Institute of Southeast Asian Studies, 1990), 4: 549.

36. Ibid., 4: 550.

37. Pasuk Phongpaichit, "Review Article: Capital Accumulation in Thailand," *Journal of Asian Studies* 22, no. 2 (1992): 383.

38. Kevin Hewison, *Bankers and Bureaucrats: Capital and the Role of the State in Thailand* (New Haven: Yale University Press, 1989), 162.

39. S. M. Waseem, "Thailand: Economic Development and ASEAN Promise," in *Proceedings of the 4th International Conference on Thai Studies* (Kunming: Institute for Southeast Asian Studies, 1990), 555; Also Pasuk, "Review," 383.

40. Hewison, *Bankers and Bureaucrats*, 206; Waseem, "Thailand: Economic Development," 557–58.

Some of the most powerful forces and major beneficiaries of this extremely recent move toward industrial capital, especially in the manufacturing sector, have been the old families of Chiang Mai, such as Nimmanhaemindha, Tantrapan, and Chinawatra. But all of Thailand seemed to inhabit the whirlwind of a phenomenally accelerating economy during the eighties and nineties. In the late 1980s and early 1990s, GDP growth rates reached as high as 12 percent per annum. The Sixth Five-Year Plan (1987–1991) recognized the potential for massive social dislocation, put forth a 5 percent growth rate as a workable ideal, and advocated balanced, structural transformation to facilitate the new capitalism.[41] In the meantime, however, land and real estate speculation, at which Khun Daeng had proven so adept, spurred the deepening divisions between capitalists and workers, producing the conditions in which the military could intervene and claim (but lose its claim) that the average person in Thailand had been betrayed by the capitalists in Chatichai Choonhaven's government. And of course, the entire system was operating on the principles of a magical impossibility: of limitless growth, of an endless capacity to sustain desire and the explosion of time.

By 1997, the whole edifice had come crumbling down, and the empty purses were finally revealed to be just that: empty purses. Once again, Sino-Thai families were put in the position of having to sacrifice themselves for the "benefit of the national good" in order to not be scapegoated for their own historical marginality. Banks were closed, family assets sold to foreign capitalists, local monopolies broken up and put on the market generated by IMF demands. The demands, of course, had been made on Thailand because it was represented to and for the international financial community as the origin of what was widely held to be a "plague." The plague was defined as an infectious principle of value destruction. At another time it would have been called witchcraft. But in the age of AIDS, the worst sin is the failure to contain within oneself the principle of one's own imminent death or loss of value. Thailand was an origin of the plague because it did not contain its crisis in the national body through the enactment of selective refusal. Economic failure became a virus: infectious before becoming visible. In its wake devotion to the nation became as necessary as sexual abstention for Siwa's patients.

Before that moment, Khun Daeng could revel in his exteriority to the Thai nation without, at the same time, destabilizing the integrity of national identification as a principle. His insistent reference to a history and an identity that lay behind him generated a kind of behindness to which he seemed always to be retreating. He was Chinese and only then Thai, and each time he invoked

41. Waseem, "Thailand: Economic Development," 558.

nationality he invoked the possibility of other nationalities, and a receding horizon of identification loomed as the specter of what Benedict Anderson calls the "comparison" inherent in all nationalism. Thus dislocating Thainess as the origin and limit of national being, Khun Daeng could become its patron, the one to confer his approving gaze on it. He could even identify with it, identification in this case being that which takes place from without: the impossible claim to a natural place compelled from the position of dislocation (what Derrida called ontopology). The point, however, is not that Khun Daeng is an ethnically marginalized subject. The point is that his exteriority to the national narrative made it impossible for him to convert his status into origins. In their place, he became the impresario of the limit.

*Ashes*

The last time I saw Khun Daeng, on a rain-soaked monsoon afternoon, he offered to entertain me with videos of his annual sacrifices. I expected the usual home video of the Praise Ceremony. Instead, the screen lit up and the voluptuous rhythms of the *tabla* took over. A Bombay film score that had been laid down next to the image track began to play. Instead of the usual *forn phii* and propitiary offerings, the video screen gave up images of a fire-walking ceremony that Khun Daeng had sponsored the previous summer. It was even subtitled.

The most dramatic part of the video, and one Khun Daeng rewound and replayed several times, showed a horrifying moment in the ceremony when one of the walkers (an assistant I had met many times) stumbled and fell headlong into the coals. In the video, the long-range camera angles permitted a panoptic view of the awful event. In seconds, Siwa leapt from his seat, reached the edge of the pit, grabbed the shocked and burning man from the coals, and was holding him in his lap as a mother would hold her injured child. He then struck the man in the head quite suddenly, and returned to his place at the head of the pit, whence the ritual proceeded. Quite "miraculously," the victim was unscarred by the experience, which fact Khun Daeng said was further proof of Siwa's curative powers.

The video was fascinatingly predictable, so perfectly scripted was its theatricality and the centrality of a crisis to its narrative. The cameraperson clearly had complete access to the ritual space and some sense of the rite's progression, for the camera angles were most advantageous. The final polish, which included production credits, indicated the public viewing for which the video was intended. So did its codification in a catalogue of videos, which Khun Daeng kept in bound volumes. In fact, Khun Daeng had videos of every major rite, from the first blessing of the ground at San Saay to the opening of the *bot*, each listed in a register with the date of the event.

Nothing signifies the modern more perfectly than the fact of being one's own archivist. Except possibly the anticipation of being seen from afar. But then, sometimes the "return to origins" is precisely the gesture of ensuring a future, or rather a future remembrance. Khun Daeng's videos were marked by that anticipation, as marked as were the democracy protests and the cultural events staged at the ruins of Thapae Gate. They were marked in their self-composure, their editorial completeness, and their captioning as performances that anticipated an audience. The degree to which the video is embedded with futurity suggests, ironically enough, that it remains within a form of signification that is based on deferral, which is to say on writing.

To suggest that these media—both photography and video—can be so located, to suggest that they are not yet the end of writing so much as its apotheosis, is perhaps to fly in the face of much media theory. That theory emphasizes simultaneity and a copresence liberated from time, counterposing that experience to the deferrals of writing. Indeed, the magic of Khun Daeng's practice at the Garden of No Worries suggests that something beyond anticipatory consciousness is also at play. A similar space "beyond" deferral was clearly being pursued by the masters of the media spectacle in the democracy protests as well. The circulation of videotapes from around the world and the blissful knowledge that people in myriad countries were watching the same thing at the same time constituted a greater threat to the nation than even the military censors probably imagined. For in the moment of such a political jouissance, in the moment that people fantasized a simultaneity between event and viewing, between the locations of origin and destination, they became postnational subjects.

Now, this consciousness was immediately mitigated by the compulsion to temporality that is entailed in every narrative gesture. Speaking about the events in Ratchadamnoen Avenue dislocated viewers from the no-time of the videographic present. This latter timelessness is also the no-time of newly modern magical power. A power that is at the same time premodern, it has been renewed, ironically enough, by being inserted in representation's economy. This magic—which is not representational but productive—seems like capital's power, especially given the descriptions of capital's fetishistic charms in Marx's own accounts. A literalized magic can only substitute for capital's violent extractions when one believes that capital itself is productive. But this is the case only when it is thought to represent actual value. And in speculative economy, such as that which dominated Thailand in the 1980s and 1990s, this is not so. Moreover, the speculative economy of those years operated primarily because Thailand (and Chiang Mai) was able to make itself attractive to those looking from without. At Khun Daeng's Garden, where the same logic of contagion defines both disease and transgressive value production, and where miracles of speculation and deferral take place through the same selective refusal, one realizes that the threshold of nationhood has been crossed. For these are logics of transnationalism's newly occult economy, and not the return of some primordially northern or even Chinese practice. Khun Daeng, one realizes, asserts his Chineseness but Siwa does not. Siwa, one might say, is before both nation and origins. He is in their place. But then, he is also afterward. So, too, the fantasy of postnational identity is made possible by the totalization of teletechnic networks (by which both capital and imagery are circulated). These networks collapse the space between origins and ends. Coming at the end of the nation, they nonetheless naturalize themselves as coming from before. Indeed, they emerge from the fantasy of a place that would exist before that impossible origin that is difference. For, as Phayaphrom well knew (and both cultural nationalism and Lannathai regionalism attempted to repress), difference *is* the origin.

# 9  AFTER ALL ELSE:
# THE END OF MEDIUMSHIP?

At the end of the introduction to this book, I warned that its structure would be marked by a certain repetitiveness. Each chapter begins anew or is haunted with the figure of Phayaphrom, the nineteenth-century poet whose astonishing modernity seemed to anticipate, so uncannily, his own return in an era marked by the sentiment of loss and the compensatory forms of nostalgic performance that accompany it. Indeed, it would not be unfair to understand the book as having been written in the enunciative form of a "stutter," where each effort to begin is somehow interrupted by a sense of the impossibility of simply "starting at the beginning."[1] Apart from performing a certain difficulty in the writing of ethnography, the "stuttering" is intended to mark the impossibility of a history that would start, simply, at the beginning and proceed in linear fashion. I have already attempted to argue—or, rather, to follow the arguments of others who have already traveled this path—that historical ethnography needs to reflect the backward glance of its writing and the futurity that is produced in such retrojection. A history of the line, a mere recitation of chronology, can never be adequate to that task. And the task is an important one. But equally important in a book that addresses the phenomena of displacement and the always incomplete process of spiritual presencing, nonlinear historiography evokes the temporal disjunctures of possession itself. It opens the possibility that possession has been remade as the oblique thematization of that logic in which it has been produced anew, as a distinctly modern phenomenon.

Having said as much, not even I could have anticipated the degree to which

---

1. I am indebted to Michael Levine for this concept of stuttering, though I use it in a rather different context and sense than that for which he developed the notion, namely, the aporia of autobiography in Christa Wolff.

the repetitiveness of this writing strategy would haunt me in later encounters with Thailand. Perhaps when one is writing of spirits, one should expect to be haunted. And yet, when I returned in Thailand in 1997, ostensibly to investigate the condition of an economy in crisis, I did not expect to be drawn again into the circle of mediums. The occasion for such a rapprochement with the topic came when one of the country's most famous mediums, Chuchad of Chantaburi, announced on national television his decision to renounce possession. The decision was accompanied by the confession of habitual dissimulation. Chuchad had, he claimed, faked his possessions and misled his clients for twenty-six years. He would reveal the techniques of his farce to the public in an extravagant press conference on 29 November.

In a narcissistic act of teletechnic encompassment that the doubt-ridden Quesalid could probably never have imagined, Chuchad not only theatricalized his newfound skepticism but also invited all mediums to join him in renouncing their dissimulating practice. Ultimately, he called for an end to mediumship itself. It was an extraordinary event, eliciting newspaper coverage and cocktail party gossip even among the rationalists of Bangkok's elite. Nonetheless, the television broadcast was merely a foretaste of an even more spectacular disclosure that Chuchad would stage in a press conference at which he would reveal everything: the tricks of his trade as well as the more scripturalist versions of *dhammic* truth to which his recent reflections had led him. After everything else, I could not resist this haunting invitation, directed as much at spectators as at mediums. So, I deferred the stock market and went to Chantaburi, southeast of Bangkok, in search of Chuchad and mediumship's end.

The events of Chuchad's revelation took place in the simulacral space of a new mediascape. By now, this context will be familiar to readers. It is a place in which there are only representations—although the meaning of representation has itself changed. And this applies to mediumship as well. Having been imagined as the sign of pastness and as a representation of tradition in its abstract mode, having been denuded of its magicality, mediumship has been reborn. It circulates along with its own images, less the double of a lost original than part of an endlessly proliferating series in which it seeks merely to be legible as an image of its displaced self. Now all mediums have photographs of themselves, and even television personalities have joined the ranks of the possessed.

It is in this newly mass-mediated space that Chuchad lured audiences with the promise of authenticity. This would be the violent authenticity of an exposure in which mediumship's representations would be renounced, save those in which the techniques of performance themselves would become the object of performative inscription.

## The Medium, the Monk, and the Message

On 29 November at 10:00 in the morning, I made my way to the shrine at which Chuchad normally held his possession performances. Outside the city, on a highway that has also become the site of a new condominium development, the medium has a semiopen shrine, made visible from the road by a sign from which hang the costumes of his possessing personae: loose satin bodysuits with patches sewn onto a background divided into two colors. To the extent that anyone recognizes these costumes as having historical reference, they are said to be of ancient Chinese style. Chuchad is himself *luuk chin* (Sino-Thai), and Chantaburi is a city whose Chinese affiliations predate the formation of the modern Thai state. He is recognized in Chantaburi as a medium of a particular (local) kind, and the body piercings and feats of endurance for which he has become famous over the past two and a half decades are not the rupture of a local tradition so much as the instantiation of its ideal form—albeit one more associated in popular imaginings with the touristified festivals of Phuket than the daily life of Chantaburi.

The occasion of Chuchad's renunciation was celebrated not at the shrine of everyday possession but in the enormous vacant lot adjacent to the strip mall and condominiums a few blocks away. Audience members were ferried to the alternative site on the backs of motorcycles driven by Chuchad's acolytes, each attired in flamboyant green and white satin. A small parade of trucks carrying posters and broadcasting systems like those used at election time had driven through the city early in the morning and even the previous day, announcing the event and inviting city residents to attend. With their raucous, crackling messages and their gaudily painted billboards, they competed with similar portable broadcasting systems that were inviting residents to attend an annual merit-making ceremony at the temple of the city pillar on the other side of town. Despite the competition, more than a thousand residents did arrive that morning and found places to sit on the hundreds of tin chairs that had been unfolded under tarpaulin canopies to make an enormous U-shaped grandstand. Embracing the chairs was a line of food vendors, with stalls selling the usual fare of sodas, distilled water, and dried cuttlefish. Behind them and at each corner, pacing across the green, were men in uniform. Several dozen military and city police, their eyes shielded by the visors of their tight helmets, stood ready along with the orange-clad personnel of the emergency services. Their agitation was dramatically countered by the laissez-faire demeanor of the audience members, who chatted idly about family and recent events and, much less frequently, about the man they had known as a medium. In the end, however, only the limp bodies of heat-stricken young women justified the mad scurrying of emergency workers as the heat rose to an unseasonal high and the event proceeded.

Chuchad's actual revelation would not begin for another two hours. In the meantime, audience members attended a broadcast tape-recorded sermon by the renowned monk of Wat Suan Kaew, Phra Phyom. Phra Phyom's extraordinary reputation among lay Buddhists as a learned and politically outspoken monk was to serve as the authority for Chuchad's extraordinary confession. A year previously, Phra Phyom had publicly attacked then–Prime Minister Chawalit Yongchaiyudh and his wife for patronizing a temple devoted to the cult of Rahu, a figure of violent power associated with a kind of Brahmanic ritualism not unrelated to Khun Daeng's, which, despite its recent popularity, has been implicitly excluded—along with mediumship—from legitimate religion since Rama IV's reign. Phra Phyom himself has an interesting place in the history of religious legitimacies, having come under serious suspicion during the 1980s when he introduced a new format of religious sermon into the radio programming of Thailand's national (military) radio station. That format was an emphatically dialogic one, which used vernacular forms and local dialects to disseminate rather conservative interpretations of the *dhamma* to rural audiences. It constituted a radical break from the format of Radio Thailand's Sunday Sermon, the didactic *Phradhamma Tesana*.

In the years immediately following the massacre of *hok tula* in 1976 and during a period of military retrenchment, the Sunday Sermon had been opened to nonconformist monks in addition to the high-ranked orthodox monks who had previously dominated the show. This in an effort to heal over the rift that had developed between those like Kithivuddho, who espoused the murder of communists, and those who joined the radical democratic students and agricultural laborers. Phra Phyom's interventions were considered too radical even in this context. Though limited to formal interventions, his sermons were censored on the grounds that their populism constituted a form of commodification to which Buddhism ought not be subject.[2] This despite the fact that their content remained deeply orthodox in their valorization of the foundational texts, and in their disavowal of both ontology and its ritualist inscriptions. The product of a fabulously technologized and mass-mediated encounter, the alliance between the populist conservative monk and the repentant medium rested on the latter's profession of epiphanic discovery, of a claim that he had received the *dhamma* while listening to Phra Phyom. In the end, however, the medium required the monk to ensure the transmission of his own antiontological, antiritualist discovery. Ironically, however, Chuchad delivered a message that openly contradicted Phra Phyom's on the stage of revelation. And the question of instrumentalization—of who was rendering whom the medium of his will—remains open to debate.

2. Ubonrat Siriyuvasak, "Radio in a Transitional Society: The Case of Thailand" (Ph.D. diss., University of Leicester, 1989), 71–72.

Stripped to its most elemental, Phra Phyom's message consisted in a denial of the persistence of spiritual entities in this world. Of the spirits whom mediums serve as mounts, he said: "They are dead. They have left this world. They cannot possess the bodies of human beings in this world when they have already moved on to others. The soul [*winyaan*] has no permanence."[3] Phra Phyom identified the spirits of northern Thailand's more famous mediums with particular care, and among these, Queen Camadevi was repeated more than any other. They were, indeed, exemplars of an unknowing belief and a false attribution.

For Phra Phyom, then, mediumship is fraudulent because there is nothing that can possess the body of the medium, merely the spectral illusion of something that has passed—irrevocably—from this plane of being. The medium who claims such a possession is therefore either deluded or, more threateningly, perpetrating a deception and confusing the minds of those common people who are in need of the real *dhamma*.

Chuchad, on the other hand, would later insist on the existence of spirits but remark on the inadequacy of the human body to facilitate their descent into this realm. The chasm that separates the materiality of the human form from the spirit that has passed into a realm of mitigated sensuousness is, for him, (now) untraversible. At best, the appearance of possession could express a desire on the part of the medium for the crossing of this space. At worst, it would be the dissimulation of the one who knows how much others share this desire. This insistence on the bodily inadequacy of the medium inevitably opens onto a discussion of the techniques of seeming prosthetization: the means by which the appearance of possession is conjured. Chuchad referred to these techniques as *tekhnikaan*, combining the English term with its Greek root, *tekhnē*, and the Thai term *kaan* for "action" or "operationalization." I will have more to say about technique, but for now we need only note that the opposition between Phra Phyom and Chuchad was one of the message versus the medium. Either there is nothing to transmit, or there is no means of transmission. Silence or white noise.

### Writing on the Tongue

The hours of waiting for Chuchad to mount the elevated stage that had been set up for his announcement were constantly interrupted by rumors of Phra Phyom's imminent arrival. The monk was coming. And then he was not com-

---

3. Phra Phyom omitted any philosophical discussion of the concept of "double-dependent origination" that would have actually insisted that it is not the self-same soul that transmigrates. But this was a popular address and not a formal sermon.

ing. He had sent his voice only. He would follow in body as well. We would hear a tape recording. We would receive a real sermon. Perhaps, someone remarked, we would hear a broadcast telephone conversation. At one point, it was even said that he had arrived in a Mercedes limousine. He had not.

Phra Phyom, in fact, had become not unlike the apparitions of deceased princes and Buddhist culture heroes whose descent into the bodies of mediums would normally be attended by clients seeking advice on love, health, and business. He was the embodiment of fame itself: a bastardized auratic presence that was always arriving, always imminent, but without specification. Chuchad paled as an object of conversation. As though anticipating this, the bus driver who had driven me to the event told me that he had never believed in Chuchad's performances, but that others did. The same combination of disavowal and attribution or even accusation circulated with generic regularity in the hours preceding the medium's performance, and only a few admitted to having been clients who took seriously the feats and the knowledges that the skeptics attributed to chicanery.

What drew these people to this performance? Why did they wait, so distractedly and with growing professions of boredom, for a man they claimed never to have believed? Was it simply to have their own skepticism confirmed? Were they seeking the ambivalent pleasure—not without violence—of having a secret unmasked? The possibility of a merely triumphalist pleasure was quickly dissolved when Chuchad did make his appearance, accompanied by two other mediums who had decided to join him in his confession. The crowd strained to see across the approximately thirty meters to the stage on which he ensconced himself upon a throne, flanked by the flags of the *sangha* and the nation. Their desire and agitation were assuaged only briefly, when the national anthem was broadcast and the many bodies of the spectators rose en masse with the soldiers.

None of the spectators were permitted to indulge their desire for proximity. Only licensed journalists, photographers, and camerapeople of the television news media were permitted the immediate view that everyone else had come for. Yet, Chuchad's acolytes took great pains to ensure a line of vision between the medium and his audience, forcing the photographers to sit when their heads rose to intrude on the scene. The medium himself narrated each moment of the unfolding events with a handheld microphone. For the most part, this worked to placate the desire for actual nearness by substituting virtual proximity, but it also generated moments of crisis. When static made of the space between us a chasm of unintelligibility and when feedback spiked the air with the trace of that seemingly impossible fact—namely, that broadcasting and recording devices are, essentially, the same thing—the promise of revelation was threatened by the emergence of opacity.[4] This opacity was not simply the failure of meaning. It was, rather, the sign of a transformation, the transformation of mass mediatization itself, in which authorship—whose emergence, we saw in a discussion of Phayaphrom, is traceable in Thailand only to the nineteenth century—has been displaced by a logic in which representation and inscription have been reduced to the "tracking of 'traces without a subject.' "

Modern mediumship has essentially come to occupy the place of the automatic. As Phayaphrom's possession of Naang Khao and the discussions of photography in recent history made clear, mediums now recognize themselves in technologies of mass mediatization. The consequences of that recognition have been twofold and contradictory. Either mediums embrace technology, and mediumship proliferates in a cycle wherein mediums and the media provide each other with metaphors. Or mediums will seek to escape the relationship altogether, in forms of ecstatic nonrepresentation or absolute renunciation. The first possibility is testified to in the language within which mediums now describe their practice: sacred sites are like batteries; the threads (*sajsin*) within which ritual space is marked off and that conduct spiritual energy are compared to telephone wires; mediums are said to be like photographic negatives; and the linkages between marked locations in the landscape are described in the idiom of railway tracks. The latter possibility is, of course, manifest both in Khun Daeng's and in Chuchad's performances. Let us now consider this last, most predictable, and yet surprising gesture of transcendence.

Chuchad began his performance, microphone next to his chin, by cutting off his tongue. Opening his mouth for the cameras to see, he pinched his tongue between his fingers and drew a long rapier across it. The tongue fell into an opaque cup held beneath his chin for the purposes, blood leaking from his lips. Another medium took the microphone and continued to speak, describing the tongue that now lay in the cup, while Chuchad stood, speechless, before his assembled audience. In perpetrating such a displacement, it appeared that Chuchad had chosen, then and there, to disavow disavowal, to repudiate his repudiation. He had rendered himself voiceless, and the only sounds of which he was capable were those of the body as machine: exhalations and inhalations. These we heard over the microphone. And as this occurred, the crowd gasped and then repeated to themselves, in a manner that confused awe and automatism, the second medium's narration: "He's cut off his tongue!"

---

4. The identity of recording with playback devices is a "discovery" of information science, particularly as formulated by Hans Magnus Enzensberger. For a discussion of this fact and its relationship to new discourse networks, see Friedrich Kittler, *Discourse Networks 1800/1900*, trans. Michael Metteer and Chris Cullens (Stanford: Stanford University Press, 1990), 316.

In fact, Chuchad did repudiate his repudiation, but only through a second gesture in which he sealed that severed organ back into its original place. The tongue was taken from the cup and placed on a piece of clean white paper, into whose fibers the blood quickly spread. For a moment it appeared as though the tongue was writing there, producing a blunt, indecipherable hieroglyph. But without reading, Chuchad took the paper and held it to his mouth, covering his face and then pressing the tongue back into its original place. Thus was his capacity to speak restored. The medium pulled the paper away, folded it carefully, and then began speaking with only a little blood reddening his lips.

The restoration of Chuchad's tongue was the enabling moment, the gesture that made possible his continued confession and thus his denunciation of possession performance. The removal of the tongue had effectively interrupted the voice, the instrument through which both language and the presence of spirits articulate themselves, and to this extent, the excising of the tongue was already the performative repudiation of mediumship. The healing back of the tongue was thus the ironic subversion of the confession it was supposed to facilitate. Yet, Chuchad could not, in fact, afford to terminate his role as interlocutor until after the confession, and so the unmasking had itself to be masked, at least temporarily. Hence, both the healing of the tongue *and* the cutting itself had to be shown to be simulated. With his tongue restored, Chuchad explained that he had substituted a pig's tongue for his own, and kept it in the cup, which he had merely spat upon. The blood, a combination of dyed water and sugar, had also been imbibed from the cup. It was all a matter of technique (*tekhnikaan*), he said: an illusion.

Like all fables, this one staged risk in the form of a bad example.[5] The object of transmission here is the truth that has been produced through a reflexive encounter with and in the medium's memory of his childhood attraction to magic and its dissimulations. Here, voice would seem to be the vehicle of a simple exteriorization, and much of mediumship would seem to be similarly organized. Yet, as the increasing frequency of untranslatable utterances and even glossolalia in contemporary spirit possession performances makes clear, mediumship is increasingly taken up by the possibility that the truth of the spirits in the mass-mediatized world is not a referential one and certainly not a universal one, but rather, a question of the difference between noise and information. This is the flip-side of Khun Daeng's libertine excess: not the rupture of representation but the displacement of that dialectic by a completely new one

5. This notion of fable comes from Tom Keenan, *Fables of Responsibility: Aberrations and Predicaments in Ethics and Politics* (Stanford: Stanford University Press, 1997).

that has been utterly severed from the demand or the compulsion to provide a mirror of the world.

Historically, what has made mediums what they are is their capacity merely to *transmit* the secrets of a reality that is thought to be populated by spirits. As we have seen mediums deny memory of their experience and their utterances during possession and repress themselves as agents of mediumship's discourse in every manner. Nonetheless, in the contemporary moment, there is no longer any guarantee of the truth of the message, no shared commitment to the real as the domain of spirits. In an era of visual hegemony, only what can be seen can be true. Indeed, it is this lack of guarantee that Chuchad seems to disavow as much as anything else. It is the possibility that mediumship has lost its identity with its message that leads him to claim that he has discovered the real truth of *dhamma*, one that is incompatible with mediumship.

In this context, it is important to know that *dhamma*, or *tham* as it is termed in Thai, denotes both law and nature, and refers to a domain of natural signification where a pure identity between signifier and signified is thought to obtain. The relationship is narrativized in the cosmological accounts of Yama, the righteous adjudicator who is described in the *Traiphum Phra Ruang* as presiding over the realm of auxiliary hells. Yama receives almost everyone immediately after death and asks, "What merit or evil deeds have you done? Quickly now, think back and speak the truth!" The deeds have been recorded by the angels or *thewada*. Those of meritorious beings have been written on luminous jewel-encrusted gold tablets, and those of evil beings have been inscribed on the hide of a dog. Under the scrutiny of Yama, meritorious beings are "miraculously" equipped with memory and find themselves able to speak of all their good deeds. But those whose evil deeds outweigh their good find themselves in an amnesiac hell, unable to recall anything or to speak at all. The *thewada* read the list of bad deeds from the dog hide, itself vulnerable to rot and putrefaction, and the shamed evildoer is left only to confess. Confession for the evildoer in this regard is really a mode of accession, of conformity to the message, and therefore resembles a mediumship whose instrumentality and apparent immediacy are summoned only in the aftermath of a rupture and a failure of spirits to proceed in the cycle of rebirth.[6]

6. Frank E. Reynolds and Mani B. Reynolds, trans. and eds., *Three Worlds According to King Ruang: A Thai Buddhist Cosmology* (Berkeley: University of California Press, 1982), 69–72. Mediums and their clients explain the necessity for a return on the part of the spirits as a function of their incomplete *kammic* progress. As princes and other founders of law (in societies in which moral law reigns), people say, these individuals have had to dip their hands in blood; in those cases where the stain is deep enough, spirits must continue to descend to earth to acquire merit to complete their

To be sure, few contemporary people treat the *Traiphum Phra Ruang* as anything but quaint tradition, and certainly the Buddhism to which Phra Phyom adheres has formally rejected the cosmology as a symptom of superstition and a relic of bygone times. But as recently as 1913, the image of Yama formed the centerpiece of the seal of the Thai judiciary and it still circulates widely in aesthetic and monumental productions, much as the blindfolded figure of Justice does in Euro-American contexts.[7] But ubiquity alone is inadequate to demonstrate relevance. It is because the logic of representation underlying the *Traiphum* recurs in mediumship—despite its repression by hegemonic Buddhism—that I invoke the chapter on "The Realm of Hell Beings" here.

The story of Yama's adjudication imagines a righteous speech marked by the identity between deed and word and figures evil as a gap between them—opened by forgetfulness in the evildoer's mind and making the sinner's speech one of deferral. To the extent that speech is not the mere instrument of truth, it is both a symptom and a cause of sin. To the extent that it corresponds to the actuality inscribed in gold—icon of purity and permanence, in which the sign of value is its substance—speech is aligned with the law. But where the law rules, there is no difference between object and sign, nor between speech and voice. This, then, explains the fact that the child who is born mute will learn "Pali, which is the language of truth,"[8] which is to say the language that is not and cannot be spoken. Personified in the speechless child, a perfect unity binds the lawful world. For those who are its subject, writing serves to legitimate the utterance of the meritorious being and to supplement the failed speech of the sinner.

But the opposition between truth's silent ideality and sin's "overnaming," to use Walter Benjamin's term,[9] is different from that which counterposes noise and information in the age of mass media. In the latter instance, something else enters. Inscription can only inscribe its own facticity. The message of mediumship becomes mediumship itself. Chuchad's performance was stretched taut between these two understandings of mediumship's representational function: that in which a referential truth could be transmitted, and that in which the

---

journey through the moral/cosmological universe. Interestingly enough, no one seems to explain the return in the language of the boddhisatta, the one who surrenders progress for others—even in cases where the returning spirit is a Thai Buddhist national hero like King Ramkhamhaeng.

7. David M. Engel, *Code and Custom in a Thai Provincial Town: The Interaction of Formal and Informal Systems of Justice* (Tucson: University of Arizona Press, 1978), 4.

8. Reynolds and Reynolds, *Three Worlds*, 122.

9. Walter Benjamin, "On Language as Such, and on the Language of Man" (1916), in *One-Way Street*, trans. Edmund Jephcott and Kingsley Shorter (London: Verso, 1979), 122.

mere technique of its transmission could be registered again and again. To restore the former, he had to make the latter visible. Chuchad occupies a moment in which "writing" can only be glyphic and representation has only itself for object. In other words, he inhabits the era of technique's fetishization, what Heidegger would have simply called the era of technology.[10]

Following the tongue cutting, Chuchad moved from station to station in what appeared to be an obstacle course of possession performance tricks. He climbed a ladder of swords and then showed the crowd how he distributed his weight across the dull blades. He walked across a bed of broken glass and explained that it had been made of bottles that were first frozen, then cracked, then spread in a box of sand, where they shifted and withstood the pressure of feet. He swung axes over his shoulder in a manner that only appeared to bring the full force of the blades onto his back. And he placed his hands in simmering oil while explaining the herbal ingredients that made the oil boil at a very low temperature. The middle point of the obstacle course, an unexpectedly literal pièce de résistance, consisted in fire walking across a bed of coals that were lit at the beginning of the confessional theater. Here, Chuchad encountered the only test of his performance. For the coal bed had been surrounded with a barrier made of rolled dried grasses. Already brittle, it had lain in the sun for the previous two days, and when a sudden wind arose, it was ignited by floating cinders. Flames leapt to the stubble of lawn, with smoke sending the camera crews and journalists running. A fire truck, standing near by, was brought in to control the blaze, but in the course of the fire, grasses had blown onto the coals. The steam itself was extremely hot and the coals were reheated to unusual temperatures. Chuchad walked across them with seeming and almost miraculous immunity, but the two mediums accompanying him both suffered minor burns.

Almost in spite of himself, Chuchad became the paragon of technical virtuosity. Indeed, at the point of the fire walking his technology of deceit was as impressive as any "real magic." The attribution of skill by audience members was cast in superlatives: "*Kaeng maak!*" (He's very clever!). Chuchad was so masterful, in fact, that his technique could almost be mistaken for the workings of spirits. This was science in its most magnificently theatrical form, and the medium had become its adept. The occult had returned in the guise of transparency. In this regard, Chuchad was reenacting his own life story. As a ten-year-old boy, he had seen a medium perform and had been awed. Innately curious, he immediately set out to discover the principles that underlay the

10. Martin Heidegger, *The Question Concerning Technology and Other Essays* (1936), trans. William Lovitt (New York: Harper & Row, 1977).

tricks, and to his own amazement, he quickly discovered them. Soon he was a master at their performance. Indeed, he was so impressive as a young magician that people began to attribute to him the power of spirits. Shortly thereafter, he established himself as a medium. One can almost believe that he had read Lévi-Strauss's account of Quesalid in "The Sorcerer and his Magic."[11]

Even after his public confession, some of Chuchad's own clients insisted that the claim to fakery was unconvincing, that he had known things about them that would have been impossible without some extrasensory powers. They seemed dismayed by the disavowal, even disappointed. For them, no technical excellence was adequate substitution for a relationship with spirits. But for most audience members, it was not only an adequate substitution, it was its own object of fascination. Men in particular spoke animatedly about how to perform the tricks, identifying with the young boy who had harbored such a natural propensity for chemistry, physics, and engineering. And it was as such a genius of science that Chuchad presented himself, remarking each trick as an example not of magic but of science (*pen witthayasaat maj chaj sayasaat*). When he called on the audience to exercise their individual powers of objectivity (*ruupatham*), he was invoking a nationalized discourse of modernity whose oppositional terms are those of science versus magic, rationality versus supernatural belief, the visible versus the invisible. Indeed, the entire event was redolent of the rhetoric of another moment, more than a century earlier, that has since been emblematized in the image of the rationalist king, Rama IV, arguing with his Christian interlocutors for the superior and more rigorous rationality of Theravada Buddhism. It was this modernist reform Buddhism that Phra Phyom had attempted to reinvigorate and popularize in his radically dialogic sermons.

Nonetheless, science could not explain why, as the afternoon proceeded, fascination was replaced by agitated disinterest. By the midpoint of the event, the audience was visibly bored, the people shifting on their tin seats and mopping their sweating brows. Many began to leave or to talk about other matters and to wonder aloud when it would all be over. "Naa bya," they said. "It's boring." In the violently climactic last moments of his revelation, when Chuchad threaded his cheek with the same rapier that had cut off his pig's tongue, and which he could explain (away) only as the result of bodily training, the audience was unable to summon itself to the task of observation. As though such observation had indeed become a labor, a form of attention no longer propelled by desire. Chuchad had exhausted his audience, and they glanced

11. Claude Lévi-Strauss, "The Sorcerer and his Magic," in *Structural Anthropology*, trans. John Russell (New York: Doubleday, 1967), 161–80.

only distractedly toward the stage as he began his verbal summary of a life lived duplicitously. Before he completed his sermon, the space had been almost entirely abandoned; all that was left to signify the having-been-there of the audience was the tangle of discarded plastic water bottles and crumpled photocopies of the statements his assistants had distributed during the course of the event.

It is helpful, I think, to recall here Friedrich Kittler's reading of the discourse network that overtook Europe in 1900 and found itself articulated in the diverse writings of Freud, Simmel, and Rilke. That network was one in which "writing [became], rather than miniatures of meaning, an exhaustion that endlessly refused to end."[12] Kittler notes that, in this context, writing "is nothing beyond its materiality. The peculiar people who practice this act simply replace writing machines." And all that can be promised them is the "mystical union of writing and delirium." Either that or death, and death itself is not far from the face dissembled by boredom, decomposed in the stare that looks stupidly and sees nothing.

Earlier, I spoke about the relationship between mediumship and writing and noted the history of mediumship's transformation alongside a gradual shift away from a belief in the actual magicality of script, to the representational capacity of inscription, to a deployment of writing in the mode of mathematics, as bureaucratic lists. I noted also that, when mediumship is overtaken by representation, it generates the possibility of both renewal and transcendence. Saeng Suong's possessions exemplified the moment of representation and the return of magic as the represented. Khun Daeng enacted the second possibility, the surpassing of representation. Chuchad's no longer scandalous renunciation is the next step in the process. That step occurs in a moment marked by the naturalization of technologies of mass mediatization in the language and performance of possession and by the discourses of lost tradition within which mediumship is now inscribed. Of course, when mediumship can no longer lay claim to truth, there is no choice but to either disavow truth or seek it elsewhere. And Chuchad chose the latter.

### Repetitions Undisclosed

What about this latter, this putative truth to which Chuchad and Phra Phyom both directed us? Where does a medium go after having repudiated mediumship? What kind of mediation is not simply the inscription of its technique, but a transmission of meaning? I went back to my hotel, where the gem sellers were

12. Kittler, *Discourse Networks*, 326.

sitting around coffee cups and sacks of uncut rubies, to ask this question. Looking across the street as the sun went down and the neon turned the sky ghoulish, I watched the prostitutes buying food from the vendors before returning to the clubs, where they could expect a couple of dollars for their labors. The hotel was extravagant by Chantaburi standards, being five stories high. But dollars were precious, the baht having slipped from 25 to 35 to 42, and so the hotel was affordable. I retreated into the newspaper, to read stories of that day's economic news and to hear what new measures had been instituted by the government to meet the stringent requirements of the IMF loan package.

It is more than incidental that the baht had been floated the previous month in an effort to have it return to a more adequate, a more natural representation of its worth, which is to say of the nation's reserves. As though money could ever be made to signify naturally! But then, Thailand seemed gripped by the fantasy of a return to meaning, to be obsessed by the possibility that the madness of its own economic excess could somehow be undone or at least overcome. The newspapers were full of stories about fiscal planning and market stabilization. And the transition from artificial stability to truer meaning seemed everywhere to incite terror. Indeed, when the prime minister fainted dramatically at a public event, he described his ordeal as one in which he "floated like the baht."

The means for mitigating this awful uncertainty took the form of a stabilization strategy that, on some levels, can be reduced to a single demand, namely, "disclosure." If banks and lending institutions would reveal the true nature of their debt, it has been repeatedly stated, then hopelessly overextended institutions could be closed, written off, and their assets centralized to permit the consolidation of national value and the restoration of the baht, as well as the nation's renown. More than sixty of Thailand's lending institutions were closed within six months of the IMF plan on the basis of this strategy. Foreclosures, downsizing, unemployment, and reruralization have become its symptoms. The baht has stabilized, though inflation has not, and unemployment continues to rise. In the midst of all this, the most dramatic growth sector of the economy has been that of "direct marketing" or multi-level marketing.[13]

Direct marketing is, in some senses, the economic counterpart of medium-

13. There have been a number of legal battles over the status of Amway concerning whether it constitutes a full pyramid scheme or not. The significance of this status is important, as such schemes are usually illegal (though national and state standards differ). The loop by which Amway escapes this representation is that in which sellers get a refund for the commodities they have bought in advance of distribution but failed to sell. When distributors have to buy their products before selling and when they, rather than the corporation, are held liable for the cost of those products, the company is eligible for prosecution under most international statutes.

ship, the mode of retailing in which the function of distribution and resale is masked in the rhetoric of directness. Directness itself is nothing but the withdrawal of an infrastructure of mediation into the person of the distributor, the occulting of technique in the very moment of display.

The end of this story can perhaps already be guessed, but it is worth narrating nonetheless. Leaving the boredom of my grotesquely functional room, I went across town to the suburban house of Chuchad's cousin, whose niece happened to work at the hotel. There, I met a woman, another relation of Chuchad's, who had just returned from Chicago, where she had been to an Amway conference. Chuchad has abandoned mediumship to be an Amway distributor. Or at least he has followed his career as a medium with a career as one of Amway's instruments. His assistants have, by and large, also become distributors and now constitute the base of his newly emergent power in the world of multilevel marketing. He has established telephone operators in three cities to field calls from the clients of his former profession, and he uses the occasion of their contact—for advice and counsel—to recruit new consumers and to convert an older form of repressed mediation into a new one. Like magic. And like all magic, Chuchad's metamorphosis entailed a repetition.

Phra Phyom had been accused of sinful affiliation with commodification when he introduced direct sermons on the radio. Following his censorship, he began to record his sermons and to sell them on cassette tape because he no longer had access to the web of radio's audiences. Thus did the accusation become a prophesy and force him to be what he already was. So too, Chuchad's abandonment of mediumship was accompanied by an overt entry into the market economy, one in which he became what he already was: a middleman disavowing the mediations that he performed in order to produce the illusion of value, or meaning, or truth.

Mediumship works only in the repression of its own operations, of course. These operations are increasingly read as the limit and totality of its truth, and so, with a combination of nostalgia and contempt for belief, Chuchad risks boredom to claim what the economists promise: that the market can substitute for magic, that the media can be themselves, that the very nature of money, its abstractions and its generality, can compensate for the differences it effaces. Not the least of the disappearances in this process are those of capital itself. Amway Japan Ltd. and Amway Asia Pacific Ltd. were estimated to have assets of over U.S. $7 billion in 1996.[14] Growth has been fabulous during the past two years, slowing in many nations as a result of the fiscal crisis in 1997 but remaining

14. James W. Robinson, *Empire of Freedom: The Amway Story and What It Means to You* (Rocklin, CA: Prima Publishing, 1997), 129.

strong in Thailand, where it achieved rates of more than 8 percent despite currency instability in the final quarter of that year.

The attraction of Asia for companies like Amway lies in the putative wealth of (at least some of) its citizens, its populousness, and the belief of North Americans that Asian business is "conducted on the strength of personal, family, and ancestral relations."[15] Precisely because it does not operate as an open economy, it is said it offers the possibility for companies like Amway to establish competitive advantages by tapping into occult networks in which conservative values can achieve the appearance of legitimacy. The notion that Asian economies are dominated not only by particular families but by the logic of family—which is to say by exclusive and unassailable ties among small communities of people— is, of course, the ideological foundation of much self-Orientalizing discourse in the Asian and ASEAN business community. Indeed, the foreign minister of Thailand, Prachuab Chaiyasan, addressed members of an Asia Society audience in October 1997, he mobilized precisely this rhetoric of Asian family values in his rejection of foreign demands for the total rationalization of local economies and the application of sanctions against such states as Myanmar and Laos, which had, at that point, resisted pressures to engage in market liberalization. The minister has been bypassed by now, and one could have prophesied as much given the degree to which he was prepared to admit the secret of new capital, namely, that it operates on the basis of invisible power and affinities, as the return of an occult whose abolition had been the project but also the ironic effect of reform.

In its slippage between the individual families so idealized in the anachronistic imaginary of transnational capitalism and the racialized family of Asian nations, Prachuab's address revealed the metaphorical ruse of kinship's discourse and new capitalism's rhetoric. The language of small business became that of state protectionism for national interests. Amway plays on this belief to extraordinary effect, the vast majority of its capital returning to the bizarre company town from which this behemoth of transnational capital is operated by two Christian men who still indulge in neocolonial fantasy that they conceal in the dream of immediacy. Holding tightly to a theologically informed market liberalism, they pursue a noiseless world where feedback is impossible. And their recruits are eager mediums of this message.

Just as Chuchad made himself a magician all over again by professing to display his technique, so the confessional disclosures of new capital, and the rhetoric of transparency with which they cloak themselves, effect the secreting of a system premised on secrecy. Siegfried Kracauer knew this well when he

15. Ibid., 120.

recalled Edgar Allan Poe's story of the purloined letter to explicate the process by which "the salaried masses" are made the media of a system in which they are denied knowledge and distracted with its entertaining simulacra.[16] It was to this realization that Chuchad returned me. And so I returned to the market, after a detour through mediumship's enthralling dramaturgy of disclosure. The indirectness of the route was constantly and ironically haunted by the fact that it led through a fantasy of restored transparency. But then, what else is transparency in the massified world but a mediation so total that it has become invisible? It is this fact, the fact of total mediation, that refuses the dream of meaning's unfolding and leaves all transmissions vulnerable to the resistant omnipresence of white noise.

The story does not end, of course, at least not here. There is no single line of historical progression here, no final resolution to the negative dialectics of history. Although Chuchad's turn to transparency, and his disavowal of mediumship (but also mediation in general) seems finally to cast the many forms of possession that Naang Khao, Saeng Suang, and Khun Daeng practice under a single rubric—thereby achieving that conceptual unity forbidden by actuality— he is himself an instrument of changes whose future are as yet opaque. Even the substitution of information's duality for representation and its transgression is unevenly established in Thailand. It will likely be haunted, not only by the sounds of technology's own transmissions, but by the resurfacing of older forms, other longings, and the almost infinitely renewable drive for origins. Although time and the principle of temporization mean that a real return is impossible, Chuchad calls for the restoration of an older, purer form of Buddhism. He believes in that possibility. And in this he is joined by many Thai people, from both the north and the south of the country. Ironically, however, he is the symptom of an unconscious recognition that such returns to the place of origins are impossible, for he is actually advocating a return to the future, the moment of modernity's eruption as the future in the present, and the simultaneous appearance of the past as an object to be trafficked in the arcades of memory's commodification. That was Phayaphrom's world. Now, Thailand is rent not only by regional, ethnic and linguistic difference, but by a class-based difference onto which is mapped the difference between information and representation. And as long as this is the case, the fantasy of being in a place of origins will return again and again, attempting to stave off the growing noise of information's self-interruption. In this context, mediumship seems doomed to inhabit this one last desire: to be bathed in the luminosity of spiritual presence,

16. Siegfried Kracauer, *The Salaried Masses: Duty and Distraction in Weimar Germany* (1930), trans. Quintin Hoare (London: Verso, 1998).

to be free of mediation, to be on the other side of an economy in which the living and the dead are irrevocably separated by a distance that no telephone line can traverse. To be on call, of course, is to be in the world as an ethical being. This book has thus been the story not only of a practice and its technologization, but of ethics and politics, of the miraculous possibility of ethics and politics, in a place where individuals must respond to the calls that come to them from within the dark nights of rationality's unreason.

# BIBLIOGRAPHY

Adis Israngkura and Luechai Chulasai. *Profile of Northern Thailand*. Chiang Mai: The Manager Company, Siam Studies, and Chiang Mai University, 1990.

Adorno, Theodor W. *Aesthetic Theory*. Gretel Adorno and Rolf Tiedemann, eds.; trans. Robert Hullot-Kentor. Minneapolis: University of Minnesota Press, 1997.

———. *Negative Dialectics*. 1966. Trans. E. B. Ashton. New York: Continuum, 1994.

Akin Rabibhadana. *The Organization of Thai Society in the Early Bangkok Period, 1782–1873*. Ithaca, NY: Cornell University, Southeast Asia Program, 1969.

Akira Suehiro. *Capital Accumulation in Thailand 1855–1985*. Tokyo: Centre for Southeast Asian Cultural Studies, 1989.

Anake Nawigamune. *Phaab kao lao tamnaan* [Old pictures and the stories they tell]. Bangkok: Matichon, 1997.

———. *Thaaj ruub müang thai samaj raek* [Early photography in Thailand]. Bangkok: Saengdaed, 1987.

Anan Ganjanapan. "The Idiom of *Phii Ka*': Peasant Conception of Class Differentiation in Northern Thailand." *Mankind* 14, no. 4 (1984): 325–29.

———. "The Partial Commercialization of Rice Production in Northern Thailand (1900–1981)." Ph.D. diss., Cornell University, 1984.

Anderson, Benedict. *Imagined Communities: Reflections on the Origin and Spread of Nationalism*. London: Verso, 1983.

———. "Murder and Progress in Modern Siam." *New Left Review* 181 (1990): 33–48.

———. "Notes on the Changing Implications of Political Killings in Thailand." In *Proceedings of the International Conference on Thai Studies*, compiled by Ann Buller. Canberra: Australian National University, 1987, 255–62.

———. *The Specter of Comparisons: Nationalism, Southeast Asia, and the World*. New York: Verso, 1998.

———. "Withdrawal Symptoms: Social and Cultural Aspects of the October 6 Coup." *Bulletin of Concerned Asian Scholars* 9, no. 3 (1977): 13–30.

Anuman Rajadhon, Phya. "The Khwan and Its Ceremonies." *Journal of the Siam Society* 50, no. 2 (1962): 11–64.

———. *Looking Back: Book One*. Bangkok: Translation Center, Chulalongkorn University Press, 1992.

——. "Me Posop, the Rice Mother." In *Popular Buddhism and Other Essays on Thai Studies.* Bangkok: Thai Inter-Religious Commission for Development and Sathirakoses Nagapradipa Foundation, 1986, 135–42.

——. "The Phii." In *Popular Buddhism and Other Essays on Thai Studies,* 99–124.

Aroonrat Wichienkaeo. *Lanna syksaa* [Lanna studies]. Chiang Mai: Teacher's College, 1982.

Asad, Talal. "The Concept of Cultural Translation in British Social Anthropology." 1986. In *Genealogies of Religion: Discipline and Reasons of Power in Christianity and Islam.* Baltimore: Johns Hopkins University Press, 1993, 171–99.

Asian Development Bank. *Changes in the Export Patterns of Asian and Pacific Developing Countries: An Empirical Overview.* Manila: Asian Development Bank, 1986.

Austin, J. L. *How to Do Things with Words,* 2d ed. Ed J. O. Urmson and Marina Sbisa. Cambridge, MA: Harvard University Press, 1975.

Bachelard, Gaston. *The Poetics of Space.* Trans. Maria Jolas. Boston: Beacon, 1964.

Barmé, Scot. *Luang Wichit Wathakan and the Creation of a Thai Identity.* Singapore: Institute of Southeast Asian Studies, 1993.

Barthes, Roland. *Camera Lucida.* Trans. Richard Howard. New York: Hill and Wang, 1981.

——. *Mythologies.* Trans. Annette Lavers. New York: Hill and Wang, 1986.

Basham, Richard. " 'False Consciousness' and the Problem of Merit and Power in Thailand." *Mankind* 19, no. 2 (1989): 125–37.

Bataille, Georges. *The Accursed Share: An Essay on General Economy, Vol. 1, Consumption.* 1967. Trans. Robert Hurley. New York: Zone Books, 1991.

——. *Visions of Excess: Selected Writings, 1927–1939.* Trans. Allan Stoeckl, Carl Lovett, and Donald Leslie Jr. Manchester: Manchester University Press, 1985.

Batson, Benjamin. *The End of Absolute Monarchy in Siam.* Singapore: Oxford University Press and Asian Studies Association of Australia, 1984.

Baudrillard, Jean. *The Mirror of Production,* Trans. Mark Poster. St. Louis: Telos, 1975.

Bell, Peter. "Gender and Development in Thailand." In *Gender and Development in Southeast Asia,* ed. Penny van Esterik and John van Esterik. Montreal: Canadian Asian Studies Association, 1992, 61–82.

Benjamin, Walter. "Berlin Chronicle." 1932. In *One-Way Street.* Trans. Edmund Jephcott and Kingsley Shorter. London: Verso, 1979, 293–346.

——. "Moscow." 1928. In *One-Way Street,* 177–208.

——. "On Language as Such, and on the Language of Man." 1916. In *One-Way Street,* 107–23.

——. "On the Mimetic Faculty." In *Reflections,* ed. Peter Demetz, trans. Edmund Jephcott. New York: Harcourt Brace Jovanovitch, 1978, 333–36.

——. "The Task of the Translator." 1923. In *Illuminations.* Trans. Harry Zohn, ed. Hannah Arendt. London: Fontana, 1973, 70–82.

——. "Theses on the Philosophy of History." 1950. In *Illuminations,* 253–64.

——. "The Work of Art in the Age of Mechanical Reproduction." 1936. In *Illuminations,* 211–44.

Bhabha, Homi. "The Commitment to Theory." *New Formations* 5 (1988): 5–24.

——. "The Other Question." *Screen* 24, no. 6 (1983): 24–36.

Bilmes, Jack. "On the Believability of Mediums." *Journal of the Siam Society* 83, nos. 1–2 (1995).

Blanchot, Maurice. *The Writing of the Disaster.* Trans. Ann Smock. Lincoln: University of Nebraska Press, 1986.

Block, M., and J. Parry. "Introduction: Money and the Morality of Exchange." In *Money and the Morality of Exchange*. Cambridge: Cambridge University Press, 1989, 1–32.

Bock, Carl. *Temples and Elephants*. 1885. Bangkok: White Orchid, 1985.

Bourdieu, Pierre. *Distinction: A Social Critique of the Judgment of Taste*. Trans. Richard Nice. Cambridge, MA: Harvard University Press, 1984.

———. *Outline of a Theory of Practice*. 1972. Trans. Richard Nice. Cambridge: Cambridge University Press, 1977.

Bowie, Katherine. "Peasant Perspectives on the Political Economy of the Northern Thai Kingdom of Chiang Mai in the Nineteenth Century: Implications for the Understanding of Peasant Political Expression." Ph.D. diss., University of Chicago, 1988.

———. *Rituals of National Loyalty: An Anthropology of the State and the Village Scout Movement in Thailand*. New York: Columbia University Press, 1997.

Brailey, Nigel. "The Origin of the Siamese Forward Movement in Western Laos." Ph.D. diss., University of London, 1968.

Brecht, Bertolt. "Alienation Effects in Chinese Acting." In *Brecht on Theater: Development of an Aesthetic*, ed. and trans. John Willett. New York: Hill and Wang, 1964, 100–103.

Brown, J. Marvin. *From Ancient Thai to Modern Dialectics*. Bangkok: Social Science Association of Thailand, 1965.

Brun, Viggo. *Traditional Herbal Medicine in Northern Thailand*. Berkeley: University of California Press, 1987.

Buck-Morss, Susan. *The Dialectics of Seeing: Walter Benjamin and the Arcades Project*. Cambridge, MA: MIT Press, 1989.

———. "The Dream World of Mass Culture: Walter Benjamin's Theory of Modernity and the Dialectics of Seeing." In *Modernity and the Hegemony of Vision*, ed. David Michael Levin. Berkeley: University of California Press, 1993, 309–38.

Bunrod Kaeokanha. "Kaan kep suaj naj samaj rattanakosin, AD 1782–1868" [Tribute in the Rattanakosin period, 1782–1868]. M.A. thesis, Chulalongkorn University, 1975.

Burr, Angela M. R. "Merit-Making and Ritual Reciprocity: Tambiah's Theory Examined." *Journal of the Siam Society* 66, no. 1 (1978): 102–8.

Butler, Judith. *Bodies That Matter: On the Discursive Limits of "Sex."* New York: Routledge, 1993.

———. *Gender Trouble: Feminism and the Subversion of Identity*. New York: Routledge, 1990.

Campbell, Jill. *Natural Masques*. Stanford: Stanford University Press, 1995.

Canetti, Elias. *Crowds and Power*. 1960. Trans. Carol Stewart. New York: Noonday, 1996.

Caruth, Cathy. *Unclaimed Experience: Trauma, Narrative, and History*. Baltimore: Johns Hopkins University Press, 1996.

Certeau, Michel de. *The Practice of Everyday Life*. Trans. Steven F. Rendall. Berkeley: University of California Press, 1984.

———. "Railway Navigation and Incarceration." In *The Practice of Everyday Life*. Trans. Steven Rendall. Berkeley: University of California Press, 1984, 111–114.

———. "Walking in the City." In *The Practice of Everyday Life*, 91–110.

Chai-Anan Samudavanija. "State-Identity Creation, State-Building and Civil Society, 1939–1989." In *National Identity and Its Defenders: Thailand, 1939–89*, ed. Craig J. Reynolds. Chiang Mai: Silkworm, 1991, 59–86.

———. *The Thai Young Turks.* Singapore: Institute of Southeast Asian Studies, 1982.

Chamlong Srimuang. *Chiwit Chamlong* [The life of Chamlong]. Bangkok: HJKAV Publishing, 1990.

Chatrayaphaa Sawatdiphon. "Laksana Wannakam Khao So" [Attributes of Khao So literature]. *Lannathai Khadii* [Lannathai research] (1978): 156–74.

Chatsumarn Kabilsingh. *Thai Women in Buddhism.* Berkeley: Parallax, 1991.

Chatthip Nartsupha, "The Ideology of the 'Holy Men' Revolts in North East Thailand." In *History and Peasant Consciousness,* eds. Andrew Turton and Shigeharu Tanabe. Senri Ethnological Studies 13. Osaka: National Museum of Ethnology, 1984, 111–34.

Chatthip Nartsupha, Suthy Prasartset, and Montri Chenvidyakan, eds. *The Political Economy of Siam, 1910–1932.* Bangkok: Social Science Association of Thailand, 1978.

Chayan Vaddhanaputi. "Cultural and Ideological Reproduction in Rural Northern Thailand." Ph.D. diss., Stanford University, 1984.

Chokechai Sutthawet. "Phuttathaat kap kaan patiruub khwaam mii haet mii phon khong khon Thai" [Buddhadasa and the rationalization of the Thai people]. *Sutsapdaa* 2, no. 65 (1993): 34–35.

Chusit Chuchat. *Lokathaat chao lanna Syksaa Caak Khao Phayaphrom* [Lanna worldview based on the study of Phayaphrom's poetry]. Chiang Mai: Chiang Mai Teacher's College, n.d.

Clifford, James. *The Predicament of Culture.* Cambridge, MA: Harvard University Press, 1988.

Coedès, Georges. *Documents sur l'histoire politique et religieuse du Laos Occidental.* Vol. 25 of *Bulletin de l'école française d'extrême orient.* Paris: École Française d'Extrême Orient, 1925.

———. *The Indianized States of Southeast Asia.* Trans. Susan Brown Cowing. Honolulu: East-West Center, University of Hawaii Press, 1968.

———. *Prachun silājāroek phak thī 2* [*Recueil des Inscriptions du Siam Deuxième Partie*]. Bangkok: Siamese Society, 1961.

Cohen, Paul T., and Gehan Wijeyewardene. Introduction to *Spirit Cult and the Position of Women in Northern Thailand.* Special issue no. 3, *Mankind* 14, no. 4 (1968): 249–62.

Comaroff, Jean. *Body of Power, Spirit of Resistance: The Culture and History of a South African People.* Chicago: University of Chicago Press, 1985.

———. "Medicine: Symbol and Ideology." In *The Problem of Medical Knowledge,* ed. P. Wright and A. Treacher. Edinburgh: Edinburgh University Press, 1982.

Comaroff, John. "Ethnicity, Nationalism and the Politics of Difference in an Age of Revolution." In *Ethnicity, Identity and Nationalism in South Africa,* ed. E. Wilmsen and P. McAllister. Chicago: University of Chicago Press, 1994.

Condominas, Georges. "Essay on the Evolution of Thai Political Systems." In *From Lawa to Mon, from Saa' to Thai: Historical and Anthropological Aspects of Southeast Asian Social Spaces.* Trans. Maria Magannon. Canberra: Department of Anthropology, Australian National University, 1998, 29–91.

Conrad, Joseph. "Karain: A Memory." In *Eastern Skies, Western Skies.* New York: Carroll and Graf, 1990, 129–60.

Cuasay, Peter. "Siamese Montage." M.A. thesis, University of Washington, 1995.

Dang Nghiem Van. "The Lac Muong (City Pillar): A Power Fetish of Thai Seigneurs." In *Proceedings of the 4th International Conference on Thai Studies.* Kunming: Institute of Southeast Asian Studies, 1990, 3:69–82.

Davis, Richard. "Muang Matrifocality." *Mankind* 14, no. 4 (1984): 263–71.

——. *Müang Metaphysics: A Study of Northern Thai Myth and Ritual.* Bangkok: Pandora, 1984.

Debord, Guy. *Society of the Spectacle.* Detroit: Black and Red, 1983.

Delaney, William. "Sociocultural Aspects of Ageing in Buddhist Northern Thailand." Ph.D. diss., University of Illinois, 1977.

de Lauretis, Teresa. "Desire in Narrative." In *Alice Doesn't: Feminism, Semiotics, Cinema.* Bloomington: Indiana University Press, 1984, 103–57.

Deleuze, Gilles. *The Fold: Leibniz and the Baroque.* 1988. Trans. Tom Conley. Minneapolis: Minnesota, 1994.

Derrida, Jacques. *Archive Fever: A Freudian Impression.* Trans. Eric Prenowitz. Chicago: University of Chicago Press, 1995.

——. *Given Time: I. Counterfeit Money.* Trans. Peggy Kamuf. Chicago: University of Chicago Press, 1991.

——. *Of Grammatology.* 1967. Trans. Gayatri Chakravorty Spivak. Baltimore: Johns Hopkins University Press, 1974.

——. *Positions.* Trans. Alan Bass. Chicago: University of Chicago Press, 1981.

——. *Specters of Marx: The State of the Debt, the Work of Mourning, and the New International.* 1993. Trans. Peggy Kamuf. New York: Routledge, 1994.

——. *Truth in Painting.* Trans. Geoff Bennington and Ian McLeod. Chicago: University of Chicago Press, 1987.

Diller, Anthony. "What Makes Central Thai a National Language." In *National Identity and Its Defenders: Thailand, 1939–89,* ed. Craig J. Reynolds. Chiang Mai: Silkworm, 1991, 87–131.

Doane, Mary Ann. "Temporality, Storage, Legibility: Freud, Marey and the Cinema." *Critical Inquiry* 22, no. 2 (1996): 171–74.

Domnern Kaandaen and Sathienpong Wanapok. *Thai-English Dictionary.* Bangkok: Amarin, 1994.

Doré, Amphay. *Aux sources de la civilization lao: Contribution ethno-historique à la connaissance de la culture louang-phrabanaise* [On the sources of Lao civilization: Ethno-historical contributions to the understanding of Luang Prabang culture]. Paris: Cercle de Culture et de Récherches Laotiennes, 1987.

Douglas, Mary. *Purity and Danger: An Analysis of the Concepts of Pollution and Taboo.* London: Routledge, 1966.

Du Bois, W.E.B. *The Souls of Black Folk.* 1903. New York: Fawcett, 1964.

Durkheim, Emile. *The Division of Labor in Society.* Trans. George Simpson. New York: Free Press, 1933.

Egerod, Søren. Introduction to *Khao sii bot [The Poem in Four Songs]: A Northern Thai Tetralogy* (1861), by Phayaphrom. Transcription, English translation, vocabulary, and introduction by Søren Egerod. Stockholm: Scandinavian Institute of Asian Studies, no. 7, 1971.

Engel, David M. *Code and Custom in a Thai Provincial Town: The Interaction of Formal and Informal Systems of Justice.* Tucson: University of Arizona Press, 1978.

Erni, John Nguyet. "Of Desire, the *Farang* and Textual Excursions: Assembling 'Asian AIDS.'" *Cultural Studies* 11, no. 1 (1997).

Fabian, Johannes. *Time and the Other: How Anthropology Makes Its Object.* New York: Columbia University Press, 1983.

Ferguson, Frances. "Sade and the Pornographic Legacy." *Representations* 36 (fall 1991): 1–21.

Feeley-Harnik, Gillian. "Cloth and the Creation of Ancestors in Madagascar." In *Cloth and Human*

*Experience,* ed. Annette B. Weiner and Jane Schneider. Washington: Smithsonian Institution Press, 1989, 74–116.

Fielding, Henry. *The Historical Register for the Year 1736; and, Eurydice Hissed.* Ed. W. Appleton. Lincoln: University of Nebraska Press, 1967.

Florida, Nancy K. *Writing the Past, Inscribing the Future: History as Prophecy in Colonial Java.* Durham, NC: Duke University Press, 1995.

Foresta, Merry A., and John Wood. *Secrets of the Dark Chamber: The Art of the American Daguerreotype.* Washington, DC: National Museum of American Art and Smithsonian Institution Press, 1995.

Foster, Brian L. "Ethnic Identity of the Mons in Thailand." *Journal of the Siam Society* 61 (1973).

Foucault, Michel. *The Birth of the Clinic.* New York: Vintage, 1975.

——. *Discipline and Punish: The Birth of the Prison.* 1975. Trans. Alan Sheridan. London: Penguin, 1979.

——. "The Eye of Power." In *Power/Knowledge: Selected Interviews & Other Writings, 1972–1977,* ed. Colin Gordon, trans. Colin Gordon, Leo Marshall, John Mepham, and Kate Sopher. New York: Pantheon, 1980, 146–165.

——. *The History of Sexuality,* vol. 1. 1976. Trans. Robert Hurley. New York: Vintage, 1990.

——. *The Order of Things: An Archaeology of the Human Sciences.* New York: Vintage, 1970. Originally published in French as *Le mots et les choses,* 1966.

——. "Préface à la transgression." *Critique: Revue Générales Publications Françaises et Étrangères* 19, nos. 195–96 (1963): 751–69.

——. "Questions on Geography." In *Power/Knowledge: Selected Interviews and Other Writings, 1972–1977,* 63–77.

Freud, Sigmund. *Beyond the Pleasure Principle.* In *The Standard Edition of the Complete Psychological Works of Sigmund Freud.* Trans. James Strachey, with Anna Freud, Alix Strachey, and Alan Tyson. 24 vols. London: Hogarth, 1953–74, vol. 18.

——. *The Interpretation of Dreams.* [1915.] Trans. James Strachey. New York: Avon, 1965.

——. *Three Essays on the Theory of Sexuality.* Trans. James Strachey. New York: Basic Books, 1962.

——. "The Uncanny." In *Writings on Art and Literature.* Trans. James Strachey. Stanford: Stanford University Press, 1997, 193–233.

Fukuyama, Francis. "The End of History?" *The National Interest* 16 (1989): 3–18.

Garber, Marjorie. *Vested Interests: Cross-Dressing and Cultural Anxiety.* New York: Routledge, 1991.

Geertz, Clifford. "Centers, Kings, and Charisma: Reflections on the Symbolics of Power." In *Local Knowledge: Further Essays in Interpretive Anthropology.* New York: Basic Books, 1983, 121–46.

——. "Found in Translation: On the Social History of the Moral Imagination." In *Local Knowledge,* 36–54.

——. *Negara: The Theatre State in Nineteenth-Century Bali.* Princeton, NJ: Princeton University Press, 1980.

Gennep, Arnold van. *The Rites of Passage.* Trans. Monika B. Vizedom and Gabrielle L. Caffee. Chicago: University of Chicago Press, 1960.

Gessick, Lorraine. "Kingship and Political Integration in Traditional Siam, 1767–1824." Ph.D. diss., Cornell University, 1976.

Giles Ji Ungpakorn. "Factors Influencing the Balance of Power in Thailand." *Asian Review 1988* 2 (1988): 79–86.

Girling, John, L.S. *Thailand: Society and Politics*. Ithaca, NY: Cornell University Press, 1981.

Golomb, Louis. *An Anthropology of Curing in Multiethnic Thailand*. Urbana: University of Illinois Press, 1985.

Gombrich, Richard. *Theravada Buddhism: A Social History from Ancient Benares to Modern Colombo*. London: Routledge and Kegan Paul, 1988.

Gray, Christine E. "Royal Words and Their Unroyal Consequences." *Cultural Anthropology* 7, no. 4 (1992): 448–63.

——. "Thailand: The Soteriological State in the 1970s." Ph.D. diss., University of Chicago, 1986.

Gregory, C.A. *Gifts and Commodities*. London: Academic Press, 1982.

Gunning, Tom. "Phantom Images and Modern Manifestations: Spirit Photography, Magic Theater, Trick Films, and Photography's Uncanny." In *Fugitive Images: From Photography to Video*, ed. Patrice Petro. Bloomington: Indiana University Press, 1994, 42–71.

Gupta, Akhil, and James Ferguson. "Beyond 'Culture': Space, Identity, and the Politics of Difference." *Cultural Anthropology* 7, no. 1 (1992): 6–23.

Halbwachs, Maurice. *On Collective Memory*. Trans. Lewis A. Coser. Chicago: University of Chicago Press, 1992.

Hale, Anne. "A Re-Assessment of Northern Thai Matrilineages." *Mankind* 12 (1979): 138–50.

Hallett, Holt. *A Thousand Miles on an Elephant in the Shan States*. Edinburgh: William Blackwood and Sons, 1890.

Hanks, Lucien. "Merit and Power in the Thai Social Order." *American Anthropologist* 64 (1962): 1247–61.

Hantrakul Sukanya. "Prostitution in Thailand." In *Development and Displacement in Southeast Asia*. Melbourne: Monash University, 1988).

Haraway, Donna. *Primate Visions: Gender, Race, and Nature in the World of Modern Science*. New York: Routledge, 1989.

Harvey, David. *The Condition of Postmodernity: An Enquiry into the Origins of Cultural Change*. Oxford: Oxford University Press, 1989.

Hass, Mary. *Thai-English Student's Dictionary*. Stanford: Stanford University Press, 1964.

Haug, W. F. *Critique of Commodity Aesthetics: Appearance, Sexuality and Advertising in Capitalist Society*. Trans. Robert Bock. Minneapolis: University of Minnesota Press, 1986.

Heidegger, Martin. *Being and Time*. Trans. John Macquarrie and Edward Robinson. New York: Harper & Row, 1962.

——. *The Question Concerning Technology and Other Essays*. 1936. Trans. William Lovitt. New York: Harper & Row, 1977.

Heine-Geldern, R. "Conceptions of State and Kingship in Southeast Asia." *Far Eastern Quarterly* 2 (1942): 15–30.

Hewison, Kevin. *Bakers and Bureaucrats: Capital and the Role of the State in Thailand*. New Haven: Yale University Press, 1989.

Hill, Ann Maxwell. "Chinese Funerals and Chinese Ethnicity in Chiang Mai, Thailand." *Ethnology* 31, no. 4 (1992): 315–30.

Horathibodi, Phra. *Cindamani, lem 1–2 lae' banthuk ruang nangsy cindamani lae' cindamani chabap phrachao borommakot* [Cindamani, volumes 1–2, with a note on the Cindamani and King Borommakat's edition]. Bangkok: Sinlapa Bannakhan, 1979.

Ingram, James. *Economic Change in Thailand 1850–1970*. Stanford: Stanford University Press, 1971.

Irigaray, Luce. *Speculum of the Other Woman.* Trans. Gillian C. Gill. Ithaca, NY: Cornell University Press, 1975.

Irvine, Walter. "Decline of Village Spirit Cults and Growth of Urban Spirit Mediumship: The Persistence of Beliefs, the Position of Women and Modernization." *Mankind* 4 (1984): 315–24.

——. "The Thai-Yuan 'Madman,' and the Modernizing, Developing Thai Nation as Bounded Entities under Threat: A Study in the Replication of a Single Image." Ph.D. diss., University of London, 1982.

Ishii, Yoneo. "A Note on Buddhistic Millenarian Revolts in Northeastern Siam." *Journal of Southeast Asian Studies* 6, no. 2 (1977): 121–26.

——. *Sangha, State, and Society: Thai Buddhism in History.* Trans. Peter Hawkes. Honolulu: University of Hawaii Press, 1986.

Ivy, Marilyn J. *Discourses of the Vanishing: Modernity, Phantasm, Japan.* Chicago: University of Chicago Press, 1995.

Jackson, Peter A. *Buddhism, Legitimation, and Conflict: The Political Functions of Urban Thai Buddhism.* Singapore: Institute of Southeast Asian Studies, 1989.

——. *Dear Uncle Go: Male Homosexuality in Thailand.* Bangkok: Bua Luang, 1995.

——. *Male Homosexuality in Thailand.* Amsterdam: Global Academic Publishers, 1989.

——. "Summary of Political Events in Thailand, 1991 and 1992." In *The May 1992 Crisis in Thailand: Background and Aftermath: Selected Papers from the 1992 Thailand Update Conference, University of Sydney, 16 October 1992,* ed. Peter Jackson. Canberra: National Thai Studies Centre, Australian National University, 1992, 4–6.

Jameson, Frederic. "Postmodernism, or the Cultural Logic of Late Capitalism." *New Left Review,* no. 146 (1984): 59–92.

Jay, Martin. "Sartre, Merleau-Ponty, and the Search for a New Ontology of Sight." In *Modernity and the Hegemony of Vision,* ed. David Michael Levin. Berkeley: University of California Press, 1993, 143–85.

Jottrand, Mr. and Mrs. Émile. *In Siam: The Diary of a Legal Adviser of King Chulalongkorn's Government.* Trans. Walter E. J. Tips. Bangkok: White Lotus Press, 1996.

Kasian Tejapira. "The Postmodernization of Thainess." In *Proceedings of the 6th International Conference on Thai Studies, Theme II: Cultural Crisis and the Thai Capitalist Transformation.* Chiang Mai, 14–17 October 1996, 385–403.

Keenan, Tom. *Fables of Responsibility: Aberrations and Predicaments in Ethics and Politics.* Stanford: Stanford University Press, 1997.

Kennedy, Victor. "An Indigenous Early Nineteenth Century Map of Central and Northeast Thailand." In *In Memoriam, Phya Anuman Rajadhon,* ed. Tej Bunnag and Michael Smithies. Bangkok: Siam Society, 1970.

Keyes, Charles F. "Ambiguous Gender: Male Initiation in a Northern Thai Buddhist Society." In *Gender and Religion: On the Complexity of Symbols,* ed. Caroline Walker Bynum, Steven Harrell, and Paula Richman. Boston: Beacon, 1986, 66–96.

——. "Buddhist Pilgrimage Centers and the Twelve Year Cycle: Northern Thai Moral Orders in Space and Time." *History of Religions* 5, no. 1 (1975): 71–89.

——. "Buddhist Politics and Their Revolutionary Origins in Thailand." *International Political Science Review* 10, no. 2 (1989): 121–42.

——. Millennialism, Theravada Buddhism and Thai Society." *Journal of Asian Studies* 36, no. 2 (1977): 283–302.

——. "Mother or Mistress, but Never a Monk: Buddhist Notions of Female Gender in Rural Thailand." *American Ethnologist* 11, no. 2 (1984): 223–41.

——. "Power of Merit." *Visakha Puja* (1973): 95–102.

——. *Thailand: Buddhist Kingdom as Modern Nation-State.* Boulder, CO: Westview, 1987.

Khin Thitsa. "Nuns, Mediums and Categories of Women." In *Women and Development in Southeast Asia.* Canterbury: University of Kent, Centre for Southeast Asian Studies, Occasional Paper No. 1, 1983, 4–45.

Kirsch, A. Thomas. "Buddhism, Sex Roles and the Thai Economy." In *Women of Southeast Asia,* ed. Penny van Esterik. Dekalb: Northern Illinois University, Center for Southeast Asian Studies, 1996, 16–41.

——. "Economy, Polity, and Religion in Thailand." In *Change and Persistence in Thai Society,* ed. G. William Skinner and A. Thomas Kirsch. Ithaca, NY: Cornell University Press, 1975, 172–96.

——. "Modernizing Implications of Nineteenth Century Reforms in the Thai Sangha." In *Religion and Legitimation of Power in Thailand, Laos, and Burma,* ed. Bardwell L. Smith, Chambersburg, PA: Anima, 1978, 52–65.

——. "The Thai Buddhist Quest for Merit." In *Southeast Asia: The Politics of National Integration,* ed. John McAlister. New York: Random House, 1973, 188–201.

Kisly, David. "Commodity Native? The Politics of Hill-tribe Tourism in Northern Thailand." M.A. thesis, York University, 1991.

Kittler, Friedrich. *Discourse Networks 1800/1900.* Trans. Michael Metteer and Chris Cullens. Stanford: Stanford University Press, 1990.

Kobkua Suwannatha-Pian. "Phibunsongkhram's Socio-Cultural Programme and the Siamese-Malay Response, 1938–1950." In *Proceedings of the 4th International Conference on Thai Studies.* Kunming: Southeast Asian Studies Institute, 1990, 1:144–61.

Koizumi, Junko. "The Commutation of *Suai* from Northeast Siam in the Middle of the Nineteenth Century." *Journal of Southeast Asian Studies* 23, no. 2 (1992): 276–307.

Kojima, Kiyoshi. *Direct Foreign Investment: A Japanese Model of Multinational Business Operations.* London: Croom Helm, 1978.

Korff, Rudiger. *Bangkok and Modernity.* Bangkok: Chulalongkorn University, Social Research Institute, 1989.

Kracauer, Siegfried. "Photography." In *The Mass Ornament,* trans. Thomas Y. Levin. Cambridge, MA: Harvard University Press, 1955.

——. *The Salaried Masses: Duty and Distraction in Weimar Germany.* 1930. Trans. Quintin Hoare. London: Verso, 1998.

Kraisi Nimmanhaeminda. "*Ham Yon,* the Magic Testicles." In *Essays Offered to G. H. Luce,* ed. Ba Shin et al. Ascona: Artibus Asiae, 1966, 133–48.

——. "The Lawa Guardian Spirits of Chiengmai." *Journal of the Siam Society* 55, no. 2 (1967): 185–226.

——. "Put Vegetables into Baskets, and People into Towns." In *Ethnographic Notes on Northern Thailand,* ed. Lucien M. Hanks, Jane R. Hanks, and Lauriston Sharp. Ithaca, NY: Cornell University Press, Southeast Asia Program Data Paper No. 58, 1965, 6–9.

Krauss, Rosalind. "Tracing Nadar." In *Illuminations: Women Writing on Photography from the 1850s to the Present*, ed. Liz Heron and Val Williams. Durham, NC: Duke University Press, 1996, 37–49.

Lacan, Jacques. "Anamorphosis." 1973. In *The Four Fundamental Concepts of Psycho-Analysis*, trans. Alan Sheridan. London: Penguin, 1977, 79–90.

Laplanche, Jean, and J.-B. Pontalis. *The Language of Psychoanalysis*. Trans. Donald Nicholson-Smith. London: Hogarth Press, 1973.

Levin, David J. *The Dramaturgy of Disavowal: Richard Wagner, Fritz Lang, and the Nibelungen*. Princeton, NJ: Princeton University Press, 1998.

Levin, David Michael. "Decline and Fall: Ocularcentrism in Heidegger's Reading of the History of Metaphysics." In *Modernity and the Hegemony of Vision*. Berkeley: University of California Press, 1993, 186–217.

Lévi-Strauss, Claude. *The Savage Mind*. 1962; Chicago: University of Chicago Press, 1966.

——. "The Sorcerer and His Magic." In *Structural Anthropology*, trans. John Russell. New York: Doubleday, 1967, 161–80.

——. *Tristes Tropiques*. Trans. John Weightman and Doreen Weightman. New York: Atheneum, 1978.

Lobe, Thomas. *United States National Security Policy and Aid to the Thailand Police*. Denver: University of Denver Press, 1977.

McCannell, Dean. "Cannibal Tours." In *Visualizing Theory: Selected Essays from V.A.R. 1990–1994*, ed. Lucien Taylor. New York: Routledge, 1994, 99–114.

McCargo, Duncan. *Chamlong Srimuang and the New Thai Politics*. New York: St. Martin's Press, 1997.

McFarland, George Bradley. *Historical Sketch of Protestant Missions in Siam 1828–1928*. Bangkok: Bangkok Times, 1928.

McGilvary, Daniel. *A Half Century among the Siamese and the Lao: An Autobiography*. New York: Fleming H. Revell, 1912.

Ma Xiaojun. "The Agrarian Change and Reform in Thailand (1850–1910): A Comparative Study with Meiji Restoration in Japan." In *Proceedings of the 4th International Conference on Thai Studies*. Kunming: Institute of Southeast Asian Studies, 1990, 4:543–52.

Maalaa Khamjan. *Cao can phom horm* [Princess of the fragrant hair]. Bangkok: Khathataron, 1992.

Manas Chitakasem. "Poetic Conventions and Modern Thai Poetry." In *Thai Constructions of Knowledge*, ed. Manas Chitakasem and Andrew Turton. London: SOAS, 1991, 37–62.

Manii Phayomyong. *Phithiikam Lannathai* [Lannathai ceremonies]. Chiang Mai: Sapkaanphim, 1986.

——. *Prapheenii sipsong dyan Lannathai* [Lanna traditions of the 12 month calendar]. Chiang Mai: Sapkaanphim, 1989.

——. *Prawat lae' wannakhadii Lanna* [Lanna history and literature]. Chiang Mai: Mitron Raakaan, 1973.

——. *Prawat lae' wannakhadii Lannathai* [Lannathai history and literature]. Chiang Mai: Khon Müang Kaanphim, 1970.

Mann, Thomas. *The Magic Mountain*. Trans. H. T. Lowe-Porter. New York: Alfred A. Knopf, 1927.

Marcus, George E., and Michael M. J. Fischer. *Anthropology as Cultural Critique: An Experimental Moment in the Human Sciences*. Chicago: University of Chicago Press, 1986.

Marcuse, Herbert. *The Aesthetic Dimension: Toward a Critique of Marxist Aesthetics.* Trans. Herbert Marcuse and Erica Sherover. Boston: Beacon, 1977.

Marx, Karl. *Capital,* 2 vols. 1887. Moscow: Progress Publishers, 1954.

——. "The Eighteenth Brumaire of Louis Bonaparte." In *Karl Marx and Frederick Engels: Selected Works.* New York: International, 1970, 1:97–180.

Maspéro, Henri. "La societé et la religion des Chinois ancients et celles des Tai modernes." In *Mélanges posthumes sur les religions et l'histoire de la Chine.* Paris: Publications du Musée Guimet, Bibliothèque de diffusion 57, 1950, 48–68.

Masquelier, Adeline. "Ritual Economies, Historical Mediations: The Poetics and Power of *Bori* among the Mawri of Niger" Ph.D. diss., University of Chicago, 1993.

Mauss, Marcel. *The Gift: Forms and Functions of Exchange in Archaic Societies.* 1925. Trans. Ian Cunnison. London: Routledge and Kegan Paul, 1966.

——. "Techniques of the Body." Trans. B. Brewster. *Economy and Society* 2, no. 1 (1973): 70–88.

Mead, George Herbert. *The Philosophy of the Act.* Ed. Charles Morris. Chicago: University of Chicago Press, 1938.

Mehlman, Jeffrey. "Trimethylamin: Notes on Freud's Specimen Dream." *Diacritics* (spring 1976): 42–45.

Merrill, James. "Lost in Translation." In *From the First Nine: Poems 1946–1976.* New York: Atheneum, 1981.

Metz, Christian. "Photography and Fetish." 1985. In *The Critical Image,* ed. Carol Squiers. San Francisco: Bay Press, 1990, 155–64.

Miller, Sonia. "In Search of Lan Na: Culture and Regional Identity in Northern Thailand." Unpublished manuscript, College Year in Thailand, 1993.

Miller, Toby. *The Well-Tempered Self: Citizenship, Culture, and the Postmodern Subject.* Baltimore: Johns Hopkins University Press, 1993.

Miller, Walter A., Jr. *A Canticle for Leibowitz.* New York: Bantam, 1961.

Mills, Mary Beth. "Attack of the Widow Ghosts: Gender, Death, and Modernity in Northern Thailand." In *Bewitching Women, Pious Men: Gender and Body Politics in Southeast Asia,* ed. Aihwa Ong and Michael G. Peletz. Berkeley: University of California Press, 1995, 244–73.

——. "Modernity and Gender Vulnerability: Rural Women Working in Bangkok." In *Gender and Development in Southeast Asia.* Montreal: Canadian Asian Studies Association, 1992, 83–92.

Ministry of Internal Affairs, Research and Evaluation Department (Thailand). *Report on Survey of Problems and Need of Women in Rural Area According to Project on Developing Women.* Bangkok: Ministry of Internal Affairs, 1981.

Mitchell, Dundi. "Politics and Glamour, the Lure of Likay Bangkok: An Anthropological Perspective." In *Proceedings of the International Conference on Thai Studies,* compiled by Ann Buller. Canberra: Australian National University, 1987.

Moerman, Michael. "Chiangkham's Trade in the 'Old Days.'" In *Change and Persistence in Thai Society,* ed. G. William Skinner and A. Thomas Kirsch. Ithaca, NY: Cornell University Press, 1975, 151–71.

Moertono, S. *State and Statecraft in Old Java: A Study of the Later Mataram Period, 16th to 19th Century.* Ithaca, NY: Cornell University Press, 1968.

Morris, Rosalind C. "Educating Desire: Thailand, Transnationalism, Transgression." *Social Text* 52–53 (1998): 53–79.

——. *New Worlds from Fragments: Film, Ethnography and the Representation of Northwest Coast Cultures*. Boulder, CO: Westview, 1994.

——. "Surviving Pleasure at the Periphery: Chiang Mai and the Photographies of Political Trauma in Thailand, 1976–1992." *Public Culture* 10, no. 2 (1998): 341–70.

——. "Three Sexes and Four Sexualities: Redressing the Discourses on Sex and Gender in Contemporary Thailand." In *Circuits of Desire*, ed. Yukiko Hanawa. Special issue of *positions* 2, no. 1 (1994): 15–43.

Muecke, Marjorie. "Mother Sold Food, Daughter Sells Her Body: Prostitution and Cultural Continuity in the Social Function of Thai Women." *Social Science and Medicine* 35, no. 7 (1992), 891–901.

Mulholland, Jean. *Medicine, Magic, and Evil Spirits: Study of a Text on Thai Traditional Paediatrics.* Canberra: Australian National University, 1987.

Munn, Nancy. "Excluded Spaces: The Figure in the Australian Aboriginal Landscape." *Critical Inquiry* 22, no. 3 (1996), 446–65.

——. *The Fame of Gawa: A Symbolic Study of Value Transformation in a Massim (Papua New Guinea) Society.* 1986. Durham, NC: Duke University Press, 1992.

Murdoch, John B. "The 1901–1902 'Holy Man's' Rebellion." *Journal of Siam Society* 62, no. 2 (1974): 47–66.

Murphy, Jock. "Changes in the Fields: The Three Seasons in the Chiang Mai Valley." In *A Northern Miscellany: Essays from the North of Thailand*, ed. Geoffrey Walton. Chiang Mai: Suriwong, 1989.

Mus, Paul. *"Cultes indienes et indigènes au Champa." Bulletin de l'École Française d'Extrême-Orient* 33 (1933): 367–410.

——. "Thousand-Armed Kannon: A Mystery or a Problem." *Journal of Indian and Buddhist Studies* (1964): 1–33.

Myoshi, Mayao. "A Borderless World: From Colonialism to Transnationalism and the Decline of the Nation-State." *Critical Inquiry* (1993): 726–51.

Nagara, Prasert N., project advisor. *Basic Research on the Ancient Lanna Law: An Analysis of Its Legal Structure and Texts as Inscribed in Palm Leaves from Time Immemorial.* 12 vols. Trans. (from Pali and Thai Yuan) Pitinai Chaisangkasukkul and Aroonrut Wichienkaeo. Bangkok: Thammasat University Press, 1989 [in Thai].

Naroll, Raoull. "Who the Lue Are." In *Essays on the Problem of Tribe: Proceedings of the 1967 Annual Spring Meeting of the American Ethnology Society.* Seattle: University of Washington Press, 1968.

Narujohn Iddhichiracharas. "The Northern Thai Peasant Supernaturalism." In *Buddhism in Northern Thailand*, ed. Saeng Chandrangaam and Narujohn Iddhichiracharas. Chiang Mai: Thippanetr Publishing House, 1980, 100–109.

Nathan, K. S. "Thailand's Role in Seato and ASEAN: Parallels and Differences." In *Proceedings of the 4th International Thai Studies Conference.* Kunming: Institute of Southeast Asian Studies, 1990, 4:610–24.

National Statistics Office of Thailand. *The Survey of Health, Welfare and Use of Traditional Medicine.* Bangkok: National Statistics Office, 1986.

——. *Warasan Satthiti Rai Traimat* [Quarterly bulletin of statistics], 1987.

Nikom Rayawa. *High Banks, Heavy Logs.* 1984. Trans. Richard C. Lair. Ringwood, Australia: Penguin, 1991.

Nithi Aeusriwongse. "Lathipetthi Sadet Phor Rama" [Beliefs and rituals regarding the Royal Father, King Rama V]. *Silapa Watthanatham* [Arts and culture] 14, no. 10 (1993): 78–102.

———. *Paak kai lae' bai rua* [Quill and sail]. Bangkok: Amarin Kanphim, 1984.

———. "Phasaa thai mathathan lae' kaan müang" [Central Thai language and politics]. *Phasaa lae' Nangsü* 17, no. 2 (1984).

———. "Sao Khrua Faa" *Silapa Watthanatham* 12, no. 6 (1991): 180–85.

Niyom Rathamarit. "Thailand and the Problem of Party Development." In *Proceedings of the 4th International Conference on Thai Studies.* Kunming: Institute for Southeast Asian Studies, 1990, 4: 596–603.

Notton, Camille. *Chronique de La:p'un: Histoire de la Dynastie de Chamt'evi,* vol. 2 of *Annales du Siam,* 3 vols. Paris: Charles-Lavauzelle, 1930.

———, trans. *P'ra Buddha Sihing.* Bangkok: Bangkok Times Press, 1933.

Obeyesekere, Gananath. *Medusa's Hair: An Essay on Personal Symbols and Religious Experience.* Chicago: University of Chicago Press, 1981.

O'Connor, Richard. "Interpreting Thai Religious Change: Temples, Sangha Reform and Social Change." *Journal of Southeast Asian Studies* 24, no. 2 (1986): 320–39.

———. "Mechanical and Organic Solidarity in Bangkok." *Contributions to Southeast Asian Ethnography* 6 (1987): 13–26.

Office of the National Culture Commission, Ministry of Education (Thailand). *The National Culture Policy and Guidelines for Preservation, Promotion and Development of Culture 2529 [1986].* Bangkok, 1987.

O'Flaherty, Wendy Doniger. *Asceticism and Eroticism in the Mythology of Siva.* Oxford: Oxford University Press, 1973.

Ong, Aiwa. *Spirits of Resistance and Capitalist Discipline: Factory Women in Malaysia.* Albany: State University of New York Press, 1987.

Ozawa, Terutomo. *Multinationalism, Japanese Style: The Political Economy of Outward Dependency.* Princeton, NJ: Princeton University Press, 1979.

Panakkhaa Bunphilaa. "Khrongkaan phatana rajngaan satrii nai phaak udsahakam kaan paan phalid: Khrongkaan syksaa ngaan satrii" [The development of women's work in the industrial sector: A study of female laborers]. M.A. thesis, Thammasat University, 1990.

Pasuk Phongpaichit. *From Peasant Girls to Bangkok Masseuses.* Geneva: International Labour Organization, 1982.

———. "The New Wave of Japan's Investment: Determinants and Possible Impact on Domestic Capital in Thailand in the Next Decade." In *Proceedings of the 4th International Conference on Thai Studies.* Kunming: Institute of Southeast Asian Studies, 1990, 4:524–42.

———. "Review Article: Capital Accumulation in Thailand." *Journal of Asian Studies* 22, no. 2 (1992): 379–86.

Pasuk Phongpaichit and Sungsidh Piriyarangsan. *Corruption and Democracy in Thailand.* Chiang Mai: Silkworm Books, 1994.

Peltier, Anatole-Roger. *Pathamamūlamūlī: Tamnan khao phii Lanna* [The origin of the world in the Lan Na tradition]. Chiang Mai: Suriwong, 1991.

Pemberton, John. *On the Subject of "Java."* Ithaca, NY: Cornell University Press, 1994.

Phayaphrom. *Khao Sii Bot [The Poem in Four Songs]: A Northern Thai Tetralogy* 1861. Transcription, English translation, vocabulary, and introduction by Søren Egerod. Stockholm: Scandinavian Institute of Asian Studies Monograph Series Number 7, 1971.

Placzek, J. A. "Phii miang: Black Thai Symbols of State and Leadership." In *Proceedings of the 4th International Conference on Thai Studies.* Kunming: Institute for Southeast Asian Studies, 1990, 3:48–68.

Poe, Edgar Allan. "The Purloined Letter." 1845. In *The Norton Anthology of American Literature,* 3d ed., ed. Nina Baym et al. New York: Norton, 1979, 1:1425–37.

Potter, Sulameith Heins. *Family Life in a Northern Thai Village.* Berkeley: University of California Press, 1977.

Prakhong Nimmanhaeminda. "Khwan lae' kham riak khwan" [The *Khwan* and the calling of the *khwan*]. In *Lannathai Khadii.* Bangkok: Caroenwit Press, 1978, 106–36.

——. *Laksana wannakam phaak nüa* [An analysis of northern Thai literature]. Bangkok: Faculty of Social Research, Institute of Thailand, 1980.

Pramoj, M. R. Seni, and M. R. Kukrit Pramoj. *A King of Siam Speaks.* Bangkok: Siam Society, 1987.

Pratt, Mary Louise. "Fieldwork in Common Places." In *Writing Culture,* ed. James Clifford and George E. Marcus. Berkeley: University of California Press, 1986, 27–50.

Prizzia, Ross. *Thailand in Transition: The Role of Oppositional Forces.* Honolulu: University of Hawaii Press, 1985.

Proschan, Frank. "Who Are the *Khaa*?" In *Proceedings of the 6th Annual International Conference on Thai Studies: Theme Four: Traditions and Changes and Local/Regional Levels.* Chiang Mai, 1996, 2:391–414.

Race, Jeffrey. "The War in Northern Thailand." *Modern Asian Studies* 8, no. 1 (1974): 85–112.

Rafael, Vicente L. *Contracting Colonialism: Translation and Christian Conversion in Tagalog Society under Early Spanish Rule.* 1988. Durham, NC: Duke University Press, 1992.

Rahula, Walpola. *History of Buddhism in Ceylon: The Anuradhapura Period.* Colombo: 1967.

Ramsey, James Ansil. "The Development of a Bureaucratic Polity: The Case of Northern Siam." Ph.D. diss., Cornell University, 1971.

——. "Modernization and Reactional Rebellions in Northern Siam." *Journal of Asian Studies* 38, no. 2 (1979): 283–97.

Randolph, Sean. "Diplomacy and National Interest: Thai-American Security Cooperation in the Vietnam Era." Ph.D. diss., Fletcher School of Law and Diplomacy, Medford, MA, 1982.

Ratanaporn Sethakul. "Political, Social, and Economic Changes in the Northern States of Thailand Resulting from the Chiang Mai Treaties of 1874 and 1883." Ph.D. diss., University of Illinois, 1989.

Reynolds, Craig J. "Buddhist Cosmography in Thai History, with Special Reference to Nineteenth Century Cultural Change." *Journal of Asian Studies* 35, no. 2 (1976): 203–20.

——. "The Buddhist Monkhood in Nineteenth Century Thailand." Ph.D. diss., Cornell University, 1972.

——. "Sedition in Thai History: A Nineteenth Century Poem and Its Critics." In *Thai Conceptions of Knowledge,* 15–36.

———. *Thai Radical Discourse: The Real Face of Thai Feudalism Today.* Ithaca, NY: Cornell University, Southeast Asia Program, 1987.

Reynolds, Craig, ed. *National Identity and Its Defenders: Thailand 1939–89.* Chiang Mai: Silkworm, 1991.

———. "The Two Wheels of Dhamma: A Study of Early Buddhism." In *The Two Wheels of Dhamma,* ed. Bardwell Smith. Chambersburg, PA: American Academy of Religion, 1972, 6–30.

Reynolds, Frank R. "Buddhism as a Universal Religion and as Civic Religion: Some Observations on a Recent Tour of Buddhist Centers in Central Thailand." In *Religion and Legitimation of Power in Thailand, Laos, and Burma,* ed. Bardwell Smith. Chambersburg, PA: Anima, 1978, 194–203.

———. "Sacral Kingship and National Development: The Case of Thailand." In *Religion and Legitimation of Power in Thailand, Laos, and Burma,* 100–110.

Reynolds, Frank E., and Mani B. Reynolds, trans. and eds. *Three Worlds According to King Ruang: A Thai Buddhist Cosmology* [Translation of *Thraiphum Phra Ruang*]. Berkeley: University of California Press, 1982.

Rhum, Michael R. *The Ancestral Lords: Gender, Descent, and Spirits in a Northern Thai Village.* DeKalb: Center for Southeast Asian Studies, Northern Illinois University, Monograph Series on Southeast Asia; Special Report No. 29, 1994.

Riggs, F. W. *The Modernization of a Bureaucratic Polity.* Honolulu: University of Hawaii, East-West Center Press, 1976.

Robinson, James W. *Empire of Freedom: The Amway Story and What It Means to You.* Rocklin, CA: Prima Publishing, 1997.

Saenhaa Bunjarak. *Wannakam Khao Khong Phaak Nüa* [Khao literature of northern Thailand]. M.A. thesis, Teacher's College, 1976.

Sahlins, Marshall. *Islands of History.* Chicago: University of Chicago Press, 1985.

Said, Edward. *Orientalism.* New York: Vintage, 1979.

Saiyud Kerdphol. *Addresses of Lieutenant General Saiyud Kerdphol, 1968–1971.* Bangkok Historical Division, SCHQ [no additional data on publication source; microfilm by Library of Congress dated 1975].

Sanguan Chotisukharat. *Phrapheenii Lannathai lae' phithiikam taang taang* [Traditions and ceremonies of Lannathai], Chiang Mai: Phrathüang Withayaa, 1971.

———. *Phrapheenii thai phaak nüa* [Thai traditions of the northern region], 2d ed. Phranakhon: Odeon, 1969.

Santi Chantasawon. "The Spirit Cults and Superstition in Thai Habitation: A Case Study in the Northern Region." Ph.D. diss., University of Michigan, 1987.

Schneider, Benjamin. "Likay: Popular Theater in Northern Thailand." In *A Northern Miscellany: Essays from the North of Thailand,* ed. Geoffrey Walton. Chiang Mai: Jareuk, 1989, 191–206.

Seidenfaden, Erik. *Guide to Bangkok, with Notes on Siam.* Bangkok: Royal State Railway Department of Siam, 1927.

———. "Siam's Tribal Dresses." *Journal of the Siam Society* 31, no. 2 (1939): 169–75.

Seremetakis, Nadia. "The Memory of the Senses: Historical Perception, Commensal Exchange, and Modernity." In *Visualizing THEORY: Selected Essays from V.A.R. 1900–1994,* ed. Lucien Taylor. New York: Routledge, 1994, 214–29.

Shalardchai Ramitanondh. *Phii cao naaj* [Spirits of the lords and masters]. Chiang Mai: Faculty of Social Sciences, Chiang Mai University, 1984.

Siegel, James T. "Curing Rights, Dreams, and Domestic Politics in a Sumatran Society." *Glyph* 3 (1978): 18–31.

——. *Fetish, Recognition, Revolution*. Princeton, NJ: Princeton University Press, 1997.

——. *Solo in the New Order: Language and Hierarchy in an Indonesian City*. Princeton, NJ: Princeton University Press, 1986.

Sila Viravong (Maha). *History of Laos*. New York: Paragon, 1965.

Simmel, Georg. "The Metropolis and Modern Life." 1900. In *The Sociology of Georg Simmel*, trans. Kurt H. Wolff. New York: Free Press, 1950, 409–24.

——. *The Philosophy of Money*. London: Routledge and Kegan Paul, 1978.

Singer, Linda. *Erotic Welfare: Sexual Theory and Politics in the Age of Epidemic*. Ed. and introduced by Judith Butler and Maureen MacGrogan. New York: Routledge, 1993.

Sinith Sitthiraksa. "Prostitution and Development in Thailand." In *Gender and Development in Southeast Asia*, ed. Penny van Esterik and John van Esterik. Montreal: Canadian Asian Studies Association, 1992, 93–108.

Sirilak Sakkriankrai. *Ton Kamnoed Chonchan Naithun naj Prathet Thai (B.E. 2398–2453)* [The origins of the capitalist class in Thailand (1855–1910)]. Bangkok: Sangsan, 1980.

Smalley, William A. *Linguistic Diversity and National Unity: Language Ecology in Thailand*. Chicago: University of Chicago Press, 1994.

Smithies, Michael. *Descriptions of Old Siam*. Kuala Lumpur: Oxford University Press, 1995.

——. "Likay: A Note on the Origin, Form and Future of Siamese Folk Opera." *Journal of the Siam Society* 59, no. 1 (1971): 33–64.

Snodgrass, Adrian. *The Symbolism of the Stupa*. Ithaca, NY: Southeast Asia Studies Program, Cornell University, 1985.

Somboon Suksamran. *Buddhism and Politics in Thailand: A Study of Socio-Political Change and Political Activism of the Thai Sangha*. Singapore: Institute of Southeast Asian Studies, 1982.

Sommai Premchit and Pierre Doré. *The Lan Na Twelve Month Traditions: An Ethno-Historic and Comparative Approach*. Chiang Mai: Faculty of Social Sciences and CNRS, France, 1991.

Sontag, Susan. *Illness as Metaphor*. New York: Farrar, Straus & Giroux, 1978.

Southeast Asian Perspective Project. *Transnationalism, the State, and the People: The Case of Thailand*. Manila: United Nations University Press, 1989.

Spiro, Melford. *Buddhism and Society: A Great Tradition and Its Burmese Vicissitudes*. New York: Harper & Row, 1970.

Spivak, Gayatri Chakravorty. "Ghostwriting." *Diacritics* 25, no. 2 (1995): 65–84.

Stallybrass, Peter. "Footnotes." In *The Body in Parts: Fantasies of Corporeality in Early Modern Europe*. David Hillman and Carla Mazzio, eds. New York: Routledge, 1997, 313–25.

Stcherbatsky, Th. *Buddhist Logic*. 2 vols. 1930. New York: Dover, 1963.

Stewart, Susan. *On Longing: Narratives of the Miniature, the Gigantic, the Souvenir, the Collection*. Durham, NC: Duke University Press, 1993.

Strong, John. *The Legend of King Aśoka*. Princeton, NJ: Princeton University Press, 1983.

Sukhrot Phanwilai. "*Bot Suu Khwan: Wannakam Thii Kiaw Khong kap Prapheenii lae' Phithiikam*" *Eekasaan Prakob Kaan Samomnaa Lannakhadii Syksaa: Phasaa lae' Wannakam*, 4–6 August (1987).

Sulak Sivaraksa. "The Crisis of Siamese Identity." In *National Identity and Its Defenders: Thailand, 1939–89*, ed. Craig J. Reynolds. Chiang Mai: Silkworm, 1991, 41–58.

Sungsindh Piriyarangson. "The Rise of the Labor Movement in Thailand: An Analysis of Public Enterprise Workers." *Asian Review 1988* 2 (1988): 54–78.

Sunthorn Phu. *Nirat Muang Klaang* [*Poem of the Middle World*]. Trans. H. H. Prince Prem Purachatra. Bangkok: National Identity Board, Office of the Prime Minister, 1984.

Sutcharit Thawonsuk. *Kaan chat san huamüang khrang raek* [Establishment of the first provincial courts]. Bangkok: Ministry of Justice, 1964.

Suwadee Tanaprasitpatana. "Thai Society's Expectations of Women, 1851–1935." Ph.D. diss., University of Sydney, 1989.

Swanson, Herbert R. *Krischak Muang Nua* [The northern Thai church]. Bangkok: Chuan, 1984.

——. "This Seed: Missionary Printing and Literature as Agents of Change in Northern Siam." Unpublished manuscript, R-MS 2/50-10, Chiang Mai, Phayap University Archives.

Swearer, Donald K. "The Northern Thai City as Sacred Center." In *The City as a Sacred Center: Essays on Six Asian Contexts*, ed. Bardwell L. Smith and Holly Baker Reynolds. Leiden: E. J. Brill, 1987, 103–13.

Swearer, Donald K., and Sommai Premchit. *The Legend of Queen Cāma: Bodhiramsi's Cāmadevīvamsa, a Translation and Commentary*. Albany: State University of New York Press, 1998.

Tagg, John. *The Burden of Representation: Essays on Photographies and Histories*. London: Macmillan, 1988.

Tambiah, Stanley J. *Buddhism and the Spirit Cults in Northeast Thailand*. Cambridge: Cambridge University Press, 1970.

——. "Sangha and Polity in Modern Thailand." In *Religion and Legitimation of Power in Thailand, Laos, and Burma*, ed. Bardwell L. Smith. Chambersburg, PA: Anima, 1978, 111–33.

——. *World Conqueror, World Renouncer: A Study of Buddhism and Polity in Thailand against a Historical Background*. Cambridge: Cambridge University Press, 1976.

Tanabe, Shigeharu. "Ideological Practice in Peasant Rebellions: Siam at the Turn of the Twentieth Century." In *History and Peasant Consciousness in South East Asia*, ed. Andrew Turton and Shigeharu Tanabe. Senri Ethnological Series 13. Osaka: National Museum of Ethnology, 1984, 75–110.

——. "The Person in Transformation: Body, Mind and Cultural Appropriation." Special lecture, Sixth International Thai Studies Conference, Chiang Mai, 15 October 1996.

——. "Spirits, Power and the Discourse of Female Gender: The *Phi* Meng Cult in Northern Thailand." In *Thai Constructions of Knowledge*, ed. Manas Chitrakasem and Andrew Turton. London: SOAS, 1991, 183–212.

——, ed. *Religious Traditions among Tai Ethnic Groups: A Selected Bibliography*. Ayutthya: Ayutthya Historical Study Center, 1991.

Taussig, Michael. *The Devil and Commodity Fetishism in Latin America*. Chapel Hill: University of North Carolina Press, 1980.

——. *Mimesis and Alterity: A Particular History of the Senses*. New York: Routledge, 1993.

——. "Reification and the Consciousness of the Patient." In *The Nervous System*. New York: Routledge, 1992, 83–109.

——. *Shamanism, Colonialism and the Wold Man: A Study in Terror and Healing*. Chicago: University of Chicago Press, 1987.

Taylor, Jim. "Contemporary Urban Buddhist Cults and the Socio-Political Order in Thailand." *Mankind* 19, no. 2 (1989): 112–25.

Thak Chaloemtiarana. *Thailand: The Politics of Despotic Paternalism.* Bangkok: Social Science Association of Thailand and Thai Khadi Institute of Thammasat University, 1979.

Thamsook Numnonda. "Phibulsongkram's Thai Nation-Building Programme during the Japanese Military Presence, 1941–1945." *Journal of Southeast Asian Studies* 9, no. 2 (1978): 243–47.

Thamthat Phaanich. *Phra Naang Chamathewii* [Queen Chamadevi]. Bangkok: Thamthaan-mulinit, 1950.

Thanet Aphisuwan, ed. *Rao Maj Lyym Hok Thula* [We haven't forgotten October 6]. Bangkok: Committee to Commemorate the 20th Anniversary of October 6, 1976, 1995.

Thipakhorawang (Chaophraya). *The Dynastic Chronicles: Bangkok Era for Fourth Reign.* Trans. Chadin Flood. Tokyo: Centre for East Asian Cultural Studies, 1965.

———. *Nangsy sadaeng kitchanukit* Bangkok: Khurusapha, 1971, (1867).

Thongchai Winichakul. "*Ramleuk 6 Thula: Thammai lae' Yangrai*" [The massacre of October 6: Why and how?]. In *Rao Maj Lyym Hok Thula* [We haven't forgotten October 6]. Bangkok: 20th Anniversary Memorial Publication, 1995, 13–22.

———. "Remembering/Silencing the Traumatic Past: The Ambivalence Narratives of the October 1976 Massacre in Bangkok." In *Proceedings of the 6th International Thai Conference on Thai Studies. Theme II: Cultural Crisis and the Thai Capitalist Transformation.* Chiang Mai: 473–93.

———. *Siam Mapped: A History of the Geo-Body of a Nation.* Honolulu: University of Hawaii Press, 1994.

Tips, Walter E. J. *Crime and Punishment in King Chulalongkorn's Kingdom.* Bangkok: White Lotus, 1998.

———. *Gustave Rolin-Jaequemyns and the Making of Modern Siam: The Diaries and Letters of King Chulalongkorn's General Advisor.* Bangkok: White Lotus, 1996.

Treaty and Legal Department (Thailand). *Bilateral Treaties and Agreements between Thailand and Foreign Countries and International Organizations.* Bangkok: Prachrandra, 1969.

Tsing, Anna Lowenhaupt. *In the Realm of the Diamond Queen: Marginality in an Out-of-the-Way Place.* Princeton, NJ: Princeton University Press, 1993.

Turner, Terence S. "The Social Skin." In *Not Work Alone*, ed. J. Cherfas and R. Lewsin. London: Temple Smith, 1980.

Turton, Andrew. "Limits of Ideological Domination and the Formation of Social Consciousness." In *History and Peasant Consciousness in South East Asia*, ed. Andrew Turton and Shigeharu Tanabe. Osaka: Senri Ethnological Studies, no. 13, 1984, 19–74.

———. "Matrilineal Descent Groups and Spirits Cults of the Thai Yuan in Northern Thailand." *Journal of the Siam Society* 60, no. 2 (1972): 217–56.

Turton, Andrew, Jonathon Fast, and Malcolm Caldwell, eds. *Thailand: Roots of Conflict.* Nottingham, GB: Spokesman, 1978.

Ubonrat Siriyuvasak. "Radio in a Transitional Society: The Case of Thailand." Ph.D. diss., University of Leicester, 1989.

van Esterik, Penny. Keynote address. Conference on Gender and Sexuality in Thailand. Australian National University, Canberra, August 1995.

———. "Lay Women in Theravada Buddhism." In *Women of Southeast Asia*, ed. Penny van Esterik.

Dekalb: Northern Illinois University, Southeast Asian Studies Occasional Paper No. 9, 1982, 42–54.

———. *Nurturance and Reciprocity in Thai Studies: A Tribute to Lucien and Jane Hanks.* Toronto: York University Thai Studies Project/Women in Development Consortium in Thailand, Working Paper no. 8, 1982.

Vandergeest, Peter, and Nancy Lee Peluso. "Fixing Property in National Space: Territorialization of the State in Siam/Thailand." Unpublished manuscript, 1993.

van Gennep, Arnold. *The Rites of Passage.* Trans. Monika B. Vizedom and G. L. Caffee. Chicago: University of Chicago Press, 1960.

Vatikiokiotis, Michael. "Ethnic Pluralism in the Northern Thai City of Chiang Mai." Ph.D. diss., Oxford University, 1984.

Vella, Walter. *Chaiyo! King Vajiravudh and the Development of Thai Nationalism.* Honolulu: University of Hawaii Press, 1978.

———. *Siam under Rama 3, 1824–1851.* New York: J. J. Augustin, 1957.

Virilio, Paul. *The Vision Machine.* London: British Film Institute, 1994.

Wales, Quaritch H. G. *Ancient Siamese Government and Administration.* 1934. New York: Paragon, 1965.

———. *Divination in Thailand: The Hopes and Fears of a Southeast Asian People.* London: Curzon, 1983.

———. *Siamese State Ceremonies.* London: Bernard Quaritch, 1931.

Wan Waithayakorn, Prince. "Thai Culture: Lecture Delivered before the Thailand Research Society [formerly the Royal Siam Society], 27 February 1944." In *The Centennial of His Royal Highness Prince Wan Waithayakon Krommun Naradhop Bonsprabandh.* Bangkok: Office of the National Culture Commission, 1991, 29–38. Originally published in *Journal of the Thailand Research Society* 35, no. 2 (1944): 135–45.

Waseem, S. M. "Thailand: Economic Development and ASEAN Promise." In *Proceedings of the 4th International Conference on Thai Studies.* Kunming: Institute for Southeast Asian Studies, 1990, 553–65.

Weber, Samuel. "The Divaricator: Remarks on Freud's *Witz.*" *Glyph* 1 (1977): 1–27.

———. "Mass Mediauras, or: Art, Aura and Media in the Work of Walter Benjamin." In *Mass Mediauras: Form, Technics, Media,* ed. Alan Cholodenki. Stanford: Stanford University Press, 1996, 76–107.

———. "The Unraveling of Form." In *Mass Mediauras,* 9–35.

Weber, Max. "The Types of Authority and Imperative Co-ordination." 1947. In *The Theory of Social and Economic Organization,* ed. and introduced by Talcott Parsons, trans. A. M. Henderson and Talcott Parsons. New York: Free Press, 1964, 324–423.

Wheatley, Paul. *Nāgara and Commentary: Origins of the Southeast Asian Urban Traditions.* Chicago: University of Chicago Press, 1983.

———. *The Pivot of the Four Quarters.* Chicago: Aldine, 1971.

Wichit Wathakan, Luang. "Aryatham" [Civilization]. In *Pathakatha lae Kham Banyai* [Lectures and talks]. Bangkok: Soemwit Bannakan, 1973, 1:54–64.

Wigley, Mark. *The Architecture of Deconstruction: Derrida's Haunt.* Cambridge, MA: MIT Press, 1993.

Wijeyewardene, Gehan. "Address, Abuse, and Animal Categories in Northern Thailand." *Man* 3, no. 1 (1968): 76–93.

———. "Introduction: History, Anthropology and Ancient Texts." In *The Laws of King Mengrai.* Trans. Aroonrut Wichienkaeo. Canberra: Department of Anthropology, Research School of Pacific Studies, Australian National University, 1986, 1–20.

———. "Matriclans or Female Cults: A Problem in Northern Thai Ethnography." *Mankind* 11, no. 1 (1977): 19–25.

———. "Northern Thai Succession and the Search for Matriliny." *Mankind* 14, no. 1 (1984): 286–92.

———. *Place and Emotion in Northern Thai Ritual Behavior.* Bangkok: Pandora, 1986.

———. "Scrubbing Scurf: Medium and Deity in Chiang Mai." *Mankind* 13, no. 1 (1981): 1–14.

Williams, Raymond. *The Country and the City.* Oxford: Oxford University Press, 1973.

Wilson, Constance. "State and Society in the Reign of Mongkut, 1851–1868: Thailand on the Eve of Modernization." Ph.D. diss., Cornell University, 1971.

Wood, W. A. R. *Consul in Paradise: Sixty-Nine Years in Siam.* London: Souvenir, 1965; rpt. Bangkok: Suriwong Books, 1991.

Wyatt, David K. "Chronicle Traditions in Thai Historiography." In *Southeast Asian History and Historiography,* ed. C. D. Cowan and O. W. Walters. Ithaca, NY: Cornell University Press, 1976, 107–22.

———. *The Politics of Reform in Thailand: Education in the Reign of King Chulalongkorn.* New Haven: Yale University Press, 1969.

———. "The Subtle Revolution of Rama I of Siam." In *Studies in Thai History.* Chiang Mai: Silkworm, 1995, 131–72.

———. *Thailand: A Short History.* New Haven: Yale University Press, 1984.

Wyatt, David K., and Aroonrat Wichienkaeo. *The Chiang Mai Chronicle.* Chiang Mai: Silkworm Books, 1995.

# INDEX

Rosalind C. Morris is Associate Professor of Anthropology at
Columbia University. She is the author of *New Worlds from
Fragments: Film, Ethnography, and the Representation of
Northwest Coast Culture.*

Library of Congress Cataloging-in-Publication Data
Morris, Rosalind C.
In the place of origins : modernity and its mediums in northern
Thailand / Rosalind Morris.
p. cm. — (Body, commodity, text)
Includes bibliographical references (p.    ) and index.
ISBN 0-8223-2481-4 (cl. : alk. paper)
ISBN 0-8223-2517-9 (pa. : alk. paper)
1. Mediums—Thailand—Chiang Mai Region.   2. Ethnology—
Thailand—Chiang Mai Region. I. Title. II. Series.
BF1242.T5M67   2000   133.9′1′09593—dc21   99-42577